Relationship Banker

MERCER
UNIVERSITY PRESS

Endowed by

TOM WATSON BROWN

and

THE WATSON-BROWN FOUNDATION, INC.

Relationship Banker

Eugene W. Stetson, Wall Street, and American Business, 1916-1959

James L. Hunt

Mercer University Press
Macon, Georgia

The publication of this book is made possible in part by generous gifts from Georgia Pine Level Foundation, Pine Level Foundation, Inc., and GFGW, Inc.

MUP/H672

1400 Coleman Avenue
Macon, Georgia 31207

First Edition.
Second Printing

Books published by Mercer University Press are printed on acid free paper that meets the requirements of American National Standard for Information Sciences—Permanence of Paper for Printed Library Materials.

Mercer University Press is a member of Green Press initiative (greenpressinitiative.org), a nonprofit organization working to help publishers and printers increase their use of recycled paper and decrease their use of fiber derived from endangered forests. This book is printed on recycled paper.

Library of Congress Cataloging-in-Publication Data

Hunt, James L. (James Logan), 1959-
Relationship banker : Eugene W. Stetson, Wall Street, and American business, 1916-1959 / James L. Hunt.
p. cm.
Includes bibliographical references and index.
ISBN-13: 978-0-86554-915-9 (hbk : alk. paper)
ISBN-10: 0-86554-915-X (hbk : alk. paper)
1. Stetson, Eugene W. (Eugene William), 1881-1959. 2. Guaranty Trust Company of New York. 3. Bankers—United States--Biography. 4. Capitalists and financiers—United States—Biography. 5. Banks and banking, American—History—20th century.
I. Title.
HG2463.S63H86 2009
332.1'2092--dc22
[B]
2009029564

Contents

For Ruth, David, and Naomi

Acknowledgments

This project began almost ten years ago when I was asked by two colleagues at Mercer University, Carl Joiner and Charles Andrews, if I would contribute a chapter to a small book about the business career of Eugene W. Stetson (1881-1959), a former student and a long-time financial supporter of the university. Originally, because of my interest in railroads, I agreed to write a section on Stetson's activities with the Illinois Central.

After finishing the paper, I was asked to write two additional sections—one addressing Stetson's banking work with the Guaranty Trust Company of New York and another that described Stetson's forty-year connection to Coca-Cola. Essentially, these few chapters were the entire project, at least as it was originally envisioned. I hesitated, knowing that this took my responsibilities to a much more demanding level. I also hesitated because I did not know very much about Stetson, and frankly I was skeptical that his career might deserve a kind of effort that I could not give. Nonetheless, I agreed to do the additional sections, if I could find suitable historical sources to write them.

After writing these sections, however, one of Eugene Stetson's grandsons, Chuck Stetson, suggested that the three-part organization (Illinois Central, Guaranty, and Coca-Cola) did not do the subject, or the research, justice. Instead, the project should be reorganized in a way that was more purely biographical and narrative. This, of course, required a substantial amount of additional time, research, and writing.

I would not recommend this sort of gradualism as the ideal manner in which to write a book. Yet it has benefits, some of which I hope are reflected in the final product. Among these advantages is that getting to know Gene Stetson has been worth the effort. Stetson was not simply a successful banker. He was at the center of American banking from 1916 into the late 1950s, the decades in which the United States became the world's leading financial power.

Less positively, I learned that the greatest challenge in writing about Stetson was the deficiency in materials available to study his banking career. By historians' standards he left very little record of his business practices. Most of the corporate records of Guaranty, Coca-Cola, or the Illinois Central, for instance, three companies with which he spent a great deal of time, are limited, non-existent, or unavailable for public inspection. The solution was to cast a broad net across business, governmental, and other kinds of records in order to "catch" the overall story.

Many persons at Mercer contributed to this goal. I appreciate especially the advice and support of faculty members William S. Mounts, Charles H. Andrews, and G. Russell Barber Jr. From the library, Susan Broome, Arlette Copeland, and Laura Botts provided assistance with the Eugene W. Stetson Papers, and Ed Miner helped with government documents. I am also thankful for the work of Marc Jolley, Marsha Luttrell, Kevin Manus-Pennings, and Barbara Keene from the Mercer University Press, Jerome Gratigny of learning technologies, and the Mercer law school's Sandy Studdard.

Archivists tend to be a historian's greatest friends. David W. Wright and Nancy Palley in New York graciously allowed me access to the Guaranty Trust archives, now housed at its successor institution, JPMorgan Chase. Philip Mooney showed the same high level of courtesy at Coca-Cola in Atlanta, as did Dawn Stanford at the IBM Archives. I also appreciate the assistance of Carl Van Ness, Curator of Manuscripts and Archives at the University of Florida's Special Collections, for his help with the large and valuable Braga Brothers papers.

Given the lapse of time since Stetson's banking career, it was difficult to find a person who had more than anecdotal or second-hand knowledge of the events described in this book. The exception was Lillian Otlowski, an executive at Guaranty and later Morgan Guaranty, who provided inside information about those banks as well as Eugene Stetson. I appreciate her enthusiastic willingness to share those memories.

I am especially thankful for the time and feedback of several outstanding business historians and scholars: Benjamin J. Klebaner, Leah Rawls Atkins, Maury Klein, and Paul J. Miranti Jr.

I also am grateful for the interest and encouragement of Eugene Stetson's descendants, especially grandsons Robert Hatcher and Chuck Stetson. As experts in finance and banking, they understand Eugene Stetson's significance. Robert Hatcher has supported the project from its inception. Chuck Stetson pushed the book in new and positive directions, effectively "raising the bar" along the way. He and his assistant, Barbara Rockefeller, made real and positive contributions to the book's content and structure. It is better because of them and their work.

Our family has had to live with Eugene Stetson, and for the most part he has been a welcome guest. During this time Ruth, David, and Naomi kept the focus on the big issues, the ones that matter the most. They deserve many thanks for their encouragement and patience.

Illustrations

Stetson's Boyhood Home and Family (c. 1892). Eugene Stetson stands on the right.
Photograph courtesy of Georgia Archives and History Division, Vanishing Georgia Collection, bib047, Morrow, Georgia.

A banking frontier: Fitzgerald, Georgia (1907). Photograph courtesy of Georgia Archives and History Division, Vanishing Georgia Collection, ben145, Morrow, Georgia.

Macon's New South: Doffer boys at Bibb Manufacturing (1909).
Courtesy Prints and Photographs Division, Library of Congress, Washington, DC.

The Guaranty Trust, 140 Broadway (c. 1910s).
Courtesy JPMorgan Chase Archives, New York, New York.

Guaranty's Main Banking Room, 140 Broadway.
Courtesy JPMorgan Chase Archives, New York, New York.

Charles H. Sabin, president of Guaranty Trust (1919).
Courtesy JPMorgan Chase Archives, New York, New York.

Stetson's Banking Neighborhood: Lower Broadway between Wall and Cedar Streets. The Equitable Building, built next to Guaranty Trust at 120 Broadway in 1915, dominates the photograph (c. 1920s). Courtesy New York Public Library, New York, New York.

Ernest Woodruff (1863–1944). Courtesy The Coca-Cola Company, Atlanta, Georgia.

Coca-Cola's board of directors, including Eugene Stetson (1931).
Courtesy The Coca-Cola Company, Atlanta, Georgia.

Robert Woodruff (1889–1985). Courtesy The Coca-Cola Company, Atlanta, Georgia.

Cutting cane in Cuba (between 1908 and 1919).
Courtesy Prints and Photographs Division, Library of Congress, Washington, DC.

Eugene W. Stetson, New York banker (c. 1924).
Courtesy Jack Tarver Library, Special Collections, Mercer University, Macon, Georgia.

Thomas W. Lamont (1925).
Courtesy Prints and Photographs Division, Library of Congress, Washington, DC.

Averell Harriman (1891–1986). Photograph between 1940 and 1946.
Courtesy Prints and Photographs Division, Library of Congress, Washington, DC.

Officers and Directors of the Illinois Central Railroad, 1950s.
Courtesy Jack Tarver Library, Special Collections, Mercer University, Macon, Georgia.

Introduction

The twentieth century could be called the Great Age of Consumer Branding. Companies competed fiercely for customers, choosing unique names and images in order to generate life-long loyalty. Their efforts were so successful that by 2000 Americans were more likely to recognize leading corporate logos than the names of their political representatives. On the other hand, most Americans probably did not know much about the people or institutions that drove the reconstruction of reality around consumer satisfaction and dissatisfaction. Most, for example, would recognize Coca-Cola, IBM, Life Savers, Canada Dry, Gillette, Ritz-Carlton Hotels, or Vick's Vapo Rub; but few could identify the individuals who created and built those brands. This concept is especially true for the financial backers of products and services; specifically the banks and bankers who helped raise the essential capital and then provided long-term support for emerging companies and their products. What was their work? What were their values and purposes?

This book is about one such person, Eugene W. Stetson. Although once one of the more powerful financial figures in the United States, memories of Stetson currently rest among the other anonymous business leaders who did nothing less than construct the modern world. At various times during the early and mid-twentieth century Stetson was connected to many companies that are familiar to contemporary consumers, including all of those mentioned in the preceding paragraph. During the 1940s, Stetson presided over the Guaranty Trust Company of New York as president and chairman, having begun his career at the bank in 1916. When Stetson was president, Guaranty operated as the largest trust company in the world. This book seeks to explain some of the characteristics of the great corporate trends of the twentieth century by describing and evaluating Stetson's experiences as a banker in the United States and abroad.

The task is complicated by the traditions of business biography. Too often such works have been reduced to overly simplistic tales of good or evil. The American capitalist is either munificent benefactor or Robber Baron. This study tries to avoid these extremes by considering the broader context and focusing on key influences and beliefs that shaped Stetson's career: his upbringing in the post-Reconstruction South; his attitudes toward business and the larger community; his beliefs about the purposes of wealth and wealth-getting; and, most importantly, his ideas and practices in developing profitable relationships with bankers and businessmen. Focusing on these influences and beliefs identifies new aspects regarding the nature of banking and business practice in the first half of the twentieth century, the period during which the American economy became globally dominant. Stetson's life was a piece of this vastly important history, and his biography sheds light on its meaning and character.

This study is also an examination of institutions, particularly in banking. American banking history has been approached from many perspectives. There are written accounts of individual institutions, the experience of particular regions, the role of state and federal governments, the impact of international banking, and the relationship between money and banking. Banking history's diverse authors include professional historians, economists, journalists, and bankers. They have applied a wide variety of methodologies, from econometrics to oral history. One of the more challenging needs of banking history is a better understanding of its human element. It is useful to consider not only the internal operations of a particular bank and the external economic and political forces operating on that bank, but also the lives of bankers and their clients. To write a worthwhile business biography of a banker requires attention to economic, social, and political trends as well as to the myriad complexities of interpreting the subject and the other individuals in his or her life. Studies that consider these operations can counterbalance the inevitability sometimes implied in other kinds of scholarship. A biography has the potential to humanize the field, helping to show the impact that individuals did and could make in the development of banking practice.[1]

---

[1] A discussion of trends in banking history, with a select bibliography, is Larry Schweikart, "U.S. Commercial Banking: A Historiographical Survey," *Business History Review* 65 (Autumn 1991): 606–61. Broad surveys of American commercial and investment banking history are Paul Trescott, *Financing American Enterprise: The Story of Commercial Banking* (New York: Harper & Row, 1963); and Vincent

Particular attention is paid here to the practice of "relationship banking." Although a large literature exists on relationship banking in current practice, there has been few efforts focus on the details of relationship banking in the first half of the twentieth century. Most scholarly writing about relationship banking considers advantages and disadvantages as compared to banking strategies focused on one-time services and increased transactional volume. Relationship banking in the early and mid-twentieth century reflected the core meaning of both banking and business, not simply the selling of bank services. Relationship banking measured success by the cultivation and delivery of multiple continuing services to a particular client over the long run, such as personal service to individual clients in the commercial banking context. The perspective of a commercial relationship banker—such as Stetson—was shaped by a desire to obtain, maintain, and expand the banking services provided to a corporate client over a long period of time. This kind of banking enterprise depended largely on such intangible human factors as personality and communication.[2]

Carosso, *Investment Banking in America: A History* (Cambridge: Harvard University Press, 1970).

[2] A survey of literature on relationship banking is Arnoud W. A. Boot, "Relationship Banking: What Do We Know?", *Journal of Financial Intermediation* 9 (2000): 7–25. Other examples of the extensive writing on contemporary issues in relationship banking are Mark S. Mizruchi and Linda Brewster Stearns, "Getting Deals Done: The Use of Social Networks in Bank Decision-Making," *American Sociological Review* 66 (2001): 647–71; Allen N. Berger and Gregory F. Udell, "The Future of Relationship Lending," in *The Future of Banking*, ed. Benton E. Gup (Westport, CT and London: Quorum Books, 2003); Dwight S. Ritter, *Relationship Banking: Cross-Selling the Bank's Products and Services to Meet Your Customer's Every Need* (Chicago and Cambridge: Bankers Publishing Co. & Probus Publishing Co., 1993) (Bankers are salespeople who should establish relationships with customers to cross-sell banking services); Dimitris N. Chorafas, *The Commercial Banking Handbook: Strategic Planning for Growth and Survival in the New Decade* (London: MacMillan Press Ltd., 1999) 163 ("The relationship banker is the consultant assigned to a specific project, and the way he acts can make or break the customer contact."); Michael T. Jacobs, *Short-Term America: The Causes and Cures of Our Business Myopia* (Boston: Harvard Business School Press, 1991) 143–70 (Arguing that the demise of relationship banking is bad and is connected to unnecessary government regulation.); Arnoud W. A. Boot and Anjan V. Thakor, "Can

The challenge for the historian who wants to describe banker-client relationships is that they usually occurred in a context where confidentiality and unrecorded conversations were the norm. Although frequently hidden, such relationships were at the center of both banking and American business. During Stetson's life experts recognized that establishing and nurturing such relationships was essential. Luther Harr and W. Carlton Harris, finance professors at the Wharton School, wrote in 1936 that among bankers, "Good *mixers* and *joiners* are advantageous, as their wide acquaintanceship may lead to extensive additions to deposit and borrowing accounts." Harr and Harris encouraged bank officers to "recognize and greet the bulk of their depositors and clients." Bank directors, as well, should be selected in part on the basis of their potential to generate new clients. H. Parker Willis, John M. Chapman, and Ralph West, faculty members at the Columbia University Business School, wrote in 1934 that bankers must understand in detail the financial standing and financial requirements of their clients. But aggressive promotion was also necessary to generate desirable business through general advertising and direct contact with clients by bank officers.[3]

In 1926 G. Prather Knapp wrote a remarkable book entitled, *How Banks Increase Their Business*. This volume laid bare the fact that modern banking was a selling game. Knapp presented strategies already in place at prominent banks, complete with photographs, for marketing a range of bank services. He suggested that bank managers should be aware of the needs of special groups: immigrants, women, children, and business. For

---

Relationship Banking Survive Competition?", *Journal of Finance* 55 (April 2000): 678–713; and Bruce W. Morgan, "Demystifying Relationship Banking," *Journal of Retail Banking* 15 (Winter 1993–1994): 9–20 ("Relationship banking means understanding how to create and preserve those customer interactions that will serve to maximize the institution's net asset value.").

[3] Luther Harr and W. Carlton Harris, *Banking Theory and Practice*, 2nd ed. (New York: McGraw-Hill, 1936) 55–304; H. Parker Willis, John M. Chapman, and Ralph West, *Contemporary Banking* (New York: Harper & Bros., 1934) 481–98. See also William H. Kniffin, *The Businessman and His Bank* (New York: McGraw-Hill, 1930) 3–4, which emphasizes banks' active search for customers; and Robert G. Rodkey, *Sound Policies for Bank Management* (New York: Ronald Press Co., 1944) 7, which stresses the need for better public relations.

Knapp, when it came to attracting customers no detail was too insignificant. He implored bank managers to "*Make the tellers smile.*" Strategies also advised that the architecture and decoration of the bank's interior, its advertising policy, and even well-timed speeches by executives could woo clients. Gimmicks, such as one bank's installation of a radio so that curious visitors could hear Calvin Coolidge's presidential inauguration, were desirable because they brought in potential customers from the street. Knapp's superman banker was the fellow who could both sell a service and understand what the service was all about. In his experience, often the bright financiers could not sell and the salesmen were not effective in operating accounts. At the top of the bank hierarchy should be men attuned to the needs of large commercial clients. Only bank executives, however, were likely to operate successfully within the requisite "business and social spheres" to pull in such business. Ultimately, according to Knapp, banking was a personal service with class and cultural components, and the sooner bank officials recognized this, the better for their profits.[4]

Stetson's career provides a unique vantage from which to evaluate the practice of relationship banking because Stetson fit the mold of Knapp's "Super Banker." By describing the career of Stetson and his bank, the meaning of "relationship" in mid-twentieth century relationship banking can be explored. The values of banking and business can be addressed. These tasks are challenging, because Stetson's relationships were complex and evolving; moreover, they were affected by institutional concerns, government actions, and by outsiders to the relationship, including other banks, corporations, and individuals.[5]

Stetson is an especially good subject for this sort of study because he held the highest leadership positions at Guaranty Trust, an important bank.

---

[4] G. Prather Knapp, *How Banks Increase Their Revenue* (Chicago: Rand McNally, 1926) 37, 169.

[5] Examples of historical studies of banking relationships include Naomi R. Lamoreaux, *Insider Lending: Banks, Personal Connections, and Economic Development in Industrial New England* (Cambridge: Cambridge University Press, 1994) and Caroline Fohlin, "Relationship Banking, Liquidity, and Investment in the German Industrialization," *Journal of Finance* 53 (October 2000): 1737–1758 (Finding limited benefits of relationship banking in Germany for industrial investment, 1903–1913.).

More significantly, he excelled at developing relationships with corporate clients. Stetson grew up in Georgia during the 1880s and 1890s and began his banking career there just after the turn of the century. He helped establish a national bank in Macon in 1907, eventually becoming its president. He was active in projects to improve Macon's infrastructure, to organize its businessmen, and to cast off the economic limitations of the Old South. Far-off Wall Street noticed his efforts, and in 1916 he was hired as a vice president with Guaranty, a behemoth on lower Broadway operating within J. P. Morgan & Co.'s expansive orbit.

Over the next thirty years, through two world wars and the Great Depression, Stetson rose in the estimation of the Morgan partners, other officers of Guaranty, and Guaranty's blue chip corporate clients. He was appointed to Guaranty's board in 1928, elected the bank's president in 1941, and chairman of its board in 1944. Stetson was instrumental in the merger of Guaranty in the late 1950s with J. P. Morgan and was a member of the new Morgan Guaranty board at the time of his death in July 1959.

This laundry list of accomplishments is useful, but it does not address what Stetson did as a banker and why it mattered, which is the critical question for this study. Stetson's real achievement was to cultivate and sustain effective banking relationships with officers and directors in his bank as well as with corporate clients. His achievements resulted from a combination of skills, including financial knowledge, social vigor, and a willingness to take the corporate client's perspective. These skills may not appear to be dramatic traits, but they determined who received money from his bank and who did not. Considering that the distribution of economic benefits, capital, is among the most basic issues in economic, political, and social history and analysis, "mere" personal relationships cannot be taken lightly.

Unfortunately, although Stetson's career is well suited to provide insight into mid-twentieth century banking, the materials available to explore his actions are incomplete. I made extensive efforts to find the history of Stetson and his bank's key clients. All the usual sources, including private manuscripts, corporate records, government records (including legal records, which are sometimes ignored by banking historians), oral history, and contemporary publications, were scoured for information. One especially imposing difficulty was the lack of much previous study of Guaranty Trust, which existed from 1864 to 1959.

Although between 1910 and 1959 Guaranty was a global leader in commercial and international banking, banking historians have not spent much time with it. The bank tends to get swallowed up by the larger Morgan presence. In the published literature, it is mentioned—and then only briefly—in the context of Morgan influence after 1910 and the merger with Morgan in the 1950s. As a result, much spadework was necessary to provide context for Stetson's work. I did not intend to write Guaranty's history, but I had to provide an outline of such a history in order to address the central task of the project. Given the study's orientation, that outline is concerned primarily with the operations of the bank, its relation with J. P. Morgan & Co., and its corporate clientele. Frankly, I doubt a sophisticated financial history of this important bank could now be written, given the extensive destruction of documents from its past.

A second research problem concerned Stetson himself. A biographer, even one focused on a portion of the subject's life, such as his or her business activities, needs a solid body of facts to construct a reasonable portrait. Yet Stetson did not leave a large amount of information about his business activities or views. Most notably, there are some speeches, a few articles he wrote, a limited number of letters, some fascinating accounts of his relationships with Cuban sugar companies, and a wonderful set of testimony he provided in a lawsuit against the Illinois Central. This is enough to capture the basic story, but it leaves many gaps and unanswerable questions. Stetson was primarily a man of action, not novel ideas. Yet the record of most of his actions has been lost.

As a result, my strategy was to relate the events in Stetson's career that I could document, focusing on his relationships within and outside the bank. This necessarily includes a good bit of contextual information about the careers of the many companies with which he was intimately involved. Despite the limitations of the sources, there is enough to show Stetson and Guaranty's views of bankers' responsibilities, including the role of a banker as corporate director. There is also information about J. P. Morgan & Co.'s connection with the Guaranty, as well as good evidence of Stetson's many personal relationships, especially with Ernest and Robert Woodruff of

Coca-Cola, Thomas Lamont of J. P. Morgan, Thomas Watson Sr. of IBM, and Averell Harriman, the heir of railroad tycoon E. H. Harriman.

What emerges is the picture of an individual, Gene Stetson, and of business institutions addressing rapid and profound changes in the American economy: global war, new financing techniques and challenges, the increased value of advertising and trademarks, the growth of economic regulation by the federal government, internationalization of markets, devastating depression, shifts in technology, and shareholder pressures. When Stetson left Georgia for New York in 1916 the Federal Reserve System was new and equity markets were hugely underdeveloped. The United States was financially a second-rate nation, automobiles were not considered a reliable means of long distance transportation, and there was no federal regulation of securities issues. Four decades later the banking and economic world had changed in unimagined ways. By the late 1950s, the fact that J. P. Morgan was an incorporated entity that needed cash from Guaranty in order to prosper demonstrated that the banking world had indeed been transformed. Altogether, Stetson's experiences provide a unique perspective on the relationship between elite bankers and corporate clients in the middle decades of the twentieth century. Men like Stetson built the modern business and financial world, in the process creating the institutions and values that continue to shape economic life as well as the American nation as a whole.

1

Surroundings

In July 1959, hefty stacks of papers from the big merger covered Gene Stetson's desk at the Morgan Guaranty Trust Company. Just a few months earlier Stetson had helped engineer a union between the Guaranty Trust and the much smaller but more prestigious J. P. Morgan & Co. This union was perhaps the most important of the large bank mergers of the late 1950s and early 1960s, and could be considered one of the key banking deals of the century. Although by summer the bargain was officially done, the hard work of integrating the two great banks remained. Stetson, a veteran of almost sixty years in banking, planned to be a key part of the effort to achieve that goal, but death intervened and he was never to see the merger's fruitful results.[1]

Just after Stetson's passing, the solemnity of his former office was abruptly disturbed by the distinctive ring of the elevator. Out burst one of Stetson's sons, Charlie, who had dropped in to inspect his father's desk. Chosen by his father to manage the estate, Charlie brushed passed the secretary guarding the office, charged into Gene's office, and started rifling through papers. Naturally, the giant trust company had expected that it would be the senior Stetson's executor. Although Stetson's bank achieved much of its wealth through the management of estates, Gene Stetson apparently thought the bank's services would be too expensive.[2] He was fully aware of the substantial fees Guaranty charged for its elite services.

As Charlie sifted, the secretary had more on her mind than Stetson's heirs. She thought, "Some of those papers deal with merger negotiations; I'm not sure he should be seeing them." Mrs. Lillian Otlowski of the trust department, Stetson's personal assistant for family business, was summoned.

---

[1] Lillian Otlowski, *Over the Walls of Wall Street with Mrs. O* (New Smyrna Beach FL: Luthers' Publishing, 2000) 27.

[2] Ibid., 26–28.

Otlowski immediately called a bank lawyer, John Early. Early calmly replied, "Thanks, Mrs. O. I'll be right down to pay him a visit." Charlie's stay ended promptly. The banker's son actually had a benign objective, far removed from any desire to discover secrets of the merger. As he stated, "About the only time I was in this office was when the old man called me in to bawl the hell out of me. I wanted to see how it felt to be in his chair."[3]

Introducing Eugene W. Stetson

The anecdote hints at Stetson's power and influence, even in death; yet it also suggests how deeply his personality and business career affected the lives of those around him, including his family. For the student of business and banking, however, there are larger and more important questions about Stetson's life. How did he rise from rather moderate circumstances in the failed South after the Civil War to be a top dealmaker in the tightly-controlled world of Wall Street? What skills, beliefs, and outside institutions, persons, and forces shaped Stetson's life and in turn shaped the kind of banking practices that Stetson followed and developed? What precisely was the role of a corporate banker in the middle decades of the twentieth century? As a young man Stetson did not possess what many people running Wall Street during his era had: family connections or personal capital. On the other hand, when Stetson came to New York from Georgia in 1916, he brought a gentlemanly southern charm, intelligence, ambition, faith in the power of banking, and a tough and disciplined focus. The last, implied by Charlie Stetson's desire to sit in his dad's chair, imposed substantial expectations on others. Gene Stetson was serious and demanding, and he expected similar efforts from colleagues and family members. When disappointed, he tended to anger and did not hesitate to show his feelings. Although he had a robust sense of humor, he was unlikely to laugh at himself. Al Gordon, former chairman of Kidder, Peabody & Co., also a legend on Wall Street, once served with Stetson as a corporate

---

[3] Ibid.

director. He recalled: "Stetson was great to work with. But I would never work for him."[4]

Even as a boy Gene Stetson wanted to reach a high level of success. Of course bountiful ambition is present in some individuals in every age and in every profession. If this aspiration was the only significance of Stetson's life his story could be very briefly told. One simply concludes that he was the sort of rational maximizer of self-interest economists so love. But self-interest does not have uniform meaning. What is really significant about Stetson, and any other important corporate leader, is precisely how he envisioned the purpose of his labor in the context of both his business interests and ultimately the whole of society. Contrary to the belief that businessmen produce social wealth without intending to, many business leaders, including Stetson, act in large part based on the assumption that what they do should benefit society broadly.

Ultimately, Stetson's vision of his life and career offered a particular understanding of the relationship between banking, business, and the general well-being of society. Like all visions, Stetson's had strengths and weaknesses. He was neither an intellectual nor a theorist contemplating abstractions. Instead, business, not art, music, or some other force, was his interest and passion. Nonetheless, he saw banking as a means to a larger goal—not simply wealth or wealth creation, but a better, more meaningful life for Americans generally. Perhaps money was a measure of man in Stetson's eyes, but this was primarily because it could be constructive in some larger sense.

This study of Stetson's business experience seeks to portray the details of this vision and how Stetson sought to implement it. The topic is important not just because some of the individuals involved were among the most influential persons in American business and banking history. Rather, it matters on a larger scale because Stetson embodied many of the assumptions and values about business, politics, and economy that

---

[4] Albert Gordon, statement to Chuck Stetson, 1982; John A. Sibley, interview by L. Kenneth Hammond, 3 March 1982; Charles P. Stetson, interview by L. Kenneth Hammond, 24 April 1982; Josephine Hatcher, interview by Adrienne M. Bond 1981–1982; Jack Tarver Library, Special Collections, Mercer University, Macon, Georgia.

triumphed during his life and have dominated American economics and society since then. In short, Stetson helped shape mainstream business. He is among America's winners and thus his life helps to shed light on what it meant to achieve power and success in the twentieth century.

Gene Stetson's career included many substantial banking accomplishments. Given their number and diversity, Stetson himself would probably not identify one undertaking as clearly preeminent. It was against his nature to collect trophies, as opposed to concentrating on doing one's duty in all events in the best possible manner.[5] A historian, however, might ask whether his key achievement was orchestrating the merger of the Guaranty Trust Company with J. P. Morgan. Or, perhaps it was serving as a key negotiator in the buyout of Coca-Cola, the largest business sale in the history of the South before 1920. There are other possibilities. Was it keeping the Illinois Central Railroad from going bankrupt during the Depression? What about helping to establish the giant Southern Company electric utility in the 1940s and 1950s, a project expressly intended to help his native region? Or, was it being among the men who made Guaranty Trust one of America's leading banks from the 1920s through the 1940s? Ultimately, the individual works are best understood as part of a pattern of behavior, with deeper meaning for Stetson and for American business and banking.

In summarizing Stetson's accomplishments, one can begin with the last, the Morgan merger, as it represents the culmination of many strands in his long banking career. In 1958, Stetson initiated the merger of his own Guaranty Trust Company with the venerable J. P. Morgan & Co. At the time, Stetson was in his late seventies—a retired chairman and former president of Guaranty. Despite retirement, he maintained an office at the bank and showed up nearly every work day. Top-level personnel needs, according to Stetson, drove the need for a deal. Prior to the merger Stetson told insiders that his replacement as chairman lacked the essential spark to keep the Guaranty on top. This deal was the last of hundreds of transactions for which Stetson served as the man in the background who inspired the action, persevered through the details, and carried it to conclusion. For his

---

[5] Charles P. Stetson interview.

efforts in the Morgan merger he received a $1 million investment banking fee years before mergers and acquisition departments were established at investment banking firms on Wall Street.[6]

The merger with Morgan provided a complex, yet fitting end to a career that began at the dawn of twentieth century, an entirely different era of American finance. When Stetson first entered Georgia banking in 1901, the gold standard reigned and national banks issued their own circulating banknotes. Deposit insurance was nonexistent. When banks failed, which they did at an alarming rate, depositors were left holding the proverbial empty bag. Only in the 1930s, long after Stetson came to New York, did the federal government mandate a national deposit insurance program. Stetson, incidentally, along with most other executives at New York's top commercial banks, thought insurance was a bad idea because it supposedly protected the faulty management of bad bankers through a tax on honest bankers.

In 1901 the world's financial center resided in London. Stetson was a member of the first generation of American bankers who could claim global supremacy in finance. During World War I, when the center of capital shifted to New York, he was a vice president at Guaranty, an institution already well-positioned as a leader in international banking. After the war, when publicly traded security markets boomed, commercial banks started to arrange public offerings. By arranging public offerings, security markets challenged a role formerly dominated by private banks, such as J. P. Morgan. Stetson was part of this trend as well; he acted as a leader in one of more significant initial public offerings in American finance—that of the Coca-Cola Company. From his position at Guaranty Stetson participated in all the subsequent great events of banking history in the middle decades of the century: the collapse of the 1930s, the challenges of financing global war in the 1940s, and the consolidations and readjustments of the 1950s.

Throughout these decades Stetson's connection to the Coca-Cola Company best reflected his role as advisor to corporations, especially as a director. When Stetson died, he was the longest standing member of the company's board of directors, having served longer than even company

---

[6] The merger is described in detail in Chapter 14.

president Robert Woodruff. Of course, the Coca-Cola story is well known. The drink is the most successful consumer product ever made. In the early twenty-first century, over one billion Cokes are sold each year, and Coca-Cola owns the single most recognized, and most valuable, brand name in the world, estimated at more than $65 billion in 2006. The Coca-Cola Company has paid dividends yearly since 1893 and during that time has increased dividends over forty times.[7]

In July and August 1919 Stetson helped put the financing together so that Atlanta's Trust Company of Georgia, a firm one-tenth the size of Coca-Cola and headed by Ernest Woodruff, along with a group of New York banks, could acquire control of Coca-Cola. There were several worrisome points that could have killed the deal. Among these problems was that a federal court had ruled the company's prized trademark invalid. While that question was on appeal in the Supreme Court, Stetson helped bring the public offering to a successful conclusion. The concept of giving significant value to a "brand" was a new feature to financing in those days, contrary to the time-honored means of valuing a business by "hard" assets, such as real estate or inventory. Stetson, Woodruff, and the New York banks valued the company at $25 to $30 million although its hard assets were only worth $5 million. They rightly saw the bulk of Coca-Cola's value in its trademark.

The Coke transaction revealed much about Stetson's salesmanship. He loved business challenges, particularly difficult situations with difficult people. In 1919 Asa Candler's family owned Coca-Cola. The Candlers had been looking for a buyer for several years as Asa's children wanted money, not the business. At that time Atlanta was a small city and in Atlanta it was well-known that Asa Candler despised Ernest Woodruff. So the Candlers were not likely to sell the company to Woodruff or his bank, the Trust Company of Georgia. Stetson had the challenge to overcome this barrier. As part of the deal, the Candlers were led to believe that the purchase offer derived from New Yorkers. This could not have been surprising because

[7] Daniel Workman, "Top Global Brands: World's Most Valuable Trademarks in 2006," http://internationaltrade.suite101.com/article.cfm/top_global_brands. Stetson's relationship with Coca-Cola, including the 1919 sale, is described in detail in Chapters 5–7.

southerners in 1919 were not likely to be able to come up with more than $20 million for a soft drink company. As a key negotiator for the purchase, Stetson traveled to Atlanta and met with the Candlers to represent the "New York interests" who were supposedly buying the company. Of course, he did nothing to suggest to the Candlers that among the New York buyers were the hated Woodruff and his bank.

This aspect of the deal reflected another dimension of Stetson's business career: his interest in southern economic development. Despite the disdain for Woodruff, would not even Asa Candler be surprised by the benefits to Atlanta and Georgia that have resulted from the fact that the company did not move to New York? In 2006, the Robert Woodruff Foundation owned $1.8 billion of Coca-Cola stock, from whose dividends the Foundation gave away approximately $100 million, primarily for cultural activities in Georgia. As a direct result of Coca-Cola's success, Emory University is among the best endowed universities in America. This, of course, is only some of the wealth that has been created by and distributed to employees and shareholders through Coca-Cola in Atlanta. Stetson's banking continues to make a permanent mark in his native Georgia.[8]

Appropriately, this is where the story should begin, in the South where Stetson grew up. Although he lived in the New York area from 1916 until his death forty-three years later, Stetson frequently returned to Georgia and was always recharged after visits home. He considered himself a loyal southerner. Born in 1881, just four years after the last federal troops departed from the Reconstruction South, he was profoundly shaped by the contrast between his region's great potential human capital and its deficiency of financial capital. He was also deeply influenced by contemporary beliefs about how to remedy these problems. To explain Stetson's business career, one must start with the place where his personality and habits were formed.

---

[8] On the Woodruff Foundation, see "About the Foundation," http://woodruff.org/about_rww.aspx.

After the Civil War

Stetson grew up in central Georgia during the 1880s and 1890s, in the economically depressed environment of the post-Civil War South. This South, including his hometown of Macon, Georgia, reeled from the effects of the Civil War. Battles had been fought and men killed within a few miles of where Stetson played as a boy. Particularly devastating to the area was Sherman's "March to the Sea," from Atlanta to Savannah, from which Macon only narrowly escaped.[9]

Before the war, the value of human property in the region, some four million slaves, exceeded $1 billion. This value was more than all of the southern capital in industry, banks, and railroads. Therefore, the abolition of slavery destroyed an entire economic system, rendering worthless the investments in human property that had accumulated since colonial times. One historian estimates that the shock caused the South to lose thirty percent of its total wealth and fifty percent of its land value. Further, over 130,000 Southern soldiers died in the War. The economic effect of this loss of life was great, considering especially that the white and black population in 1860 numbered only about ten million. In addition, by one estimate, as many as 50,000 civilians may have perished. At the end of the war southern income was less than thirty percent of the North's average.[10]

The end of slavery ruined the plantation system but it did not destroy the strong demand for its most valuable crop, cotton. Short staple, or "upland" cotton, grows almost anywhere in the Deep South, including in the area of central Georgia where Stetson lived as a boy and a young man. During the 1790s Eli Whitney's cotton gin resolved short staple's key limitation, a sticky fiber from which it is difficult to remove seeds. Throughout the nineteenth century cotton was labor intensive to cultivate

---

[9] On central Georgia during the war, see generally Richard W. Iobst, *Civil War Macon* (Macon GA: Mercer University Press, 1999).

[10] Claudia Goldin and Frank Lewis, "The Economic Cost of the American Civil War," *Journal of Economic History*, 35 (June 1975): 299–326; Jonathan Hughes and Louis P. Cain, *American Economic History*, 7th ed. (Boston: Pearson Education, Inc., 2007) 265–73; Roger L. Ransom, "The Economic Consequences of the American Civil War," in *The Political Economy of War and Peace*, ed. by M. Wolfson (Norwell MA: Kluwer Academic Publishers, 1998).

and harvest. Yet the crop flourished because of nearly insatiable demand from the textile manufacturers of Europe, New England, and eventually the South itself. Cotton became an American crop whose production exploited some of the best resources of the nation.[11]

In addition to ruining slave-based agriculture, the Civil War brought destruction to Georgia's other economic institutions. Both Confederate and Union soldiers seized or destroyed large amounts of property in their path. Government borrowing to finance the war produced spectacular inflation that ruined banking and finance and made even the necessities of life inaccessible. The state's education system, including its colleges, essentially ceased to function. Railroads, the key to agricultural markets, which had been highly developed in 1860, suffered from neglect and intentional destruction.[12]

The subsequent Reconstruction period, from 1865 to 1877, failed to resolve the pressing racial, political, or economic issues raised by the end of slavery and the collapse of the slave-based economy. One statistic summarizes the experience: in 1880, the year before Stetson's birth, the South had been unable to raise per capita output back to its 1860 level. Most of the blame for this rests with reactionary white southern leadership. The federal Congress passed a sweeping series of laws, including the act establishing the Freeman's Bureau, technically called the Bureau of Refugees, Freedmen and Abandoned Lands, which addressed some of the changes effected by war. Soon the country saw the Thirteenth, Fourteenth, and Fifteenth Amendments to the Constitution, which ended slavery and sought to guarantee the freed slaves certain civil rights, including voting rights. Such laws could have revolutionized the role of the federal government in economic and racial matters and dramatically improved the operation of markets. For a brief period, southern state governments,

---

[11] Timothy C. Jacobson and George D. Smith, *Cotton's Renaissance: A Study in Market Innovation* (New York: Cambridge University Press, 2001) 41–68.

[12] Among the many accounts of the Civil War in Georgia are Kenneth Coleman, ed. *A History of Georgia*, 2nd ed. (Athens: University of Georgia Press, 1991) 187–204; T. Conn Bryan, *Confederate Georgia* (Athens: University of Georgia Press, 1953).

including in Georgia, were controlled by leaders anxious to transform life in the region.[13]

Most southern whites, however, and especially those with land, wanted to return to a system as close to slavery as possible. Committed to the continued subjugation of black people, they formed terrorist organizations such as the Ku Klux Klan that targeted blacks and white Republican supporters of Reconstruction. Ultimately, through force, fraud, and intimidation, they regained power state-by-state, including in Georgia, during the 1870s. The key to this revived white power was as much economic as political. The end of Reconstruction not only meant that the uniformed Yankees would go home; it also meant white southerners regained control of the both the land and the black labor that were needed to produce cotton and other crops for market.[14]

The economic system that emerged from Reconstruction was grossly inefficient. In general, the best land remained controlled by wealthier whites. Given the labor-intense nature of cotton production and the refusal of newly freed blacks to work in slave-like gangs for wages, a system of renting and sharecropping emerged. Many poorer blacks and whites grew cash crops on shares, paying landlords with a portion of the crop. If they had their own mules or equipment, perhaps they might rent for money, an arrangement that held out a hope for greater profit and independence. Of course, all market-based agriculture needs credit to get a crop planted and to tide a farmer over during the growing season. In the South, banking and credit, both in a primitive state after the war, devolved to merchants, many of whom were also larger landowners. These landowners provided advances to renters and sharecroppers, but at extremely high rates, often exceeding fifty per cent per year. The system produced a self-defeating cycle of debt

---

[13] On Reconstruction-era Georgia, see William H. Bragg, "Reconstruction in Georgia," http://www.georgiaencyclopedia.org/nge/Article.jsp?path=/History-Archaeology/CivilWarandReconstruction/Topics-12&id=h-2533; Coleman, *History of Georgia*, 207–37; Eric Foner, *Reconstruction: America's Unfinished Revolution, 1863–1877* (New York: Harper & Row, 1988) 564–601; Allen Trelease, *White Terror: The Ku Klux Klan Conspiracy and Southern Reconstruction* (New York: Harper & Row, 1971) 226–42.

[14] Ibid.

and excessive dependence on cash crops, particularly cotton. This was a recipe for social and economic poverty.[15]

Not all Southerners, however, were willing to accept the low standard of living imposed by this system. By the 1880s, a strong movement had emerged to effectively refashion the South in a northern image through industrialization. Industrialization did not mean racial equality, as the best jobs would be reserved for whites. Nonetheless, railroad expansion and textile manufacturing were perhaps the most prominent early examples of this thinking. A leading voice in the call for a "New South" was Henry W. Grady of the *Atlanta Constitution*. Grady broadcast his views with religious fervor. Predictably, the movement centered in the new and growing cities of the piedmont, such as Atlanta, Birmingham, Charlotte, and Durham. Unfortunately, lacking capital, the South turned to northern, and especially New York, sources of money. Railroads in particular were dominated by northern investors, who naturally reaped any dividends and made key decisions about their operation. Much investment was forthcoming, but the larger price was to produce a kind of regional colonialism that did not always serve the interests of southerners.[16]

American Finance

The economic and social plight of the South is only one piece of the larger world into which Stetson was born. To be sure, he grew up in a Georgia characterized by inefficient agriculture, the triumph of white supremacy, a slowly emerging colonial industrialization, and the lingering disabilities of war. Yet, he was also born at the very beginning of modern American finance, which included the rise of modern investment and commercial banking. Not long before Stetson was a toddler in Macon, Jay

---

[15] Foner, *Reconstruction*, 399–409; Hughes and Cain, *American Economic History*, 273–80; Harold D. Woodman, *New South—New Law: The Legal Foundations of Credit and Labor Relations in the Postbellum Agricultural South* (Baton Rouge: Louisiana State University Press, 1995).

[16] C. Vann Woodward, *Origins of the New South, 1877–1913* (Baton Rouge, LA: Louisiana State University Press, 1951) 107–58, 291–320; Harold E. Davis, *Henry Grady's New South: Atlanta, A Brave and Beautiful City* (Tuscaloosa: University of Alabama Press, 1990).

Cooke became the first American to raise significant capital from Americans, not Europeans, to finance American economic activity.[17]

Traditionally, nineteenth century American railroads and industry were financed by raising money from Europe, primarily Britain. During the Civil War, however, financier Jay Cooke of Philadelphia found a way to tap the mass of individual savers in the United States by using the new technology of the telegraph and door-to-door sales. Cooke placed war securities through aggressive salesmanship and advertising. He sold more than $350 million of these securities, an astronomical sum at the time. Cooke also supported prices in the secondary securities market. After the war Jay Cooke & Co. continued to open channels for raising money on a national basis from individuals. Once again, Cooke used advertising and individual salesmen to sell securities.[18]

A corollary to growing American investment was the rise of relationship banking, particularly through private banking partnerships. In the absence of extensive government regulation prohibiting such activities, leading private bankers became personally active in client companies, joining their corporate boards and finance committees. These bankers routinely provided inside and outside financial advice and services. Such potentially long-term relationships became very profitable and prized as companies began to choose selected banking firms as their "principal bankers"—meaning that the banking firms did not have to compete with other bankers for the client's business.[19]

The large capital needs of railroads drove the early evolution of American finance. Railroads demanded a steady stream of capital, but the financial practices that developed around them created an environment with

---

[17] On Cooke, see Charles R. Geisst, *Wall Street: A History* (New York: Oxford University Press, 1997) 49–58; Henrietta Larson, *Jay Cooke: Private Banker* (Cambridge: Harvard University Press, 1936).

[18] Geisst, *Wall Street*, 53–58; Larson, *Jay Cooke*, 119–37; Hughes and Cain, *American Economic History*, 388; Samuel L. Hayes III and Philip Hubbard, *Investment Banking: A Tale of Three Cities* (Boston: Harvard Business School Press, 1990) 92.

[19] Benjamin J. Klebaner, *American Commercial Banking* (Boston: Twayne Publishers, 1990) 14–16, 91; Hughes and Cain, *American Economic History*, 394–96.

few rules. The enormous databases, credit ratings, and information that bankers can call up in the twenty-first century at a moment's notice did not exist. As a result, bankers relied on personal relationships and personal knowledge of companies. Of course, benefits flowed to and from the railroads and their bankers. The railroads gained prestige as well as advice and services from the bankers, including the endorsement of supporting banks. In turn, bankers received big fees for securities distribution, including registrations and transfers.[20]

According to finance historian Samuel L. Hayes III, a few private banks, created along the lines of the British and European continental merchant banks, led the way in American finance. Private banks provided their own capital based on wealthy partners in the firm and formed syndicates of smaller banking houses that distributed securities. In the last half of the nineteenth century, the securities of choice were mostly bonds paying three to five percent after the lead firm or firms pocketed a management fee of one and one-half percent. Among the outstanding private banks were J. P. Morgan & Co., Drexel & Co., and Kuhn Loeb and Co., led by Jacob Schiff. The revolutionary change produced by these institutions is well summarized in an example by historians Jonathan Hughes and Louis P. Cain:

> In the late 1860s, [Andrew] Carnegie, then a Pennsylvania Railroad official, had gone to London to raise money. It could not be done in the United States. In 1900, when Carnegie decided to sell out, he wrote his price, more than $400 million, on a piece of paper, and handed it to his boy-wonder executive, Charles Schwab, who delivered it to Pierpont Morgan. Schwab reported that Morgan merely glanced at the paper and said, "I'll take it." The result was the biggest industrial merger to date, United States Steel, which had two-thirds of the industry's ingot capacity, $550 million of common stock, $550 million of preferred stock, and $304 million in bonds. The

---

[20] Albro Martin, *Railroads Triumphant: The Growth, Rejection and Rebirth of a Vital American Force* (New York: Oxford University Press, 1992) 333–38 ("The need to marshal unheard-of amounts of capital into fixed, long-term investments, of which railroads were the chief and for a long time almost the only form, created American investment banking as it existed down to the Great Depression.").

American capital market, by then centered in Wall Street, had come into its own with investment bankers like Morgan filling the pilot role. It all happened in a single lifetime, in the business career of a single person, such as Carnegie or Morgan.[21]

The rise of private investment banks took place in a larger environment of growing complexity, wealth, and sophistication of financial institutions. Commercial banks and insurance companies, in particular, experienced steady development. Outstanding commercial banks in this period included National City Bank, the forerunner of Citigroup, Chase National Bank, First National Bank of Boston, eventually part of Bank of America, and, especially after 1910, Stetson's Guaranty Trust Company of New York. J. P. Morgan, of course, was linked to many of these and other financial companies, a factor that led to the industry's concentration in New York.[22]

On the one hand, Gene Stetson was born to the legacy of a failed economic system rooted in slavery, white supremacy, the disaster of Civil War, and inefficient cash crop agriculture. Yet, at this same moment the American industrial economy and its financial structures were undergoing

---

[21] Hayes and Hubbard, *Investment Banking*, 91–112; Samuel L. Hayes III, A. Michael Spence, and David Van Praag Marks, *Competition in the Investment Banking Industry* (Cambridge: Harvard University Press, 1983) 5–16; Hughes and Cain, *American Economic History*, 381, 396.

[22] See Harold van B. Cleveland and Thomas F. Huertas, *Citibank, 1812–1970* (Cambridge: Harvard University Press, 1985); John Donald Wilson, *The Chase: Chase Manhattan Bank, 1945–1985* (Boston: Harvard Business School Press, 1985); Ben Ames Williams, *Bank of Boston 200: A History of New England's Leading Bank, 1784–1984* (Boston: Houghton Mifflin, 1984).

spectacular change, including in the South. Stetson's generation of southerners was the inheritor of both the Klan and its political consequences as well as to new visions of wealth and industry. Georgia's Henry Grady, Jay Cooke, and other financial kings such as Jay Gould and J. P. Morgan were creating a foundation in thought and finance upon which Stetson would build his own ideas and career. Stetson's task was to take selectively from these different influences and apply them to the larger forces of change in American business and banking in the twentieth century.

2

Preparing for Wall Street

Eugene William Stetson was born on 5 December 1881, in Hawkinsville, Georgia, a town on the Ocmulgee River in the south central part of the state. His father, James D. Stetson, worked as a cashier at the Hawkinsville Bank and Trust Company. The family was typically southern in some ways and, yet, decidedly unique in others. James had grown up in Milledgeville, attended Oglethorpe University, and served as an officer in the Confederate army. Eugene's mother, Eugenia Sophia Pate, called the Hawkinsville area home, where her father, also a former Confederate officer, was a farmer and merchant. Certainly it was ordinary for children of Gene's generation to grow up in a small town or rural environment, to parents who had lived in the region since birth. On the other hand, his parents were plainly well above average in terms of education and community standing. Not many boys in middle Georgia had a father who had attended college and was not earning a living by manual labor.[1]

Gene remained in Hawkinsville until he was about ten years old when the family moved to nearby Macon after his father took a position in another bank. There he attended a public school and then Gordon Institute, in Barnesville, named for Confederate General John B. Gordon. Stetson finished his studies at Gordon in 1897, the year he turned sixteen. The amount of time Stetson was able to stay in school was indeed a great luxury.

---

[1] Adrienne Moore Bond, *Eugene W. Stetson* (Macon GA: Mercer University Press, 1983) 1–4. Stetson's southern heritage was stronger on his mother's side, which immigrated to Virginia from Europe in the colonial period. The Stetson line, by contrast, was originally from New England and moved South in the early nineteenth century. A branch in the family tree was John B. Stetson (1830–1906), the hat maker. William J. Northen, ed., *Men of Mark in Georgia* (Atlanta: A. B. Caldwell, 1912) 298–300.

As late as the 1930s, the average white Georgian had less than six years of formal education.[2]

The family held high expectations for their children, including young Gene. He sensed this and was eager to take advantage of his chances. After all, it was the Victorian era, and in the South that meant a certain level of seriousness and a sharp sense of responsibility. Boys, such as Stetson, had great reverence for Robert E. Lee's admonition that "Duty is the most sublime word in our language." In fact, Lee was Stetson's lifelong hero. This partly explains his deep sense of personal loyalty to friends and family as well as a strong work ethic. Early on, Gene determined to do well. At the tender age of nine, young Stetson gave his father, then working in Macon preparing to start a new banking job with a national bank, the very sober advice to "Do right and fear not." At fourteen, the future banker wrote letters home praising standard virtues such as loyalty—more evidence of the impact of values represented by solid and manly figures such as General Lee. He spoke disparagingly of dishonorable traits he disliked, such as tattle-telling.[3]

Although many of his youthful letters were formal and even business like, they also expressed deep affection. From Gordon he wrote his father that "of course, I am very homesick and want to come home, but intend to study hard and make something of myself." Much of Stetson's ethic can be explained by his religious upbringing, which had a lasting impact. His father was a Baptist deacon and Scripture was required learning. As a teenager Stetson wrote his father, "I received your exceedingly loving letter and was glad that we have pleased you. You know what the Bible says, 'A wise son maketh a glad father.' I have tried to work and have been rewarded as will anyone when they believe."[4]

Yet there was also something very worldly about his efforts. The future Wall Streeter reported he was "keeping an account in my little book of how much I get from home. I will be as economical as I can." In 1895 Stetson

---

[2] Bond, *Stetson*, 4–11.

[3] Ibid., 4–11; Charles P. Stetson, interview by L. Kenneth Hammond, 24 March 1982, Jack Tarver Library, Special Collections Mercer University, Macon, Georgia.

[4] Bond, *Stetson*, 6–10.

successfully saved, borrowed, and amassed fifty dollars, a huge sum for a boy, especially in the midst of the greatest national depression in American history, to go on a church-sponsored trip to Washington, Baltimore, and New York. There he set eyes on Central Park and the almost new Brooklyn Bridge. The trip ignited a permanent fascination with railroads, travel, and perhaps most importantly, New York City.[5]

After Gordon, Stetson received another big opportunity. In 1897, he entered Mercer University, a Baptist school established in the 1830s in Penfield, Georgia, and moved to Macon in 1871. From his home on College Street, Stetson could walk the few blocks to the small campus. In the 1890s Mercer's curriculum and environment was similar to that of other American colleges. Most of the coursework was required, as the almost 200 male, white, and largely Baptist students moved lockstep through a liberal arts curriculum that featured Greek, Latin, mathematics, literature, history, and science. Traditionally, the close-knit school aimed to prepare men for the ministry, teaching, or other learned professions. Although some economics classes were offered, mere commerce, which would become Stetson's life work, was not yet given academic attention. On the other hand, schools like Mercer—perhaps recognizing that many students would become preachers and lawyers—encouraged oratory, sponsoring formal debating societies. Stetson, however, disliked this sort of performance and even applied for an exemption from public speaking duties.[6]

Although the course of study did not direct anyone to high finance, Mercer offered other valuable opportunities. Perhaps most importantly, Stetson discovered abilities to lead others, especially on money matters. Sports were popular during Stetson's student days and proved a useful vehicle for fun and learning. In 1899, Stetson probably attended the football game in Macon when Mercer was crushed by Coach John Heisman's famous Auburn squad. Stetson especially loved baseball, and although he

---

[5] Ibid., 4–5.

[6] Ibid., 13–21; Spright Dowell, *A History of Mercer University, 1833–1953* (Macon GA: Mercer University, 1958) 217-230; *Catalogue and Annual Announcement of Mercer University, Macon 1897–1898* (Macon GA: J. W. Burke, 1898) 22–23; Charles P. Stetson interview.

did not make the university team he gladly became its manager. In an era before scholarships, professional staff, and athletic "departments," this work required making travel arrangements and raising money to pay the team's expenses. Stetson's aggressive approach included persuading his father to guarantee payment while he set about raising money. The young businessman quickly erased the chronic debt of the school's association responsible for athletics and kept it in a surplus. As a contemporary newspaper reported: "Stetson did things on a flourishing scale: there was nothing too big for him to tackle and as a result the people of Macon had the best college baseball team here that season the old town had ever had before. He gave his men the best there was. The best hotel service in every city was at their disposal." This early effort made impressions and friends that lasted a lifetime.[7]

At Mercer Stetson was determined to succeed, but not as a scholar. He was socially popular, and considered an underachiever academically and happy-go-lucky. As he wrote a few years after leaving college, in his "sophomore year at Mercer I conceived the idea of having a good time rather than studying, and now I find that when I want to study that it is harder for me to do so than it would have been should I have taken the full advantage during my college course." So, in addition to managing the baseball team, he joined the Phi Delta Theta fraternity. The handsome Stetson was interested in girls from the neighboring women's school, Wesleyan College, attended by his sister and located distractingly close, just a few blocks from Mercer.[8]

Stetson's life changed abruptly in the spring of 1901, his senior year. First, tragedy struck in March when his father succumbed to Bright's disease, a kidney ailment, and died. Second, he quit Mercer. In the 1940s Stetson recalled that there was a "row with the math professor" which caused his departure. He was naturally sensitive about the episode and during his life gave inconsistent accounts of the experience. In 1956, for example, he wrote that he "took an elective course, in my junior and senior years, in order to help rehabilitate Mercer athletics," and that was the reason he did not graduate; however, a dispute seems a more likely reason.

---

[7] Bond, *Stetson*, 16–18; *Mercer University Kinetoscope 01* (N.d.: n.p. [1901?]).

[8] Bond, *Stetson*, 16.

In February 1901 the faculty expressed concerns when Stetson proposed taking the baseball team to the University of Alabama, and in April it allowed a student to drop Latin because of class absences related to baseball. All this is evidence of tension between Stetson and the administration. More important, a clash developed over a planned game between the University of South Carolina and Mercer, and in May the South Carolina school demanded $75 that it may have been promised for expenses by Stetson. The matter was resolved, but not without cost. Perhaps overreacting from these events and realizing that at any rate his college days were practically over, Stetson left Mercer without a degree.[9]

The behavior is noteworthy because he later made persistence under adversity a hallmark of his business practice. His departure from Mercer may have contributed to this persistence. After 1901, moreover, he had a need and desire to be on his own financially. With a deceased father, the lazy days of dependence were gone for good. Although the family was better off than most, it was not wealthy. Equally important was that Stetson had no intention of using such a petty dispute to cut deeper ties, so his departure was not intended to leave a permanent scar. He soon made amends with the math professor, who later joined the faculty at Columbia University when Stetson was in New York. More revealing, Stetson became a loyal Mercer alumnus, regularly attending reunions, sponsoring trips with old baseball buddies, and providing substantial financial support. He always admired Pinckney D. Pollock, Mercer's president during his senior year. Despite the fact that he did not graduate he considered himself a full member of the Class of 1901. Ultimately, for Stetson the meaning of Mercer went beyond books or baseball. The experience was about relationships and an early appreciation for the fact that institutions and leaders can enrich and change lives.[10]

---

[9] Ibid., 18–20; Eugene W. Stetson to J. W. Norman, 16 February 1956, Eugene W. Stetson Papers; Mercer University Faculty Minutes, 1898–1907, 4 February, 19 April, 13 May 1901, Jack Tarver Library, Special Collections, Mercer University, Macon, Georgia.

[10] Bond, *Stetson*, 19–21; Eugene W. Stetson to J. W. Norman, 16 February 1956, Eugene W. Stetson Papers.

Learning Banking

With college behind him, Stetson started his first full-time job as a teller and debt collector at the American National Bank in Macon. This bank was the same bank where his father had been vice president and where he had worked in the summers during college. The choice of banking as a profession seemed inevitable, perhaps too inevitable, given that the job seemed entirely explained by family connections. Stetson had wide interests, but from the beginning he rejected life as a preacher, a doctor, a lawyer, or a teacher, the careers chosen by most other Mercer students and educated young men in the Georgia of his day.[11]

Actually, going into banking was a kind of political statement. In the South agriculture was still king, at least culturally. For many, especially the rural majority, banking, bankers, and even corporations in general represented the evil and corrupt ways of urban life. The banking profession was also burdened by unhealthy overtones of Yankee imperialism. Bankers did not wear overalls, they did not get their hands dirty and most important to the man who worked in the field or the factory, they did not produce anything tangible. Suspicion and, in some cases, hatred was directed at national banks, precisely the kind of institution where Stetson began banking. The Populist Party, which was very popular in Georgia in the 1890s, supported the abolition of national banks. Georgia's loudest Populist, Tom Watson, opposed the Democrats' nominee for vice president in 1896 in large part because he was a national banker. To the Populists bankers manipulated the money supply to farmers' detriment through their support of a gold standard and privately issued bank notes. Banks were also associated with Jews, still the object of intense bigotry in both Georgia and

---

[11] Ibid., 21; Northen, ed., *Men of Mark*, 298. The American National Bank of Macon was chartered in 1891 and voluntarily liquidated in December 1916, apparently into the Citizens and Southern Bank of Savannah, which many decades later became associated with the Bank of America. See, John Hickman and Dean Oakes, *Standard Catalog of National Bank Notes* (Iola WI: Krause Publications, 1982) 158.

the United States. While Stetson was a banker in Macon a wild mob lynched Leo Frank in Marietta, one of the most notorious examples of anti-Semitism in American history. So by choosing banking Stetson was taking sides, allying himself with a particular vision, one that was not even respectable in parts of rural Georgia.[12]

After three years of learning about banking in Macon, Stetson was recruited by the Exchange Bank, later Exchange National Bank, in Fitzgerald, Georgia, to the higher position of cashier. This position paid more than the Macon job. At the time, Stetson's supervisor from the American National Bank praised the young banker for having been "exceedingly accurate in all of his work and honest and straight in all of his transactions." Further, Stetson's "father helped to organize the American National Bank and was its managing Officer up to the time of his death. We believe the Son has inherited much of the business sagacity and conservatism for which his Father was famous." The choice of the word "conservatism" is revealing. In a small town Georgia bank with slender resources and no deposit insurance to protect customers, perceived caution in guarding bank assets was essential.[13]

Although Stetson's new title of "cashier" seems menial, in fact it denoted the role of treasurer or senior operating officer. As cashier, Stetson was in charge of ensuring that the bank's assets matched its liabilities. This meant deposits were sufficient to fund the loans extended towards local businesses. If the deposits were in surplus, then they were reinvested in a security with the best return. The cashier also oversaw the mechanical side of paying and receiving money, which required security and proper documentation. The cashier held a critically important job in a small Georgia bank, just subordinate to the general manager. A cashier had to know and practice the nuts and bolts of banking.

---

[12] On Populism, see Barton C. Shaw, *The Wool-Hat Boys: Georgia's Populist Party* (Baton Rouge: Louisiana State University Press, 1984), on Watson, C. Vann Woodward, *Tom Watson: Agrarian Rebel* (New York: Macmillan, 1938), and on Frank, Leonard Dinnerstein, *The Leo Frank Case* (Athens: University of Georgia Press, 1997).

[13] Bond, *Stetson*, 23–24. The Exchange bank became a national bank in May 1906. Like many other Georgia small town operations, it closed during the 1930s Depression. Hickman and Oakes, *Standard Catalog*, 155–56.

Stetson's willingness to take a new job says something about his growing ambition. As the son of a former bank officer living in his hometown, he had plenty of connections and was well-placed to find a foothold on the local economic ladder of Macon. Yet, he left and took the Fitzgerald job. In an important sense the decision represented Stetson breaking out of his father's mold, a move that would be repeated on an even larger scale when he moved to New York twelve years later.

Fitzgerald was a small, isolated place located approximately seventy-five miles southeast of Macon. Naturally the new cashier in town missed his family, friends, and particularly his fiancée, Josephine Moulton Shaw. But the young couple wrote often and frequent letters bound them closer. Josephine encouraged and consoled Stetson: "You are miserable, I know. It is going to be hard for you. There are many struggles before you. Would that God would grant that I could help you bear them.... Write me everything—don't forget—that may help. You are brave and strong, dear and must conquer." Six months of loneliness was apparently enough, and in December 1904, Stetson showed he was ready for a higher level of independence and adulthood. Now 23, he married Josephine in her parents' home and they set up a household in Fitzgerald.[14]

Fitzgerald influenced Stetson's views about economics and banking. An unusual town with about 5,000 residents, it was incorporated only a few years before Stetson's arrival, partly by immigrant Union soldiers. In 1895, Northern veterans formed a company and acquired 50,000 acres of Georgia wiregrass. Creating Fitzgerald on this property from scratch, they named the town's streets after Union and Confederate generals and christened the local hotel the "Lee-Grant." Fitzgerald was a "new" town as far as Georgia was concerned and, more important, not unduly unhampered by the ideals of the Old South. The drive for profit, especially in lumber and cotton, shaped the local economy. Fitzgerald had three banks, was a cotton shipping center, and resided at the junction of two branches of the Atlantic Coast Line Railway. In Fitzgerald, Stetson could easily see that the railroad and cash crops from the land were keys to economic development.

---

[14] Ibid., 24–28.

Fitzgerald was also where Stetson learned the core of banking practice—the creation of money through lending and through banker's acceptances.[15]

In Fitzgerald Stetson witnessed the bank-lending process in its most basic form. If a farmer went to the local bank to borrow money to buy necessities for the upcoming planting and growing season, he left behind a note with the bank that would be redeemed, with interest, after the harvest. When the farmer bought seed, fertilizer, and equipment from a local merchant some of this money could find its way back into the bank. The bank "reserved" some of each deposit, retaining it at the bank, but then it was free to lend out the remainder to other borrowers. For example, some of a loan to a farmer could be returned to the bank in the form of a deposit from a merchant, and, after the reserve process, the bank lent a portion of it to another borrower, who in turn spent it on goods whose sellers deposited some of the money in the bank, whereupon after the reserve process, the bank loaned out another sum against the reserves. This cycle of relending the same money over and over again, albeit in ever-smaller amounts, was the core source of profit for the Fitzgerald bank.[16] On one hot South Georgia afternoon, Stetson experienced this process directly. He liked to tell this story:

> One day, when the sun was doing its best, and Mr. Stetson's collar was down like a dish rag, he stood around the bank mopping his brow and whewing and cussing the weather. Finally, the elderly gentleman who owned the bank got tired of his complaining and called him over.

---

[15] For views of Fitzgerald, see, Georgia Writers' Project, *Georgia: The WPA Guide to Its Towns and Countryside* (Columbia: University of South Carolina Press, 1990) 333; Bond, *Stetson*, 24–30.

[16] Discussions of the process from this time period are David Kinley, *Money: A Study of the Theory of the Medium of Exchange* (New York: Macmillan & Co., 1913) 358–59, and Ray B. Westerfield, *Banking Principles and Practice* (New York: Ronald Press Co., 1928) 70 ("[A]ny banks receiving deposits of cash can proceed to loan an amount larger than the deposit received."). For a general overview, see also Jonathan Hughes and Louis P. Cain, *American Economic History*, 7th ed. (Boston: Pearson Education, Inc., 2007) 239 (discussing fractional reserve banking).

> "Listen here, young man," he said. "We have got a drawer full of notes here that will be due this fall. Every time the sun shines down like this, one of these notes becomes money. It means that the cotton is growing and the farmers will be able to pay us. The weather is what they need. Every time you get disgusted with hot weather in the middle of summer, just figure out how much those notes would be worth without it."
>
> Mr. Stetson said the hot weather has never bothered him since, and he never "whews" any more.[17]

In addition to straight loans, Stetson also learned how to finance trade outside Fitzgerald through letters of credit. In an ordinary business transaction, the seller did not know the buyer and could not trust him to make payment after the goods were shipped, and the buyer did not know the seller and could not trust him to make the shipment of the goods in the amount and quality specified in their agreement. The letter of credit placed two banks as the middlemen between a commercial buyer of goods and the seller of the goods in another location. [18]

If one bank knew the buyer and another bank knew the seller, and the banks knew each other, then the connection between the two banks was a "correspondent" relationship. The buyer's bank issued a letter of credit to the seller to be paid at the seller's bank, and once the seller's bank verified that the shipment was in order, it paid the seller. The seller's bank was counting on the buyer's bank to reimburse it for its payment to the seller. This process sped up the seller getting his payment and relieved the buyer of having to pay for goods that were still in transit or in a warehouse. Once the buyer received the goods and sold them, he had the funds to repay the bank that issued the letter of credit on his behalf. In Fitzgerald, Stetson learned how this important practice worked.[19]

---

[17] Bond, *Stetson*, 29–30.

[18] For a nearly contemporaneous account of letters of credit, see Westerfield, *Banking Principles*, 789–826.

[19] On the significance of correspondent banks and their relationship to New York banks, see Stuart Bruchey, *Enterprise: The Dynamic Economy of a Free People* (Cambridge: Harvard University Press, 1990) 312–17; William H. Kniffin, *Better*

Stetson also learned how to build a bank's assets. For businesses other than banks, assets consisted of such things as cash, marketable securities, raw materials, inventory, and plant and equipment. Liabilities were accounts payable, loans, and other debt. Whatever money was left over was equity, or the owners' capital. However, it was exactly the reverse on a bank balance sheet. Assets, for example, consisted of loans. Aside from the bank's own cash and marketable securities representing its saved earnings, deposits belonged to other parties and were a liability, money that had to be paid back to someone else. To a bank, loans were not liabilities, but were rather assets or money that borrowers were expected to return with interest.[20]

While at the Exchange National Bank, Stetson was a key part of the lending effort that more than doubled the bank's assets from $223,000 in 1905 to $485,000 in 1906, making it the largest bank in town. Doubling the bank's assets meant that the bank basically had twice as many loans. If the loans were of high quality, meaning the borrowers were going to repay the money, earnings could potentially double. To increase lending so much the Fitzgerald bank had to have increased deposits by a lot, since fractional reserve banking allowed the bank to use the same money more than once. This meant in addition to making loans, Stetson and the rest of the bank's staff had to bring in more deposits through effective salesmanship, and apparently they did just that.[21]

Opportunities

The valuable experiences gained in Fitzgerald gave Stetson the confidence to seek a broader field of operation. In 1907, at the age of 25, he returned to Macon as cashier of a new bank, the Citizens National. Of course, as with any new venture, this move was risky and the timing seemed especially bad. In 1906 and 1907, three Macon banks failed. Nationally, in

---

Banking: A Treatise on Bank Management in the Light of the Depression (New York: McGraw-Hill, 1934) 345–52.

[20] O. M. W. Sprague, ed. *Chapters on the Theory and History of Banking* (New York: G. P. Putnam's, 1904) 20–38.

[21] Bond, *Stetson*, 28–29. On the unceasing drive for deposits, see also Westerfield, *Banking Principles*, 70.

1907, there had been a severe panic on Wall Street. The collapse in share prices was so great that even the New York Stock Exchange was temporarily insolvent. In the absence of any government-controlled central bank, the elderly J. Pierpont Morgan organized infusions of private capital to prevent further damage. Even after the worst of the crisis was over, when Stetson returned to Macon from Fitzgerald the American economy still lagged.[22]

Nonetheless, an optimistic Stetson looked toward a brighter future. He and a group of other prominent Maconites joined together in September 1907 to raise the initial capital of $250,000 to start Citizens National. By November the *Macon Telegraph* reported that half the subscribed capital was already deposited and the rest would be contributed within a month. Stetson's large ambition is suggested by the bank's first major transaction, the purchase of $50,000 in United States bonds for the Panama Canal construction. Faith in "Progress," whether in far-off Latin America or at home in Georgia, was contagious, and Stetson caught the disease and planned to make the most of it.[23]

In a more profound sense the hopeful banking venture suggests how Stetson's hometown, with 40,000 residents in 1910, was being transformed from its agricultural and Confederate past into a New South community. Stetson counted himself among the outstanding cheerleaders for this sort of economic and social change. The directors of his bank were not nostalgic for the Old South, at least as long as money was to be made in more modern ways. They included cotton mill officers, the local Coca-Cola bottler, the president of a brick company, and two other men who forthrightly identified their profession as "Capitalist." Stetson's glad acceptance of the booster role showed that even in his mid-twenties he already believed banking was not just accounts and balances. Banking was about people and the successful integration of capital, industry, and public

---

[22] Bond, *Stetson*, 31–32; Charles R. Morris, *The Tycoons: How Andrew Carnegie, John D. Rockefeller, Jay Gould, and J.P. Morgan Invented the American Supereconomy* (New York: Henry Holt and Company, 2005) 249–51; and generally, Robert F. Bruner and Sean D. Carr, *The Panic of 1907: Lessons Learned from the Market's Perfect Storm* (New York: Wiley, 2007).

[23] Bond, *Stetson*, 32–34. To Stetson, progress generally meant economic growth, but it also included moral, intellectual, and scientific advancement.

policy. As he understood it, this kind of cooperation was the wave of the future. He exuberantly told the press, "[E]verybody will be welcome and well treated at the Citizens and we want the little fellows as well as the big ones."[24]

Similarly, Stetson placed no geographical limitations, no time-worn distinctions between North and South, on Citizens' prospects. Establishing contacts with larger banks outside the region was essential to create correspondent banking relationships as well as to get first-hand information on economic conditions in the national economy. Stetson believed a small-town bank needed big-town banks to help it make credit and pricing decisions. When a local customer was selling to an out-of-town buyer, the buyer was probably using credit from his own bank. It was prudent for the seller's banker to know the buyer's banker and to get assurances that the buyer was good for the transaction and that the out-of-town bank stood behind its customer. These mutually beneficial relationships, as Stetson had learned in Fitzgerald, were a key part of modern banking.

In January 1908, prior to Citizens' opening, Stetson took his first business trip to New York to make just these sorts of correspondent banking arrangements. According to a news article, he reported that after the recent panic, "things are normal again…and that business is resuming on a lively scale everywhere." Such hopeful statements became a Stetson trademark. When Citizens officially opened on 31 January 1908, he was quoted as saying: "Well, you see, the prospects are excellent for good deposits right from the start. By the end of business tomorrow, I hope to see deposited about one hundred and fifty thousand dollars for we have been told that a number of substantial deposits would be placed with us on the first day. The assurances that have been received from the people of the city and the surrounding territory are calculated to make the stockholders feel

---

[24] Ibid., 32–36. Macon's growth between 1900 and 1920 reflected the "progress" ideal. Population increased from about 23,000 in 1900 to almost 53,000 in 1920, making it the third largest city in Georgia, behind Atlanta and Savannah. United States Bureau of the Census, *Fourteenth Census of the United States, State Compendium: Georgia* (Washington: Government Printing Office, 1924) 8.

mighty good." Six months later, a newspaper noted "Cashier Eugene W. Stetson, who is working so hard to make the bank a great success, is well pleased over the showing made as are the other officers and directors." After another trip to New York later in 1908 Stetson told Macon newspapers that "Business conditions are improving everywhere and things look good in the East." The young banker knew that perceptions and confidence counted for much in banking.[25]

In fact, the new bank and its cashier did make progress. In February 1909 Stetson returned to New York, increasing his circle of bank acquaintances and getting the latest national outlook. By June, total resources at the Citizens National Bank exceeded $1.4 million. In October, Stetson even proposed the creation of another institution, a savings bank: "Mr. Eugene Stetson of the Citizens National Bank wants to encourage the savings of the working class and thinks that there is no better way than to do this than to place a bank as near to their doors as possible.... There are a number of the best mechanics of the city living in this section of the city, [and] not a few of them among them own homes." In December, 1909, Stetson led his first banking merger. A group of Citizens shareholders bought the local Central Georgia Bank.[26]

Sensing they had something good on their hands, the Citizens board elevated Stetson from cashier to bank president in 1910, just before his thirtieth birthday. According to a prideful *Macon News*, "Mr. Stetson is probably the youngest bank president in the United States." His enthusiasm, spirit of salesmanship, and public awareness, which attracted both confidence and deposits, cast him as a model commercial banker.[27]

---

[25] Bond, *Stetson*, 34–38.

[26] Ibid., 36–39. Nonetheless, the state of banking, especially national banking, was not particularly strong in Georgia. In 1909, there were only 91 national banks with just over 23,000 depositors. At the time, Georgia had approximately 2.5 million residents. United States Department of Commerce and Labor, *Statistical Abstract of the United States* (Washington: Government Printing Office, 1910).

[27] Bond, *Stetson*, 39–41.

The New South

The larger significance of these achievements is how Stetson, in the decade after leaving Mercer, absorbed, developed, and acted within an emerging ideology that linked banking, community, and modern forms of economic growth. Despite the earlier exhortations to take up this sort of work by Henry Grady, between 1900 and 1910 the New South ideal was still a somewhat new social and economic ideal in middle Georgia. Much of the region was part of the Creek frontier as late as the 1820s, and for decades thereafter it developed within the bounds set by the rural slavocracy. By contrast, Stetson embraced and promoted the New South concept with religious ebullience.

To Stetson the New South meant economic and social transformation using northern examples of prosperity: railroads, industry, commercial agriculture, urban pride and development, salesmanship, and growth-generating capital. The sources of this vision were complex: the family's banking background (and not agriculture), his time in the Yankee-influenced town of Fitzgerald, reading the popular and business press (the local *Macon Telegraph* specialized in Grady-like optimistic boosterism), and simply the hopes of a new generation seeking wealth and liberated from the need to defend slavery. Stetson was fully aware of class differences and conflict. He knew of progressive efforts to improve working conditions in industry and certainly read of organized labor efforts in the United States and Europe. Still, he always thought tying everyone to capitalism and its inevitable profits was the best answer to conflict. Also, as a white Southerner at the height of Jim Crow, Stetson accepted the racial status quo. A contemporary biographer reported that Stetson was an "Independent Democrat"—the racial context would have made it difficult for a white banker to affiliate with Lincoln's party in Macon. Yet, he also assumed a New South would lift the living standards of all southerners, black and white. More revealing, it was said that Stetson was "one of that stirring group of young Georgians who believe that the State is and has been suffering from too much political action and that the people should devote themselves to the development of manufacturing and farming interests." Stetson's vision assumed the effects of a New South would be dramatic: it would lead to urbanizing a rural region, bring the masses into a money economy, and destroy the discredited institutions of the Old South.[28]

A good demonstration of Stetson's early economic faith was his eagerness to sit on local boards of directors and invest in corporate stock. From the perspective of the twenty-first century, an appreciation of the corporation as a relatively new business device in Stetson's Georgia is difficult. In fact, the corporation represented a wholly new model for economic order. Stetson understood this. Early in his banking career he became a director or part owner of a small railroad, in the Hawkinsville Bank and Trust Company, the Merchants and Mechanics Bank, the Macon Railway and Light Company, and in the Continental Trust Company, which performed trustee services for individuals, corporations, and executors.[29]

The best example of Stetson's initial corporate experiences began in 1910, when he was elected director of the Bibb Manufacturing Company, an important Macon textile operation. Stetson took a long term view of corporate leadership, and he remained associated with Bibb in some form, including as a director and a member of its executive committee, from 1910 until the early 1950s. During most of these years the dominant figure in the company was William D. Anderson, who served as its president from 1919 to 1947.[30]

Bibb Manufacturing was a perfect example of the kind of business that reflected and reinforced Stetson's faith in industry as a transforming force. Emerging from the ashes of the Civil War, Bibb Manufacturing was the product of an early wave of Southern capitalists who seized the business

---

[28] Northen, ed., *Men of Mark in Georgia*, 299. On the possibilities and limitations of the New South ideal in Georgia, see Numan V. Bartley, *The Creation of Modern Georgia* (Athens: University of Georgia Press, 1983) 83–87. It is doubtful, however, that Stetson was interested in the variety of full-blown "Yankeefication" that has overtaken his home region since the 1960s—even though he contributed mightily to its causes. On this theme, see Richard N. Current, *Northernizing the South* (Athens: University of Georgia Press, 1983) 83–117.

[29] Bond, *Stetson*, 40–42; Northen, ed., *Men of Mark*, 298.

[30] Mary P. Whitlock, "Bibb Manufacturing Company and Payne City, Georgia: An Historical Perspective, 1876–1986" (Specialist in Education thesis, Georgia College and State University, 1986) 47–58.

opportunity presented by the availability of cotton and underemployed labor. Georgia businessmen, led by H. M. Comer of Savannah and J. F. Hanson of Macon, incorporated the company in 1876 and constructed its first textile mill in Macon. Over the next thirty years, slow but persistent expansion turned it into a powerhouse, one of the largest cotton manufacturers in the South. When Stetson joined its board, Bibb Manufacturing already operated three mills in Macon, one in Columbus, and two others (in Porterdale and Reynolds, Georgia). In its early years the company focused on the production of yarns and twine.[31]

Bibb had much in common with other Southern textile mills of the early to mid-twentieth century. Over the decades it gradually shifted from simpler products, such as cotton thread and twine, to more complex and finished products, such as bed sheets. Bibb maintained paternalistic and whites-only mill "villages," where workers and their families lived, and it took a staunchly anti-union position. When Stetson was a young banker in Macon, the company employed child labor, as famously documented by photographer Lewis Hine. Some of its communities, including Payne City, were incorporated as self-contained municipalities. At its height Bibb's Macon villages included five regular schools, nineteen vocational schools, six churches, six free medical clinics, one hospital, forty-nine social clubs, numerous athletic teams, two gymnasiums, and four auditoriums. Anderson believed the company's "duty and responsibility to the people who work for us in shop and factory do not end when these employees walk out of the mill gates at the end of their tour of duty, or when they receive their weekly pay check." Because the workers had "a lot of spare time," Anderson's company assumed an interest in seeing that "this spare time is employed in

---

[31] Whitlock, "Bibb Manufacturing Company," 1–2. Later, in New York, Stetson was a director with two other cotton-related companies, the Gulf Atlantic Warehouse Company (1940s and 1950s) and the Southeastern Compress and Warehouse Corporation (1930s). Southeastern was a Georgia-based cotton processing and warehouse business with facilities in the southeast. See *Metropolitan Life Insurance Co. v. Daniel*, 64 Ga. App. 620 (1941) (involving injury to worker at company's Savannah plant). Similarly, while Stetson was a director Gulf Atlantic operated warehouses in various cities, focusing on cotton storage. See *Gulf Atlantic Warehouse v. Bennett*, 36 Ala. App. 33 (1951) (case involved labor-management dispute at company's Birmingham, Alabama, facility).

such a way that the comfort, health, and happiness of the workers and their families will show an improvement and development making for better citizenship, better educational facilities for their children, and a fine type of recreation."[32]

By the 1930s Bibb Manufacturing was a publicly traded corporation with national and international business. With headquarters still in Macon, the corporation also maintained offices in New York; Chicago; Philadelphia; Greensboro, North Carolina; and Akron, the latter a consequence of its production of tire material. The company manufactured more than seventy-five million pounds of textile products annually. In the early 1950s, Bibb employed over 7,200 persons with an annual payroll of more than $14 million.[33]

Stetson was proud of the fact that Bibb Manufacturing was the most successful business to emerge out of his hometown and that he was closely connected to its operation. Bibb Manufacturing represented the kind of hope, change, and progress he believed was possible when finance and industry worked together. Stetson also had a long and confidential relationship with Anderson, Bibb Manufacturing's politically conservative president who ruled the board of directors. For example, he worked with Anderson on the Southern Business Committee, a group of executives that held meetings and discussed common problems in the late 1940s. For many years after he moved to New York Stetson scheduled trips to Georgia around Bibb Manufacturing's board meetings.[34]

---

[32] Whitlock, "Bibb Manufacturing Company," 12; Bibb Manufacturing Company, *The Story of Cotton* (Macon GA: Bibb Manufacturing Co., [1939?]); W. D. Anderson, *A Bench Mark: Bibb Manufacturing Company, Macon, Georgia, U.S.A.* (New York: Newcomen Society, 1950) 14–17.

[33] Whitlock, *The Story of Cotton*; Anderson, *A Bench Mark*, 12–13, 17.

[34] John A. Sibley to F. S. Keeler, May 12, 1949, John A. Sibley Papers, Manuscript, Archives, and Rare Book Library, Emory University, Atlanta, Georgia. The widespread restructuring, perhaps better characterized as collapse, of the textile industry in the southern United States in the 1980s and 1990s ended the history of Bibb Manufacturing. There were fundamental changes in the company's ownership in the 1980s, which eventually led to the 1996 bankruptcy of its successor, The Bibb Company. Bibb was sold to Dan River, Inc., a Virginia textile firm, in 1998. Dan River itself filed bankruptcy in 2004. In late 2005 Dan River was acquired by the Indian company GHCL Ltd. GHCL planned "to outsource most of the production

Stetson's broader vision, energy, and purpose were also on display in Macon's business and civic groups. Some of these were traditional Southern institutions, such as the Methodist church, the local militia, and social clubs, while others were business-related, specifically new kinds of organizations meant to solidify a profession or advance the community's economic cause. As a young man, Stetson won election as president of both the Georgia Bankers' Association and the Macon Chamber of Commerce. As Chamber of Commerce president he erased the organization's debt in one year. Stetson was also vice president of the Georgia Chamber of Commerce and a member of the executive council of the American Bankers Association. In May 1909, he was elected vice president from Georgia to the American Bankers Association. Stetson was also a member of and treasurer to the Bibb County board of education. He was active in raising money for charities and was a leader in arranging for the construction of a new passenger train station in Macon, an impressive structure completed in 1916. He supported improved public utilities and promoted his city's Georgia State Fair. He even lobbied, unsuccessfully, for the removal of the state capital from Atlanta to Macon.[35]

A major promotional device of the day was the "booster train," on which businessmen, trying to drum up sales, traveled through the countryside and advertised what their city had to offer. Both Cincinnati and Nashville, for example, sponsored heavily-advertised booster trains. Cincinnati's effort included one hundred businessmen who traveled to thirty-seven cities in five days. Nashville sent out eight booster trains with more than eight hundred business leaders. Not to be out done, Stetson organized a booster train for the Macon Chamber of Commerce in September 1912. The train carried about one hundred businessmen from Macon to Columbus and Albany, Georgia, as well as to other nearby towns.[36]

---

to units in India, Pakistan and China and shut down several [of] Dan River's production units in the US." See, "GHCL Acquires Dan River for $17.5 m," http://www.blonnet.com/2005/12/28/stories/2005122802550200.htm.

[35] Bond, *Stetson*, 45–50; Northen, ed., *Men of Mark in Georgia*, 298–99.

[36] Bond, *Stetson*, 47–48.

Before the Federal Reserve

The character of Stetson's early career—banker, board member, New South devotee and promoter—suggests that he never envisioned banking work as limited to a wholly private sphere. Banks and bankers always had substantial public responsibilities. Stetson's perspective was partly influenced by the broad legal powers available to banks, especially national banks such as Citizens. A most important example of this power was that in the absence of a central bank or Federal Reserve, even small national banks, including Citizens, printed their own circulating notes. Citizens issued more than $1.7 million in notes during its brief existence between 1908 and 1916. This circulation included roughly 211,000 notes in denominations of five, ten, and twenty dollars. The sources of money, such as these kinds of notes, had a long and contentious history in America. In the 1890s, for example, Georgia's Populists considered the idea of privately owned banks issuing their own circulating notes as primitive, inefficient, and a usurpation of the public interest in the money supply. The political failure of the Populist Party, however, did not end the contest over the money supply. The Federal Reserve Act of 1913, adopted during the midst of Stetson's presidency of Citizens National, finally ended the era of national bank notes.[37]

Controversy over central banking existed from the very beginning of the nation's history. Throughout the late eighteenth and nineteenth centuries there was vigorous and near constant debate about a central bank and the closely related issues of money and currency. Under President George Washington, a famous disagreement between Alexander Hamilton (who favored a bank) and Thomas Jefferson (who opposed it) shaped national politics. Hamilton's commercial interests won the first round, and

---

[37] Important views on the history and theory of the Federal Reserve are James Livingston, *Origins of the Federal Reserve System: Money, Class and Corporate Capitalism, 1890–1913* (Ithaca: Cornell University Press, 1986); Richard H. Timberlake, *Monetary Policy in the United States* (Chicago: University of Chicago Press, 1993) 214–34; Robert C. West, *Banking Reform and the Federal Reserve, 1863–1923* (Ithaca: Cornell University Press, 1977). A review of the literature is Elmus Wicker, *The Great Debate on Banking Reform* (Columbus: Ohio State University Press, 2005) 8–21.

the Bank of the United States, with the government as part owner, was established in 1791. But Jefferson's agrarians had their day, allowing the charter of Hamilton's bank to expire twenty years later. Congress created a second bank in 1816, but President Andrew Jackson, who loathed it as an exercise of unconstitutional federal power and as a treacherous eastern monopoly, saw to it that the bank disappeared in the 1830s. No new central bank would be approved by Congress for the rest of the century. Only the National Bank Act, passed during the trials of the Civil War, and a hodgepodge of often contradictory currency laws concerning federal coinage of silver and gold, provided slender organization to the national currency in the late nineteenth century. Congress formally adopted a gold standard in 1900.[38]

How can one explain the intensity and persistence of the money and banking debate? The contest was so heated partly because it involved nothing less than choices about the nation's fundamental values. Many Americans distrusted a central bank's power. The idea smacked of special financial privilege, something political leaders, including Jefferson and Jackson, detested. From this perspective no real American wanted to give power to same kind of self-appointed elite allowed to run European central banks, especially the Bank of England. A central bank put the national economy in the hands of non-producers, "money-changers" who made a living by sharp practices. In the absence of central banking, state-chartered banks, which were presumably more democratic, remained somewhat acceptable to this view. A general anti-banking perspective especially targeted at national banks was alive and well when Stetson practiced banking in Georgia.[39]

---

[38] A recent historian's account of financial debates involving Jefferson, Hamilton, and Jackson in a broad context is Sean Wilentz, *The Rise of American Democracy: Jefferson to Lincoln* (New York: W.W. Norton, 2005), while an economist's discussion of the background on central banking is Timberlake, *Monetary Policy*, 1–186.

[39] During the 1890s the most powerful white fraternal organization in Georgia, the Farmers' Alliance, banned members of Stetson's future profession, bankers, from membership, along with other "undesirables," such as lawyers and black people. Shaw, *Wool-Hat Boys*, 27.

By the 1890s, however, various forces built up momentum for more centralized control of the national money supply. An important moment was the presidential election of 1896, which pitted Democrat William Jennings Bryan of Nebraska, who favored an inflationary unlimited silver coinage, against Republican William McKinley, who supported gold. This dramatic "Battle of the Standards" focused public attention on money and financial issues. After the election, which McKinley won, there was an increasing movement to replace the existing chaotic banking system with something resembling a central bank. The movement picked up steam after the 1907 panic. This time, bankers, academics, and politicians, not radical farmers, rallied to the cause. Henry Davison and his J. P. Morgan firm supported centralized banking. Paul Warburg of the investment bank Kuhn, Loeb, published papers and promoted the idea of a central bank. Among the key arguments for a central bank was that it could create greater elasticity in the money supply by allowing for more flexibility in the issuance of legal tender notes. This sort of flexibility, as shown by the 1907 panic, was clearly lacking under current arrangements.[40]

In 1913 Congress passed the Federal Reserve Act and it was duly signed by President Woodrow Wilson. The Act, although a revolutionary exercise of government power, did not threaten Wall Street. The New York City branch of the Federal Reserve, the "Fed," acquired special influence. Leaders in the new Federal Reserve were well-connected by family or business ties to established investment banks and to the J. P. Morgan firm. The sponsoring Republican of an early version of the law was Senator Nelson Aldrich of Rhode Island, a friend of J. Pierpont Morgan and an in-law of John D. Rockefeller. The first president of the important New York branch was Benjamin Strong, formerly a vice president of Bankers Trust, a Morgan-controlled institution. The five-member Washington-based Board of Governors of the Federal Reserve included a partner with Kuhn, Loeb (Paul Warburg); Frederic A. Delano, former president of the Rockefeller-controlled Wabash Railway and uncle of Franklin Delano Roosevelt; William P. G. Harding, an Alabama banker whose wife's family's manufacturing company had board members with both Morgan and

---

[40] Michael Kazin, *A Godly Hero: The Life of William Jennings Bryan* (New York: Knopf, 2006) 45–79; Wicker, *Great Debate*, 22–69.

Rockefeller interests; and an economist, Adolph C. Miller, whose wife was a Sprague, a Chicago business family associated with Morgan.[41]

Just as New South thinking influenced Stetson, so did the dramatic financial events of the late nineteenth and early twentieth centuries. To a young student, bank officer, and bank president, shifts in national bank powers and the creation of the Federal Reserve would have been of intense interest and impact. Although only fifteen at the time of the 1896 election, with a banker father it seems likely that the debate between Bryan and McKinley over currency was staple fare at the Stetson dinner-table. In Macon and in Fitzgerald, including during the 1907 panic, Stetson worked at national banks. His clients were individuals and businesses caught in the uncertainties of currency fluctuation. After 1907 he regularly traveled to New York and was an active member of both the Georgia and American Bankers Association, the latter of which was a strong proponent of a central bank. Ambitious young bankers were attuned to the drama and significance of the Federal Reserve and the tremendous influence of J. P. Morgan and New York banking. America was becoming a financial powerhouse, and New York was its center. The increasing centralization of American banking naturally affected Stetson's interests and ideas. The creation of the Federal Reserve, and the expanding New York and Morgan-focused financial world, had a gravity-like pull on Stetson, calling him to even larger aspirations.[42]

Stetson turned thirty-two during the month the Federal Reserve was created. He had already developed a particular understanding of the world around him and had begun to implement a personal vision linked to the ideals of the New South. He displayed a buoyant optimism based on the prospects of growth. More specifically, he viewed finance, railroads, textiles, and efficient agriculture as the proper foundation for a community's

---

[41] Ron Chernow, *The House of Morgan: An American Banking Dynasty and the Rise of Modern Finance* (New York: Atlantic Monthly Press, 1990) 181–82. For the Washington members of the board in 1914, see "Membership of the Board of Governors of the Federal Reserve System, 1914–Present," http://www.federalreserve.gov/bios/boardmembership.htm.

[42] On the American Bankers Association's support for a central bank, see West, *Banking Reform*, 126.

wealth and greatness. But because of his religious and Victorian upbringing Stetson believed a community was measured by more than money. Business leaders should recognize the dignity of work and support public and private institutions that would advance growth. A corporation, such as a bank, had an obligation and a purpose that exceeded returns to shareholders. All of these ideas are reflected in Stetson's banking practice, his membership in civic organizations, and his commitment to Macon. At the same time, Stetson was not in favor of political change in the status of blacks, who made up more than half of middle Georgia's population, or in radical redistributions of wealth. Altogether, Stetson represented well the "informed" values of his generation, which meant his beliefs were not particularly original. Instead, it was his enthusiasm, energy, and skill in carrying them forward that distinguished him from his peers.[43]

It is hard not to imagine that Stetson had his sights aimed high from the very beginning. As a young man he trained to acquire technical banking skills. This brought him to the attention of important men in the modernizing world of Georgia business, and it would soon result in Stetson's recruitment to the center of the American banking universe. New York's increasingly powerful banks were interested in having banking relationships around the country and they often hired small-town bankers to achieve this goal. Employment at one of the private banking firms, such as Morgan, would have been impossible for Stetson. Such firms were partnerships that required an inside social track and a large sum of capital, which he did not have. Luckily, there were eligible substitutes, and by 1916 Stetson had prepared himself well for one of them, the Guaranty Trust Company of New York.

---

[43] On the theme of "business progressivism" in the South and in Georgia, see George B. Tindall, *The Emergence of the New South, 1914–1945* (Baton Rouge: Louisiana State University Press, 1965) 223–33; and Bartley, *Creation of Modern Georgia*, 147–78.

3

Guaranty Banking

In 1915, Citizens Bank celebrated its eighth anniversary. On the occasion the *Macon Telegraph* expressed high praise for its young president: "Mr. Stetson has invested the Citizens National Bank with a degree of personality. He has made it conspicuously a young man's establishment.... Safe and conservative are some of his distinguishing characteristics, but he also combines with these traits a happy measure of progressive spirit." The combination of "young" and "safe," "conservative" and "progressive," as well as the linking of Stetson to the "personality" of the bank, expressed a very appealing image. Stetson and his bank were young, but conservative. They were safe, but progressive. Was not this the essence of the New South? As it turned out, many of the nation's leading banks, based in New York, valued just such attributes. One of those banks was the Guaranty Trust Company of New York, with which Citizens National maintained a correspondent banking relationship.[1]

About this time, through a friend of his at Guaranty, Stetson met Charles H. Sabin in New York, who had recently become Guaranty's president. Stetson hinted to Sabin that he was in the job market. Sabin, a dynamic leader, was intensely interested in international finance and not hidebound to the standard ways of banking. He was more than willing to delegate substantial authority to key assistants. During the first three months of Sabin's presidency, the assets of Guaranty grew by almost one-third, to more than $350 million. Total foreign transactions in 1915 exceeded $6 billion, the equivalent in 2007 of almost $130 billion. These

---

[1] Adrienne Moore Bond, *Eugene W. Stetson* (Macon GA: Mercer University Press, 1983) 58.

values put Guaranty among the largest and most internationally-focused banks in the United States.[2]

Sabin perceived that continued growth required the addition of new banking officers, at least some of whom with extensive experience outside New York. These men would be "go getters," bringing in business and expanding the financial expertise of the firm. At the end of 1911, Guaranty had eighteen officers, with four vice presidents. Five years later, the bank had forty-three officers, including thirteen vice presidents. Guaranty showed an especially strong interest in increasing its role in cotton financing, which naturally required knowledge of the American South. A relatively young, sales-oriented southern banker, such as Stetson, with experience ranging from agriculture to railroads and textiles represented an attractive acquisition.[3]

Impressed by their initial meeting, Sabin recruited Stetson to work at Guaranty Trust in 1916. Stetson later said this was not his first opportunity in the city. But he turned down an earlier job, telling the banker, "You would not be happy with me, sir. You and I do not see banking in the same light. You would be making a mistake if you took me on, and I would be making a mistake if I came." The substance of not seeing banking "in the same light" is unclear, but the recollection implies that Stetson did see eye-to-eye with Sabin. On 25 September 1916, Sabin sent Stetson a formal offer for a vice-presidency at $18,000 a year. This was the chance Stetson wanted, a very big step up from his first position as a teller and debt collector at his father's bank fifteen years earlier. The title of vice president meant he

---

[2] "Guaranty Trust Company of New York, 1864–1927," 46–55, J. P. Morgan & Co., Inc. Papers, JPMorgan Chase Archives, New York, New York; Josephine Hatcher, interview by Adrienne M. Bond, 1981–1982, Jack Tarver Library, Special Collections, Mercer University, Macon, Georgia. According to Ms. Hatcher, after meeting Sabin, Stetson stopped by Washington, DC on the way back to Macon and obtained government permission to sell Citizens National—just in case a job offer was forthcoming. Josephine Hatcher interview. Value in 2007 dollars calculated with reference to Consumer Price Index. See "Six Ways to Compute the Relative Value of a U.S. Dollar Amount," http://measuringworth.com/calculators/uscompare/# .

[3] "Our New Vice-President," *The Guaranty News* (November 1916): 324.

would be one of a very few senior officers, and his salary was the stunning equivalent of about $350,000 in 2007 dollars. He accepted immediately.[4]

It may be that Stetson was partly influenced to start a new life because of family tragedy. In 1912, his beloved wife Josephine developed scarlet fever and died, leaving him with the care of two small children. Only eight years after their wedding and first household in Fitzgerald, the event naturally had a profound effect. The loss prompted Stetson to join his deceased wife's Episcopal church and to move out of the home he had shared with Josephine and their children. In 1915 Stetson married Iola Lamar Wise, a Macon native. They had just celebrated the birth of their first child when Stetson received the Guaranty offer. Together, perhaps, the Guaranty offer signaled that the time was right to start a new life.[5]

After accepting the job, Stetson oversaw the voluntary liquidation of Citizens National Bank. Shareholders received $150 for the shares they purchased for $100 eight and a half years earlier, in addition to having received regular six percent dividends. Celebrating, the directors resolved that Stetson was "an associate and leader of rare ability and of unswerving integrity, whose power to weigh large business problems accurately has ever been matched by his keen and discriminating moral judgment." They congratulated "the Guaranty Trust Company upon securing a man who brings to it these gifts of mind and heart which are destined to make him conspicuous among men who 'do things,' no matter where he may go."[6]

Guaranty Trust

One of the leading American banks of the twentieth century, Guaranty Trust has received only limited attention from banking historians. Yet, from

---

[4] Mercer University, Eugene W. Stetson Memorial Library, *Dedication Ceremonies, The Eugene W. Stetson Memorial Library, Mercer University* (Macon GA: Mercer University, 1965) 39–40; Charles H. Sabin to Eugene W. Stetson, 25 September 1916, Eugene W. Stetson Papers, Jack Tarver, Special Collections, Mercer University, Macon, Georgia. Value in 2007 dollars calculated with reference to Consumer Price Index. See "Six Ways to Compute the Negative Value of a US Dollar Amount," http://measuringworth.com/calculators/ uscompare/#.

[5] Bond, *Stetson*, 51–57.

[6] Ibid., 42, 60–61.

its beginning the bank had big plans. On 13 April 1864, only a few weeks before Union General Ulysses S. Grant commenced his assault on Robert E. Lee's Army of Northern Virginia in the Wilderness campaign, the New York state legislature chartered a new corporate entity, the New York Guaranty and Indemnity Company. Given the powers they bestowed, bank charters were a matter of public concern, and Guaranty's was no exception. The *New York Herald* was suspicious that its creation might be "a big swindle." The reason for this criticism is unknown, other than the normal corruption associated with the New York legislature at the time, but Guaranty won the support of Democratic Governor Horatio Seymour, a future presidential candidate, and that apparently was sufficient for the charter's success. The bank's legal authority was unusually broad:

> [The bank was authorized to] guaranty the payment, punctual performance, and collection of promissory notes, bills of exchange, contracts, bonds, accounts, claims, rents, annuities, mortgages, evidences of debt, and certificates of property or value, and the titles to property real or personal, upon such terms as may be established by the Board of Directors of said company; to receive upon storage, deposit, or otherwise, merchandise, bullion, specie, plate, stocks, bonds, promissory notes, certificates and evidences of debt, contracts or other properties, and to take the management, custody and charge of real and personal estate and property, and to advance money securities, and credits upon any property, real or personal, on such terms as may be established by the Directors.

After receiving the coveted charter, Guaranty opened its first office in Manhattan, on lower Broadway near the stock exchange.[7]

Because the company's legal power included the right to "receive upon storage, deposit, or otherwise" a wide range of items, including "merchandise," its directors could approve loans secured by goods in warehouses, a significant and previously limited source of financing for

---

[7] "Guaranty Trust Company of New York, 1864–1927," 2–4, J. P. Morgan & Co., Inc. Papers; Guaranty Trust Company of New York, *One Hundred Years of Banking Service* (New York: Guaranty Trust Company of New York, 1939) 19–20.

domestic and foreign trade. The original shareholders of Guaranty, capitalized with 1,000 shares at $100,000, included New York bankers and merchants, both of whom knew the need for warehouse receipts. The company raced into this business, charging seven percent on the receipts, the maximum allowed by law. An opportunity for further expansion presented itself when the New York legislature in 1871 amended the company's charter to allow it to "accept and execute any trust created by mortgage made by any railroad or other corporation, to secure its bonds or other obligations...[by] appointing such Company trustee, and to act as trustee." However, full exploitation of the corporate trust business, especially for railroads, a variety of work not then legally available to most other banks, would not take place for some years.[8]

Despite this auspicious beginning, by the mid–1870s Guaranty had difficulty competing with other banks for loan business and its assets dwindled to an office building at 52 Broadway and some real estate on Long Island. The directors decided to abandon the warehouse receipts trade. John Jacob Astor, one of the wealthiest men in the United States, bought Guaranty's Broadway office for $1,000,000 in 1883, a notable real estate transaction for the time. During the next eight years, the company existed merely to collect rents on its Long Island property and distribute the proceeds as dividends. Guaranty's sole part-time employee kept a desk at 52 Broadway in order to present, in formal hand-delivered fashion, the semi-annual dividends.[9]

Guaranty, however, was soon rescued from this near-death experience. In 1891 men connected to Guaranty and another New York corporation, the Mutual Life Insurance Company, perceived the special opportunities presented by Guaranty's broad charter. Mutual Life, of course, was not just any insurer. In the early 1890s it was the largest insurance company in the

---

[8] Guaranty Trust Company, *One Hundred Years*, 3–5. For a survey of trust company growth after the Civil War, see Benjamin J. Klebaner, *American Commercial Banking* (Boston: Twayne Publishers, 1990) 72–74. For a description of early trust companies and their functions, see Eugene N. White, *The Regulation and Reform of the American Banking System, 1900–1929* (Princeton: Princeton University Press, 1983) 38–42.

[9] Guaranty Trust Company, *One Hundred Years*, 5–7.

world. Samuel Babcock, George Griswold Haven, and Richard McCurdy (the latter its president) led Guaranty's rejuvenation. They quickly increased the bank's capital to $2,000,000. They elected a new board which reflected the high expectations of the operation. Among the directors were Oliver Harriman, Frederick W. Vanderbilt, Augustus D. Juilliard, William C. Whitney, and Robert Goelet, all wealthy and prominent New Yorkers. From the beginning, Mutual planned to use the broad lending authority permitted by Guaranty's charter to develop new business, including in the potentially lucrative field of lending on Mutual's life insurance policies. The first official transactions under new leadership were the purchase of $1,000,000 in United States bonds and $500,000 in New York City bonds.[10]

Guaranty was thus reborn as a significant commercial institution. In its new incarnation the bank invested assets in government bonds, railroad securities, and demand loans. Venturing into the trust business for the first time, Guaranty became a trustee for mortgage bonds of the Galveston City Railroad. Adding the powerful New York banker George F. Baker to the board augmented its already formidable personal and business connections. At the beginning of 1892 the company possessed about $3.7 million in assets. The next year this increased to more than $14 million. The company even hired an agent in London to handle the financing of grain shipments, an innovative international venture for an American commercial bank.[11]

During the next fifteen years Guaranty experienced substantial growth despite the national economic crises of the 1890s and 1907. Many banking institutions in New York collapsed during the panic of 1893, at the time the

---

[10] "Guaranty Trust Company of New York, 1864–1927," 8–14, J. P. Morgan & Co., Inc. Papers; Guaranty Trust Company, *One Hundred Years*, 23–24. Mutual merged into the global AXA Group in 2004. See, "A Message to Our Valued Clients," http://www.mony.com/.

[11] "Guaranty Trust Company of New York, 1864–1927," 13–14, J. P. Morgan & Co., Inc. Papers. George Baker had unusually broad connections in the New York financial community, including with J. P. Morgan. He was a Mutual Life director and his brother was the law partner of Charles Peabody, who became president of Mutual. See Maury Klein, *The Life and Legend of E. H. Harriman* (Chapel Hill: University of North Carolina Press, 2000) 345–46.

most severe downturn in the nation's history. Guaranty, however, continued to pay dividends. An increasing amount of this prosperity derived from trust business, most of which was linked to railroads. Two important examples of the company's trust activities were the reorganization of the Atchison, Topeka, and Santa Fe Railroad in 1895 and the consolidation of the Edison General Electric and Thompson-Houston Electric into the General Electric Company in 1894. Guaranty thereby placed itself at the forefront in the institutional restructuring of American business. Guaranty also built check, deposit, and certificate of deposit services. By the beginning of 1896, assets neared $16 million, a four-fold increase in just four years. Guaranty's clients were important persons, representatives of burgeoning railroad companies, industries, and utilities. Its expanding services, particularly trust services, resulted in 1896 in a name change to the Guaranty Trust Company of New York.[12]

The bank's eagerness to accommodate the corporate customers who were transforming American life led the directors to open the first full-fledged branch of an American bank on London's Lombard Street in 1897. Federal law then prohibited national banks from creating foreign branches, but the state-chartered Guaranty faced no such barrier. In New York, the company opened an Exchange Department, with two employees, to facilitate international financing. The path-breaking work of that department, a tiny toehold serving American capitalism in Europe, was later described by one of the two employees:

> At first, business consisted entirely of buying cotton and grain bills on London, and selling our own demand against them. I did all the clerical work, drew drafts, made entries, and wrote the letters forwarding the bills. We soon opened a mark account with the Dresdner Bank in Hamburg, and a franc account with the Credit Lyonnais in Paris. The business we did on other countries was handled through our London account. There was no trading in exchange at that time. The "Book-keeping Division" of the Foreign

[12] "Guaranty Trust Company of New York, 1864–1927," 14–19, J. P. Morgan & Co., Inc. Papers; Guaranty Trust Company, *One Hundred Years*, 25–26.

Department consisted of a ledger and a remittance register, for which I was responsible.

Guaranty expanded its international operations to the Far East after American victory in the Spanish-American War of 1898 gave the United States possession of the Philippines. Guaranty astutely followed the flag, opening a branch in Manila, where it was appointed depositary for the new American-dominated Philippines government.[13]

Dramatic new challenges, however, soon threatened Guaranty. In 1905, future Republican presidential candidate and United States Supreme Court Chief Justice Charles Evans Hughes led an investigation of fraud and corruption in the New York insurance business. Hughes's work uncovered outrageous salaries to executives, bribery of public officials, and sweeping malfeasance of policyholder funds. The investigation produced a series of state laws requiring insurance companies to divest themselves of investments in other corporations. Mutual Life owned enormous blocks of stock in more than fifteen banks and trust companies, including Guaranty, and under the new laws Mutual had to sell this stock.[14]

As part of Mutual's compliance with the regulations, Edward H. Harriman, the famous railroad tycoon who controlled the Union Pacific and Illinois Central Railroads, bought half the shares in Guaranty owned by Mutual and thus obtained a controlling interest in the bank. In 1911, the remainder of Mutual's Guaranty stock was sold to the by-then deceased Harriman's estate.[15]

The bank also confronted the economic crisis of 1907, which focused on New York's trust companies. According to one historian, in October of that year "country and small-town bankers withdrew their [deposits in New York banks], city bankers called in their loans to meet demand, and the

---

[13] "Guaranty Trust Company of New York, 1864–1927," 19–23, J. P. Morgan & Co., Inc. Papers.

[14] Ibid., 23–25; Merlo J. Pusey, *Charles Evans Hughes*, 2 vols. (New York: MacMillan Co., 1951) 1: 140–68.

[15] Klein, *Life and Legend of E. H. Harriman*, 55–57, 352, 425. Harriman began his business relationship with the Illinois Central in 1881, became a director in 1883, and obtained control of the company in 1906. Harriman's relationship with Guaranty and the Illinois Central would have a profound effect on Stetson's career.

credit structure collapsed like a house of cards." Fortunately for Guaranty, its officers perceived potential problems before the downturn, successfully calling in loans and strengthening cash reserves. Many other trust companies, by contrast, despite low cash reserves, had invested heavily in speculative ventures and issued risky loans on stocks and bonds. Ultimately, J. Pierpont Morgan led a coalition of financial interests that propped up the tottering system, and Guaranty participated in these efforts. Although the bank's assets fell dramatically during the episode, by mid–1909 they had rebounded to an all time high of more than $84 million.[16]

Divestiture by Mutual Life, Harriman's entry, and the 1907 crisis provided a basis for even greater expansion. The most important force in these changes was J. Pierpont Morgan and his firm, which made Guaranty the largest trust bank in the world. The Morgan intrusion, perhaps better described as an anointment, was part of a grand scheme to consolidate New York banking. The crux of the Morgan plan was to obtain control of Guaranty and enlarge it through mergers. One early Guaranty merger was with Morton Trust, headed by Levi P. Morton, a former vice president of the United States and governor of New York. Another merger was with Morton's Fifth Avenue Trust. Henry P. Davison, a Morgan partner, arranged this deal through purchases of the holdings of Morton, Thomas Fortune Ryan, the William C. Whitney estate, and Mutual Life. As a result, Levi Morton became chairman of Guaranty's board and Ryan, one of the wealthiest men in the United States, became a Guaranty director. Further suggesting the tight interrelationships among the "consolidating" leadership, Morton Trust's office had been in the same Mutual Life building on Nassau Street occupied by Guaranty. The mergers left Morgan, George Baker of the First National Bank, and James Stillman of the

---

[16] "Guaranty Trust Company of New York, 1864–1927," 25–27, J.P. Morgan & Co., Inc. Papers. On Morgan and the 1907 Panic, see Ron Chernow, *The House of Morgan: An American Banking Dynasty and the Rise of Modern Finance* (New York: Atlantic Monthly Press, 1990) 121–38; Robert F. Bruner and Sean D. Carr, *The Panic of 1907: Lessons Learned from the Market's Perfect Storm* (New York: Wiley, 2007).

National City Bank as the controlling figures of American commercial banking.[17]

The mergers also produced several years of spectacular, profitable growth. In 1910 Guaranty possessed assets of more than $150 million. The directors that year declared a dividend of thirty-two percent; by 1912 the dividend was thirty-eight percent. The blossoming company began construction of a large building at Liberty and Broadway on a parcel purchased from Mutual Life. In 1912, Guaranty absorbed another trust, the Standard Trust Company, which raised its assets to almost $250 million. By this time the board of directors included such financial luminaries as George F. Baker, Henry P. Davison, James B. Duke, Daniel Guggenheim, Thomas W. Lamont, Thomas F. Ryan, Harry Payne Whitney, and Albert H. Wiggin. Morgan and other prominent New York banks dominated. Lamont, chairman of Guaranty's executive committee, and Davison were Morgan partners. The Guggenheim family had close relations with the Morgan interests for a long time, Baker was with First National Bank, and Wiggin was associated with Chase. The dominance of private and national bankers reflected the desire of those banks, which were legally prohibited from trust activities, to have control of a leading state-chartered trust.[18]

---

[17] "Guaranty Trust Company of New York, 1864–1927," 27–31; Articles from *The Chronicle*, 8, 15, 22, 29 January, 5 February 1910, J. P. Morgan & Co., Inc. Papers; Guaranty Trust Company, *One Hundred Years*, 30–32; Vincent P. Carosso, *The Morgans: Private International Bankers, 1854–1913* (Cambridge: Harvard University Press, 1987) 619–21; Thomas M. Lamont, *Henry P. Davison: The Record of a Useful Life* (New York: Harper & Brothers, 1933) 116–21; Fritz Redlich, *The Molding of American Banking: Men & Ideas*, 2 vols. (New York: Hafner Publishing Co., 1951) 2:186–89. Levi Morton objected to the loss of his name from the Morton Trust, but Pierpont Morgan convinced him it was for the best: "You will become associated with one of the great financial institutions in the world. I'll make that stock worth $1000 a share." Eventually, Guaranty stock did reach that plateau. Jean Strouse, *Morgan: American Financier* (New York: Random House, 1999) 603–604.

[18] "Guaranty Trust Company of New York, 1864–1927," 29, 31–32; "To The Board of Directors, Guaranty Trust Company of New York," 15 January 1912, J. P. Morgan & Co., Inc. Papers. On the interrelationships in New York finance, see also Frederick Allen, *The Lords of Creation* (New York: Harper & Brothers, 1935) 177–78.

After 1912 a particularly important component of Guaranty's escalating growth was railroad financing. In 1913 Alexander J. Hemphill, originally a railroad executive, became Guaranty's president. The railroad focus was symbolized by a special display case installed in the directors' room, which featured large maps of the lines. No other industry received this kind of attention. The railroad business involved the bank as financial agents, in securities transactions, as depositary, and included placement of bank officers on railroad boards. By 1917 Guaranty held more than $30 million in deposits just from railroads; but transportation was only part of the ongoing growth. Anticipating the great boom in public equity sales during the 1920s, in which Stetson would play an important part, Guaranty also expanded its work to include the distribution of securities, which required hiring salesmen. It increased its operations in foreign exchange and international business.[19]

Although political and legal developments had always been important to Guaranty, in 1913 two new laws deeply impacted and enhanced its operations. First, in 1913 Congress approved a federal income tax. Rather than harming the bank, the expertise required for handling income tax issues for the wealthy provided a considerable amount of new business. Second, as already described, Congress passed the Federal Reserve Act in 1913, which created a new centralized structure for banking. The law allowed banks to borrow money from new regional Federal Reserve Banks in order to meet quickly changing needs, thereby supplying flexibility to the money supply. The Act had direct benefits for Guaranty. Although it did not become a Reserve member until 1917, the Reserve System encouraged the development of a market for "acceptances," time drafts or bills of exchange, as investments. Guaranty quickly became a national leader in this kind of commercial paper.[20]

---

[19] "Guaranty Trust Company of New York, 1864–1927," 35–37, J. P. Morgan & Co., Inc. Papers.

[20] Ibid., 37–39. An analysis of the growth, success, and importance of bankers' acceptances in the United States is J. Peter Federer, "Institutional Innovation and the Creation of Liquid Financial Markets: The Case of Bankers' Acceptances, 1914–1934," *Journal of Economic History*, 63 (September 2003): 666–94.

Another transforming development was the outbreak of World War I, in August 1914. Before the war the United States was a debtor nation. American railroads and other industries, for example, traditionally depended on capital from Europe. This gave enormous power to English banks and relegated New York bankers, however powerful they appeared to average citizens, to second-class status. The diplomatic and military stupidity of European leaders, however, caused a shift in the world's financial capital during the long years of war. Guaranty, with already established foreign interests and solid connections with other American institutions interested in overseas opportunities, was primed to benefit from the growth in American power.[21]

Guaranty's aggressive actions before April 1917, when the United States declared war on Germany, illustrated the enormous opportunities provided by global conflict. These opportunities undoubtedly helped create the need for new officers, such as Stetson, whom the bank hired during this period. Between 1914 and 1917 Guaranty sold bank services to Americans in Europe, propped up gold supplies, and financed huge amounts of grain and cotton shipped to Britain and France. In 1914, Great Britain closed its banks for four days and declared a moratorium on debt payments for three months. In contrast, Guaranty's London office never closed and paid gold on letters of credit—it ignored the moratorium. Britain and France expected continued payment for securities debts in gold, and Guaranty and other New York banks ensured that a loan due in early 1915 met that expectation. Guaranty also facilitated the transfer of American products to Britain, particularly grain and cotton. The company participated in the Cotton Loan Fund under the direction of the Federal Reserve Board. The Fund generated confidence in the international market for cotton and improved money supply problems in the southern United States. Guaranty financed the purchase of American cotton by the French government and French and British companies, even establishing special cotton offices in Liverpool and Havre. Between 1913 and 1925 the bank financed more

[21] A first-hand account of some transactions that were part of this shift is Lamont, *Henry P. Davison*, 186–230.

cotton exports than any other American bank, an amount that exceeded more than half the entire exported crop of the United States.[22]

Guaranty's intense international activity resulted in part from the global perspective of Charles Sabin and his Morgan backers. Soon after Sabin's appointment as president, Guaranty participated in the largest private loan ever made to a foreign government. Europe was running out of money, and looked to Americans for cash. Under the direction of J. P. Morgan & Co., Guaranty joined in a massive $500 million loan to Britain and France. Soon other international loans, to Italy and Canada, followed. Technically, the United States was still neutral, but Guaranty's actions made it clear which power the New York banks supported. In addition, Guaranty made loans to American industries, such as Remington Arms and Bethlehem Steel, which produced products for the Allied effort. In effect, the bank loaned money to Britain and France, who used money to buy goods from American companies, while the American companies expanded using money from American banks, including Guaranty. The potential profits from this multiplying business caused the price of a share of Guaranty stock to soar to more than $600 by 1916.[23]

For Gene Stetson, the great significance of Guaranty's distinguished history was that by 1916, when he came to New York, Guaranty was one of the leading financial institutions in the world. Starting with a favorable charter and a niche business in warehouse receipts, it nearly expired in the 1880s. Yet, the possibilities offered by the charter interested Mutual Life's savvy leaders. The insurance giant's takeover of Guaranty in 1891 and the linking of Guaranty after 1905 to trust and international business, as well as to elite sponsors from the heights of New York banking, especially J. P. Morgan, renewed a moribund operation. Divestment by Mutual in 1911, a series of mergers in 1910 and 1912, and an enormous expansion of international operations helped by connections to the most prominent New York individuals and banks, including the Harriman family and J. P. Morgan & Co., set the stage for Guaranty's spectacular growth during the First World War. These developments, as well as the company's special

---

[22] "Guaranty Trust Company of New York, 1864–1927," 39–46, J. P. Morgan & Co., Inc. Papers.

[23] Ibid., 46–55.

interest in cotton and railroads, two businesses with which Stetson was already familiar, helped make Stetson an attractive candidate for Sabin and the Morgan colossus.

The Right Place at the Right Time

As an informed banker who had made numerous trips to New York, Stetson would have known much of this history. He was certainly aware that Guaranty offered a fantastic opportunity for an ambitious and young, but seasoned, banker such as himself. In the early twentieth century, there were just a handful of major "deal doers" on Wall Street and they were concentrated in several private banks, the most prominent of which was J. P. Morgan & Co., which had only a few partners. Stetson would have been aware that as an outsider the only way to get to the top of finance was to join one of the rising commercial banks. Guaranty had massive capital, relationships with private banks and wealthy clients, and could meet the rapidly increasing need of American industry for loans and especially investment underwriting. As a result, a large, global bank like Guaranty, which also had the decided advantage of intimate relations with the true insiders of Wall Street, including Morgan, was a perfect match for Stetson. The New South was very much at home in lower Manhattan.[24]

Charles Sabin's career provided precedent for the outsiders' path to banking prominence, so Stetson probably looked to Sabin as a model. Sabin, like Stetson, began at a small regional bank before moving to New York, where he made an outstanding record. Sabin, like Stetson, had strong leadership skills and solid social ability. They even shared a life-long love for baseball. In fact, Sabin was offered his first job at an Albany, New York,

---

[24] According to Charles R. Geisst, "Banking in the United States prior to World War I was somewhat different from the banking practiced later in the century. It was based upon cozy, informal relationships rather than simple credit evaluations and client history. Bankers granted loans and agreed to issue securities for corporate clients based on the social and economic standing and general reputation of the client. Clients had to court bankers in order to get good terms for loans and negotiated securities deals rather than the other way around." Charles R. Geisst, *Deals of the Century: Wall Street, Mergers, and the Making of Modern America* (Hoboken NJ: John Wiley and Sons, 2004) 7.

bank because he agreed to pitch for the bank's baseball team. Each man had a penchant for unusual deals and foreign adventures. In 1916, a prominent national publication described Sabin as "independent" and "progressive," a man making a mark on Wall Street in the aftermath of J. Pierpont Morgan's death. Stetson had consistently been described in similar terms on the smaller stage of Macon. Sabin, like Stetson, was also interested in the relationship between business and community, including charities.[25]

Stetson had the excellent fortune to arrive in New York at the exact time that the mantle of world financial power was shifting from London to Wall Street. He started his new job in November 1916, in the midst of Guaranty's massive lending to Allied nations and just two years after Britain entered a period of financial desperation, effectively ending Britain's dominance of international finance. Europe's need for cotton, and Guaranty's leadership in cotton financing, was Stetson's special door-opener. An expert in financing the cotton trade from his Georgia banking days, he was positioned to help expand Guaranty's cotton business by leaps and bounds. In fact, it may be that this was the most important factor in Sabin's decision to hire Stetson.

Stetson had worked at Guaranty for less than six months when the United States declared war against Germany in April 1917, and he undoubtedly played an important role in the bank's wartime efforts. The end of neutrality placed Wilson's government at the forefront of war finance, but it also created new and essential tasks for the bank. In fact, Guaranty's war-related work transformed its operations. Between June 1917 and June 1919, bank resources grew spectacularly, from $600 million to

[25] A breezy account of Sabin's career, written just before Stetson came to New York, is in B. C. Forbes, *Finance, Business, and the Business of Life* ([New York]: The Author, 1915). See also Henry Cushing, "The New Wall Street," *The World's Work* 32 (June 1916): 215–23; "Our New Vice-President," *The Guaranty News*, 324; "Eugene W. Stetson," 20 April 1951, J. P. Morgan & Co., Inc. Papers; Charles H. Sabin to Eugene W. Stetson, 25 September 1916, Eugene W. Stetson Papers. Sabin's personal appeal is also suggested by the fact that in 1933 more than 1,000 persons attended his funeral. The mourners included John D. Rockefeller Jr., John J. Raskob, Thomas Lamont, George F. Baker, and many other financial notables. *New York Times*, 14, 23 October 1933.

more than $820 million, with outstanding loans increasing by more than twenty percent. Much of this growth was the result of Guaranty's heavy involvement with the government's Liberty Loan program. President Sabin belonged to the Liberty Loan Committee for New York and even marched in a Liberty Loan Parade beside J. P. Morgan Jr.[26]

When the first Liberty Loan, for $2 billion, was issued in May 1917, Guaranty helped sell the bonds. Joining other financial institutions and large employers, it subscribed its own name to $25 million. Guaranty also authorized officers to invest trust funds in the loan. In the second Liberty Loan, the bank placed more than $110 million with the public, the largest single subscription in the United States. After the fifth and final loan in 1919, the company's total wartime placements exceeded $500 million, or roughly $6 billion in 2007 dollars.[27]

Marketing, of course, was a big part of these sales. Guaranty erected huge red, white, and blue posters at its Broadway office that urged passersby to purchase bonds. Branches stayed open past regular hours and Guaranty employees, each of whom purchased at least one bond, went "door-to-door" in the area around Wall Street to sell bonds. Guaranty operated a bond booth on the steps of the recently completed New York Public Library on Fifth Avenue, which produced at least one revealing display of financial patriotism:

> A very small girl emerged from the crowd that surrounded [the] Liberty Loan Booth at Forty-second Street and Fifth Avenue. She

---

[26] "Guaranty Trust Company of New York, 1864–1927," 56–73; "Condensed Statements," Guaranty Trust Company of New York, 20 June 1917; 30 June 1919, J. P. Morgan & Co., Inc. Papers; J. T. W. Hubbard, *For Each, the Strength of All: A History of Banking in the State of New York* (New York: New York University Press, 1995) 183. Guaranty's relationship with Morgan undoubtedly assisted its ability to get business in Britain and France. See Harold van B. Cleveland and Thomas F. Huertas, *Citibank, 1812–1970* (Cambridge: Harvard University Press, 1985) 82. World War I's impact on commercial banking, including the significance of government securities, is noted in Klebaner, *Commercial Banking*, 116–17.

[27] "Guaranty Trust Company of New York, 1864–1927," 56–73, J. P. Morgan & Co., Inc. Papers. Value in 2007 dollars calculated with reference to Consumer Price Index. See "Six Ways to Compare the Releative Value of a U.S. Dollar Amount," http://measuringworth.com/calculators/uscompare/#.

> carried a pasteboard box tightly clasped in her hands. Attracting the attention of a Guaranty Trust Company salesman stationed at the booth, she dumped the contents of her box on the counter. Slowly and accurately she counted the pennies, nickels, dimes, and quarters that she had hoarded in her "safety deposit" box since last Christmas. The total was $49. Her mother contributed an extra dollar, and the child became the possessor of a Liberty Bond.

It is no wonder that when King Albert of Belgium rode down Broadway in a 1919 parade he saluted Guaranty as he passed.[28]

War affected the bank in other ways. More than five hundred employees went into government service, including four of the fourteen vice presidents. Altogether, about seventy-five percent of the work force had to be replaced. One vice president, Lewis Franklin, became director of the War Loan Organization in the Treasury Department. In the fall of 1917, when Guaranty joined the Federal Reserve System, President Sabin explained the bank's membership on the grounds that, given the emergency, national finances had to be conserved and yet responsive to demand. Concentration in the Federal Reserve, accordingly, was an appropriate way to achieve this goal. Sabin also realized that membership allowed the bank to discount some acceptances at a better rate and to rediscount commercial paper and bills of exchange to a larger amount. Another impact of the war was that in early 1918 the federal government took over operation of the nation's railroads, many of which were Guaranty customers. As part of this process, the government ordered removal of more than $30 million in railroad company deposits from Guaranty.[29]

Seeing itself as an adjunct of the military effort, Guaranty plunged headlong into Europe itself, creating a banking flank on the Western Front. The bank opened new facilities in London near the American Embassy, the Army and Navy headquarters, and the Red Cross. Similar expansion occurred in Paris, where the emphasis was on service to soldiers. The bank even constructed a special railroad car to shuttle money, including soldiers'

---

[28] "Guaranty Trust Company of New York, 1864–1927," 56–73, J. P. Morgan & Co., Inc. Papers.

[29] Ibid.

pay, from Paris to the environs of the trenches. Painted military gray, Guaranty's field operation had windows where men-in-arms could cash checks and buy Liberty Bonds, all within hearing distance of German guns. At one point Guaranty maintained approximately 10,000 accounts of American soldiers in France.[30]

Failure: The Mercantile Bank Crisis

Stetson's arrival at Guaranty is also illuminated by events after the November 1918 armistice. Peace confronted the bank with new challenges. The transition turned out badly, even threatening to destroy the ambitious Guaranty and thus Stetson's career. Victorious in war, Stetson's boss Sabin actually became a noteworthy casualty of the peace. Not fully perceiving the risks, Sabin wrote a January 1919 report to shareholders that summarized the situation with too much optimism:

> The outlook for the year 1919 seems to be on the whole encouraging, although many problems must obviously be faced. The readjustments of business from war to peace conditions will in many instances be difficult, and your Company, to some extent, must share in these difficulties. An easier money market may operate to reduce interest rates, and deflation of credit may reduce the demand. In spite of the relatively sound position which this country finds itself at the close of the war, we shall be affected to some degree by conditions throughout the world. Only by the most intelligent cooperation all along the line shall we be able to avail ourselves of the advantages offered in foreign markets.

Sabin's reference to expanding foreign investments was revealing, if misguided. To Guaranty's leadership it seemed the demand for American

---

[30] Ibid., 70–73. A discussion of J. P. Morgan's British affinity, which worked to the disadvantage of the French, is Martin Horn, "A Private Bank at War: J. P. Morgan & Co. and France, 1914–1918," *Business History Review* 74 (Spring 2000): 85–112.

goods and American financing was nearly unlimited, and the bank planned to look to foreign transactions for success.[31]

As early as 1915, Guaranty obtained a large interest, with investing partnerships J. & W. Seligman & Co. and Brown Brothers & Co., in the Mercantile Bank of the Americas, which had subsidiaries in Peru, Nicaragua, Venezuela, Brazil, Colombia, and Cuba. The purpose of the bank was "to assist in the development of trade between the Republics of this hemisphere." This meant financing agriculture, exporters of coffee, sugar, and cocoa, and assisting in the sale of the products. For example, in Cuba, a subsidiary, the Banco Mercantil Americano de Cuba, financed sugar to market. Guaranty also invested heavily in the Asia Banking Corporation, with headquarters in Shanghai. In Europe, the company opened an office in Brussels to compliment the London and Paris operations. It initiated an agreement with the new Polish government that helped facilitate credit in the United States. Guaranty also entered into an alliance with Banca Italiana di Sconto in Italy and in 1920 opened an office in Constantinople, signaling the potential importance of the Middle East to American business. In the early 1920s the sun never set on Guaranty's empire, as representatives of the bank also operated in Scandinavia, India, and Australia.[32]

One overseas operation which illustrates the bank's intense search for accounts involved the soon-to-be formed Soviet Union. The Bolshevik revolution of 1917 necessitated unusually imaginative banking, even for Guaranty. Simply put, the new communist government needed the assistance of capitalist financiers for foreign transactions. In 1920 three ships carrying gold owned by the revolutionary Soviet government left

---

[31] "Condensed Statement," 31 December 1919, Guaranty Trust Company of New York; "To the Stockholders of the Guaranty Trust Company of New York," 6 January 1919, J. P. Morgan & Co., Inc. Papers.

[32] "To the Stockholders of the Guaranty Trust Company of New York," 6 January 1919, J. P. Morgan & Co., Inc. Papers; Herbert Hoover to Charles Evans Hughes, 21 May 1921, Herbert Hoover Papers, Herbert Hoover Presidential Library, West Branch, Iowa; "Memorandum on Mercantile Bank of the Americas [1918?]," Braga Brothers Collection, George A. Smathers Libraries, University of Florida, Gainesville, Florida; Ross L. Muir and Carl J. White, *Over the Long Term: The Story of J. & W. Seligman & Co.* (New York: J. & W. Seligman, 1964) 119.

Russia bound for Guaranty Trust. Importing gold, however, presented legal problems because the United States did not officially recognize the Soviet government, which of course assumed power in a bloodbath of murder, civil war, and confiscation of property. When the gold arrived, Guaranty turned it over to the Treasury Department for sale, but the government refused to pay the $7 million selling price. Eventually Guaranty convinced officials that the gold was not of Bolshevik origin but had actually been produced by melting French and Belgian coins. The Treasury then paid for the gold, the money was credited to a Russian account at Guaranty, and Comrade Lenin became a loyal customer of the J. P. Morgan-controlled bank. By mid–1920 the bank was Lenin's agent in the United States. Soon thereafter Secretary of Commerce Herbert Hoover, not exactly a Marxist sympathizer, promoted Guaranty's idea of a formal exchange relationship with the New State Bank at Moscow. Hoover wanted a more "rational" approach to Bolshevik business transactions in the United States, particularly if Russian money was used to purchase American goods. Guaranty also helped establish the first Soviet international bank in Moscow and a Guaranty employee was hired as head of its foreign department.[33]

Unfortunately, in 1921 the foreign boom burst. Guaranty was most affected by troubles in Latin America, especially a spectacular collapse in the price of sugar, from 22 to 3.5 cents per pound, but other tropical products faced steep price declines as well. The resulting pressures on the Latin America-based Mercantile Bank of the Americas, forty percent of

---

[33] "Guaranty Trust Goes to Russia," http://reformed-theology.org/html/books/bolshevik_revolution/. Herbert Hoover to Charles Evans Hughes, 10 January 1922, Herbert Hoover Papers. A different chapter of Guaranty's relationship with the Soviets was less friendly to the revolutionaries. In December 1917 Guaranty held several million dollars in old tsarist Russian accounts. The money was not returned to Russia until the United States government sued the bank on behalf of the Soviets in the 1930s. In 1947 a judgment was rendered against the bank for approximately $3.5 million. "Annual Report to Stockholders for the Year 1947," J. P. Morgan & Co., Inc. Papers. A sophisticated discussion of Hoover's encouragement of foreign investment is Joan Hoff Wilson, *Herbert Hoover: Forgotten Progressive* (Boston: Little, Brown, 1975). The interests of other New York bankers in Russia is presented in Priscilla Roberts, "Jewish Bankers, Russia, and the Soviet Union, 1900–1940: The Case of Kuhn, Loeb and Company," *American Jewish Archives Journal* 49 (1997): 9–37.

which was owned by Guaranty, led to the Mercantile Bank's failure. Guaranty's enormous losses, up to more than $40 million, caused one observer to admit that "Guaranty's credit structure, while it did not actually fail, was strained to the breaking point." Overextensions in foreign banking ended one era in the bank's history, the great expansion of 1910 to 1921, and began another, a period of retrenchment and slow renewal that ended favorably in 1929 in a merger with the National Bank of Commerce.[34]

The most important long-term effect of the crisis of the early 1920s, which would have a profound affect on Gene Stetson's career, was the shifting of Guaranty's leadership even more firmly in the direction of influence and control by J. P. Morgan & Co. At the time of Mercantile Bank debacle, the key link between Morgan and Guaranty was Thomas W. Lamont, a Morgan partner. Lamont was a consummate relationship banker who became an important role-model for Stetson. Beginning the 1910s, as a member of Guaranty's board of directors and as chairman of its executive committee, Lamont participated in a wide range of Guaranty activities, including cotton financing, the selection of potential directors, war finance, steering corporate business to the bank, and the decision to become a member of the Federal Reserve. He lobbied politicians on behalf of the bank, writing one United States Senator to let him "drop in and let me have a word with you about the Guaranty Trust Company." Lewis Franklin sought Lamont's approval when he resigned as a Guaranty vice president in 1918 in order to take a position in the Treasury Department.[35]

---

[34] "Guaranty Trust Company of New York, 1864–1927," 75–80; Siegfried Stern, *The United States in International Banking* (New York: Columbia University Press, 1951) 131–32, 159–60; "Percentage of Interests in the Mercantile Bank of the Americas," 3 May 1921, Braga Brothers Collection. An extended discussion of the Mercantile Bank's problems, focusing on the intervention of Morgan partner Edward R. Stettinius, Sr., is John Douglas Forbes, *Stettinius, Sr.: Portrait of a Morgan Partner* (Charlottesville: University Press of Virginia, 1974) 137–49.

[35] Wilbur Wamsley, "Wall Street's New Leaders," *Munsey's Magazine* 68 (December 1919): 412–27; Thomas W. Lamont to Alexander J. Hemphill, 24 May 1911; James M. Pratt to Thomas W. Lamont, 15 December 1914; Thomas W. Lamont to Alexander J. Hemphill, 19 February 1915; G. Murphy to Thomas W. Lamont, 10 January 1916; Maxwell M. Upson to Thomas W. Lamont, 11 January 1916; Charles H. Sabin to Thomas Lamont, 17 September 1917; Thomas W. Lamont to Charles Sabin, 1 October 1917; Thomas W. Lamont to W. Murray

Lamont was well aware of the risks and opportunities of international trade. Even before the collapse of the Mercantile Bank, he feared extensive liabilities, which primarily consisted of loans to tropical planters. He knew Sabin was chairman of the board of Mercantile. He was familiar with Guaranty's efforts to expand its influence overseas after the war, in part because these efforts occasionally conflicted with the interests of J. P. Morgan. Morgan, in fact, assumed the position of global clearinghouse with Guaranty, often seeking to grant or deny it rights to develop international business. Sabin, for example, in response to a complaint from J. P. ("Jack") Morgan Jr. about competition with Morgan regarding French loans, wrote Lamont,

> We have previously negotiated, as you undoubtedly remember, the largest commercial credit for France. Brown Brothers also arranged a credit, as did Bonbright and the Bankers Trust Company. We, therefore, cannot feel that we are infringing upon your territory, or Brown Brothers' territory, or anybody else's territory in such negotiations.... The matter has all been threshed out with Mr. Morgan—and I believe to his entire satisfaction.

As early as November 1920, Lamont expressed pessimism to Sabin about the overall economic situation, counseling that Guaranty should "do only such business as may be necessary until the situation clears up."[36]

Within weeks of that warning the Mercantile Bank's difficulties threatened Guaranty itself with collapse. At Lamont's urging, an "advocacy committee" was formed. There were efforts to call up bank stock. Sabin,

---

Crane, 18 October 1917; L. B. Franklin to Thomas Lamont, 16 March 1918, Thomas W. Lamont Collections Baker Library Historical Collections, Harvard Business School, Boston, Massachusetts. On Lamont generally, see Edward M. Lamont, *The Ambassador from Wall Street: The Story of Thomas W. Lamont, J. P. Morgan's Chief Executive* (Lanham MD: Madison Books, 1994).

[36] "Mercantile Bank of the Americas [1918]"; Charles H. Sabin to Thomas W. Lamont, 22 April 1919; Thomas W. Lamont to Charles H. Sabin, 9 May 1919, 5 November 1920, Thomas W. Lamont Collection.

however, still failed to appreciate the gravity of the threat. His annual letter to the shareholders, issued in December 1920, contained only vague hints of the deepening crisis. He admitted deposits decreased from 1919 to 1920, yet the current difficulty was merely "a reflection of the natural reaction and the general readjustment of business which is in progress." In short, there was no need to worry: "Our large gold reserve, our sound financial situation, our tremendous crops, our improved transportation and industrial conditions, our foreign markets and our great natural resources all underlie the business situation and give promises of future prosperity and progress."[37]

More willing to see the danger, Lamont and his partners opted to exercise the Morgan muscle. In May 1921, they formed a syndicate of eighteen banks, including Guaranty, to advance $35 million to the failing Mercantile Bank, with the eventual goal of liquidation. Leading stockholders of the Mercantile Bank, including Guaranty, raised another $20 million to encourage hesitant bankers to participate. Fear of a Guaranty failure, including the potential for personal liability of Guaranty directors if it did fail, was a key motive for syndicate participation. But even these moves were not enough. By the end of the summer Lamont, Jack Morgan, and Morgan partner Edward Stettinius stepped in more forcefully. In September Guaranty's board reduced the dividend to three percent, charged off all losses, and established extraordinary reserves of more than $15 million. Although these actions seemed drastic—to cut dividends implied bad management—they were preferable to an immanent bank run. According to the board, the measures covered "any losses that may be sustained from banking operations in Central and South America, where the shrinkage in the value of customers' loans, due to the unprecedented fall in

---

[37] Thomas W. Lamont to W. Ripley Nelson, 23 December 1920; Thomas W. Lamont to Charles Sabin, 10 February 1921, Thomas W. Lamont Collection; "To the Stockholders of the Guaranty Trust Company of New York," 31 December 1921," J. P. Morgan & Co., Inc. Papers; "Minutes of a Special Meeting of the Board of Directors of Banco Mercantile Americano de Cuba," 2 May 1921; Manuel Rionda to Victor Zevallos, 14 February 1922, Braga Brothers Collection. Sabin was chairman of the Cuban subsidiary's board.

the price of commodities and the fluctuation in exchange, has been excessive."[38]

The source of all this activity was a raw exercise of power by Morgan's partners. Lamont wrote a Guaranty director that "we at No. 23 [Wall Street, the location of Morgan's offices] have conferred almost constantly about the Guaranty situation." This discussion led to a restructuring of Guaranty's leadership. The tainted Sabin was bumped up to chairman of the board, while William C. ("Bill") Potter assumed the presidency. Stettinius and George Whitney, two Morgan partners, were added to Guaranty's board and executive committee. Their job would be to keep a close eye on the company, as the Morgan men believed some of the blame for the financial mess rested on current board members who had not been properly overseeing bank operations. In addition to Jack Morgan, who gave his seal of approval, Lamont consulted Harry Payne Whitney, Thomas F. Ryan, and Daniel Guggenheim. Lamont developed the plan while Sabin was out of New York and presented it to him when he returned. He did so on 30 September 1921, in a polite, but firm letter: "We have all had some severe lessons, and these make it imperative for us all to rally together and to see that the Guaranty Trust Company—both as to interior management and in the eyes of the public—occupies an impregnable position and moves forward to increasing success." Sabin was not left to doubt that the Morgan firm, including Morgan himself, was behind the move.[39]

[38] Thomas W. Lamont to Charles H. Sabin, 29 June 1921; Thomas W. Lamont to Benjamin Strong, 18 August 1921; William C. Potter to Thomas W. Lamont, 15 August 1921; J. P. Morgan Jr. to Thomas W. Lamont, 11 August 1921; Thomas Lamont to Harry P. Whitney, 12 August 1921; Thomas W. Lamont to Daniel Guggenheim, 30 September 1921; George H. Gardiner to W. C. Potter, 29 June 1925; Folders 220–27, 28, 29, 30, Thomas W. Lamont Collection; "To the Stockholders of the Guaranty Trust Company of New York," 16 September 1921, J. P. Morgan & Co., Inc. Papers. For more on Stettinius's role, see Forbes, *Stettinius*, 137–49.

[39] Thomas W. Lamont to A. H. Harris, 30 September 1921; Thomas W. Lamont to Edward Stettinius, 27 September 1921; Thomas W. Lamont to Charles H. Sabin, 30 September 1921; Thomas W. Lamont to Cuyler, 1 October 1921, Thomas W. Lamont Collection; Forbes, *Stettinius*, 142–43.

The new leadership, particularly Potter and Lamont, immediately began to restore faith. Potter was a good choice. Born in Chicago and trained as a mining engineer at the Massachusetts Institute of Technology, as a young man he worked in mines in the West and in central and South America, partly for the Guggenheims. He came to Guaranty in 1912 after a brief presidency with the Intercontinental Rubber Company. For his part, Lamont took the lead in generating positive publicity. He forthrightly confronted lingering concerns in the banking community. A letter he wrote Frank B. Anderson of the Bank of California suggested the degree of lost confidence caused by the Latin American collapse and the detailed repair work needed:

> A sheaf of gossip comes to us, probably just as inaccurate as all gossip is, to the effect that your criticism of the Guaranty Trust Company and of its officers, etc., has been very severe....
>
> The way that we [Morgan] look at the situation is this: The whole country, including the banking institutions, ran into a period of great inflation and when the bubble broke almost all of them had to suffer severe losses. The Guaranty Trust Company was the biggest trust company in the country and its operations were on a correspondingly large scale. We think that it outgrew its organization and in that way began, after a time, to lack the detailed personal supervision which you, of all men, know is so necessary to the proper conduct of a large institution. Moreover, as we see it, the Guaranty Trust Company was anxious to respond generously to the appeals made from Washington that American institutions should take their place in furnishing ample credit facilities to the foreign markets of the world, especially those of South and Central America. It was this last desire on the part of the officers of the Guaranty Trust Company that led them into the investment in the Mercantile Bank of the Americas, which [performed] badly owing to the terrific commodity losses in cocoa, coffee, rubber and other products indigenous to the countries served. As a matter of fact, with the improvement in Central American exchange, the situation is not

> nearly as bad as it was, but nevertheless there was no doubt plenty to criticize in the way of lack of complete organization and foresight. At the same time, neither Sabin nor any of his associate officers in the Guaranty Trust Company could ever be accused of anything but the best of good faith, and if one had been obliged to analyze their transactions day by day, I doubt whether his judgment would have been anything like as severe as his judgment is likely to be after the event.
>
> In any event, the Guaranty Trust Company is now in a position that is sound and its earnings good. It was because of our faith in the situation and our strong desire to assist it and to make it better that we encouraged two more of the members of our firm, Ed Stettinius and George Whitney to go on the Executive Committee. Thus you see we are very closely identified with the institution and are anxious that good friends like you should do everything to help us. Please, therefore, when the subject comes up again, do your best, not simply for the Guaranty Trust, but for your friends in this firm by explaining that the storm is completely over and the situation sound and the outlook excellent.[40]

Despite Lamont's support, the turnaround was slow and expensive. In 1922, there were false rumors that Guaranty's European offices would be closed. The Constantinople outpost, despite strong encouragement from Secretary of Commerce Hoover to keep it open, did become a casualty. Lamont, ever the booster, told the bank's representative in Paris that he should convey to one skeptical customer "that we are one family and that the Guaranty has had and would, according to our present ideas, continue to have a place in the Morgan-Baring Group." Eventually the Guaranty board voted to pay off losses to banks that participated in the 1921 syndicate in order to improve its credit and good will. Of course, Morgan was one of

---

[40] "The Corporate History of Guaranty Trust Company of New York [1952]," 45–46, J. P. Morgan & Co., Inc. Papers; E. Marshall Young to Thomas W. Lamont, 13 October 1921; Thomas W. Lamont to Frank B. Anderson, 31 December 1921, Thomas W. Lamont Collection; Forbes, *Stettinius*, 149. On Potter's life, see *New York Times*, 3 January 1957.

the banks to receive payment. Guaranty's assets showed a steady decline through the mid-twenties. Peaking at about $960 million in 1919, they fell to $890 million in February 1921 and $540 million by the end of 1921, a catastrophic loss. In 1923 assets had climbed back to $620 million, but they remained under $750 million as late as 1927.[41]

Lessons

Guaranty's experiences from 1916 through the Mercantile crisis had a powerful effect on Stetson's career. Dramatic events involving no less than the reshaping of world finance meant that Stetson had to hit the ground running. In moving from Macon to Manhattan he stepped from the simpler world of New South boosterism to the highest levels of an evolving international scene in which American banks had acquired new and far-reaching powers. Equally important, in Guaranty's case, both during and after World War I its banking practice was fundamentally linked to the Morgan partnership. In order to survive and succeed, Stetson needed to retain the positive lessons of his youth while adapting quickly to the aggressive values of demanding Wall Street sponsors. A Guaranty job came with rare and valuable connections, resources, and opportunities. But it also

[41] A. Breton to William C. Potter, 13 April 1922; Thomas W. Lamont to Mr. Hebmann, 5 May 1922; George Gardiner to William C. Potter, 29 June 1925; Thomas W. Lamont to George Whitney, 2 July 1925; Thomas W. Lamont to Clarence H. MacKay, 31 January 1924, Thomas W. Lamont Collection; "Guaranty Trust Company of New York, 1864–1927," 79; "Condensed Financial Statements," Guaranty Trust Company of New York, 31 December 1919, 28 February 1921, 30 June 1921, 6 September 1921, 15 November 1921, 10 March 1922, 30 September 1922, 15 November 1922, 27 March 1923, 10 September 1923, 31 December 1923, 30 June 1924, 31 December 1924, 31 December 1925, 23 March 1927, J. P. Morgan & Co., Inc. Papers. A detailed discussion of the mechanisms for resolving the Mercantile Bank's problems is Forbes, *Stettinius*, 144–49. Regarding the Constantinople branch, Hoover wrote Charles Sabin that "the United States has as great a need of patriotic action today as ever before in its history and...the United States still demands sacrifices from its citizens. I believe we are of one mind in realizing the important effect that American business must have on the future civilization of the world." Herbert Hoover to Charles Sabin, 9 September 1921, Herbert Hoover Papers. See also William C. Potter to Herbert Hoover, 17 September 1921, Herbert Hoover Papers.

carried the burdens of acting under the intense pressures of global financial power and responsibility.

Stetson's role in the Mercantile crisis was limited but significant. He belonged to the Latin American bank's board of directors. And, according to the *New York Times*, he was the "guiding mind" in the decision to close the subsidiary Banco Mercantile Americano de Cuba, working with Morganites Martin Egan and Dwight Morrow. As a result, he joined in the Morgan-sponsored clean-up and avoided any blame associated with Sabin. More broadly, the Mercantile failure imparted some valuable lessons. First, it signaled the absolute necessity of paying attention to Lamont and working with the Morgan firm. Perhaps Sabin's reputed "independence" had carried too high a price. During the 1920s, failure in Morgan's eyes meant the end of any ambitions to a higher place. This, apparently, was a key part of the quid pro quo of Stetson's Guaranty opportunity. Stetson also must have perceived the need for extreme caution in international banking. The rewards were assumed to be great, but so were the risks. Finally, the Mercantile episode seems to have enhanced Stetson's sense of the long and sometimes lonely preparation and monitoring necessary to make effective financial decisions. Sabin may have lost that edge, and Stetson apparently promised himself that if he ever failed it would not be for lack of effort.[42]

---

[42] On Stetson and the Cuban bank's closing, see *New York Times*, 4 October 1921.

4

New York

Stetson, of course, knew that despite the Mercantile Bank mess, Guaranty had a lot going for it. Its potential as a commercial bank was always enormous. An important reflection of this fact was the bank's carefully chosen culture and physical presence. Guaranty tried to impress well-heeled clients with a temple-like dignity. Within its offices, solemnity was imposed on employee and visitor alike; loud talking was expressly prohibited. According to written rules, employees could not "work without their coats in any place visible to the public, except in the summer time, and then only under rules prescribed by the Chief Clerk." No detail was too small. A clear line of power and status separated officers and other employees, just as an even clearer line distinguished the bank's elite clients from the average citizen.[1]

The Guaranty building where Stetson came to work had only recently opened, in 1913, at 140 Broadway. Adjacent to Wall Street and other leading financial institutions, the building's gray New England granite exterior carried forward the dignity theme, exuding confidence and stability. The main floor featured a massive banking room, roughly one hundred feet on one side and one hundred and thirty-five feet on the other, with towering Corinthian columns rising four stories. The room held teller stations where ordinary customer business was transacted. Marble from France made up the walls and columns, and marble also covered the floor, which incorporated mosaics copied from originals in The Vatican and Pompeii. Massive doors to the street contained carvings of Greek coins, suggesting ancient origins and lasting dependability, and three huge

---

[1] "Guaranty Trust Company of New York, 1864–1927," 32–34; "Morgan News Story," 16 April 1991, J. P. Morgan & Co., Inc. Papers, JP Morgan Chase Archives, New York, New York.

chandeliers of bronze and glass hung from a blue and gold ceiling.[2]

Even less public spaces gave an impression of wealth and security. In the basement a polished steel vault held millions in securities and cash. The Directors' Room, as well as the President's Office, perched above the main entrance, facing Broadway. According to an impressed company historian, the executive area was "designed to carry out the effect of strength, simplicity, and space while the detail both in ornament and in furnishing, shows the same restraint in color and the same exquisite workmanship that one would expect to find in a beautiful private home."[3]

The working culture of Guaranty showed there was substance beneath the sophisticated image. After World War I an important contributor to revived growth was the company's venture into the underwriting and marketing of debt and equity securities. Guaranty had been active in securities since the early years of the century, but the real development of the business did not occur until after 1915, when a young man named Harold Stanley arrived. Before 1920, operating within the Bond Department, Stanley's securities group participated in international, federal, state, and municipal government issues, as well as offerings of public utilities, industrials, and railroads. Hopes for further expansion resulted in the formation of the Guaranty Company of New York in 1920, a wholly owned subsidiary of Guaranty Trust. The Guaranty Company responded aggressively to the new retail market for equity securities by opening twenty-seven offices throughout the United States. Stanley led the Guaranty Company from 1921 to 1928.[4]

During the 1920s Guaranty purchased, distributed, and marketed original issues of securities. As a full-fledged investment bank, it participated in selling syndicates for securities and handled government issues. The company provided information to investors, but did not express opinions on stocks or on trends in the market. The investment policy was

---

[2] Ibid.

[3] Ibid.

[4] David Rogers, *The Future of American Banking: Managing for Change* (New York: McGraw-Hill, Inc., 1993) 201; "Guaranty Trust Company of New York, 1864–1927," 81–83; J. P. Morgan & Co., Inc. Papers; Benjamin J. Klebaner, *American Commercial Banking* (Boston: Twayne Publishers, 1990) 126–27.

that "every customer on its books shall have a carefully studied financial plan, shall own none but sound investments, and that these investments shall be wisely diversified as to type and maturities, and possess yields as high as is consonant with safety of principal." Investor information was based on the work of in-house analysts and statisticians, who used Guaranty's extensive financial library. Clients could also receive special reports on foreign investments.[5]

Another important characteristic of Guaranty during this period was the incredibly sophisticated scope and customer-oriented focus of its activities. Guaranty and its officers, including Stetson, were expected to be models of commercial relationship banking. Attention to detail and the development of long-term customers were hallmarks. This work included an impressive array of domestic, foreign, fiduciary, and securities banking. Domestically, Guaranty organized services geographically, following the boundaries of the branches of the Federal Reserve. Officers such as Stetson received regional territories to oversee. The bank offered checking and deposit accounts and paid interest on those accounts. However, the bank specialized in service to business: "Beginning with the organization of a corporation, and at each later stage in its existence, this Company can aid in the safe and expeditious transaction of every phase of present-day business." The bank handled notes, bond coupons, and commercial paper across the United States. It employed shipping experts skilled in dealing with bills-of-lading for goods entering New York. Funds could be transferred by telegraph. Clients obtained information about the creditworthiness of other individuals and businesses. The bank made secured and unsecured loans, utilizing a wide range of devices, including stocks and bonds as collateral, drafts drawn on foreign countries, and staple commodities as collateral. Guaranty developed an extensive business assisting other banks, facilitated by membership in the Federal Reserve System and the New York Clearing House Association. The trust company would collect credit instruments,

---

[5] Guaranty Trust Company of New York, "Guaranty Service (1923)," 47–61, J. P. Morgan & Co., Inc. Papers. Ron Chernow, *The House of Morgan: An American Banking Dynasty and the Rise of Modern Finance* (New York: Atlantic Monthly Press, 1990) 304, suggests that the company invented American depository receipts, which "enabled Americans to buy overseas stocks without currency problems."

deal in acceptances, act as an agent for other banks in numerous kinds of transactions, serve as a trustee, deal in securities, accept deposit accounts, issue letters of credit, and even provide meeting, library, and secretarial services for visiting bankers.[6]

Guaranty also offered specialized international banking through its five overseas offices and correspondent banks throughout the world. The bank aimed to provide American-level banking services abroad. Individuals maintained accounts in the Guaranty's foreign offices and obtained letters of credit and travelers' checks. For businesses, the bank could collect bills drawn on foreign customers in dollars or foreign currencies. Loans, especially on commodities, were arranged, facilitating the shipment of goods across national boundaries. The company provided services regarding foreign exchange rates and transactions and the purchase and sale of gold and silver. It issued commercial letters of credit as a means of financing imports and exports. In addition, the bank acted as an agent in the United States for foreign governments and corporations.[7]

The largest work was trust business, which in the 1920s employed more than 600 persons. Individuals, including trustees and executors under wills, received trust services, from probate to payment of taxes. The bank managed insurance proceeds, real estate, cash, and securities as trust property. Guaranty advertised its conservative approach to trust management: "Constant and close watch is kept over the investments, and no effort is spared in safeguarding such funds." Guaranty also performed trustee duties for corporations, serving as fiduciary for public utilities, railroads, and mining corporations. It issued mortgage bonds, collateral trust bonds, convertible bonds, debenture bonds, notes, and income bonds. The bank was escrow and transfer agent on complex matters, paid coupons and mature bonds, and prepared and paid federal income taxes for corporations. Guaranty provided similar services to state and local governments.[8]

---

[6] Guaranty Trust Company of New York, "Guaranty Service (1923)," 5–19, J. P. Morgan & Co., Inc. Papers.

[7] Ibid., 20–33.

[8] Ibid., 34–46.

The bank engaged in an enormous variety of other tasks, making its New York offices a city unto itself. At its Fifth Avenue branch, Guaranty maintained a vault with 16,000 safety deposit boxes. Ninety feet long, forty feet wide, and two stories tall, the vault possessed walls of solid concrete, heavy steel bars, and a lining of armor steel. Its entrance door weighed more than 70,000 pounds and locked with twenty-four bolts. Daily mail poured into the bank in enormous quantities that required a sophisticated postal service. More than 130,000 pieces a month arrived from outside the United States. Employees prepared over 7,000 letters to foreign addresses each day. The company employed fifteen persons whose only job was to translate and compose documents in twenty-seven languages. Forty messengers, a corps of fifty-six security officers, signature checkers, and printers carried out other essential tasks. Eighteen telephone operators manned the largest switchboard of any bank in the world, handling more than 12,000 calls each working day. The company also published sophisticated information about income taxes and international trade. Guaranty employees wrote and distributed *The Guaranty Survey*, a monthly devoted to analyses of financial developments around the world, and *The Guaranty News*, which contained information for employees and customers. Guaranty held a large library of 20,000 volumes, including books on banking and finance, more than 400 periodicals, and its own collection of data on the nation's most important corporations.[9]

Altogether, Guaranty employed more than 3,000 persons. The company offered unusual working conditions, including an above average scale of wages. Employees could become students in the Educational Department, which featured lectures on banking topics, including investments. The Guaranty Club, with its own rooms, sponsored social, athletic, and educational activities. The Club administered a "thrift fund"

---

[9] Ibid., 62–91. *The Guaranty Survey* was distributed to newspapers, Cabinet members, and Members of Congress. "Corporate History of the Guaranty Trust Company of New York (1952)," 68B, J. P. Morgan & Co., Inc. Papers. A fascinating document showing employee organization is the "Guaranty Club Notebook (1911–1916)," J. P. Morgan & Co., Inc. Papers, which describes how Guaranty employees before World War I, organized a wide range of recreation, entertainment, and athletics activities.

composed of employee investments. This reflected the company's desire to have employees "who have the peace of mind and self-respect that result from savings." The bank provided free annual physical examinations and a resident physician and nurse gave free medical care at the fully equipped hospital in the main office. The company owned a "Country House" outside the city for persons recovering from illness. Another benefit was a pension system, inaugurated in 1914. The main office even housed a restaurant, which, contrary to the claims of economists, gave free lunches to all employees and dinner and breakfast to employees working after hours. Employees could visit the company store, which sold meat, butter, eggs, flour, canned goods, tobacco, and fruit at less than market prices.[10]

The Guaranty expected a lot in exchange for these benefits, enacting detailed rules prohibiting such things as crowding or pushing in halls and elevators and encouraging employees to keep expenses to a minimum. Workers were told to examine wastepaper baskets at the end of each day to ensure nothing important was thrown away. The last employee leaving each department was supposed to turn out overhead lights. And, there was a mandated distinction between different levels of staff. Officers had their own eating areas, and the directors' room was strictly off limits to employees.[11]

Early Relationships

Stetson became a key participant in this complex work immediately upon his arrival in New York, quickly adapting to and learning Guaranty's relationship banking culture. From the beginning, his efforts tackled both domestic and international finance. On the international side, Guaranty proudly offered "its facilities to bankers, manufacturers and merchants, and

---

[10] Guaranty Trust Company of New York, "Guaranty Service (1923)," 92–99; "Morgan News Story," 16 April 1991, J. P. Morgan & Co., Inc. Papers. On the Guaranty restaurant, see "The Lunch Problem," *New York Globe and Commercial Advertiser*, 26 November 1920, J. P. Morgan & Co., Inc. Papers.

[11] Guaranty Trust Company of New York, "Guaranty Service (1923)," 92–99; "Morgan News Story," 16 April 1991, J. P. Morgan & Co., Inc. Papers; Lillian Otlowski, telephone interview with author, notes in possession of author, 8 June 2004.

invite[d] them to consult the officers of its Foreign Department regarding the most economical and practical methods of financing the foreign business that is resulting from the new position of the United States among the nations of the world." Guaranty plainly intended to use this "new position," and its bankers such as Stetson, to oil the American investing machine around the globe.[12]

An early example of Stetson's international work involved The Asia Banking Corporation. Asia Banking promoted itself as "An American Bank for Trade with the Orient." Although its headquarters was just down the street from Guaranty on lower Broadway, the company operated through branches in Shanghai, Peking, Hong Kong, Canton, and Manila. Asia Banking sought the business of Asian merchants, manufacturers, importers, and exporters. The bank dealt in bills of exchange, issued letters of credit, compiled credit ratings, financed international shipments, and provided economic information to clients. In the early 1920s it was owned and managed by a consortium of American banks, including Guaranty, Bankers Trust, National Shawmut, the National Bank of Commerce in Seattle, and the ill-fated Mercantile Bank of the Americas. At the end of the first year of its operation, assets totaled more than $42 million.[13]

In effect, the Asia bank was Guaranty's eastern front. Of the eighteen board members in 1920, five were Guaranty officers, including Sabin and Stetson. Guaranty owned a much larger share of ownership than any other entity. Given that some board members lived on the west coast and meetings were held in New York, Guaranty clearly controlled the operation. For example, at the 6 January 1920, weekly board meeting, held at Guaranty's offices, four of the eight directors present were Guaranty officers. Sabin, as president of Asia Banking, presided. On 13 January 1920 four of the five directors present, including Stetson, were Guaranty officers.

---

[12] Guaranty Trust Company of New York, *Banking Service for Foreign Trade* (New York: Guaranty Trust Company of New York, 1919) 1, 2, 8, 10.

[13] Asia Banking Corporation, *Asia Banking Corporation* (New York: Asia Banking Corporation, 1918); Asia Banking Corporation, *Asia Banking Corporation* (New York: Asia Banking Corporation, 1919); Asia Banking Corporation, *Asia Banking Corporation* (New York: Asia Banking Corporation, 1920). The corporation is mentioned in Ji Zhaojin, *A History of Modern Shanghai Banking: The Rise and Decline of China's Finance Capitalism* (Armonk NY: M. E. Sharpe, 2003).

In 1920 the board received frequent reports of assets and liabilities, including information about transactions from the Asia branches such as acceptances held, futures contracts, and outstanding loans. The loans appear to have been primarily to American businesses operating in China. The board rendered decisions about the staff of the bank and significant transactions, especially credit extension. In March 1920, the board assigned Stetson the task of investigating whether a trust receipt line of $500,000 should be extended to a dealer in leather hides.[14]

Another example of Stetson's international work was the trip he made to Europe with Harold Stanley in mid–1920. The men spent two months evaluating the prospects of European recovery after the war. Stetson traveled to the defeated Germany and Austria as well as to the new nation of Czechoslovakia. He found considerable unease and uncertainty. A perennial optimist himself, he "did not meet any optimists in Germany." Similarly, Austria was "crushed," and "there is little semblance of industrial or productive activity." In Czechoslovakia matters were better, but Stetson recognized it was early in the nation's history "and that the making of a nation is a long process." The contrast between Stetson's reservations and Stanley's glowing reports about economic conditions in Britain, France, and Belgium reflected the chasm between East and West that soon produced an even greater cataclysm than the Great War.[15]

Stetson had his own miniature version of the Mercantile Bank crisis in 1921, thanks to his directorship in another bank that sought foreign trade. After World War I, Guaranty obtained an interest in Italian Discount and Trust, a New York institution founded in 1918. Stetson was made chairman of the board of this small bank. Unfortunately for him and for depositors, in December 1921 Italian Discount had difficulties related to the failure of a bank in Italy. Depositors in New York made a panicked run on Italian

---

[14] See *Asia Banking Corporation*. This resource contains copies of minutes from weekly board meetings, 1918-1920. Part of Stetson's international work at this time also involved communicating with government agents. Paul Phillip Abrahams, for example, cites a letter Stetson wrote to the federal Bureau of Foreign and Domestic Commerce in 1921. See Abrahams, *The Foreign Expansion of American Finance and its Relationship to the Foreign Economic Policies of the United States, 1907–1921* (New York: Arno Press, 1976) 175.

[15] *New York Times*, 9 July 1920.

Discount, and the police had to be called to maintain order. Guaranty's president, Bill Potter, told the press that at the time of the run Guaranty had already sold its interest in Italian Discount to an Italian bank, and the bank reopened successfully in early 1922. The incident did not indicate any failures on Guaranty's part, but as with the Mercantile bank fiasco it again signaled to Stetson the risks of international banking.[16]

Stetson was also associated with various Guaranty operations in cotton. Clearly, the bank was interested in taking advantage of Stetson's Georgia experiences with cotton production and manufacturing. Guaranty always viewed cotton, accurately, as a global commodity. The bank was deeply interested in facilitating trade through more efficient financing at all levels of production and it expected officers such as Stetson to carry forward the work. Guaranty sponsored the Textile Banking Company, for which Stetson became a director at its founding in 1919. At his death, forty years later, he was Textile's chairman. Guaranty also invested in Independent Warehouses, Inc. Stetson not only sat on its board, he became the company's president in the 1920s. Guaranty, and Stetson, believed the absence of good warehouses was a major deficiency in marketing cotton. The independent warehouse system, constructed at ports of entry and at key places in the southern United States, enhanced the credit system by allowing storage of cotton for market and the issue of negotiable warehouse receipts. Textile manufacturers were unwilling to tie up their own capital in warehouse construction and storage.[17]

Stetson and Harriman

Social connections and alliances with wealth were particularly important in New York elite banking. This is a key reason why the status, organization, and history of Guaranty were so important to Stetson's opportunities. Guaranty possessed both the capital and the personal

---

[16] Ibid., 1 July 1919; 5 May, 30 December 1921; 22 February 1922.

[17] Guaranty Trust Company of New York, *The Fabric of Civilization: A Short Survey of the Cotton Industry in the United States* (New York: Guaranty Trust Company of New York, 1919) 19–35. Stetson also was a director of the European Textile Corporation, a position that probably involved the same kinds of cotton finance.

connections a talented banker needed to further cultivate business relationships. One especially revealing example of the early opportunities presented by Guaranty's connections was Stetson's association with the Barnsdall Corporation. Barnsdall, formed in 1919, included Stetson on its initial board. The corporation originally consisted of the assets of the estate of oil baron Theodore N. Barnsdall. It was a complex group of oil and mining operations scattered across the United States, Canada, and Mexico. Oil, coal, zinc, gas, and gold were all part of the Barnsdall empire. At the end of 1919, assets of the companies exceeded $24 million. Stetson served on Barnsdall's executive committee from 1919 to 1921 and, then, again from 1927 to 1930. Despite radical price shifts among its commodities, the 1920s were quite profitable, and its assets grew to more than $75 million by 1928.[18]

Stetson's work with Barnsdall was most important, however, because it was his first significant opportunity to work with W. Averell Harriman and a cast of other important financiers. The relation between the late E. H. Harriman, Averell's father, and Guaranty has already been noted: before 1912, the elder Harriman and his estate bought a huge chunk of Guaranty's stock when Mutual Insurance was forced to divest its interest in the bank. In 1919, when Stetson went on the Barnsdall board, Averell Harriman was still a young man, only a few years out of Yale. Thanks to a princely inheritance, he was already one of the wealthiest men in America. Harriman's involvement with Barnsdall expanded through the presence of George H. Walker, president of Harriman's securities firm, on the Barnsdall board. Walker became the grandfather and great-grandfather, respectively, of two subsequent American presidents, George H. W. Bush and George W. Bush.

---

[18] Barnsdall Corporation, *Annual Report* (New York: Barnsdall Corporation, 1919); Barnsdall Corporation, *Annual Report* (New York: Barnsdall Corporation, 1920); Barnsdall Corporation, *Annual Report* (New York: Barnsdall Corporation, 1921); Barnsdall Corporation, *Annual Report* (New York: Barnsdall Corporation, 1927); Barnsdall Corporation, *Annual Report* (New York: Barnsdall Corporation, 1928); Barnsdall Corporation, *Annual Report* (New York: Barnsdall Corporation, 1929); Barnsdall Corporation, *Annual Report* (New York: Barnsdall Corporation, 1930). In 1930, Stetson was a director with another oil outfit, the New York Petroleum Royalty Corporation, but I could not determine its connection with Barnsdall.

Walker and Stetson served on the Barnsdall executive committee together. Further, Barnsdall's president was Matthew C. Brush. Brush was also president of Georgian Manganese, a Harriman mining company operating in the Soviet Union. Brush would later serve with Stetson as fellow directors of W. A. Harriman Securities, another Harriman investment firm.[19]

Stetson's work with Harriman interests increased during the 1920s, a clear sign of Harriman's growing trust. In addition to Barnsdall, Stetson was on the board of W. A. Harriman & Co., an investment company largely supported by Harriman's substantial fortune. This venture had merged with Morton & Co., another New York investment firm, in 1920. Morton was partially owned by Guaranty, so Stetson went on the W. A. Harriman board, along with Guaranty's Harold Stanley, in order to represent Guaranty's interest. When Guaranty sold its stake in W. A. Harriman &

---

[19] George H. Walker (1875–1953) was the father-in-law of Prescott Bush (1895–1972), who was the father of President George H. W. Bush (b. 1924) and the grandfather of President George W. Bush (b. 1946). Matthew C. Brush was also president of American International Corporation, a joint venture of important New York financial interests created in 1915, including Guaranty, to invest and gather political intelligence for the United States government in Europe and Russia. Kevin Phillips, *American Dynasty: Aristocracy, Fortune, and the Politics of Deceit in the House of Bush* (New York: Viking, 2004) 151–52, 179. Phillips associates Barnsdall Corporation with Harriman's oil exploits in the Soviet Union in the 1920s. Yet this was perhaps a different entity, Barnsdall International Corporation. The annual reports for Barnsdall Corporation describe North American activities. Nonetheless, the links among Stetson, Guaranty, Harriman, Brush, and Walker and their extensive support for foreign investment during and after World War I are clear. Stetson was later a director with Cuba Distilling Company, a subsidiary of U.S. Industrial Alcohol. George H. Walker had an ownership interest in U.S. Industrial Alcohol and was a Cuba Distilling director in the 1930s. See George H. Walker to W. Averell Harriman, 25 September 1930, W. Averell Harriman Papers, Library of Congress, Manuscripts Division, Washington, DC (indicating Walker's ownership in both U.S. Industrial Alcohol and Barnsdall Corporation). In 1918, *Forbes* listed Mrs. E. H. Harriman as the eleventh wealthiest person in the United States, with a fortune of $80 million, the equivalent of more than $1.1 billion in 2007 Consumer Price Index dollars. Kevin Phillips, *Wealth and Democracy: A Political History of the American Rich* (New York: Broadway Books, 2002), 56; "Six Ways to Compute the Relative Value of a U.S. Dollar Amount," http://www.measuringworth.com/calculators/uscompare/result.php.

Co. in 1922, this function was no longer necessary, and Stetson left the Harriman board.[20]

Although many of the details of Stetson's contributions to this complex assortment of companies are unclear, there is no doubt that he made a very favorable impression on Harriman, especially in the areas of investment advice and corporate management. Stetson's successes led to a better documented opportunity, when Harriman jumped into the fledging airplane business. In 1929 Harriman created an ambitious holding company, Aviation Corporation. The corporation planned to pioneer passenger and freight services in the United States and included some of the early leaders of commercial flight, such as the Embry-Riddle Company, Louis Piper, and Fairchild Aircraft Corporation. Stetson became one of Aviation's initial directors, as did his friends Robert Woodruff of Coca-Cola and Robert Lehman of Lehman Brothers. Harriman handpicked Stetson for the job, a sure demonstration of his confidence. In quick order Aviation acquired thirty-three operating companies. This was truly the exciting, if not-so-profitable, dawn of an industry. Aviation faced hiring untested executives, purchasing vast amounts of property, and dealing with the government over potentially lucrative mail routes. It also had the misfortune of beginning simultaneously with a national depression. Although one of its airlines in 1931 offered a then-speedy thirty-six hour flight from Atlanta to Los Angeles, with only nine stops, the enormous cost of $147.15 (one-way) deterred all but the wealthiest of travelers.[21]

---

[20] "Merger File [1969]," Brown Brothers Harriman & Company Collection, New-York Historical Society, New York, New York; *New York Times*, 12 October 1920.

[21] "Digest of Transactions Since Incorporation of the Aviation Corporation [1929]"; "Brochure for Southern Air Fast Express, Atlanta to Los Angeles (October, 1930)," W. Averell Harriman Papers. The Atlanta to Los Angeles fare would be the equivalent of over $2,000 in 2007 Consumer Price Index dollars. See "Six Ways to Compute the Relative Value of a U.S. Dollar Amount," http://measuringworth.com/calculators/uscompare/. For Robert "Bobbie" Lehman's dominance in the Lehman firm from the 1920s to the 1960s, see Charles R. Geisst, *The Last Partnerships: Inside the Great Wall Street Money Dynasties* (New York: McGraw-Hill, 2001) 76–77.

Stetson's most important job with Aviation was as a member of its finance committee. Originally, Aviation was well-off from a cash standpoint and the board sought to invest the cash in various securities through a subsidiary, Aviation Shares Corporation, of which Stetson was also a director. Stetson apparently received an invitation to join the finance committee because of his enthusiasm for the business as well as for his financial expertise. The committee's work involved decisions on investments, mostly publicly traded stocks. Many small meetings were held involving only Harriman, Robert Lehman, and Stetson. This was heady business, but the record of those meetings shows that Stetson was often willing to disagree with Lehman and Harriman about investment policy. The board sometimes discussed investments in other companies for which Stetson was a director, such as Coca-Cola.[22]

Eventually, shrinking revenues and not-so-unusual losses in the early 1930s took a toll on Harriman and Stetson's hopes for Aviation. Then, a dispute over the acquisition of North American Aviation, Eastern Air Transport, and Sperry Gyroscope destroyed unity on the board and led to the exit of both Harriman and Stetson. The protagonist was E. L. Cord, a flamboyant Indiana industrialist interested in cars and airplanes. Cord, who manufactured the famous Duesenberg Model J automobile, bought a large amount of Aviation stock during 1932. Cord complained about management and investment policy, prompting one board member, not Stetson, to condemn Cord's "pugnacity, selfishness, and…strong tendency to the use of vulgar profanity." In the end, Harriman recognized that Cord had the upper hand in terms of shares and agreed to reorganize the company in late 1932. Stetson also disliked Cord and resigned. He wrote Harriman, "It is, of course, my purpose to fully cooperate with you in the settlement," and he would certainly "continue to pull for [the company's] permanent success." Within months Harriman himself could not stand the drift of affairs and exited. He apparently planned his own version of a last

---

[22] "Aviation Shares Corporation Folder (1930–1933)," W. Averell Harriman Papers.

laugh on Cord, dumping his large block of Aviation stock on the market at his departure, with a predictable effect on its price.[23]

Stetson also enjoyed a relationship with W. A. Harriman Securities, an investment trust formed in the 1920s. Stetson was elected to its board and finance committee in March 1929 and remained through the 1930s. As with Aviation, the job was primarily to recommend investments. At one committee meeting Stetson "spoke at length," endorsing a purchase of Coca-Cola common stock. Later, he was asked by the committee for a special report on American Cyanamid. Given Stetson and his bank's connection with much of the publicly traded market, conflicts of interest were likely, but as yet unpoliced by federal regulation. Particularly significant was that the position required repeated contact with Harriman, Matthew Brush, and George H. Walker. W. A. Harriman Securities was decidedly an elite fund. Although possessed of over $11 million in assets in 1931, it had less than seventy-five shareholders, one of whom was Stetson's wife Iola.[24]

The adventures with Harriman, Lehman, Cord, Walker, and Brush placed Stetson in powerful company almost from the beginning of his Guaranty career. The value of these relationships was further enhanced in 1930 when Harriman's core investment business, W. A. Harriman & Co., merged with Brown Brothers, a venerable private banking partnership that traced its origins to 1825. Both companies focused on foreign investment, but the merger addressed complementary needs. According to Brown

---

[23] "To the Stockholders of the Aviation Corporation, November 14, 1932"; "To the Stockholders of the Aviation Corporation, November 15, 1932"; Harold Kondolf to W. Averell Harriman, 8 August 1932; Eugene W. Stetson to W. Averell Harriman et al., 18 November 1932; Chandler Harvey to W. Averell Harriman, 30 November 1932; G. C. Thayer to W. Averell Harriman, 2 February 1933, W. Averell Harriman Papers.

[24] Digest of Minutes of Meeting of the Finance Committee," 8 March, 24 May, 10 June 1929; "W. A. Harriman Securities Pro Forma Balance Sheet," 31 March 1931; "W. A. Harriman Securities Directors," 11 July 1929; "List of Stockholders," 19 September 1929, W. Averell Harriman Papers. Another Harriman-related company for which Stetson was a director in the 1920s was Small Issues Corporation. On the variety of investment trusts in the 1920s, see Maury Klein, *Rainbow's End: The Crash of 1929* (New York: Oxford University Press, 2001) 144, 151–52.

partner Robert Lovett, Harriman had plenty of capital but not much business, while Brown had plenty of business but not enough capital. Another young banker who joined the Harriman firm in 1926 and later became a partner at the new Brown Brothers made essentially the same observation. He was Prescott Bush, son-in-law of George H. Walker, Stetson's fellow director in Barnsdall. In the early 1930s Brown Brothers, Harriman possessed more than $55 million in resources and provided corporate and industrial financing, commercial letters of credit, foreign exchange, and investment advice.[25]

Stetson enjoyed an excellent relationship with Brown Brothers, Harriman and its partners. In 1939 the firm's Robert Lovett wrote Harriman that Stetson had successfully lobbied for federal legislation, probably with Stetson's friend United States Senator Walter F. George of Georgia, that allowed Harriman to continue to serve on Guaranty's board for another year. According to Lovett, "We are all indebted to [Stetson] and know he would greatly appreciate some word from you." Knight Wooley, another partner, told Harriman that World War II inflation necessitated higher pay and that "In this respect, we and other New York banks have followed along the general plan established by Gene Stetson in the Guaranty Trust Co." By this time Stetson's son, Eugene Jr. had taken a position with Brown Brothers, Harriman. The links among these men persisted. In the early 1950s, when Prescott Bush decided to run for the United States Senate from Connecticut, Stetson was a supporter and hosted a campaign gathering for Bush at the Stetson home.[26]

---

[25] "Robert Lovett Oral History," 8 June 1981, 36–37, Robert Abercrombie Lovett Papers, Yale University Library, Manuscripts and Archives, New Haven, Connecticut; "Condensed Statement of Condition," Brown Brothers, Harriman & Co., 31 December 1933, Brown Brothers Harriman & Co. Collection; "Reminiscences of Prescott Sheldon Bush (1966)," 11, in the Columbia University Oral History Research Office Collection, New York, New York. For additional background on Brown Brothers Harriman and its creation, see Geisst, *The Last Partnerships*, 81–97, and John A. Kouwenhoven, *Partners in Banking: An Historical Portrait of a Great Private Bank, Brown Brothers Harriman & Co.* (New York: Doubleday & Co., 1968) 7–9.

[26] Robert Lovett to W. Averell Harriman, 26 July 1939; Knight Wooley to W. Averell Harriman, 18 March, 12 August 1942, W. Averell Harriman Papers.

Stetson and Watson

Another long-lasting relationship Stetson commenced soon after arriving at Guaranty was with Thomas J. Watson Sr., president of the Computing-Tabulating-Recording Company (CTR), the predecessor of International Business Machines (IBM). In 1916 CTR was already a Guaranty customer. In fact, Watson's son later told the story that his father had requested a loan of $40,000 for research and development from Guaranty, apparently prior to Stetson's arrival. The bank responded that CTR already owed $4 million and that a new loan was unjustified. Watson answered boldly: "Balance sheets reveal the past. This loan is for the future." Although this is the sort of debtor's reply a banker could laugh off, Watson, the great salesman, got the loan. His son later remarked that it was an important break in the company's history. One of Stetson's first accounts after coming to Guaranty was with Watson's fledgling CTR, and as with Harriman and his businesses, he did not mishandle the opportunity.[27]

Stetson's typical banking practice, followed in Watson's case, was not to view Watson as merely a client with occasional financial needs. Instead, he tried mightily to combine ongoing business and social relations. Beginning in the late 1920s, when IBM was still a relatively small operation, Stetson invited Watson to be his guest at formal dinners in New York, a practice that continued into the 1940s. He also faithfully sent Watson Christmas notes. Stetson encouraged Watson to use his brother, James D. Stetson, as a securities broker. He even managed to get Watson, a New Yorker by birth, to serve on the committee seeking to preserve Stratford, the Virginia birthplace of Confederate General Robert E. Lee. Stetson passed along information about local real estate to Watson and invited him to play golf with Guaranty executives.[28]

---

[27] Thomas J. Watson Jr. and Peter Petre, *Father Son & Co.: My Life at IBM and Beyond* (New York: Bantam, 1990) 14–15. On Watson as salesman, see Richard S. Tedlow, *The Watson Dynasty: The Fiery Reign and Troubled Legacy of IBM's Founding Father and Son* (New York: HarperBusiness, 2003), and Kevin Maney, *The Maverick and his Machine: Thomas Watson Sr. and the Making of IBM* (New York: J. Wiley & Sons, 2003).

[28] Eugene W. Stetson to Thomas J. Watson, 10, 20 December 1928; 3 May, 4 December 1929; 25 January 1932; 17 November 1933; 6 December 1934; 20

Watson appreciated the attentions of a fellow salesman. In 1938 he invited Stetson and other Guaranty executives to the dedication of IBM's new World Center Building in Manhattan. He wrote Stetson that "had it not been for the cooperation of the Guaranty Trust Company in [the] early days [of IBM], we would never have been able to carry on at the rate of development which we have enjoyed." He remembered "very well my first contact with [Stetson] when you came to the Guaranty, and it has been a great satisfaction to me, personally, to note your steady progress and I congratulate you on the well-earned recognition which you have received."[29]

The friendship thrived throughout both men's careers. In early 1942, Watson told Stetson that "it has always been most gratifying to do business with you, and, as an old friend, I want you know how proud I am to be associated with you now in your new capacity as President of the Guaranty Trust.... [N]o man could be better qualified for the position than you are." The next year, Watson wrote that "among my greatest pleasures during this past year were the many occasions on which I have had the opportunity of being with you.... I warmly congratulate you on the outstanding manner in which you are handling the great responsibility which rests on your shoulders, and you know that you will always have my full cooperation." Similar kind words followed when Stetson was elected Guaranty chairman in 1944. Watson, famous for his attention to friendly details, even forwarded a message from a former member of his executive staff who met one of Stetson's sons while on a Navy ship. The correspondence continued until Watson's death in 1956.[30]

November 1939; 9 September, 20 December 1941; 18 December 1942; 1 June 1943, Thomas J. Watson Sr. Papers, IBM Corporate Archives, Somers, New York.

[29] Thomas J. Watson to Eugene W. Stetson, 24 January, 11 April 1938; 20 November 1939; 9 September, 20 December 1941, Thomas J. Watson Sr. Papers.

[30] Thomas J. Watson to Eugene W. Stetson, 7 January 1942; 21 December 1943; 31 January 1944; 2 November 1951; 20 October, 5 December 1955; L. C. Schumm to Eugene W. Stetson, 12 July 1944; Eugene W. Stetson to Thomas J. Watson, 6 December 1955, Thomas J. Watson Sr. Papers.

Stetson may have been influential in encouraging IBM to enter into the voting machine business. In his typical way of introducing one client to another with the goal of both fellowship and profit, he encouraged Watson to become, with him, a board member of the Automatic Registering Machine Company and the Automatic Voting Machine Company, both Guaranty clients. The companies were headquartered in Jamestown, New York, near IBM's headquarters. They designed and manufactured mechanical voting devices and were early leaders in the field. Stetson also knew about Automatic Voting Machine because Guaranty served as the company's transfer agent.[31]

Compared to many of Stetson's other clients, Automatic Voting Machine was small, possessing less than $2 million in assets in late 1929, about a third of which was directly related to production facilities. Automatic Voting Machine claimed twelve million voters used its products in the 1944 elections. To a forward-looking banker and entrepreneur, this signaled a largely untapped market, considering that almost fifty million votes were cast in the presidential election that year. Watson did not act immediately, but later his company did get into the voting machine business.[32]

Ultimately, the nearly forty-year relationship between Watson and Stetson was about more than finance. The friendship flourished based on Stetson's ability to see the potential in Watson's business, Stetson's skill in cultivating that potential when IBM was in start-up condition, and then Stetson's continuing personal commitment to Watson. The strategy and behavior reflected a pattern repeated many times during Stetson's career.

---

[31] Douglas W. Jones, "A Brief Illustrated History of Voting," http://www.cs.uiowa.edu/~jones/voting/pictures/; Automatic Voting Machine Corporation, *Annual Report* (Jamestown NY: Automatic Voting Machine Corporation, 1929); Automatic Voting Machine Corporation, *Annual Report* (Jamestown NY: Automatic Voting Machine Corporation, 1930).

[32] Ibid.

From Georgia to New York

Stetson's move to New York was perfectly timed to put him in one of the most exciting places in financial history at just the right moment. The banking system had been rationalized with the Federal Reserve Act. Thanks to World War I, America and New York emerged as the center of the banking world just as Stetson landed on Wall Street. He and his bank moved head-long into the two most dynamic areas of finance: international banking and retail securities sales. Moreover, Stetson was fortunate enough to be hired by an institution that was intimately linked to the center of financial power, the Morgan firm. This allowed him immediate access to both the super wealthy, such as Harriman, and up-and-coming entrepreneurs such as Watson. When his bank needed propping up in the wake of the Mercantile Bank crisis, none other than Tom Lamont and his Morgan colleagues were there to supply both cash and optimism.

Stetson was willing and able to make the most of his chance. As demonstrated by his relations with Harriman and Watson, from the beginning he fully engaged clients on both a professional and social level, providing what was perceived as very valuable assistance. This was precisely the sort of proactive relationship banking in which Morgan and Guaranty excelled, especially in the competitive banking climate of the 1920s. Stetson worked hard to sell himself and Guaranty and to provide sound financial advice that benefited a range of constituencies. However, there was no better demonstration of Stetson's ability and potential in his early years with Guaranty than his leadership in one of the most remarkable public offerings of the era, the sale and reorganization of Georgia's Coca-Cola Company.

5

Coca-Cola for Sale

On 22 August 1919, Georgians woke up to dramatic news: "Coca-Cola BOUGHT BY ATLANTANS," and "Trust Company of Georgia Gets National Drink." It was the first time they learned that local interests were spearheading the purchase of the Atlanta-based company. A few days after the headlines, brokers offered more than 400,000 shares of Coca-Cola stock to the public. The sale opened at 9 a.m. and by 3:45 that afternoon it was oversubscribed by 140,000 shares. At the time, the multimillion dollar deal was the largest business transaction in southern history. A southerner in New York, Guaranty's Gene Stetson, was one of the men who helped make the deal happen.[1]

The Coca-Cola sale was a spectacular opportunity for Stetson to take advantage of his Georgia connections and to display high level financing and deal-making skills. The sale had even broader potential. Keeping Coca-Cola in Georgia was consistent with Stetson's long-standing vision for a New South. In fact, the vision advanced an even more dramatic ideal: creating a truly national, publicly-traded business with headquarters and majority ownership in his home region. Not surprisingly, there were a number of major obstacles. The Asa Candler family, which owned Coca-Cola in 1919, wanted top dollar, and this was not likely to be found among the southern buyers who were most familiar with the product. In fact, the Candlers had tried for some years to sell without success. A second problem was that the buyer's financial institutional, the Trust Company of Georgia, was merely the seventh largest bank in Atlanta, still a small city by national standards. Atlanta counted only about 200,000 persons in 1920, less than

---

[1] *Atlanta Constitution*, 22, 23, 26, 27 August 1919.

Louisville, Akron, or Toledo. In essence, Atlanta's Trust Company hoped to buy a company ten times its size.[2]

For Stetson, it all started with an act of chance, a reference from an old acquaintance. The acquaintance was A. B. Simms, a former officer at Stetson's Citizens National Bank in Macon. About the time Stetson departed for New York, Simms left Macon for the greener pastures of the Fulton National Bank in Atlanta. Fortuitously, Simms happened to be a relative by marriage to Ernest Woodruff, the head of the Trust Company of Georgia. Woodruff and his bank lacked the resources to obtain Coca-Cola, so he looked to New York to raise the needed capital. Simms knew Stetson was on the spot in Manhattan and he gave Woodruff an introduction. Stetson and Woodruff first met in New York in the summer of 1919. That meeting was the start of one of the most extraordinary deals in American financial history.[3]

Rainmaker

In the Coca-Cola deal Stetson acted as the quintessential rainmaker, a deal-leader who navigates a complex and indirect business journey from concept to completion. In Stetson's era the rainmaker ideal was among the principal expectations of relationship banking as practiced at Guaranty and at private banks such as J. P. Morgan. The rainmaker was an executive who

---

[2] In 1920, per capita income in Georgia was only a little more than half the national average; in 2004, it was ninety-one percent of the national average. Jon Moen, "Still Playing Catch-Up: Mississippi and the South" (July 2006), http://www.olemiss.edu/winterinstitute/documents/econo-study1.pdf. An official history of Woodruff's bank is Trust Company of Georgia, *Story of the Trust Company of Georgia on its 60th Anniversary* (Atlanta: Trust Company of Georgia, 1951).

[3] A. B. Simms to Mark Pendergrast, 23 April 1992, Mark Pendergrast Papers, Manuscript, Archives, and Rare Book Library, Emory University, Atlanta, Georgia; "Depositions Taken in Georgia Cases," 2483 (Charles Candler), Appeal Record, *Coca-Cola Bottling Co. v. Coca-Cola Co.*, Nos. 2650, 2651 (1920), United States Court of Appeals for the Third Circuit, National Archives and Records Administration, Philadelphia, Pennsylvania; Clipping, *Macon News*, 27 November 1907 (mentioning A. B. Simms as the assistant cashier), Box 5, Eugene W. Stetson Papers, Jack Tarver Library, Special Collections, Mercer University, Macon, Georgia.

grasped the worth of a business idea and did everything in his power to turn it into reality. Rainmaking was not simply marketing or getting clients. Instead, rainmaking involved commitment to the business of the client after the initiation of the relationship. The process meant strategizing many moves ahead, anticipating setbacks, criticism, and competition. Rainmaking meant sharing the vision with the client and, by valuing the customer as a friend, keeping it on track to succeed. If the customer was a cantankerous or unlikable person, such as the Trust Company's Ernest Woodruff, it meant exercising courtesy and perseverance to move the project forward anyway.[4]

For Stetson, the rainmaking role required strong powers of persuasion and an unwavering devotion to removing obstacles. This took sales skills to overcome the objections of doubters and the risk-averse within the banker's own firm, partner banks, and sometimes the clients' customers. At the same time, the rainmaker had to be open-minded and flexible, so that if a roadblock existed, the business plan could be modified. This, in turn, required even wilier salesmanship, convincing everyone involved that a new direction must be taken.

As Stetson and other successful relationship bankers of his period understood it, the rainmaker was a steward of the client's business, on par with the client's chief executive officer. The rainmaker considered the interests of shareholders, employees, other bankers, consumers, and the larger community. In Stetson's mind, this role carried a moral and social commitment. The idea that a banker should accept a self-imposed duty to the public welfare seems quaint and naïve, in fact contrary to the patent fraud, theft, and hardball tactics that marked some banking practice. But, much as he latched onto the public aspects of the New South ideal, Stetson believed in the broad obligations of bankers and tried to define his behavior by this ideal. By the time Stetson came to New York, the era of the celebrity banker and the dominant private banking firm had waned. Deals were simply too big and too complex for the older methods of J. Pierpont

---

[4] For a modern advice manual, see Harry Mills, *The Rainmaker's Toolkit—Power Strategies for Finding, Keeping, and Growing Profitable Clients* (New York: American Management Association, 2004). A perspective contemporary to Stetson emphasizing salesmanship is G. Prather Knapp, *How Banks Increase Their Revenue* (Chicago: Rand McNally, 1926) 37, 169.

Morgan. As a result, gigantic bureaucratic institutions, such as Guaranty, were the present and the future, and Stetson's rainmaking, including its moral component, took place in this context.[5]

In 1919 Stetson possessed the key technical tools of a banker-rainmaker, but he also possessed imagination. While bankers needed to be able to evaluate a balance sheet and income statement projections, every extraordinary business deal took a leap of imagination. In Coca-Cola's case, Stetson's appreciation for the power of the "brand" concept, the real value of the trademark, as well as his sense of the public's excitement about the product, made the difference in obtaining his and Wall Street's backing. Coca-Cola, after all, was the first major food product to be traded on the New York exchange, and it took insight to sense that the drink's popularity could be translated into financing by public sale.

The Coca-Cola buyout involved fractious relationships, an element of family betrayal, cloak-and-dagger secrecy, and long train rides between Atlanta and New York. The process culminated in a series of dramatic financial transactions that made personal fortunes and put Stetson's native region on the financial map in a new way, setting the stage for a genuinely southern-based business with national and international markets. It represented the New South ideal realized.

The Coke Story

According to *BusinessWeek*, in 2006 Coca-Cola was the most valuable brand in the world, worth more than $67 billion. This was billions more than high-tech Microsoft or IBM and more than twice the value of trademark powerhouses McDonald's and Toyota. Stetson would probably be pleased that even the Morgan Stanley and J. P. Morgan brands were far behind, with each measured at less than a meager $10 billion. The Coca-Cola achievement represents quite a feat for a company whose core product was developed more than one hundred years ago from mostly water, sugar, and caffeine. The key to the drink's success, however, lies not only in flavor, but also in precisely the *BusinessWeek* measure: branding. Partly by design

---

[5] On one aspect of this change, of which Stetson was a reflection, see Ron Chernow, *The Death of the Banker* (New York: Vintage Books, 1997).

and partly by luck, Coca-Cola achieved the first global brand identity in American sales and marketing.[6]

From the beginning, the drink's marketing grabbed the consumer's attention. According to an early ad, Coca-Cola was not only "Delicious!" and "Refreshing!", it was also a "brain tonic and nerve stimulant." Of course, the product's flavor and alleged health benefits were only part of the story. The power of the drink really came from the bond that Coca-Cola forged with consumers. Over time, this bond was cemented by numerous branding factors, including its price, the wide availability of the product, its uniformity, the famous logo, the shape of the company's bottles, and the colors of ubiquitous advertising posters.[7]

Even in 1919 the Coca-Cola Company was among the marvels of business history. Its prized formula was invented by a pharmacist, John Pemberton. Pemberton grew up in middle Georgia, was a Confederate soldier wounded in the Civil War, and became a druggist in the river town of Columbus, Georgia. He moved to Atlanta in 1869, where he mostly failed as a businessman. Pemberton was a morphine addict. Despite personal and financial tribulations, his great passion was pharmaceutical experimentation. In the mid–1880s he developed "Pemberton's French Wine Coca," a potent mixture of coca (from which cocaine is derived), kola nuts, and grape wine. Consistent with Pemberton's general run of bad luck, prohibition briefly went into effect in Atlanta in 1886 and killed French Wine Coca. The ex-Confederate went back to his laboratory and came up with a new drink without the alcohol but retaining coca and caffeine. The first batch was made in a three-legged brass kettle in his backyard. Pemberton's partner and bookkeeper, Frank Robinson, suggested the name Coca-Cola and wrote it out in his excellent penmanship. This became the symbol now known around the world. Predictably, given Pemberton's track record, first-year sales at a local Atlanta pharmacy were a less-than-impressive fifty dollars, compared to seventy dollars in production costs. Yet

---

[6] Daniel Workman, "Top Global Brands: World's Most Valuable Trademarks in 2006," http://internationaltrade.suite101.com/article.cfm/top_global_brands.

[7] Frederick Allen III, *Secret Formula: How Brilliant Marketing and Relentless Salesmanship Made Coca-Cola the Best-Known Product in the World* (New York: HarperBusiness, 1994) 36.

Pemberton and Robinson persisted, and in 1887 Pemberton formally trademarked the product.[8]

Like many other innovators, Pemberton did not realize the potential of his concoction. Financially strapped and physically diminished, he engaged in a complex set of deals that ultimately transferred ownership of Coca-Cola to a more sober and businesslike Atlanta druggist, Asa Candler. Candler incorporated the first version of a Coca-Cola Company and by 1889 claimed sole ownership of the drink and its trademark. He paid about $2,300 for them.[9]

Unlike Pemberton, Candler knew how to turn a dollar. He purchased a share in a drugstore at twenty-six and eventually established his own operation, Asa G. Candler & Company, in 1886. After buying Coca-Cola, Candler gave it the sort of push Pemberton could not. He hired salesmen to cover the territory around Atlanta, pitching Coca-Cola syrup to fountain operators. At the time, the drink was exclusively a pharmacist's product, mixed and sold at drugstores. Among thirsty southerners sales increased dramatically. In 1889 Candler sold 2,171 gallons of syrup; six years later he sold 76,244 gallons. Aggressive advertising, new plants in cities across the nation, and increases in a determined and modern marketing force led to even more spectacular growth.[10]

Bottled Coca-Cola became an important part of this success. In 1899, Candler gave two Chattanooga lawyers, Benjamin Franklin Thomas and Joseph Brown Whitehead, the right to produce a bottled version of Coca-Cola using Candler's syrup. Thomas and Whitehead got what has to be one of the all-time bargains in American history. They paid one dollar, and in exchange Candler retained merely the right to cancel the agreement if the lawyers failed to meet demand. Wrongly, as it turned out, Candler thought bottling was a bad idea that would never appeal to consumers. More positively, in exchange for zero investment, from the bottlers he eventually obtained a nationwide network of Coca-Cola producers and distributors. A

[8] Mark Pendergrast, *For God, Country & Coca-Cola: The Definitive History of the Great American Soft Drink and the Company That Makes It*, rev. ed. (New York: Basic Books, 2000) 7–33; Allen, *Secret Formula*, 18–30.

[9] Pendergrast, *God, Country & Coca-Cola*, 34–68; Allen, *Secret Formula*, 34–37.

[10] Ibid.

franchise approach, even if unintended, was the perfect solution to the capital and administrative barriers to Coca-Cola's rapid expansion in the early years of the twentieth century.[11]

In addition to Candler's unwitting farsightedness on bottling, the company's marketing energies were Herculean. Coca-Cola's spending on advertising grew from $85,000 in 1900 to over $1 million in 1912. This meant, according to Mark Pendergrast, that in 1913 "the company advertised on over one hundred million items, including thermometers, cardboard cutouts, and metal signs (50,000 each); Japanese fans and calendars (a million each), 2 million soda fountain trays, 10 million matchbooks, 20 million blotters, 25 million baseball cards, and innumerable signs made of cardboard and metal." Put another way, Coca-Cola produced 100 million items of advertising, one for every man, woman, child, baby—and quite a few dogs and cats—in the United States.[12]

Amidst the prosperity, however, there was trouble. Moralists attacked the drink because of the drug caffeine and because of its connection to cocaine. The alleged traces of cocaine, which was not then illegal, were removed in 1902. New Progressive Era government regulations on foods then produced charges that Coca-Cola was unsafe, largely because of its caffeine. More challenging from a business standpoint was the host of copycats offering similar names and tastes, forcing the company to defend its increasingly valuable trademark in court. Further, federal taxes imposed significant costs on Asa Candler, who owned almost eighty percent of the company's shares and received the lion's share of escalating profits. Then, there was the issue of family fatigue. As Candler aged, he was 68 in 1919, the need for a successor became apparent. Candler attempted, without overwhelming success, to groom his son Howard for the top job. He hoped Howard would continue the business and assure its future for the rest of the

---

[11] Pendergrast, *God, Country & Coca-Cola*, 69–91; Allen, *Secret Formula*, 40–43. An argument for the benefits of the company's franchise system is Humphrey McQueen, *The Essence of Capitalism: The Origins of Our Future* (New York: Black Rose Books, 2003) 71–77.

[12] Pendergrast, *God, Country & Coca-Cola*, 69–91; Allen, *Secret Formula*, 40–43.

family. Ultimately, however, the best plan seemed to be sale of the company while providing for Howard's continued involvement.[13]

Coke for Sale

Candler began to discuss a sale as early as 1908. He first approached Samuel Brown, banker and cotton-broker from Albany, Georgia. Brown was the father-in-law of Harold Hirsch, an Atlanta attorney who eventually became Coca-Cola's general counsel. Suggesting the marginal prospects, Brown hoped to finance a deal through European banks as well as with a public sale of stock in the South. The bargaining ceased for a time, but resumed in 1911, when Brown and Candler agreed on a price of $8 million. Brown, however, was unable to raise the money—a telling indication that financing a sale in pre-World War I Georgia would be difficult, if not impossible. In 1916 Candler, now sixty-five, displayed an even greater willingness to unload Coca-Cola. Early that year he resigned, made his son Howard president, and notified Brown and Hirsch that the company was back on the block.[14]

This time, reflecting increasing profits and the changing state of American finance, the price was $25 million. The new offer, however, still aimed to keep the Candler family in control. Family members would receive $15 million in common stock, while the remaining $10 million of shares would be sold for $5 million in cash to the underwriters. Hirsch and Brown hired Max Pam, a Chicago lawyer, to push the deal. Pam brought in the New York investment bank Kuhn, Loeb & Company. This plan collapsed when the Candlers balked at including family real estate in the sale. The failure was soon followed by an arrangement with Bainbridge Colby, a highly connected New York attorney who later became Woodrow Wilson's Secretary of State and law partner. Colby would get a fat fee of $1 million,

---

[13] Pendergrast, *God, Country & Coca-Cola*, 87–122; Allen, *Secret Formula*, 43–85.

[14] Allen, *Secret Formula*, 55–56, 64, 85–88; "Copy of Notice to Beneficial Certificate Holders, Minute Book," 6 January 1919, The Coca-Cola Company, Atlanta, Georgia; "Depositions Taken in Georgia Cases," 2241–44 (Dobbs), Appeal Record, *Coca-Cola Bottling Co. v. Coca-Cola Co.*, Nos. 2650, 2651 (1920), United States Court of Appeals for the Third Circuit, National Archives and Records Administration.

to be paid in Coca-Cola shares, if he could make a sale. The Candlers, however, again backed out.[15]

Asa Candler and his family were clearly difficult sellers, but the relatively primitive state of southern finance was also a factor. Asa did not help matters in late 1917, when he gave practically all of his Coca-Cola shares to his wife and their five children. Mrs. Candler received sixty-four of the 500 shares outstanding, while each child received sixty-nine shares. This led to a formal restructuring in August 1918, when $25 million of new ownership certificates were divided among the family. The effect of all this was to fragment ownership and give the Candler children control of Coca-Cola. Perhaps most important, none of the family, including Howard, the reluctant company president, felt strongly about continued Candler ownership. Like many children of entrepreneurs, the kids preferred cash over the trials of the founder's business.[16]

Not surprisingly, personal grievances arising from Candler's distribution influenced the likelihood of a sale. One relative not overly favored in the 1917 gift of shares, holding a mere twenty-three shares, was Sam Candler Dobbs, Asa's nephew. Dobbs came to Atlanta in 1886 to work for his uncle. During the following three decades he labored diligently to develop the Coca-Cola sales force and advertising clout that generated the company's success. Although Dobbs's salary as vice president of sales and advertising rose to the substantial sum of $15,000 in 1919, he was smart enough to know this was small potatoes compared to the possibilities offered by sale. Dobbs's twenty-three shares were worth $1.15 million if the company was sold for $25 million. This was more than enough motivation to become an inside force for sale, and perhaps gain a bit of revenge.[17]

---

[15] Ibid.

[16] Allen, *Secret Formula*, 66–91; "Waiver of Jury Trial and Stipulation of Facts," 16 January 1928, 2–3, *Trust Company of Georgia v. J. T. Rose*, No. 794, United States District Court for the Northern District of Georgia, National Archives and Records Administration, Atlanta, Georgia; "Minutes of the Board of Directors," 17 January 1919, The Coca-Cola Company.

[17] Ibid. A salary of $15,000 in 1919 was the equivalent of a healthy (and less taxed) $180,000 in 2007. Dobbs's share value, however, would approach $14,000,000 in 2007 consumer price index measured dollars. See "Six Ways to

The Buyer

Coca-Cola's next potential buyer represented a more substantial likelihood of success. Ernest Woodruff (1863–1944), a steel-eyed, bare knuckles Atlanta banker and businessman was president of the Trust Company of Georgia, an institution that could be used in important ways to advance the sale. The son of a Yankee mill owner, he grew up in Columbus, Georgia, and became president of the Trust Company in 1904. Through several important merger and underwriting deals, Woodruff dramatically expanded his Atlanta bank. Woodruff also knew a great deal about Coca-Cola. He had his eye on it as early as 1907 and later said that owning the company became his dream. He even made an offer through Samuel Brown to buy Coca-Cola for $22 million in 1912. According to Woodruff, Brown took the offer to Asa Candler, without disclosing its source, who declined it. The deal provided for half payment in preferred stock or bonds, and the remainder in cash over as much as three years, with interest. Woodruff discussed financing this proposal with a New Orleans bank as well as with New York's Chase National. Candler remembered the deal a bit differently, recalling later that the initial proposal was for $20 million, and later $22 million. It is not entirely clear why Candler refused the offer; perhaps the mechanism of delayed payment was unattractive.[18]

In 1919, things would be different. After the war American finance and its public securities markets were undergoing revolutionary change. Moreover, not only had the Candler family's ownership been redistributed in 1917, eliminating Asa as the determining factor, this time Woodruff had seen to it that there was inside support for a sale. The dissatisfied Candler nephew, Sam Dobbs, just happened to be on the board of directors of Woodruff's Trust Company, worked with Woodruff on several business deals, and was a member of the boards of other Woodruff companies.

Compute the Relative Value of a U.S. Dollar Amount," http://measuring-worth.com/calculators/ uscompare/.

[18] Allen, *Secret Formula*, 91–95; "Depositions of Ernest Woodruff and Asa G. Candler Sr.," 27 January 1925, 3–30, *United States v. Coca-Cola Co.*, No. 738, United States District Court for the Northern District of Georgia, National Archives and Records Administration, Atlanta, Georgia.

Woodruff described Dobbs as a "close personal friend." Another Trust Company board member was Harold Hirsch, Coca-Cola's lawyer.[19]

Woodruff enlisted Dobbs's support for a deal, but carefully. By the spring of 1919 Dobbs knew Woodruff wanted to arrange a purchase and that $25 million was a realistic offering price. He met with Woodruff in early July to discuss the possibilities at a New York hotel. This was a cloak-and-dagger move, since both men resided in Atlanta and already knew each other well. From Woodruff's vantage, the purpose of meeting in New York was two-fold: it covered his interest in Coca-Cola from Atlantans and provided support for the useful suggestion that perhaps New Yorkers were really behind the deal. Woodruff supposedly told Dobbs that "certain interests" would like to buy Coca-Cola and asked if he thought it could be sold. Dobbs later said that he replied, "I thought probably it could; that I would be willing to sell out, that I would like very much to sell out." Woodruff likely offered Dobbs ownership and power in the new company. Dobbs later denied he was offered the presidency, but Stetson, in 1947, stated Woodruff promised Dobbs the post. It is likely that Stetson was at the New York meeting, or at least was already (July 1919) involved in arranging financing for the sale with Woodruff and knew about its purpose.[20]

Returning to Atlanta, Dobbs discussed the proposal with the Candlers, including Asa and Howard. He did not mention the names of any of the proposed buyers, including Woodruff: "I simply stated certain financial interests in New York City would buy Coca-Cola and were anxious to buy it." Dobbs's representations to the Candlers about the buyer were plainly

[19] Allen, *Secret Formula*, 94–95; "Depositions of Ernest Woodruff and Asa G. Candler Sr.," 27 January 1925, 12–14, *United States v. Coca-Cola Co.*, No. 738, United States District Court for the Northern District of Georgia, National Archives and Records Administration.

[20] "Depositions Taken in Georgia Cases," 2205–2208, 2251 (Dobbs), 2359 (Wardlaw), Appeal Record, *Coca-Cola Bottling Co. v. Coca-Cola Co.*, Nos. 2650, 2651 (1920), United States Court of Appeals for the Third Circuit, National Archives and Records Administration.

and intentionally misleading. Why not simply tell them Woodruff and his Trust Company were the wizards behind the curtain?[21]

The short answer is that Asa Candler despised Woodruff. Given Atlanta's modest size, it was not hard to know the reputations of leading businessmen. Woodruff's reputation was all-too-well-known. Woodruff's interests in Atlanta included coal and ice delivery, steel, street railways, and of course, the Trust Company. Woodruff's modus operandi did not recommend him as an executive capable of enlisting the support and collaboration of subordinates. Woodruff's methods sometimes irritated and offended fellow businessmen and the public. He was widely suspected, for example, of entering and searching a lawyer's office without permission. All this goes a long way toward explaining the need for Woodruff's indirect offer in 1912 as well as in 1919. It certainly meant Woodruff could not count the upright Methodist, Asa Chandler, as a friend.[22]

Woodruff was a big fish in Atlanta, but Atlanta was a mere minnow in the larger pool of American finance. To be sure, Woodruff had worked with J. P. Morgan as a Georgia agent in raising funds for World War I loans, and his Trust Company was among the first state-chartered banks to become a member of the Federal Reserve. But for all of his experience, bravado, and success, he was still a provincial pip-squeak when it came to pulling off a multimillion-dollar purchase. Woodruff was fully aware of his limitations. Given that his bank's entire worth was only $2 million, he knew it would take all of its resources, plus outside assistance, to participate in a $25 million sale.[23] This is where Stetson and Guaranty came in.

Selling the Candlers

Woodruff's timing was ideal. Because of special taxes imposed during World War I and still in force in 1919, the extremely profitable Coca-Cola was, according to Woodruff's later comments, "being murdered [by federal

---

[21] Ibid.

[22] Allen, *Secret Formula*, 91–95; "Depositions of Ernest Woodruff and Asa G. Candler Sr.," 27 January 1925, 3–30, *United States v. Coca-Cola Co.*, No. 738, United States District Court for the Northern District of Georgia, National Archives and Records Administration; McQueen, *The Essence of Capitalism*, 57.

[23] Allen, *Secret Formula*, 94–95.

taxes] and that if there was ever a time the property could be bought it was then." Further, as Woodruff put it, during the summer of 1919 the "Candlers were more disposed to sell than they had ever been, on account of [a trademark] decision" pending in the federal courts. This lawsuit, involving a former partner of Pemberton, J. C. Mayfield, and his knock-off "Koke" product, raised the specter of total annihilation. Mayfield argued that Coca-Cola had no right to trademark protection because although its name was connected with cocaine, it did not contain any remnant of the kola nut. In short, "Coca-Cola" was false and deceptive. A federal appeals court had actually agreed with Mayfield, and the case was pending in the United States Supreme Court. If the company lost, all the hard-earned value of the prize trademark, its most important asset, would evaporate. Yet Woodruff, a born speculator, viewed this grave risk as an opportunity for a bargain. The offer's mechanism was also important. In making his bid, Woodruff decided to obtain short-term options to buy first instead of concluding an outright purchase of the company's shares. This would allow time to arrange financing and establish the details of control. It would also advance Woodruff's desire to keep his name out of the bargaining.[24]

In July 1919 Woodruff pitched his plan to Stetson and probably to Stetson's boss, Charles Sabin. Thanks to Stetson and Sabin's favorable response, Guaranty jumped on the bandwagon. As a practical matter, this meant Guaranty's name would appear prominently in the written option agreement, hiding Woodruff's involvement. The option agreement, in fact, implied only New York institutions were interested in Coca-Cola by giving them key roles in the sale. Under the agreement, for example, a restructured Coca-Cola Company had the right to repurchase any issued preferred stock by deposits to the trust departments of Guaranty or Chase National Bank. The $15 million in cash to be paid the sellers "may be deposited to the

---

[24] Allen, *Secret Formula*, 121–24; "Depositions of Ernest Woodruff and Asa G. Candler Sr.," 27 January 1925, 3, 9–10, 13, 15, 29, *United States v. Coca-Cola Co.*, No. 738, United States District Court for the Northern District of Georgia, National Archives and Records Administration; "Depositions Taken in Georgia Cases," 2457, Appeal Record, *Coca-Cola Bottling Co. v. Coca-Cola Co.*, Nos. 2650, 2651 (1920), United States Court of Appeals for the Third Circuit, National Archives and Records Administration; *Appeal of W. C. Bradley*, 1 B.T.A. 111, 112 (1924).

respective accounts of the Sellers at the Guaranty Trust Company of New York." The president of Coca-Cola, Howard Candler, agreed to deposit with Guaranty the famous drink formula: "a written statement showing in detail the process of manufacture of Coca-Cola, which shall include all the ingredients and quantities thereof, and the entire procedure and method of manufacture." The formula would be placed in a sealed envelope and opened only upon joint agreement of the presidents of Guaranty and Chase. If the options were exercised, the Candlers would turn over their certificates to Guaranty, endorsed in blank.[25]

Woodruff gained additional cover when he employed Robert C. Alston, a prominent Atlanta attorney, to obtain the options in Alston's own name. Alston appeared to the Candlers to be acting for the "New York interests." According to Woodruff's subsequent testimony, "[I]n finally closing up the business [Alston] represented me but nobody knew it. Mr. Candler didn't know it." In 1925 Asa Candler admitted as much: "I have never had any negotiations with Mr. Woodruff in my life." In fact, the senior Candler was not informed that his family eagerly departed with Coca-Cola ownership until 26 July 1919. Not one of them asked his opinion before agreeing to the options. Because less than fifteen persons owned the Coca-Cola Company in 1919 and because these owners were family members anxious to sell out and become millionaires, the work of obtaining options took only a few weeks. By the end of July, Alston had assigned his ownership in the options to Woodruff's Trust Company of Georgia, which had until 28 August 1919 to exercise the option rights. If exercised, the Candlers would receive $10 million in seven percent cumulative non-voting preferred shares in a new Coca-Cola Company, probably to be organized in Delaware, and $15 million in cash. The options were apparently not sold for a separate price and required the buyers to pay

---

[25] "Depositions Taken in Georgia Cases," 2483 (Charles Candler), Appeal Record, *Coca-Cola Bottling Co. v. Coca-Cola Co.*, Nos. 2650, 2651 (1920), United States Court of Appeals for the Third Circuit, National Archives and Records Administration; "Waiver of Jury Trial and Stipulation of Facts," 16 January 1928, 3, Exhibit 2, *Trust Company of Georgia v. J. T. Rose*, No. 794, United States District Court for the Northern District of Georgia, National Archives and Records Administration.

any federal taxes up to the date of transfer. Under the options, the Candlers could participate in management in the new company, but were not given management rights.[26]

According to the later testimony of Sam Dobbs, the all-important efforts to convince the Candlers to sell the options included not just Alston, but also Gene Stetson. Stetson traveled to Georgia to discuss the sale with the Candlers, thereby becoming the critical personal link between the New York banks and the sellers. According to Dobbs, Stetson's presence during the negotiations gave credence to the suggestion that "New York interests" were behind the offer. Of course, as the key suppliers of finance and banking services, New York interests were in fact involved and necessary. But Dobbs's later description of the process was disingenuous at best: "There was no purpose of any concealment, because while this negotiation was going on Mr. Stetson, of the Guarantee [sic] Trust Company, came to Atlanta and was in open negotiations with the stockholders of the Coca-Cola Company." While in Georgia, Stetson also met with Hirsch and Dobbs.[27]

---

[26] *Atlanta Constitution*, 22 August 1919; Charles H. Candler, *Asa Griggs Candler* (Atlanta: Emory University, 1950), 184–85; "Waiver of Jury Trial and Stipulation of Facts," 16 January 1928, 2–4, *Trust Co. of Georgia v. J. T. Rose*, No. 794, United States District Court for the Northern District of Georgia, National Archives and Records Administration. The option agreement was reproduced as Exhibit 2 to the Waiver document. The eleven certificate holders who signed the options were Howard Candler, John Candler, Florrie G. A. Candler, Walter G. Candler, Flora C. Candler, William Candler, Sam Dobbs, Lucy C. Heinz, Asa Candler Sr., Asa Candler Jr., and Harold Hirsch. After 1916, Asa Candler's children controlled a majority of the company. See "Board of Directors Minutes," Coca-Cola Company, 4 June 1918, The Coca-Cola Company (containing a list of the owners of the company's 500 shares).

[27] "Depositions Taken in Georgia Cases," 2205–2208, 2251 (Dobbs), 2359 (Wardlaw), Appeal Record, *Coca-Cola Bottling Co. v. Coca-Cola Co.*, Nos. 2650, 2651 (1920), United States Court of Appeals for the Third Circuit, National Archives and Records Administration.

Bankers Rule

With options in hand, Woodruff, Stetson, and other New York bankers hammered out the financing details. Who, exactly, would provide the $25 million purchase price and how would control over the new Coca-Cola be distributed? There is strong evidence that these details evolved over time. Originally, in fact, Woodruff seems to have favored selling the options for a quick profit. But then the bankers agreed this would fail to make the most of the opportunity. Their arrangement was formalized on 21 August in a "Bankers' Agreement."[28]

The Bankers' Agreement provided that the Trust Company of Georgia, as trustee, would initially "hold and exercise for the benefit of others" certain rights of common stock ownership of the new Coca-Cola in the following proportions: the Trust Company of Georgia (30%); the Newmont Corporation (10%); the Shermar Investing Corporation (30%); and Charles Sabin, president of Guaranty Trust (30%). Individuals connected with Bankers Trust and Chase National controlled Newmont and Shermar. The Trust Company of Georgia would then form a new Coca-Cola Corporation in Delaware, issue $10 million in preferred stock to the Candlers, and issue 500,000 shares of common stock for public sale. Of these 500,000 shares, 83,000 were reserved for the bankers, in the proportions mentioned above, at a price of five dollars per share. The remaining 417,000 shares would be sold through a wholesale common stock syndicate for thirty-five dollars per share. They would then be resold at retail for forty dollars per share. Of the $25 million purchase price, $15 million would be raised by public sale, and the remaining $10 million, in the form of preferred shares, would be retained as a liability of the new Coca-Cola. The August 1919 prospectus stated that the preferred shares would be converted to voting shares if the company failed to pay semiannual dividends. Further, Coca-Cola had the right to retire the preferred shares from the Candlers at par, plus required dividends. The common shares were to be deposited with Guaranty, which would act as agent for the trustees of

---

[28] Allen, *Secret Formula*, 97–98.

a five-year voting trust for the common shares. The trustees of the voting trust would be Woodruff, Dobbs, and Stetson.[29]

The agreement was especially friendly to Woodruff, his Trust Company of Georgia, and its shareholders. On 13 August the Trust Company board agreed to participate up to $4.5 million in the purchase of common shares. This was more than twice the entire assets of the bank. The Trust Company board planned to raise most of this money by asking its shareholders to deposit $195 for each Trust Company share they owned. The Trust Company would then allot each shareholder Coca-Cola stock, not to exceed one share of stock for each share held by the stockholder in the Trust Company.[30]

The New York banks, including Guaranty, Chase, and Bankers Trust and their stand-ins, Shermar and Newmont, shared in the potential bonanza. Sabin, for the Guaranty, received 24,900 shares, Shermar received 24,900 shares, and Newmont received 8,300 shares at the five dollars per share price. At a forty-dollar share value, this meant Guaranty, the Trust

---

[29] "Waiver of Jury Trial and Stipulation of Facts," 16 January 1928, 4–5, Exhibit 3, *Trust Co. of Georgia v. J. T. Rose*, No. 794, United States District Court for the Northern District of Georgia, National Archives and Records Administration; "Minutes of Meeting of Beneficial Ownership Certificate Owners," 16 January 1919, The Coca-Cola Company; "Depositions Taken in Georgia Cases," 2329–30, 2348–49 (Wardlaw), Appeal Record, *Coca-Cola Bottling Co. v. Coca-Cola Co.*, Nos. 2650, 2651 (1920), United States Court of Appeals for the Third Circuit, National Archives and Records Administration; "Prospectus, The Coca-Cola Company," August 1919, Box 1 (King and Spalding), Robert W. Woodruff Papers, Manuscript, Archives, and Rare Book Library, Emory University, Atlanta, Georgia.

[30] "Trust Company of Georgia Minutes," 2, 13 August 1919, Harold H. Martin Papers, Manuscript, Archives, and Rare Book Library, Emory University, Atlanta, Georgia; "Waiver of Jury Trial and Stipulation of Facts," 4–6, *Trust Co. of Georgia v. J. T. Rose*, No. 794, 16 January 1928, United States District Court for the Northern District of Georgia, National Archives and Records Administration. By Mark Pendergrast's estimation, each of the 1919 shares, if dividends were reinvested in stock, would have been worth $7 million in 2000. SunTrust Bank, successor to the Trust Company of Georgia, still owned 1919 shares in 2007, but sold nine percent of its Coca-Cola shares in the latter year. Before the transaction, SunTrust's Coke stock was carried on the bank's books at the 1919 amount of $110,000, while the current market value of the shares was $2.5 billion. "SunTrust Selling Coca-Cola Shares Held Since 1919," http://en.epochtimes.com/news/7-5-15/55355.html.

Company of Georgia, and Shermar stood to benefit about $870,000 each for their participation. Newmont would gain a little more than $290,000. To put it another way, Guaranty, the Trust Company of Georgia, and Shermar each promised to guarantee $4.5 million towards the purchase in exchange for about $870,000 in fees, paid in common stock. Woodruff and the New York bankers retained absolute control over the company even after the public sale through the voting trust.[31]

On 21 August, the same day of the Bankers' Agreement, the syndicate sent a "confidential" letter to approximately 600 bankers and stockbrokers in the United States and Canada, inviting them to purchase 417,000 shares of common stock of the new Coca-Cola Company at $35 per share. They were told that the current owners of the company, the Candlers, would receive $10 million in non-voting preferred stock, while "All of the common stock is to be deposited under a Voting Agreement which is to continue for not less than five years." Further details of the voting agreement were not disclosed. The brokers could sell the shares for $40, with a $1 commission fee. Estimates suggested that, after the sale, these sellers profited approximately three dollars per share, plus the one-dollar commission per share. Altogether, the proposal meant the bankers' syndicate offered to sell voting trust certificates for almost $14.6 million to pay off the Candlers while giving the purchasers no control over the business.[32]

---

[31] "Trust Company of Georgia Minutes," 2, 13 August 1919, Harold H. Martin Papers; "Waiver of Jury Trial and Stipulation of Facts," 16 January 1928, 4–6, *Trust Co. of Georgia v. J. T. Rose*, No. 794, United States District Court for the Northern District of Georgia, National Archives and Records Administration. The ownership structure of the public offering:

Entity	Common Shares	Percent of Company	Amount Raised
Bankers	83,000	16.6%	$415,000
Public	417,000	83.4%	$14,595,000
Bankers and Public	500,000	100%	$15,010,000

[32] *Appeal of Ernest Woodruff*, 1926 WL 523 (B.T.A. 1926); "Waiver of Jury Trial and Stipulation of Facts," 16 January 1928, Exhibit 4, 8, *Trust Co. of Georgia v. J. T. Rose*, No. 794, United States District Court for the Northern District of Georgia, National Archives and Records Administration; "Depositions Taken in Georgia

Despite the absolute lack of power for future shareholders, public reaction to the sale was extraordinary. This was truly the dawning of mass interest in shares of American companies. On 22 August, the Trust Company wrote its shareholders:

> As you are probably aware, we, associated with strong New York interests, will share in the profits to be derived from the acquirement of the Coca-Cola Co. assets and business. This is a large transaction, involving a large sum of money, and we have made a large commitment in connection with the financing of the enterprise. We made this commitment expecting to offer to our stockholders the privilege of participating in the profits of the enterprise on the same basis that the Trust Co. will share in such profits, provided such stockholders will contribute to the financing of the enterprise in proportion to the number of shares which they hold in the Trust Co.[33]

Although it was not clear from the letter that the shares would be purchased for the bargain price of five dollars and the recipients were warned that the money had to be received in just a few days, the response was overwhelming. The owners of 9,233 shares of Trust Company stock, more than ninety percent of the shares outstanding, deposited $195 for each share with the Trust Company, a total of more than $1.8 million in less than a week. Ernest Woodruff provided $390,000 to personally reserve two thousand shares, although he owned less than 700 shares in the Trust Company. Altogether, the bank raised more than $2.1 million from its shareholders in very short order. A little over a month later, after the deal was closed, participating shareholders received $190 plus one share of Coca-Cola stock for every $195 contributed. Trust Company shareholders purchased 11,233 Coca-Cola shares, while the bank itself retained the

---

Cases," 2352–53 (Wardlaw), Appeal Record, *Coca-Cola Bottling Co. v. Coca-Cola Co.*, Nos. 2650, 2651 (1920), United States Court of Appeals for the Third Circuit, National Archives and Records Administration.

[33] *Appeal of Ernest Woodruff*, 1926 WL 523 (B.T.A. 1926). The opinion in this federal tax case lists a number of prominent Trust Company shareholders who participated in the purchase, including W. C. Wardlaw, David Woodward, Edward H. Inman, and W. C. Bradley.

remaining 13,677 shares of the total of 24,900 it received from the syndicate. This was just under five percent of the outstanding shares.[34]

Trust Company shareholders were not the only bargain hunters, as other buyers eagerly snapped up the $40 shares. Record books for the sale of 417,000 shares opened on 26 August. Orders, generally from brokers, were taken by mail and telegram. The process closed less than seven hours later with an over-subscription of 143,000 shares. The over-subscription required a pro rata allotment for purchases of greater than fifty shares. A huge number, about 250,000 shares, was sold to persons in the Atlanta area. Some of this may have resulted from Woodruff's promise to loan money at six percent to anyone who would buy the stock. The Trust Company of Georgia itself obtained 70,000 of the $35 shares, while Ernest Woodruff may have received 20,000. Here the room for immediate profit was not as great as with the five-dollar shares, but it was still significant. Amazingly, the sales generated more than $15 million in one day, effectively eliminating any earlier risk to the banking syndicate. Never before had this much money been raised so quickly from the public for a company whose primary asset was a trademark on a food product.[35]

Undoubtedly Georgia buyers acted on Coca-Cola's reputation as well as the rare opportunity to invest in a local business with national potential. Also, in this era before federal securities regulation, the *Atlanta Constitution* vigorously pumped up the stock. Although the newspaper first reported the deal only a few days earlier, and conceded many details were uncertain, it glowingly described how the Coca-Cola Company had "developed with

---

[34] Ibid.

[35] "Waiver of Jury Trial and Stipulation of Facts," 9–11, 16 January 1928, *Trust Co. of Georgia v. J. T. Rose*, No. 794, United States District Court for the Northern District of Georgia, National Archives and Records Administration; "Depositions Taken in Georgia Cases," 2334–35 (Wardlaw), Appeal Record, *Coca-Cola Bottling Co. v. Coca-Cola Co.*, Nos. 2650, 2651 (1920), United States Court of Appeals for the Third Circuit, National Archives and Records Administration; McQueen, *The Essence of Capitalism*, 57; *Atlanta Constitution*, 22, 23, 26 August 1919. Syrup production in 1918 was actually reduced because of World War I restrictions. The paper also tempted buyers by describing impressive revenues and net income, including the fact that in the first seven months of 1919, pretax income was $3,250,000, which gave a predicted income for the year of $5,571,428.

marvelous rapidity," even adding a table showing the sensational growth in syrup gallons sold, from just over 2 million in 1906 to more than 11 million in 1918. Declaring that demand for Coca-Cola exceeded supply, the paper noted that based on the first seven months of sales in 1919 of 11 million gallons, it was expected that Coca-Cola would sell 20 million gallons that year. Adopting the role of broker and New South community booster, the *Constitution* further proclaimed that Coca-Cola consumption was the highest of any soft drink in the world. Thirsty men, women, and children drank two hundred and eighty million glasses and bottles in July 1919. Almost 70,000 soda fountains sold it and over 1,500 bottlers bought Coca-Cola syrup. The new management even expressed an interest in entering the international field "in the near future."[36]

Individual buyers outside Georgia may also have been influenced by a short prospectus issued by the bankers. The circular contained a mixture of accurate, misleading, and incomplete information and was sent to brokers and published in selected newspapers. The Candler leadership appeared as the reason for Coca-Cola's growth, but it was rather falsely promised that the "present management...will continue and also be interested through the ownership of a substantial amount of the stock of the Company." The prospectus further claimed that "To insure for the Company a continuity of management" a voting trust agreement had been created, with Dobbs, Stetson, and Woodruff as trustees. Similarly, reports in the *Atlanta Constitution* emphasized that the existing leadership would retain strong influence, even claiming that there would be no change in the active management of the company. Of course, the real purpose of the voting trust was to concentrate power in the men and institutions that were replacing the Candlers, not to maintain "continuity." Further, the prospectus said nothing about the arrangement to sell 83,000 shares at five dollars each to syndicate members. More accurately, the prospectus held out the promise of enormous profits, partly because cheap, easily replaced unskilled labor could produce the drink. The clearest risk, according to the prospectus, was

---

[36] *Atlanta Constitution*, 26 August 1919.

the pending lawsuit in which a federal appeals court had held that the Coca-Cola "name, labels and advertising were deceptive." The prospectus, however, emphasized that the United States Supreme Court had agreed to hear Coca-Cola's appeal and that company lawyers thought the earlier decision was erroneous.[37]

On 5 September a new Coca-Cola Company was born as a Delaware corporation. The leadership reflected the bankers' triumph. Woodruff, Stetson, and Dobbs, the voting trustees, selected a new fourteen-person board that included Woodruff; Stetson; E. V. R. Thayer, president of Chase; W. C. Bradley, a Woodruff ally from Columbus, Georgia; Thomas K. Glenn, a Woodruff ally from Atlanta; Merrill Callaway of Guaranty; and William D'Arcy of St. Louis, a friend of Dobbs and head of Coca-Cola's advertising agency. Hirsch, Dobbs, and Howard Candler also went on the board. Others, particularly William Leggett, president of United Drug Company of Boston; W. E. McCaw, president of Proctor & Gamble of Cincinnati; and Robert B. Atkins, president of the Alegre Sugar Co. of Boston, represented an increased national orientation. The new executive

---

[37] Ibid.; "Waiver of Jury Trial and Stipulation of Facts" (Exhibit 5, Statement of W. C. Wardlaw), 16 January 1928, *Trust Co. of Georgia v. J. T. Rose*, No. 794, United States District Court for the Northern District of Georgia, National Archives and Records Administration; "Prospectus, The Coca-Cola Company," August 1919, Box 1 (King and Spalding), Robert W. Woodruff Papers; Eugene W. Stetson, "'Advertising Good-Will' as a Bankable Asset," *The Red Barrel* 3 (May 1924): 3–5. Wardlaw later conceded "the trade mark was the real value of Coca-Cola. Without that [the company] would have been of little value. Yes, the formula was worth something but the trade name was the thing that was established." More succinctly, according to Sam Dobbs, "The trade-mark was the basis of the business." The company's financial statement, dated 31 December 1918, showed $3.4 million in tangible assets, yet the Candlers issued themselves $25 million in beneficial certificates that year. "Board of Directors Minutes," 17 January 1918; "Copy of Notice Sent to Stockholders," 30 May 1918; "Balance Sheet of the Coca-Cola Company," 31 December 1918, The Coca-Cola Company; "Depositions Taken in Georgia Cases," 2227 (Dobbs); 318, 2353–55, 2358–59 (Wardlaw), Appeal Record, *Coca-Cola Bottling Co. v. Coca-Cola Co.*, Nos. 2650, 2651 (1920), United States Court of Appeals for the Third Circuit, National Archives and Records Administration. On trademarks as assets in business history, see Mira Wilkins, "The Neglected Intangible Asset: The Influence of the Trade Mark on the Rise of the Modern Corporation," *Business History* 34 (January 1992): 66–95.

committee consisted of Stetson, Woodruff, Thayer, Glenn, Bradley, Dobbs, and Howard Candler. Dobbs, the once unhappy nephew who later claimed he did not make a deal to become president, became president.[38]

On 8 September, the directors authorized the issue of the 83,000 five-dollar-shares to Sabin, the Trust Company of Georgia, Shermar, and Newmont. The next day they allowed the Trust Company, as manager of the common stock syndicate, to purchase the remaining 417,000 shares for $35 per share in order to then resell them to the public buyers. Four days later, the Candlers' 1918 beneficial trust was terminated and all of the stock in the old company was issued to the Trust Company of Georgia. Also on 13 September, at what must have been a rather odd meeting of the board of directors of the old Coca-Cola Company, with Asa Candler nowhere in sight, the board authorized the sale of all its assets to the new Coca-Cola Company.[39]

The final transfers of stock and cash, which took place on 13 September, were complex. They demonstrated the crucial cooperation between the Trust Company of Georgia and Guaranty. Just over $15 million, derived from the public equity sale, was placed in the account of the new Coca-Cola Company at Guaranty. Guaranty then "loaned" the Trust Company of Georgia $10 million, which was then transferred to the new

---

[38] Franklin M. Garrett, *Atlanta and Environs: A Chronicle of Its People and Events*, 3 vols. (New York: Lewis Publishing Co., Inc., 1954) 2: 768; "Waiver of Jury Trial and Stipulation of Facts," 16 January 1928, 11–13, Exhibit 8, *Trust Co. of Georgia v. J. T. Rose*, No. 794, United States District Court for the Northern District of Georgia, National Archives and Records Administration; "Depositions Taken in Georgia Cases," 2255 (Dobbs); 2292 (Wardlaw); 2448–49 (Howard Candler), Appeal Record, *Coca-Cola Bottling Co. v. Coca-Cola Co.*, Nos. 2650, 2651 (1920), United States Court of Appeals for the Third Circuit, National Archives and Records Administration.

[39] "Board of Directors Minutes," 13 September 1919, The Coca-Cola Company; Garrett, *Atlanta and Environs*, 2: 768; "Waiver of Jury Trial and Stipulation of Facts," 16 January 1928, 11–13, Exhibit 8, *Trust Co. of Georgia v. J. T. Rose*, No. 794, United States District Court for the Northern District of Georgia, National Archives and Records Administration; "Depositions Taken in Georgia Cases," 2255 (Dobbs); 2292 (Wardlaw); 2448–49 (Howard Candler), Appeal Record, *Coca-Cola Bottling Co. v. Coca-Cola Co.*, Nos. 2650, 2651 (1920), United States Court of Appeals for the Third Circuit, National Archives and Records Administration.

Coca-Cola, which in turn transferred to Guaranty $10 million par value preferred stock of the new Coca-Cola Company. On the new Coca-Cola's instructions, Guaranty then transferred $25 million from the account of the Delaware Coca-Cola corporation to the old Georgia Coca-Cola corporation, consisting of $15 million in cash and $10 million in seven percent cumulative preferred shares. Finally, 500,000 shares of common stock certificates were deposited by the Trust Company of Georgia at Guaranty, to be held under the terms of the voting trust.[40]

Making Personal Fortunes

Although notable for its size and scope, which was commented upon at the time, the sale is especially revealing in showing how bankers at this stage in Stetson's career were motivated and rewarded. This included, above all, Ernest Woodruff. Woodruff sought to generate a large profit for himself and his bank and, even more remarkably, obtain ownership-like control over the company without paying much for it. In the end, a small group of shareholders of the Trust Company of Georgia acquired control of a business ten times the size of their bank using capital primarily from a public sale. The key was that there was a substantial public demand for Coca-Cola shares, even when investors knew their shares would carry no voting rights. Coca-Cola was sold for $25 million in preferred and common stock, not one share of which carried any direct voting rights.

Instead, control of the election of directors and all other shareholder voting rights resided in the three-man voting trust, one of whom was Woodruff. Because two members of the voting trust constituted a majority, Woodruff and just one other trustee could leverage the "ownership" further to exercise power over company affairs. Nonetheless, because two members of the voting trust would be chosen by Albert Wiggin of Chase and Charles

---

[40] "Waiver of Jury Trial and Stipulation of Facts," 16 January 1928, Exhibit 8, *Trust Co. of Georgia v. J. T. Rose*, No. 794, United States District Court for the Northern District of Georgia, National Archives and Records Administration; "Depositions Taken in Georgia Cases," 2293–94, 2303–2306 (Wardlaw), Appeal Record, *Coca-Cola Bottling Co. v. Coca-Cola Co.*, Nos. 2650, 2651 (1920), United States Court of Appeals for the Third Circuit, National Archives and Records Administration.

Sabin of Guaranty, the New York banks initially acted as a counterforce to Woodruff. Woodruff also acquired an enormous volume of shares, well over 20,000 at discounted prices. His Trust Company of Georgia, of which he was the largest shareholder, received more than 80,000 shares, a significant portion of which was priced at five dollars. Altogether Woodruff and the Trust Company acquired more than 100,000 of the 500,000 common shares.

The New Yorkers, including Stetson, also did well. The transaction shows clearly the dynamics and incentives of investment banking as practiced by Stetson and Guaranty immediately after World War I. Later in the twentieth century it would be considered a conflict of interest to structure the transaction directly in the name of bank officers, such as Sabin, but it was accepted practice in 1919. In effect, Guaranty and Chase did not really finance the deal—they merely acted as agents through which preferred individuals, including bank officers, could obtain stock. Under the Bankers' Agreement, President Charles Sabin, and not Guaranty, was entitled to receive 24,900 shares at five dollars a share. In 1919 Sabin was already quite wealthy.[41] It would not have been very difficult for him to pay the entire $124,500 price for the 24,900 shares, particularly when they were really worth about $1 million. More likely, however, the shares were sold and distributed among the various Guaranty personnel that assisted in the transaction, including Sabin, Stetson, Harold Stanley, and Merrill Callaway. Also possible was that additional shares were transferred to Guaranty itself or Guaranty shareholders, much as they were received by Woodruff's Trust Company of Georgia. Enormous personal benefits were obtained in exchange for the banks' responsibility for thirty percent of the cost of the exercise of the options.

---

[41] In July 1919, only weeks before the Coca-Cola IPO, Sabin and his glamorous wife celebrated the opening of their new Long Island retreat. The 314-acre Southampton property, "Bayberry Land," near the National Golf Links of America, featured eight buildings, the largest of which, a "Manor House," included 28 rooms, 11 bedrooms, and 11 bathrooms. See "Bayberry Land: Rest and Refuge in Southampton," http://www.town.southampton.ny.us/specialgallery/bayberry/ bayberrynobleed.pdf.

Stetson was also a big winner, and not simply because he likely acquired bargain-priced Coca-Cola stock. Although the surviving records make it difficult to trace many details of the transaction, Stetson performed a central role. He was brought into the deal through a mutual Georgia acquaintance of his and Woodruff's. He was closely involved in evaluating Coca-Cola's value, an essential decision that helped determine the price. He played a pivotal role in going to Georgia to discuss the deal with the Candlers, Dobbs, and others, where his Georgia background was used to good effect. He negotiated with Woodruff, was elected to Coca-Cola's executive committee, and was named as one of the three voting trustees. Stetson worked as the personal representative of bank president Charles Sabin.

As a result, Stetson played the role of the rainmaking relationship banker in several crucial areas: a significant amount of money was at stake; the value of a corporation had to be assessed; a number of financial institutions were involved; several high profile bankers expected to jointly oversee the purchase of a company; the bankers expected to participate personally in the distribution of equity; and the bankers planned to exercise considerable direct control of the new entity into the indefinite future. Stetson's voting trust appointment as well as his election to the executive committee of the new Coca-Cola board demonstrated that he was not viewed as simply the facilitator of a one-time financing.

The actions of Chase and the Bankers Trust are less easy to ascertain, but the outlines are clear enough. Unlike Guaranty, they did not provide important banking services during the deal. Their role seems to have been to connect Woodruff with outside investors who would share responsibility for the purchase price. This action reflected a common practice among New York banks of spreading risks and rewards among insiders. The vehicles for their involvement seemed fuzzy. Some documents refer to them as the Newmont Company and Shermar Investing Corporation. The records of the Delaware Coca-Cola Company indicated that on 8 September 1919, Newmont received 8,300 shares, but that a "Sherman" Investing Corporation received 14,900 shares and a "Muslyn" Corporation received 10,000 shares. At the time, the persons behind "Newmont," "Shermar," and "Muslyn" were mysterious to many participants. Even the names of the companies: Shermar and Sherman, Muslyn, Moerline, and Murlyn, were inconsistently presented in the records. Dobbs and Howard Candler testified in 1920 that they did not know anything about them. A Trust Company of Georgia officer remembered vaguely that Newmont's offices were located in the Bankers Trust Company and that "Murlyn" and "Sherman" were "corporations which the Chase officers—some of the Chase officers are probably interested."[42]

Not until years later, during the scandals of the Great Depression, did it become clear that "Murlyn" and "Shermar" were two secret Canadian companies formed by Chase president Albert Wiggin and named for his daughters. In the late 1920s and early 1930s Wiggin used the corporations for manipulative purposes, profiting $4 million dollars at the time of the 1929 Crash by short-selling Chase stock owned by the corporations. It is likely that Newmont was associated in a similar way to E. V. R. Thayer of Bankers Trust, if not used for similarly nefarious ends. After all, both Thayer and Wiggin had official duties under the voting trust and on the new board. Much like Woodruff and his Trust Company of Georgia, the New York underwriters benefited personally with limited risk.[43]

The Candlers' part in the sale is more easily evaluated. The price was deemed adequate. Apparently, that was enough since family members did not want to run the business. They seemed to believe that the option buyers represented New York banks and could assume the risks facing the company. More important, they believed the buyers would be able to come up with the purchase price. They had no idea that Woodruff, Dobbs, Hirsch, Alston, and Stetson, all Georgians, would ultimately decide to keep the company in Atlanta. They mistakenly believed "New York financial interests" were the real party buying the company. On the other hand, they

---

[42] "Depositions Taken in Georgia Cases," 2197 (Dobbs); 2484–85 (Howard Candler); 2320–22 (Wardlaw), Appeal Record, *Coca-Cola Bottling Co. v. Coca-Cola Co.*, Nos. 2650, 2651 (1920), United States Court of Appeals for the Third Circuit, National Archives and Records Administration; J. T. W. Hubbard, *For Each, the Strength of All: A History of Banking in the State of New York* (New York: New York University Press, 1995) 209.

[43] Ibid. On Wiggin's use of Shermar and Murlyn in the late 1920s, see Maury Klein, *Rainbow's End: The Crash of 1929* (New York: Oxford University Press, 2001) 150, 171, 246–47.

probably did not care whether the buyer was a New Yorker or the Devil himself. There is no evidence the Candlers bothered to inquire too deeply about who Alston or Stetson really represented, or that Alston or Stetson misrepresented anything. The fact that Woodruff, Stetson, and the other bankers secretly engineered the sale is more a testament to the Chandlers' lack of interest in the buyers, excepting their ability to pay, than it is proof of Woodruff or anyone else's ability to deceive.

Coca-Cola and American Finance

The Coca-Cola sale demonstrates many key characteristics of the sort of investment and commercial banking practiced at Stetson's Guaranty. First, it shows that through an imaginative combination of common and preferred equity, a coalition of Georgia and New York banks could arrange a major purchase in the economically backward South. Almost sixty years after the Civil War, the deal symbolized the southern transition into an urban industrial economy led by two exemplars of the New South ideology: Woodruff and Stetson. On the other hand, the financing showed the continuing dependence of southern businessmen on northern capital. Woodruff thought that both the prestige and cash of New Yorkers was necessary for the transaction.

Second, the deal showed new investing opportunities in mass produced and well-branded food and drink products. The early history of American financing reeked of railroads, steel, mining, and other forms of "heavy" industry. A sugary drink with minimal labor costs, but with a valuable trademark, would not have been considered fit for Wall Street's attention just a few years earlier.

Third, the deal demonstrated how, given the generous availability of capital for investment, bank officers could make this sort of financing with minimum risk and maximum personal gain. The sale displayed the enormous potential for profit from managing such sales, including the distribution of highly discounted shares.[44] It is not surprising that Guaranty

---

[44] The bankers made considerable profits from the transactions. Woodruff's Trust Company of Georgia purchased 24,9000 shares at $5 per share, paying $124,500. At the $40 market price these shares were worth $996,000 for a gain of $871,500. In 2007 dollars, this gain is more than $10.4 million. Guaranty's Charles

eagerly sought this variety of lending and securities transaction after World War I, especially when the bank could put one of its officers, such as Stetson, in a continuing role as a voting trustee and director of the new corporation. Moreover, in an era before federal securities regulation, personal profit taking could be accomplished without disclosure to the purchasers of common stock.

Finally, the transaction showed that investors, while eager to find profitable bargains, depended heavily on personal connections, meaning trust, to make investment decisions. The public prospectus for the new Coca-Cola was brief and incomplete, particularly as to plans for the management of the company. Yet investors, many of them Georgia residents, swarmed to the opportunity. In turn, this reflected the huge demand for equity, not debt as in previous decades, as a form of investment, a fact that would radically alter Wall Street during the "Roaring Twenties."[45]

Because of its importance to American business history, the Coke deal is also worth considering from the comparative perspective of the twenty-first century, when corporate sales of enormous size and scope are common. In any age, complex transactions with difficult parties take patience,

---

Sabin acquired the same number of shares (24,900) at $5 and thus experienced the same benefits. Thayer and Bankers Trust, through Newmont, acquired 8,300 of the $5 shares for $42,500. The value of these shares at $40 was $332,000, for a gain of just over $290,000, an amount equivalent to about $3.4 million in 2007 dollars. Chase Wiggin, using the Shermar and Murlyn companies, acquired 24,900 shares at $5, which had a market value at the IPO of $871,500, for a gain of more than $10.4 million in 2007 dollars. Altogether, the bankers' gain from the $5 shares was more than $3.3 million, or just under $35 million in 2007 dollars. Values in 2007 dollars calculated using Consumer Price Index, "Six Ways to Compare the Relative Value of a U.S. Dollar Amount," http://measuringworth.com/calculators/uscompare.

[45] On the idea that American finance was revolutionized by the exploding public interest in equity investment after World War I, see Jonathan B. Baskin and Paul J. Miranti Jr., *A History of Corporate Finance* (New York: Cambridge University Press, 1997) 127–209.

creativity, and teamwork. The Coca-Cola sale had more than its share of complexity. In fact, the deal involved such substantial challenges that it may not have happened later in the century.

First, later buyouts generally had more substantial tangible or "hard" assets, such as real estate. In fact, in the nineteenth century the normal preference of bankers was also for hard assets. They are easier to liquidate when a company fails. But the Coca-Cola sale took place in an era when J. P. Morgan and others had already challenged this way of thinking, at least in such traditional high capital industries as steel.[46] The Coke deal expanded and applied this new approach to valuation to the trademark of a beverage company, where tangible assets were less than about one tenth of the purchase price. All of the key players, Woodruff, Stetson, Sabin, the Candlers, and, ultimately, the public investors, agreed that hard assets were only a small part of the true value of Coca-Cola.

A second threat was the unsettled state of Coca-Cola's key intangible asset. The lack of an ironclad trademark in a market where many upstart companies were using a version of the Coca-Cola name threatened the company's existence. Practically any entrepreneur could try to pass off something called Coke-Ola, Coo-EE-Ola, Koca-Nola, Toca-Cola or even Pepsi-Cola, and many did.[47] Before the sale a federal court of appeals had ruled that the Coca-Cola trademark was deceptive, and thus invalid, partly because it implied ingredients that in fact were no longer in the drink. The case was pending in the United States Supreme Court at the moment of the public offering, and was not resolved in the company's favor until 1920.

---

[46] According to Charles R. Morris, in the late 1890s "Conservative practice focused on book value: a business was worth no more than its actual investment in plant, inventory, and other hard assets plus undistributed profits, less liabilities and depreciation. Carnegie Steel's book value in 1898 was $49 million, while the coke company's was $5 million. Anything more, in the traditional view, was just 'water,' an unsecured claim on future success. Normal valuation rules, however, were just then being turned upside down by Pierpont Morgan's highly capitalized deals in steel and other industries." Carnegie reorganized his steel and coke business for $320 million, more than five times book value. Charles R. Morris, *The Tycoons: How Andrew Carnegie, John D. Rockefeller, Jay Gould, and J.P. Morgan Invented the American Supereconomy* (New York: Henry Holt and Company, 2005) 209–15.

[47] Allen, *Secret Formula*, 73.

This uncertainty would have been crippling later in the twentieth century because the company's value depended almost entirely on the trademark.

A third challenge was that the government price control on sugar, half the ingredients in the syrup, was about to expire. By 1919, the Coca-Cola Company was the largest single user of granulated cane sugar in the world, consuming nearly 100 million pounds a year. For years prior to the sale, sugar had been cheap, selling for about four to six cents per pound. During World War I, shortages and demand produced price controls by the American government, sustaining relatively low prices during the crisis. Of course sugar was likely to go higher when price controls were lifted. In fact, the price controls were eliminated in the fall of 1919, the very moment of the sale. Sugar prices soared in 1920, briefly rising to near twenty-three cents per pound.[48]

The fourth problem came from Coca-Cola's best customers, the bottlers, who provided forty percent of the company's revenue. Unfortunately for the company, in 1919 the bottlers thought they had a perpetual contract to purchase syrup, the original 1899 contract obtained by Thomas and Whitehead from Asa Candler, at the rate of about one dollar per gallon. This kind of fixed cost arrangement, without of course a similar prospect of fixed expenses for Coca-Cola to produce the syrup, made continued profitability suspect. Among the earliest tasks of new management was a more favorable relationship with the bottlers.[49]

At a later date any of these items could have stopped the transaction from moving forward. A final modern barrier to the deal is that federal securities regulation in effect after the early 1930s would have made the sale even less likely. The securities laws subject underwriters to potential liability for any material misrepresentations or omissions contained in a registration statement or prospectus. As a consequence, the insiders' benefits and other details about Coca-Cola would have been revealed to the government and the public. The prospectus issued by the underwriters in

---

[48] Allen, *Secret Formula*, 104–105. On Cuban sugar prices, see Muriel McAvoy, *Sugar Baron: Manuel Rionda and the Fortunes of Pre-Castro Cuba* (Gainesville: University Press of Florida, 2003) 69–70, 75 (3–4 cents, 1909–1914); 101–102 (5–6 cents, 1917); 148 (12–13 cents, 1919); 152 (22.57 cents, 1920).

[49] Allen, *Secret Formula*, 109, 113–14.

1919, as well as the patent boosterism of the Atlanta press, would fail the requirements of current law.

Stetson and the Sale

Stetson was certainly aware of the challenges. Yet one factor he never seemed to worry about was his own relative youth and inexperience. His confidence depended in large part on the strong backing of Guaranty's president, Charles Sabin. This says a great deal about the mutual trust Sabin and Stetson had developed over the previous three years. In addition, with Stetson's direct knowledge of both Atlanta and New York, he was in the best position of any individual to make critical judgments about the persons involved. As a native Georgian, Stetson was very familiar with Coca-Cola's history: Coca-Cola advertised in his university annual in the 1890s and he had the Macon bottler on his bank's board by 1908.

The specific financial devices used in the sale demanded creativity, and Stetson played a key role in formulating the details. Part of the financing for the $25 million sale was $10 million preferred stock with a dividend of seven percent to the Candler sellers. In 1919 this would not have been viewed as a disguised form of debt or, for that matter, anything particularly novel. The preferred shares, in fact, became voting shares if semi-annual dividends were not paid to the Candlers. Similarly, Andrew Carnegie had received more than $300 million in gold bonds and $93 million in preferred shares in payment for his Carnegie Company in 1901, almost twenty years earlier.[50]

Indeed, the most novel aspects of the Coca-Cola deal were its reliance on public equity, the southern locale of the issuer, and the nature of the issuer's product: a sugary soft drink. The hardest part of the sale was the $15 million of cash that would have to be raised immediately to pay the seller. How could that be obtained? The answer was provided by Stetson and the others' faith in the overwhelming power of the public offering. The

---

[50] Morris, *The Tycoons*, 362. Debt, not equity, was preferred in early railroad financing because it could be backed by other property, especially land. See Baskin and Miranti, *Corporate Finance*, 127–209.

great equity boom of the 1920s was underway, and Stetson, Guaranty, and Coca-Cola were among its frontrunners.[51]

Ernest Woodruff has to be given credit for the essential form of the deal. Woodruff's idea, not Stetson or the New Yorkers', was to phase the acquisition, starting first with a short-term option to buy the company rather than an outright purchase. Most likely Woodruff also developed the idea to structure the sale with common and preferred shares, since this is essentially what he proposed in 1912, seven years earlier, although then Woodruff contemplated the explicit use of debt, not preferred shares, as part of the payment. The $25 million valuation was also already determined by Woodruff and the Candlers even before the New York bankers got involved. This was the amount of the ownership certificates issued to the Candler family in 1918. Yet Woodruff wanted options without the Candler family knowing that he and his Trust Company were the buyers. Woodruff knew his Atlanta reputation and he perceived the Candlers would refuse to sell him their company. Perhaps most importantly, he knew that only New York could help him come up with the needed backing, and that meant a New York-supported public offering.

Stetson's greatest contribution was that he saw Woodruff had both the creativity and the chutzpah necessary to pull off the deal. At their first crucial meeting, he could have rejected the scheme as just false ambition by a small-time provincial, and the idea would have died. From the beginning Stetson understood the spectacular depth of the opportunity. He believed $25 million reflected an accurate value, despite the lack of "hard" assets. Stetson's willingness to take on the project shows why as early as 1919 he was a successful rainmaker and relationship banker.

For Stetson, the Coca-Cola sale was a big break that promised well for his Guaranty career. The deal required solid salesmanship and being able to maneuver among a host of different interests and personalities, each looking to maximize its profit. These personalities included some of the biggest names in twentieth century American business: Sabin, Thayer, Wiggin, and Ernest Woodruff. Further, the deal necessitated balancing the interest of his bank and his boss, Sabin, with the need to create a new business that would

---

[51] As Charles Morris notes, a mere $25 million in J. P. Morgan's 1901 U.S. Steel deal, a $1.4 billion transaction, was raised as new cash. Morris, *The Tycoons*, 254.

have a good chance of success. Finally, it required imagination in the use of public equity. After the sale Stetson was positioned to convert the goodwill he developed into a long-term banking relationship with Coca-Cola.

6

Relationship Banking at Coca-Cola

The Coca-Cola sale began a relationship between Stetson, the new company, and its leaders that lasted for the rest of Stetson's life. His work included sitting on the Coca-Cola board; helping with marketing strategies; arranging financing; restructuring operations; finding acquisition opportunities; and assisting in carrying all of these tasks to completion. It also included a long and close social and business friendship with Bob Woodruff, president of Coca-Cola during most of this time. The experience exemplified Stetson's vision of relationship banking and fulfilled his role as rainmaker for Guaranty.

Rainmaking is a key part of relationship banking, which to Stetson meant "Know your Customer." In relationship banking, some transactions might actually be unprofitable. But by getting a high percentage of the customer's business, a relationship-oriented bank in Stetson's day was in the best position to make the more profitable transactions, which included secured loans and the underwriting of new securities. If a bank sought and attracted well-managed companies in growing industries and built the appropriate relationships, it secured its own growth. Also, relationship banking partially insulated a bank from competition. The inside information about client needs and history inherent in a continuing bank-client relationship gave a bank a semi-monopoly position. When a client had a choice between taking a commercial bank loan or issuing a bond, the final choice may have had more to do with which banker the client trusted to support it in the event of real need. The customer perceived that the banker put the interest of the customer's business first and was not just trying to profit from a deal.[1]

---

[1] For current views on relationship banking, see Howard Bodenhorn, "Short-Term Loans and Long-Term Relationships: Relationship Lending In Early America," *Journal of Money, Credit and Banking* 35 (August 2003): 485–505; Michael

"Transactional banking" was and is an ideological counterpoint to relationship banking. Transactional banking means the bank does not know the customer or its needs and desires—it just wants to make a small amount from each of the customer's transactions. As a result, the bank values the customer according to how many transactions it makes. In transactional banking, a business that clears a lot of checks is a valuable client. In practice, of course, financial institutions have used and continue to use both transactional and relational strategies simultaneously. The precise mix and emphasis depends on strategic orientation. For Stetson's Guaranty the strategic orientation was always relationship banking.[2]

Good relationship banking, especially the sort practiced by Stetson and his colleagues at Guaranty, required both broad and specialized knowledge. To "know your customer" was to understand his business just about as well as he did, including on such diverse issues as trademarks, competition, market share, devotion to product development, and promotional style. A relationship banker identified with the customer beyond his financial needs, and in many cases became a social friend as well. The closeness of the relationship could easily lead to abuse otherwise known as "crony capitalism." So the relationship banker was given an extra and difficult task,

---

T. Jacobs, *Short-Term America: The Causes and Cures of Our Business Myopia* (Boston: Harvard Business School Press, 1991); and Dwight S. Ritter, *Relationship Banking: Cross-Selling the Bank's Products and Services to Meet Your Customer's Every Need* (Chicago and Cambridge: Bankers Publishing Co., Probus Publishing Co., 1993). For views contemporary to Stetson, see L. H. Langston and Nathan R. Whitney, *Banking Practice: A Textbook for Colleges and Schools of Business Administration* (New York: Ronald Press Co., 1921); and William H. Kniffin, *American Banking Practice* (New York: McGraw-Hill Book Co., Inc., 1921).

[2] Regarding lending, two recent writers noted that under a transactional approach "the credit decision and lending terms are based primarily on hard quantitative information that is gathered around the time that the credit is originated. Each transaction stands on its own.... In contrast, [with relationship lending] the credit decision and lending terms are based in significant part on soft...information that is gathered through continuous contact over time with the firm, its owners, and other members of the local community." Allen N. Berger and Gregory F. Udell, "The Future of Relationship Lending," in *The Future of Banking*, ed. Benton E. Gup (Westport CT and London: Quorum Books, 2003) 212.

to draw a line between the interest of the bank and client while at the same time identifying with both.

When Stetson arrived in New York, relationship banking was the standard, not only at Guaranty, but also among its peer banks on Wall Street. Stetson and Guaranty operated in an environment in which institutions sought deep and continuing relationships with good corporate customers. A practical reason for this strategy was that at least through the 1930s financial market stability could not be taken for granted. In fact, instability was the norm. Even the best-managed company could find itself in a severe cash or capital crunch, and having an ongoing bank relationship would be necessary for survival. Pierpont Morgan, a master of relationship banking, appointed his banks, including Guaranty, as guardians of their clients' interests. As a result, banking clients benefited from relationships in which bankers met their day-to-day needs and supported them even when an objective evaluation of their financial condition might indicate that they did not deserve it.[3]

From the bankers' perspective another reason for relationship banking was the tradition and preeminence of railroad financing. Railroads needed massive amounts of capital. Yet, in the late nineteenth century, the United States lacked the institutional infrastructure to provide capital to these enterprises. Railroad entrepreneurs turned to Europe, where banking firms like the Rothschilds and Barings were able to tap large investors. A distinction developed between the financial firms that could commit their own capital and pools of capital to an undertaking and firms that contracted to distribute new securities to their network of investors. The emergence of the middlemen, who bought securities for resale, marked the beginning of investment banking in the United States. The emerging investment banks formed a clear hierarchy, with the top firms determined by access to capital, a reputation for reliability, and an ability to control security prices. Most relevantly, the structure of this investment business evolved around personal relationships. Those at the top of the investment bank pecking order

---

[3] See Samuel L. Hayes III, A. Michael Spence, and David Van Praag Marks, *Competition in the Investment Banking Industry* (Cambridge: Harvard University Press, 1983) 11–12; Samuel L. Hayes III and Philip Hubbard, *Investment Banking: A Tale of Three Cities* (Boston: Harvard Business School Press, 1990) 92–93.

brought in the business and took a cut off the top for organizing syndicates. However, other firms participated in a transaction to make sure the securities would be well distributed.[4]

This basic structure was still in place at the time Stetson came to New York. A 1913 Congressional investigation, the famous Pujo hearings into the "money trust," found that the officers and directors of the top banks, Morgan, First National, National City, Bankers Trust, and Guaranty Trust, had wide influence in American business and finance. Officers at those five banks "had 118 directorships in 34 banks and trust companies, 30 directorships in 10 insurance companies, 105 directorships in 32 transportation companies, 63 directorships in 24 producing and trading companies, and 25 directorships in 12 utility companies. Thus, this group of men held 341 directorships in 112 companies having aggregate resources of $22 billion." To Congress, the extent of concentration suggested a threat to both political democracy and economic competition. Of course, the fact that a favored few had "insider" access was a rather intentional product of the values and practice of relationship banking. One connection led invariably to another.[5]

This last fact helps demonstrate why, above all other reasons, Stetson practiced the relationship banking model at Guaranty. The process was successful. Far from being an outdated concept, from Stetson's vantage it was supremely modern. Relationship banking was the key that unlocked the most profitable aspects of the banking business, from commercial lending to investment securities. As a result, it is not surprising that after the Coca-Cola deal Stetson was eager to apply the principles of relationship banking to the reorganized Atlanta soft drink company.

---

[4] Hayes and Hubbard, *Investment Banking*, 91–94, 97–98; Hayes, Spence, and Marks, *Competition in the Banking Industry*, 12–13.

[5] Hayes, Spence, and Marks, *Competition in Investment Banking Industry*, 13–14; Vincent P. Carosso, *The Morgans: Private International Bankers, 1854–1913* (Cambridge: Harvard University Press, 1987) 627–41; Vincent Carosso, *Investment Banking in America: A History* (Cambridge: Harvard University Press, 1970) 137–55 (Guaranty among "inner group" of Morgan-controlled banks).

Coca-Cola and Its Bottlers

In 1919 the Coca-Cola Company did not produce the final drink so desired by its customers. Rather, the company produced syrup, which was sold to fountain operators and bottlers for mixing and then resale to the consumer. The fates of the company and the bottlers had been linked ever since Asa Candler's 1899 bottling deal with Chattanooga lawyers Thomas and Whitehead. That relationship was made more complicated by the fact that the businesses developed by Thomas and Whitehead chose to operate as "parent bottlers," middlemen who in turn franchised bottling rights to the "actual" bottlers, local businesses that actually put Coca-Cola into bottles for consumption.[6]

Given the money and power at stake, the dealings between Coca-Cola, the "parent bottlers," and the "actual bottlers" have frequently been tense. One side could not easily dispose of the other. As recently as the late 1990s, when Coke imposed a 7.6% price hike on bottlers, the bottlers' complaints resulted in the ouster of Coca-Cola's CEO. The first serious dispute between the company and the bottlers dates to the period just after Woodruff, Stetson, and the New York banks won control over Coca-Cola.[7] Stetson, Woodruff, and the new owners eventually decided to wage a determined battle against the parent bottlers. On the surface, the contest was over the contract price the company could charge the parent bottlers for syrup and whether the parent bottlers had exclusive rights to the bottling franchises. The real fight, however, was about the company's future: would it remain a coalition of producers or would decisive control of the drink be returned to the company that created it?

---

[6] On the bottlers from 1899 to 1919, see Frederick Allen III, *Secret Formula: How Brilliant Marketing and Relentless Salesmanship Made Coca-Cola the Best-Known Product in the World* (New York: HarperBusiness, 1994) 105–13.

[7] In 1986, Coke created a new wholly-owned subsidiary, Coca-Cola Enterprises, which bought up and merged formerly independent bottlers. By 2007 Coca-Cola Enterprises produced more than eighty percent of all bottles and cans sold in North America. On the departure of CEO Doug Ivester in 1999, see M. K. Hartley, "Cola Wars: Coca-Cola vs. PepsiCo," http://media.wiley.com/product_data/ excerpt/16/04717432/0471743216–3.pdf. Coca-Cola Enterprises' self-description is "About Us: Overview," http://www.cokecce.com/pages/allContent.asp?-page_id =81.

Initially, the Woodruff-led bankers had indicated that they wanted a friendly relationship with the bottlers. On 8 August 1919, just before the public offering, Harold Hirsch wrote George Hunter, president of the Coca-Cola Bottling Company, assuring him that "Powerful interests are taking this proposition [that is, Coca-Cola] over and will make a big go of it, but the bottlers' rights will be absolutely protected without any thought of annulling the same." Sam Dobbs told Hunter, "There is a deal on whereby certain interests in The Coca-Cola Company will retire and a reorganization will take place, and some stock will be offered to the public." He asked Hunter to send Stetson a list of all the bottling plants, noting, "Some of them may want to invest in some of the new stock issue."[8]

Yet, in the weeks after the sale, Woodruff complained loudly about the need to raise the per gallon price of syrup because of rapidly increasing sugar prices. The parent bottlers agreed to price increases in the latter half of 1919 and again in early 1920. These "temporary" price changes expired on 1 March 1920. As it turned out, Woodruff was not satisfied with marginally higher syrup prices. He and eventually most of the rest of the new ownership believed the maneuvering over syrup prices presented a golden opportunity to get rid of the parent bottling companies, the Whitehead and Thomas entities that had obtained the original bottling rights from Asa Candler. In Woodruff's view, the parent bottling companies were superfluous middlemen and he wanted to deal only with the actual bottlers.[9]

---

[8] S. C. Dobbs to George T. Hunter, 12 August 1919; Harold Hirsch to George T. Hunter, 8 August 1919, Case Documents, *Coca-Cola Bottling Co. v. Coca-Cola Co.*, Nos. 2650, 2651 (1920), United States Court of Appeals for the Third Circuit, National Archives and Records Administration, Philadelphia, Pennsylvania; *Coca-Cola Bottling Co. v. Coca-Cola Co.*, 296 F. 796, 799–803 (D. Del. 1920).

[9] "The Coca-Cola Company to The Actual Bottlers of Coca-Cola," 9 April 1920, Case Documents, *Coca-Cola Bottling Co. v. Coca-Cola Co.*, Nos. 2650, 2651 (1920), United States Court of Appeals for the Third Circuit, National Archives and Records Administration.

Sugar Water and a Contract

As a result, in 1920 Coca-Cola coupled its request for increases in syrup prices with the threat that the 1899 parent bottler's contract was terminable at the will of the company. The parent bottlers called the bluff by refusing to accept further price increases unless the company agreed their contract was perpetual. Coca-Cola responded by attempting to terminate the parent bottlers' contract and contacted the actual bottlers, indicating its desire to supply them directly with syrup. On 13 April 1920, the parent bottlers sued the company in Fulton County Superior Court in Atlanta, asking the court to hold that their contract with Coca-Cola was perpetual.[10]

In the lawsuit the parent bottlers blamed the recent sale to Woodruff and the New Yorkers for the company's attempt to terminate the contract. They played anti-banker and anti-Wall Street sentiment for all it was worth. The company's decision to declare the bottling contract an at-will agreement was portrayed as part of a nefarious plot driven by Wall Street greed: "Sometime in the summer of 1919 a number of promoters and high financiers conceived a scheme to get control of the stock of [the] corporation." This "scheme" was facilitated by World War I inflation and "the willingness of the people to speculate in stocks of corporations capitalized on the basis of earning power," and not hard assets. Yet the new corporation never really received anything for its stock sales:

> As a part of said scheme and manipulation, the promoters and high financiers, after being underwritten by some syndicate, projected said common stock into Wall Street, and proceeded by divers schemes, well known only to the trade manipulators, to lure the public to so invest in said stock that they finally succeeded in unloading it at a profit to themselves and the various trust companies and others connected with the manipulations to the extent of approximately five million dollars, this profit costing them nothing but their cleverness and energy in putting the matter over.

---

[10] Ibid.

Consistent with this "manipulation," the attempt to cut off the parent bottlers resulted from "cupidity and avarice and greed." Not surprisingly, Coca-Cola responded that all this was nonsense, or more to the point, was irrelevant to the narrow legal question of whether the company could terminate the 1899 contract between the company and the parent bottlers.[11]

The legal proceedings in Fulton County proved to be a mere preliminary to the main bout. Nonetheless, they showed the weaknesses and strengths of both sides' positions. Initially, the Georgia court issued a restraining order prohibiting the company from terminating the bottlers' contract while the case was pending. The order also required the company to sell syrup to the actual bottlers at $1.72 a gallon with a seven and one-half cents "rebate" to the parent bottling companies.[12]

In April and May 1920 the Fulton court listened to a great deal of testimony relating to the contract from Sam Dobbs, Asa Candler, W. C. Wardlaw, Harold Hirsch, and Howard Candler. Judge John T. Pendleton was not overly impressed by the parent bottlers' argument and informally indicated he did not think the contract was perpetual. Perhaps he was influenced by the fact that Robert Alston, the Coca-Cola attorney who had helped obtain options from the Candlers, brought Judge Pendleton's grandson, a young lawyer in Alston's firm, to the courtroom. At any rate, fearing defeat, Jack Spalding and John Sibley, attorneys for the parent bottlers, decided to try again in a friendlier forum. They voluntarily dismissed their Georgia case on 31 May. Coca-Cola, sensing victory, promptly terminated the parent bottlers' contract and told its employees to stop shipping them syrup. The next day, however, the bottlers filed another suit, again based on the alleged perpetual nature of the 1899 contract, but this time in federal district court in Delaware, the domicile of the new

---

[11] "Proceedings in Fulton Superior Court," 1743–1755, 1789–1791, Appeal Record, *Coca-Cola Bottling Co. v. Coca-Cola Co.*, Nos. 2650, 2651 (1920), United States Court of Appeals for the Third Circuit, National Archives and Records Administration.

[12] "Transcript of Record," *Coca-Cola Co. v. Coca-Cola Bottling Co.*, No. 2650, 4 March 1921; "Brief for Appellant," 33–34, *Coca-Cola Co. v. Coca-Cola Bottling Co.*, Nos. 2650, 2651 (1920), United States Court of Appeals for the Third Circuit, National Archives and Records Administration; "Memorandum to Wilbur G. Kurtz Jr. from Pope F. Brock," 22 July 1974, The Coca-Cola Company.

Coca-Cola Company. The bottlers also obtained a restraining order requiring the company to renew syrup shipments.[13]

The bottlers' shift in venue paid off. On 8 November 1920, the Delaware court issued a ruling in their favor. After concluding that Coca-Cola had the power to sell exclusive bottling rights, the court tried to "search for the meaning of the contract from the agreement as a whole, from all its terms considered together, remembering that in a contract of many provisions the entire intention of the parties is not expressed by any single stipulation." In simple terms, the parent bottlers argued they acquired exclusive property rights to bottle Coca-Cola in 1899. The company argued, conversely, that the old agreement conveyed a right only to purchase syrup at its will. To federal Judge Hugh Morris, the most telling part of the contract was a provision in which the company expressly granted the bottlers "the sole and exclusive right to use the name Coca-Cola and all the trade-marks and designs for labels now owned and controlled by" the company. He concluded this language meant Coca-Cola permanently sold the use of its trademarks, the company's most valuable asset, to the bottlers. The court issued an injunction prohibiting any interruption in the flow of syrup, hoping this would be enough to force the parties to work out a new agreement on their own. Naturally, given the high stakes, an appeal by Coca-Cola followed.[14]

By this time, however, it was becoming increasingly clear that a forced result was in no one's best interest. A critical factor pushing the parties to compromise was the improving sugar market. In March 1920, at the beginning of the fight with the bottlers, the new leadership at Coca-Cola had become seriously concerned about reduced sugar supplies and rising prices. It purchased a literal boatload of expensive sugar from the American Sugar Refining Company, using Guaranty to help finance the deal. Stetson was directly involved in the purchase and its financing. He had represented

---

[13] Ibid.

[14] "Brief for Appellant," 33–34, *Coca-Cola Co. v. Coca-Cola Bottling Co.*, Nos. 2650, 2651 (1920), United States Court of Appeals for the Third Circuit, National Archives and Records Administration; *Coca-Cola Bottling Co. v. Coca-Cola Co.*, 296 F. at 796–814.

Guaranty for several years in Cuban sugar financing and he knew something about both sugar markets and Coca-Cola.[15]

The purchase, however, turned out to be an almost cataclysmic mistake. Soon after the transaction, the price of sugar plummeted. Coca-Cola was now stuck with an enormous stock of high-cost sugar that would take months to consume. A Coca-Cola historian revealed the deep scars of the decision to buy twenty-cents sugar and its subsequent fall to six cents per pound by describing it as "the most serious situation ever faced by the company." Fresh multi-million dollar loans from Guaranty were necessary, and the new owners engaged in some fancy accounting to prop up the share price, which nevertheless fell dramatically. The sugar storm brewed throughout the legal contest between the bottlers and the company. The good news was that by early 1921, during the appeal of the Delaware decision, the stock of expensive sugar rapidly waned and sugar prices remained low. Under these conditions it became easier to imagine a compromise that would serve the interests of both the bankers and the bottlers.[16]

Internal upheaval within Coca-Cola also helped drive a new strategy. During 1920, the first full year of operation under the bankers, important disputes erupted between Dobbs, Woodruff, and the New Yorkers. For Dobbs and Woodruff, the short-lived honeymoon was over. Dobbs wanted more money spent on advertising. He complained to board member William D'Arcy that "Woodruff and Thayer are tearing their hair, howling for retrenchment, because they want dividends. Stetson in a way is agreeing with them and of course Bradley always plays up to the New York crowd."

---

[15] "Memorandum to Wilbur G. Kurtz Jr. from Pope F. Brock," 22 July 1974, The Coca-Cola Company; "Docket Book," *Coca-Cola Co. v. Coca-Cola Bottling Co.*, Nos. 2650, 2651 (1920), National Archives and Records Administration; "The Story Behind a Name Which You Probably See More Often than any Other," 5, The Coca-Cola Company; Humphrey McQueen, *The Essence of Capitalism: The Origins of Our Future* (New York: Black Rose Books, 2003) 57.

[16] "Memorandum to Wilbur G. Kurtz Jr. from Pope F. Brock," 22 July 1974, The Coca-Cola Company; "Docket Book," *Coca-Cola Co. v. Coca-Cola Bottling Co.*, Nos. 2650, 2651 (1920), National Archives and Records Administration; "The Story Behind a Name Which You Probably See More Often than any Other," 5, The Coca-Cola Company; McQueen, *The Essence of Capitalism*, 294–95.

Dobbs considered Woodruff "ignorant" about advertising. He was also at odds with Stetson. At one board meeting "Stetson expressed himself as feeling that I had exceeded my authority in [an advertising] matter, but that he was unwilling to take the position that in doing so I had acted unwisely and asked for more facts and figures. That, of course, is always Stetson's attitude."[17]

In his roles as banker, voting trustee, and director Stetson believed he should be actively involved in the operation of the company, and this included marketing. Years later, Stetson stated that directors had an obligation to require a company's advertising executive to "state his plan—where he is going, where he is to start and what he is to do in between, with plenty of convincing reasons for everything." This is precisely what he demanded from D'Arcy and Dobbs in 1920.[18]

The negative feelings went beyond advertising. Dobbs complained that Woodruff had a bad habit of "butting-in and interfering" in just about everything, criticizing the company's attorneys without foundation, and getting mad when others disagreed with him. Allegedly, Woodruff called an all-night meeting where there was an effort to "emasculate and supercede the Board of Directors" led by Woodruff, Stetson, Thayer, and Bradley. Dobbs believed some of the other directors were also failures: McCaw of Procter and Gamble, for example, "will do whatever Stetson tells him to." The fission extended to the bottler conflict. Dobbs, unlike Woodruff, did not want to eliminate the parent bottlers, perhaps because of his longer history with them. Yet the locus of power was clearly with Woodruff and the New Yorkers. Board meetings were frequently held at Guaranty in New York. Dobbs became so disenchanted that he resigned the presidency in October 1920, in the midst of the bottler lawsuit.[19]

---

[17] Sam Dobbs to William D'Arcy, 24, 26 April, 18 May, 29 July, 6 August 1920; Harold Hirsch to W. C. Bradley, 27 December 1920; "Minutes of Meeting of the Coca-Cola Executive Committee," 15 December 1919; 19 January, 15 March 1920, Mark Pendergrast Papers, Manuscript, Archives, and Rare Book Library, Emory University, Atlanta, Georgia.

[18] Eugene W. Stetson, "Banker Sees Continuing Need of Advertising," *Printers' Ink* (23 November 1933) 43–45.

[19] Sam Dobbs to William D'Arcy, 24, 26 April, 18 May, 29 July, 6 August 1920; Harold Hirsch to W. C. Bradley, 27 December 1920; "Minutes of Meeting of the

From the parent bottlers' perspective, compromise was always the preferred option. They simply could not survive without the company's trademark. They knew their strongest course was to create incentives for both Coca-Cola and the actual bottlers. In December 1920, H. H. Ward, one of the attorneys for the bottling companies, wrote co-counsel John Sibley stating, "we should not, except upon the most weighty grounds, fail to reach an agreement with our adversaries." Negotiations gained a renewed hopefulness toward the end of the year after a very favorable ruling in the *Koke* case by the United States Supreme Court, which affirmed the validity of Coca-Cola's trademark. No less a jurist that Oliver Wendell Holmes Jr. confirmed the company's rights. In January 1921 Charles Rainwater, for the parent bottlers, and W. C. Bradley, for Coca-Cola, exchanged detailed settlement proposals addressing syrup prices. Nonetheless, the bottlers rejected it as unfair. Fed up with Coca-Cola, they now began to argue that a legal attack on the validity of the voting trust, the entire governing structure of Coca-Cola, was in order. In the spring of 1921 negotiations seemed to have reached a standstill, deadlocking over the syrup price and division of profits.[20]

Stetson and Settlement

Lawyers for both sides presented oral arguments to the federal Court of Appeals in Philadelphia in May 1921. While preparing their brief, the bottlers had worried about the high quality of the company's arguments. To counter, they leaned heavily on District Judge Morris's reasoning about the contract, particularly his belief in the unfairness of allowing Coca-Cola to terminate the contract after the bottlers completed the hard work of building a national network. In the end, the bottlers did not need to be overly concerned. Their attorney, John Sibley, recorded his impression of the oral arguments:

Coca-Cola Executive Committee," 15 December 1919; 19 January, 15 March 1920 (from court records), Mark Pendergrast Papers.

[20] H. H. Ward to John A. Sibley, 4 December 1920, "Appendix," 7–10, *Coca-Cola Bottling Co. of Elizabethtown, Inc. v. Coca-Cola Co.*, No. 81-48 MMS, United States District Court for the District of Delaware, National Archives and Records Administration, Philadelphia, Pennsylvania.

> The indications are certainly very favorable. In fact the Court almost affirmed Judge Morris's opinion from the bench. The presiding justice indicated in emphatic language that he did not see how it would be possible to construe the Whitehead and Thomas contract of 1899 in such a way that would give to the Coca-Cola Company the right to terminate it whenever they pleased so as to practically destroy the investment of the bottlers. At the close of the hearing and after court had adjourned, the presiding judge called the attorneys up before the bar and suggested to them that there was really nothing between the parties except the question of price and as the attorneys on both sides had indicated that the one side would be willing to pay and the other would be willing to accept a price which would be reasonably profitable to the manufacturer, they ought to try to get together and agree on a price and save the damage to the business which would result from the continuance of the litigation.

With this encouragement, Harold Hirsch, for the company, approached Sibley and indicated he would recommend the appointment of a special master to determine a price. Hirsch also suggested that because of their past failures, Bradley and Rainwater should resign as negotiators. Sibley believed this prospect was "far better" than any court judgment.[21]

Hirsch returned to Atlanta to a special meeting of the Coca-Cola board of directors. After more than a year of trying to eliminate the parent bottlers by litigation, it was now clear that the courts were not going to go along with the plan. Candler, Bradley, D'Arcy, Dobbs, Hirsch, Woodruff, Stetson, and Callaway listened to a presentation by Hirsch and resolved to seek a settlement. The board appointed Stetson, D'Arcy, and Candler to negotiate with the bottlers. It is clear, however, that Stetson was the point

---

[21] John Sibley to Crawford Johnson, 6 May 1921; H. H. Ward to John Sibley, 6 April 1921, "Appendix," 103–108, 111–13, *Coca-Cola Bottling Co. of Elizabethtown, Inc. v. Coca-Cola Co.*, No. 81-48 MMS, United States District Court for the District of Delaware, National Archives and Records Administration.

man. D'Arcy and Candler had little influence with either Woodruff or the New York bankers.[22]

Stetson promptly informed the bottlers that "he has been vested with full authority on behalf of The Coca-Cola Company to negotiate with the authorized representatives of the bottling companies," and that he desired a conference as soon as possible. The bottlers appointed attorney Jack Spalding to lead their side. In Atlantic City, Stetson, Candler, and Hirsch appeared for the company, while Spalding, Hunter, Rainwater, and Crawford Johnson represented the bottlers. Over the next two weeks the men worked out a settlement, and Stetson and Spalding signed a formal memorandum of agreement on 18 June 1921.[23]

The memorandum resolved all key differences. Stetson and Spalding agreed the contractual relationship would be "perpetual." They set a price per gallon for sales from the company to the parent bottlers, to be adjusted depending the costs of sugar and syrup production. Future sugar prices would be calculated on a quarterly basis, a practical choice despite the fact that such prices fluctuated daily. A price for syrup sold by the parent bottlers to the actual bottlers was also established. Any future disputes would be arbitrated, and the company got the all-important right to prosecute and defend all trademark matters without prejudice to the bottlers.[24]

On 6 July 1921, the companies signed a new contract incorporating the terms worked out by Stetson and Spalding. Three weeks later, at a meeting of Coca-Cola Company directors, the board officially "ratified and affirmed" the contract. The bottler litigation ended in early October, after

---

[22] *National Bottlers' Gazette*, 15 July 1921; *Atlanta Constitution*, 27 June 1921; Jack Spalding to Crawford Johnson, 30 May 1921; "Memorandum," 16 June 1921, Mark Pendergrast Papers; John Sibley to Crawford Johnson, 26 May 1921; John Sibley to Jack Spalding, 26 May 1921; Jack Spalding to J. T. Lupton, 27 May 1921, "Appendix"; "Plaintiff's Trial Brief," 155, *Coca-Cola Bottling Co. of Elizabethtown, Inc. v. Coca-Cola Co.*, No. 81-48 MMS, United States District Court for the District of Delaware, National Archives and Records Administration.

[23] Ibid.

[24] "Appendix," 122–31, *Coca-Cola Bottling Co. of Elizabethtown, Inc. v. Coca-Cola Co.*, No. 81-48 MMS, United States District Court for the District of Delaware, National Archives and Records Administration.

formal judicial recognition of the settlement. In the end, both sides achieved positive results: the bottlers got the coveted perpetual contract and the company received a mechanism for profitable syrup sales.[25]

The bottler litigation of 1920–1921 represents more than an ordinary moment of turmoil in the history of Coca-Cola. Viewed from the perspective of the financial reordering that preceded it, it sheds light on the character of banker control as well as Stetson's understanding of relationship banking.

First, the lawsuit demonstrated the aggressiveness of the new board members, especially Woodruff, Stetson, Bradley, and Thayer, all of whom were bankers, not soft drink executives. Often meeting in Guaranty's building near Wall Street, far from the company's operations in Georgia, they took the bold step of trying to throw off the shackles of the old bottler contract. Unlike Dobbs, they lacked personal reasons for keeping the 1899 agreement in effect. Yet their decision proved to be a mistake. The federal court repudiated the "at will" legal argument of the company, giving the bottlers a perpetual contract on a silver platter.

Second, the litigation was simply one of several examples of the inexperience of the banker-dominated board in dealing with beverage issues. The decision to buy high-priced sugar nearly destroyed the company. Competitors, not saddled with expensive sugar, undersold Coca-Cola. The stock price of the company fell below thirty dollars in 1920, a loss of more than a fourth of the 1919 sale price.

Third, and more happily for the company, the bottler settlement showed that the new leadership was willing to learn from its mistakes and could change directions. When it became clear that they could not force out the bottling companies, compromise on good terms was possible. That is what Stetson and Spalding accomplished in 1921.[26]

---

[25] Ibid.

[26] Predictably, the 1921 contract did not produce "perpetual" harmony. Even in the 1980s and 1990s a protracted series of disputes developed between the company and the actual bottlers over their relationship. See, e.g., *Coca-Cola Bottling Co. of Elizabethtown v. Coca-Cola Co.*, 988 F.2d 386 (3d Cir. 1993); *Coca-Cola Bottling Co. of Shreveport v. Coca-Cola Co.*, 988 F.2d 414 (3d Cir. 1993); *Coca-Cola Bottling Co. v. Coca-Cola Co.*, 654 F. Supp. 1388 (D. Del. 1986); *Coca-Cola Bottling Co. of*

Finally, Stetson's role as relationship banker during this period was critical. He acted as a Coca-Cola executive and as a Guaranty vice president. In fact, the history of Coca-Cola between 1919 and 1921 was fundamentally shaped by Stetson's leadership. Because of the power inherent in the voting trust, of which Stetson was one of three trustees, the line between bank and client blurred. During the bottler contest Stetson participated actively in executive committee meetings, as voting trustee, and as key settlement negotiator. In fact, John Sibley, Coca-Cola's lawyer, later stated that Stetson deserved credit as the "architect" of the settlement.[27] Stetson also contributed to the discussion of advertising costs. He addressed such management details as eliminating the bottlers, maximizing the syrup price, propping up the stock value, and increasing dividends. Perhaps his negotiator role is most telling. The leading Atlantans on the board, Woodruff, Howard Candler, and Bradley, were not good candidates for achieving compromise with the bottlers, so that job was left to Stetson, the only person with the proper knowledge and personality. He moved compromise forward in a way that advanced the interests of both Guaranty and Coca-Cola.

Ernest Woodruff's Coup

Not long after the bottler settlement Ernest Woodruff was ready to once again test his skill at a corporate takeover. This time he wanted to get rid of the New York bankers, presumably including Stetson. The clock was running on the five-year voting trust, and it was unclear who would control the company when the voting trust expired. Woodruff apparently decided that he and his fellow Atlantans would make a bid for power, in the process usurping any claims of the New York banks. Perhaps the move could have been predicted by Woodruff's indelicate past. But the new ambition reflected much higher levels of gall than the secretive purchase from the Candlers.

Elizabethtown, Inc. v. Coca-Cola Co., 98 F.R.D. 254 (D. Del. 1983); *Coca-Cola Bottling Co. of Elizabethtown, Inc. v. Coca-Cola Co.*, 95 F.R.D. 168 (D. Del. 1982).

[27] John A. Sibley, interview with L. Kenneth Hammond, 3 March 1982, Jack Tarver Library, Special Collections, Mercer University, Macon, Georgia.

The vehicle for Woodruff's planned coup was Coca-Cola International Corporation ("International"), a company he organized on 18 November 1922—without telling his now former New York allies. Woodruff established International as a holding company with 251,000 shares of common stock. The choice of 251,000 signaled its purpose—to take over the functions of the voting trust. Of course, 251,000 is just over half of 500,000, the number of outstanding Coca-Cola common shares controlled by the voting trust. Woodruff's plan was to exchange one share of International stock for every share of Coca-Cola stock surrendered to International. Thus, control of International would mean control of Coca-Cola. Woodruff and W. C. Bradley, a Woodruff supporter in International, already held huge chunks of Coca-Cola stock, certainly more than 100,000 shares. In fact, it is likely that Woodruff and the Trust Company of Georgia together held more than 125,000 shares, or about enough to leverage control of International. Through rather simple manipulation, Woodruff and his friends could dominate Coca-Cola, a company they could not have obtained without Stetson, Guaranty, and the other New York banks. Woodruff was not a mathematician, but he knew enough about numbers to know what constituted a majority.[28]

Woodruff's maneuvering proceeded under the same shroud of secrecy that helped the Candler sale. Accordingly, the scheme would be revealed only when it would be too late for any opposition. That dramatic moment came just over a week after the formation of International, in November 1922. At a Coca-Cola board meeting Woodruff abruptly announced that International controlled a majority of Coca-Cola stock. Of course, this did not in itself alter legal control of the company. Under the voting trust, no shares of common stock, including those exchanged for International shares, currently carried any voting rights. However, at the time of the announcement the voting trustees were Woodruff, Stetson, and Woodruff ally W. C. Bradley. With the announcement, it was clear that the leaders of International, Bradley and Woodruff, controlled the voting trust and Coca-Cola and would be able to maintain this control. Ironically, Guaranty's President Sabin had appointed Bradley to replace Dobbs as the third trustee

[28] *Woodruff v. Commissioner of Internal Revenue*, 46 B.T.A. 727, 728–29 (1942).

when Dobbs resigned from the company. As a result, the ultimate leverage in Woodruff's grand leveraging plan was in the form of one person, Bradley. The deeper effect of International was to settle the question of what would happen after the dissolution of the voting trust. Woodruff, and not the New Yorkers, would determine Coca-Cola's future.[29]

What was the connection between Stetson and International? Coca-Cola historian Frederick Allen has written that the New Yorkers were stunned by the creation of International and that Stetson objected to it. Stetson did not consider himself a "friend" of Ernest Woodruff. Also, he did not agree with some of Woodruff's ideas about Coca-Cola. Yet if Woodruff's goal was to eliminate all New York influence, including Stetson and Guaranty, he failed. Stetson and his bank stayed well-connected to Coca-Cola long after 1922. In the early 1950s Stetson owned more than 14,000 shares of Coca-Cola stock, a large number of which were International shares. He began to acquire these in the early 1920s, when International was created. More important, he was reelected to the Coca-Cola board for more than thirty-five years after Woodruff's bid for control. He was even a member of the Coca-Cola International board in the early 1930s. Unlike other the Manhattan bankers who helped fund the Candler sale, who were quickly replaced in the 1920s, he remained on the Coca-Cola executive committee for decades. It seems Stetson was able to convey to Woodruff that he and his bank—in the early 1920s a major Coca-Cola creditor—could continue to be useful.[30]

Ultimately, Woodruff's scheme seems more a betrayal of the support the New York banks gave him in 1919 than a grand takeover. It is doubtful Wall Street would have expected to continue the same leadership role after the expiration of the voting trust. On the other hand, it is unlikely the New Yorkers would have given Woodruff control over the company on quite the same terms. Stetson himself later gave credit where it was due, describing Ernest Woodruff as the best "trader" he ever knew. Between 1919 and 1922 Woodruff certainly made several good trades in becoming Coca-Cola's master.

---

[29] Allen, *Secret Formula*, 128–29.

[30] Allen, *Secret Formula*, 128–29; *Coca-Cola Annual Report, 1923*; *Coca-Cola Annual Report, 1924*, Box 4, Mark Pendergrast Papers.

The most long-lasting result of International, which eventually provided much of the reason for Stetson's staying power, was Ernest Woodruff's desire to get his son Robert a good job. Robert W. Woodruff was among the shareholders and directors of the newly-created International. Already more than thirty years old in 1922, the younger Woodruff did not enter Coca-Cola history until the board meeting in which Ernest announced the creation of International. Within a few months, in March 1923, Ernest managed Robert's election as Coca-Cola's president. Robert turned out to be a much better business associate for Stetson than Ernest. He was a hard worker and had a penchant for the company's greatest needs, salesmanship and promotion, issues Stetson also understood well. Bob Woodruff and Stetson quickly developed a close business and personal relationship that lasted for more than four decades.

Stetson's first years with Coca-Cola provided substantial challenges in relationship banking. There was the decision to purchase sugar during a time of escalating prices, an enormous mistake. There was disagreement among directors as to many policies, including advertising. Of course there was the long legal battle between the company and the bottlers, with an eventual settlement of the dispute. In late 1922, Ernest Woodruff's Coca-Cola International rearranged the sources of power in the company, leading to Bob Woodruff's presidency. Considered together, Stetson's experiences with Coca-Cola provide an apt illustration of the meaning of relationship banking in the years after World War I.

7

Coca-Cola in the Long Run

After the turmoil of the early 1920s, the key force shaping the relationship between Stetson and both Woodruffs was Coca-Cola's enormous success. Profits grew steadily, allowing the company to pay off its debts and restructure equity. Just before the Depression, Coca-Cola reached a valuation of more than $240 million, an amazing ten-fold increase from 1919. In 1930, retail sales exceeded $170 million. This produced a net profit of $13.5 million, compared to net profits of just over $2 million in the early 1920s. Altogether, by the end of the 1920s the product was sold at more than 120,000 fountains and by more than 800,000 bottler retailers. Coca-Cola boasted that its name appeared on more than 400 million pages of magazine and newspaper ads. The cost of producing this liquid gold, however, stayed small, thanks in part to the cheap labor described in the 1919 sale. As the company explained, "If for any reason [the workers] should leave their jobs there would be no difficulty in securing a competent force to start work the next morning."[1]

All this profit naturally had a dramatic effect on the company's financial structure. During 1925 and 1926 Coca-Cola retired all of the $10 million in preferred stock issued in 1919, effectively ending the Candler connection. In 1927 the company paid a 100 percent dividend on common stock and doubled the number of outstanding shares to 1,000,000. In 1928 it issued as a dividend another 1,000,000 shares, designated Class A cumulative common, to existing shareholders. Of course, International, as

[1] "The Story Behind a Name You Probably See More Than Any Other," The Coca-Cola Company.

holder of 251,000 of the common shares of Coca-Cola in 1922, also benefited from these distributions.[2]

The implications for the fortunate owners of the original 500,000 shares of common issued in 1919 were clear. Such shares, sold for $40 to the public investors, had a market value in 1930 of $200 each. The Class A shares issued in 1928 were worth about $100 each. Put another way, shares offered at $40 per share, multiplied by subsequent stock distributions, had a market value of $300 in 1930—a seven and one-half times return in nine years. As if this was not enough, between 1919 and 1931 Coca-Cola paid more than $91 million in dividends. Obviously the banking needs of such a company were considerably different than they had been ten years earlier, when a slump in sales, the sugar crisis, the trademark lawsuit, and the bottler litigation portended disaster. The old issues of managing debt and declining share prices disappeared in a caffeine-laced flood of profits.[3]

Stetson realized growth did not end a bankers' job, but actually created new relationship opportunities. These included assistance in issuing and registering the kinds of securities just mentioned, a service performed by Guaranty. Stetson also thought that perhaps the company's greatest banking need in the 1920s was merger, a long-time favorite of American financial advisors. The "bigger is better" approach was long taken by J. P. Morgan & Co. toward Guaranty itself and by Guaranty towards its other clients. In any era, the call for "consolidation" and "rationalizing" an industry went to the core of the banker's need to minimize uncertainty and risk. Of course, there was the added benefit of requiring expensive banking services. Indeed, by the 1920s, the push for mergers was among the leading characteristics of Wall Street banking, and Stetson's Guaranty devoted enormous resources to facilitate corporate reorganizations.[4]

---

[2] Ibid.; *Woodruff v. Commissioner of Internal Revenue*, 46 B.T.A. 727, 728–29 (1942); "Statement of Stock Actions," Box 1, Robert W. Woodruff Papers, Manuscript, Archives, and Rare Book Library, Emory University, Atlanta, Georgia.

[3] Ibid.

[4] On the growth of mergers in the 1920s and Wall Street's role in the trend, see Charles R. Geisst, *Deals of the Century: Wall Street, Mergers, and the Making of Modern America* (Hoboken NJ: John Wiley and Sons, 2004) 92–95; Maury Klein, *Rainbow's End: The Crash of 1929* (New York: Oxford University Press, 2001) 152–53.

Stetson and Another Thirst Quencher

In 1925 Stetson, at the urging of company president P. D. Saylor, became a director of Canada Dry Ginger Ale, Inc., a competitor of Coca-Cola. One can assume that Canada Dry was fully aware of Stetson's Coca-Cola record, because his formal connection to the Georgia company had been public information for years. Perhaps with thoughts of merger in the background, no one seemed too concerned about a conflict of interest. Indeed, the relationship was likely viewed as an asset by Canada Dry. What banker would be in a better position to provide advice and assistance, including consolidation, regarding a soft drink business? After his election to the board a business publication reported that the "notable banker" Stetson was "at home in [Canada Dry's] management group."[5]

The broader history of Canada Dry helps illuminate Stetson's work. Canada Dry, like Coca-Cola, originally emerged from the work of a pharmacist, John L. McLaughlin. McLaughlin began manufacturing carbonated water in Toronto, Ontario, in 1890. After several years experimenting with soft drinks, he marketed "McLaughlin's Pale Dry Ginger Ale," which was soon renamed "Canada Dry Pale Dry Ginger Ale." McLaughlin obtained a Canadian trademark in 1907 and sold his drink widely in eastern and western Canada. In 1919 Canada Dry moved into the American market, initially to New York City. The company constructed a plant there in 1922 and organized a local corporate subsidiary. P. D. Saylor became the American general manager.[6]

Like Coca-Cola, Canada Dry boomed during Prohibition. Saylor and J. M. Mathes purchased McLaughlin's company in the 1920s and reformed it as Canada Dry Ginger Ale, Inc., a publicly-traded corporation. Terrific success, despite a pricey twenty-five cents for a twelve-ounce bottle,

---

[5] Frederick Allen III, *Secret Formula: How Brilliant Marketing and Relentless Salesmanship Made Coca-Cola the Best-Known Product in the World* (New York: HarperBusiness, 1994) 184–87; "Canada Dry," *Fortune* (June 1937); "Up From Pop," *Fortune* (August 1931), Mark Pendergrast Papers, Manuscript, Archives, and Rare Book Library, Emory University, Atlanta, Georgia.

[6] Roy W. Moore, *Down From Canada Came Tales of a Wonderful Beverage* (Princeton: Newcomen Society, 1961) 9–13.

followed an ambitious national marketing campaign. Large new plants appeared in New York, Chicago, and Los Angeles.[7]

Unlike Coca-Cola, however, the Depression hurt Canada Dry. One reason was the lack of local bottlers. The low number of bottlers raised transportation costs and reduced profits. Sales dropped dramatically, forcing a new and dramatically different strategy. With the end of Prohibition in 1933, that strategy was alcohol. Key brands—including Johnny Walker Scotch Whiskey—became part of the Canada Dry beverage family. As for soft drinks, the aggressive solution to the problem of high transportation costs, which meant shipping product from New York to Miami or from Chicago to Houston, was to build plants in as many markets as possible. This evolved into a full-blown franchise system that resembled Coca-Cola's, in which the company supplied syrup and technical advice while a local franchisee owned the bottling facility and produced soft drinks. In 1934, Canada Dry's national market share of soft drinks was a respectable six million cases of the 168 million total.[8]

As a director from 1925 to 1941 Stetson participated in practically all of these developments. Only five men served on Canada Dry's board for the entire period—Stetson, Saylor, Mathes, Carleton Palmer, and Charles S. Munson. Palmer was president of E. R. Squibb & Son, while Munson was an officer with the Air Reduction Company, Inc., which supplied carbon dioxide for carbonated drinks. In addition to Stetson's board work, Guaranty was transfer agent for Canada Dry's common and preferred stock into the 1950s. Between 1928 and 1941 Canada Dry's assets increased dramatically, from $7.7 million to $16.1 million.[9]

Perhaps Stetson's greatest contribution was his role in a 1934 management shake-up, a move caused by the shrinking sales and profits of the early 1930s. Stetson suggested that the company hire Roy W. Moore, at the time a Guaranty vice president. Not by coincidence, Moore had been

---

[7] Ibid., 13–14.

[8] Ibid., 14–21.

[9] Canada Dry Ginger Ale, Inc., *Annual Report* (New York: Canada Dry Ginger Ale, Inc., 1929) 5–6, 12; Canada Dry Ginger Ale, Inc., *Annual Report* (New York: Canada Dry Ginger Ale, Inc., 1941); Canada Dry Ginger Ale, Inc., *Annual Report* (New York: Canada Dry Ginger Ale, Inc., 1936).

brought to Guaranty by Stetson in 1929 and was a Macon, Georgia, native as well as related to Stetson through Stetson's first wife. Moore graduated from Harvard Law School in 1915 and practiced law in Macon during the 1920s. Like Stetson, Moore made a mark as a young man in the smaller Georgia city and was lured to New York. On Stetson's recommendation, he became president of Canada Dry in 1935 and remained head of the company for the next twenty-five years. Moore expanded the number of company-owned and franchised bottling plants. He also cut the price of smaller bottles of Canada Dry products to five cents in order to compete with Coca-Cola and other drinks. Moore even took the company into the cola market.[10]

Because of his connection to both soft drink makers, Stetson was in an ideal position to promote a merger between Canada Dry and Coca-Cola. The merger idea seems to have come from Stetson's old partner in the Coca-Cola acquisition, Ernest Woodruff. The senior Woodruff came to New York in May 1928 to discuss it with Stetson. A possible financial vehicle for the deal was the sale to Canada Dry of the ever useful Coca-Cola International stock. Ernest's discussions were apparently begun without the consent or knowledge of his son Robert, Coca-Cola's president. Ernest simply informed Stetson that he and other International holders wanted to sell out.[11]

---

[10] Canada Dry Ginger Ale, Inc., *Annual Report* (New York: Canada Dry Ginger Ale, Inc., 1934); Moore, *Down From Canada*, 5–6; Canada Dry Ginger Ale, Inc., *Annual Report* (New York: Canada Dry Ginger Ale, Inc., 1946). Stetson's presence continued in the person of his son, Eugene W. Stetson Jr., initially of Brown Brothers, Harriman & Co., and later of the Chemical Bank. He became a director in 1942 and remained on the board in the 1950s. Canada Dry Ginger Ale, Inc. *Annual Report* (1941); Canada Dry Ginger Ale, Inc., *Annual Report* (New York: Canada Dry Ginger Ale, Inc., 1950). After a series of ownership changes, in 1986 Cadbury Schweppes acquired Canada Dry. See Canada Dry Ginger Ale, Inc., *Annual Report* (1934); Moore, *Down From Canada*, 5–6; Canada Dry Ginger Ale, Inc., *Annual Report* (1946); "Canada Dry: Tales of a Wonderful Beverage," http://www.brandspeoplelove.com/csab/Brands/CanadaDry/CanadaDry/tabid/151/Default.aspx.

[11] Allen, *Secret Formula*, 184–87; "Canada Dry," *Fortune* (June 1937); "Up From Pop," *Fortune* (August 1931), Mark Pendergrast Papers; *New York Times*, 10 May 1928.

Stetson's position was complex and conflicting, a reflection of the typical kinds of overlapping interests common in relationship banking. He was Coca-Cola's banker at Guaranty, an International shareholder, a member of Coca-Cola's seven-person executive committee, a Canada Dry board member, an advisor to Ernest Woodruff, and a friend of Bob Woodruff. Stetson was also a director in the Air Reduction Company, which supplied the carbonation for both Coca-Cola and Canada Dry products. Although the exact terms of the proposed merger are unclear, *Fortune* magazine reported in 1937 that "Coca-Cola [was] cast in what now seems the fantastic role of mergee," presumably because of the proposed sale of International to Canada Dry. In the end, the deal collapsed for unknown reasons. Perhaps the idea of Coca-Cola producing more than Coca-Cola was ahead of its time. Or, perhaps Ernest Woodruff was as difficult a seller as the Candlers. More important for Stetson, the discussions showed that his network of ties throughout the business world had unique value.[12]

Life with Ernest Woodruff

After the failed Canada Dry merger Stetson's work with Ernest Woodruff persisted intermittently until Woodruff's death in 1944. They discussed financial matters, especially securities transactions. Woodruff occasionally brought his son Robert into the dialogue. In 1931, for example, Ernest informed Bob that "Mr. Potter [of Guaranty] and Mr. Stetson are to let me know tomorrow what amount they will advance on the underwriting" of an issue of Class A Coca-Cola stock. Several months later, Ernest told Robert that he had "an interesting talk" with Stetson about the stock. In June 1931, Stetson sent Ernest a sketch of proposed financing:

[12] Ibid. Stetson resigned as a Canada Dry director in 1941. See William J. William to Eugene W. Stetson, 14 February 1941, Box 1, Eugene W. Stetson Papers, Jack Tarver Library, Special Collections, Mercer University, Macon, Georgia.

> Call 25% of the present outstanding Class "A" $5. stock at $52.50 per share. This would aggregate in dollars, approximately $10,000,000.
>
> Give the privilege of exchange to the old stockholder, one new $2. Class "B" stock callable at 50; have the new Class "B" stock convertible at any time within twelve months into five year 4% debentures.
>
> The Coca Cola Company should retain the privilege of giving extension of conversion privilege into debentures. Have debentures callable at option of company on ninety days notice at par. Make debentures mature July 1, 1936.
>
> After transaction is completed, make a survey of same and repeat according to the then prevailing conditions. Under this plan, there is no need for any underwriting fee to be paid.

This particular proposal was not adopted. Nonetheless, it demonstrated the detailed nature of Stetson's continuing work with the senior Woodruff, as well as Stetson's efforts to stress the financial benefits of continuing the banking relationship with Guaranty.[13]

Ernest was never an easy client. His imperious manner and suspicious nature were on full display in another matter involving Coca-Cola stock. Woodruff aggressively sought to keep company stock among friends by controlling certain sales. In March 1933, in the midst of the Depression, a major shareholder was in rather desperate straits, with loans on shares. Woodruff told Tom Glenn, a Coca-Cola board member, that he did not want the shareholder to part with the stock at its current low price, and that the Trust Company of Georgia would cover the shareholder's loans.

---

[13]Ernest Woodruff to Robert W. Woodruff, 7 August, 5 October 1931; 8 May 1935; Eugene W. Stetson to Ernest Woodruff, 1 June 1931; Ernest Woodruff to Emory Flinn, 2 November 1932, Robert W. Woodruff Papers. In 1935 the company split its 1,000,000 common shares into 4,000,000 shares. International then received three additional shares for each Coca-Cola common. "List of Stock Transactions, 1919–1937," Box 1, Robert W. Woodruff Papers.

Woodruff perceived that a large stock sale at low prices might undermine the confidence of stockholders.[14]

Woodruff later learned that just after his conversation with Stetson, Charles Hayden, a New York banker who served on the Coca-Cola board, placed orders to buy the distressed investor's 600 shares. Woodruff saw this as a betrayal by Stetson and Hayden, who supposedly were working together to take advantage of the low price for the valuable stock and then saddle his Trust Company with the loan. Woodruff lamented, "God help the fellow who places any dependence in a cock-eyed man," referring to Stetson. He concluded: "This, and other events, make me rather inclined to favor substituting [two bottling company owners] for Stetson's as well as Hayden's place" on the board of directors. The validity of Woodruff's suspicions of unfair dealing is open to question, but the episode shows his generally low opinion of others and his lingering desire to rid the company of northeastern financiers.[15]

Another incident demonstrates Woodruff's sometimes tense relationship with Stetson. As a conscientious relationship banker, Stetson always sent Christmas greetings to valued clients. They were short notes, mailed under a Guaranty letterhead. On 19 December 1932, he addressed such a card to Ernest Woodruff. At the time, of course, the nation was in the depths of a massive economic downturn, waiting anxiously to see what the newly-elected Franklin Roosevelt would do about the crisis. Stetson's flowery note tried to reflect the uncertainty of the moment:

> One of the lessons which adversity is forcing upon us is the essential unity of the human family.... We discover daily the interrelationships that exist between us all as individuals and peoples. If, out of this depression, we gain greater understanding, greater sympathy, a greater sense of responsibility for each other, and a truer sense of the values in life and all of its associations, we shall not have suffered in vain.... In this Christmas season above all other we should

---

[14]Ernest Woodruff to T. K. Glenn, 17 March 1933, Robert W. Woodruff Papers.

[15]Ibid.

> feel that greater unity of spirit which brings us closer in joy or sorrow, in gain or loss.[16]

Woodruff, a crusty veteran of countless downturns, corporate warfare, foreclosures, and financial scraps, could not take such sugary stuff from Wall Street without a rejoinder: "You know, Gene, there is an old saying—'Charity begins at home,' and I am just wondering if, while you are broadcasting such Christian doctrine among your friends, you have overlooked using your good offices with your associates at 140 Broadway, in an effort to instill in them 'greater understanding, greater sympathy, a greater sense of responsibility for each other, and a truer sense of values in life and all of its associations,' and I might add, a greater sympathy for their patrons during these strenuous times." To keep it friendly, Woodruff added that Stetson should not take his comments "too seriously," and to remember "the pleasure that it has afforded me to value you among my best and most loyal friends." He signed it, "Sincerely yours, (still out of debt)."[17]

The exchange captured the mixture of favorable and unfavorable feelings that characterized the twenty-five-year-long relationship between Stetson and Ernest Woodruff. On the favorable side, Stetson and Guaranty helped Woodruff and his Trust Company of Georgia acquire Coca-Cola in 1919. He continued to act as a financial advisor, banker, and director to the company for the remainder of Ernest's life. He respected the elder Woodruff. On the other hand, Ernest was not interested in being captive to a Wall Street bank or anyone else. He was never hesitant to forcefully make that point to Stetson. In 1944, Stetson dutifully attended Ernest's funeral, probably with a sense of relief.

Bob Woodruff and White Motor Company

Stetson's relationship with Bob Woodruff was always friendlier. There is no evidence the younger Woodruff knew Stetson before Stetson's

---

[16] Eugene W. Stetson to Ernest Woodruff, 19 December 1932, Robert W. Woodruff Papers.

[17] Ernest Woodruff to Eugene W. Stetson, 23 December 1932, Robert W. Woodruff Papers.

participation in the 1919 sale, although they both grew up in Georgia. Stetson was about eight years older than Bob. The two developed a close business relationship during the mid–1920s, when they began to discuss business and personal matters frequently. Other than Averell Harriman, no client had a greater impact on Stetson's career than Bob Woodruff.

A compelling example of Stetson's early relationship with the younger Woodruff was his brief connection with Cleveland's White Mo-tor Company. At Bob's behest, Stetson was elected to the White board in 1929 and served there for just over two years. Guaranty had been the lender of choice for White during the 1920s, so there was already an existing connection between Stetson's bank and the truck maker. More important was that Woodruff needed a financial ally on the board in troubled times.[18]

Woodruff commenced his relationship with White in 1912, when he purchased White trucks for his father's Atlantic Ice & Coal Company. At the time, the younger Woodruff was in his early twenties. Walter White, the company president, was impressed with the deal and offered Woodruff a sales job. The opportunity deeply affected Woodruff's life. Coming at the end of an extended period of youthful drifting, Bob Woodruff emerged as a hero salesman, convincing both businessmen and the government to buy White trucks in large numbers. One of the most important of those businessmen was his father, who eventually purchased thousands for Coca-Cola. In 1921 Woodruff became a vice president and director with White. In turn, in 1923 Walter White was elected to the Coca-Cola board. Four years later, Woodruff joined White's executive committee. Another significant personality in the White orbit in the 1920s was Bill Potter, Charles Sabin's successor as president of Guaranty. Potter acquired a large

[18] "Average Monthly Bank Balances—Eastern Banks [1932]," John A. Sibley Papers, Manuscript, Archives, and Rare Book Library, Emory University, Atlanta, Georgia.

plantation in South Georgia and White and Woodruff also bought large tracts of land there.[19]

In September 1929 Walter White died in an automobile accident, and the board selected Woodruff as his replacement. Of course, Woodruff was already quite occupied as president of Coca-Cola, but he was induced to take the second presidency by loyalty to the company, his substantial stock holdings in White, and fond memories of his suddenly departed friend. After a year of seemingly constant travel between Cleveland and Atlanta, in late 1930 Woodruff helped choose Aston Bean as White's new president. Woodruff remained on the board, but only briefly.[20]

During this period of interrupted leadership and deepening economic depression Woodruff called Stetson to White's board. The 1920s had been good years for the company. In 1928 and 1929 profits neared $3 million, with assets at more than $50 million. Then, a slide began. In 1930 White lost $83,000; the next year it lost almost $3 million. Assets tumbled to $43 million. Woodruff and the board, including Stetson, believed a sale was in order. White had substantial cash left from the heady 1920s, making it an attractive buy. The board consummated a deal in 1932 to sell White to Studebaker, to be held as a subsidiary, for cash, notes, and Studebaker shares. Within a few months Stetson was no longer on White's board, and Woodruff had agreed to only a minor and temporary role as a Studebaker director. This may have been a somewhat happy end to Stetson's automotive career, but unfortunately it was not.[21]

Studebaker quickly developed serious debt problems. It fell into receivership, a legal process that allows a debtor's property to be reorganized without bankruptcy and liquidation, not long after the White

---

19 Allen, *Secret Formula*, 146–47, 156, 178–79, 187–88; Rosemary S. Hritsko, "The White Motor Story" (Ph.D. dissertation, University of Akron, 1988) 92, 94, 103–107.

20 Allen, *Secret Formula*, 190; Hritsko, "The White Motor Story," 109.

21 Hritsko, "The White Motor Story," 110–19; White Motor Corporation, *Annual Report* (Cleveland: White Motor Corp., 1928); White Motor Corporation, *Annual Report* (Cleveland: White Motor Corp., 1929); White Motor Corporation, *Annual Report* (Cleveland: White Motor Corp., 1930); White Motor Corporation, *Annual Report* (Cleveland: White Motor Corp., 1931); White Motor Corporation, *Annual Report* (Cleveland: White Motor Corp., 1932).

purchase, leaving White's future uncertain. In July 1933, Studebaker's president, Albert Erskine, who had been a strong advocate for the purchase, shot himself. White managed to stay afloat during these bad times, although it lost about $11 million between 1932 and 1935. In 1935, Studebaker sold White. Although continuing to struggle for a time, the company lost another million dollars between 1936 and 1939; White revived with the help of wartime government contracts in the early 1940s. Sales in 1935 of about $20 million grew to more than $156 million in 1943. The transformation led to a new and profitable era in the company's history.[22]

Stetson's role as a White board member between 1929 and 1932 was primarily to serve as advisor to Woodruff and facilitator of the Studebaker sale. When Walter White died, the key shareholders of White Motor were Woodruff, White's heirs, and Walter Teagle of Rockefeller's Standard Oil. None of these persons was interested in carrying on White's legacy. Woodruff continued to trust Stetson and relied on his counsel under such stressful circumstances. From Stetson's perspective, this was a relatively unusual situation. The ethic of relationship banking generally required that he make long-term commitments to a business when he agreed to serve as a director. The fact that he did not in this instance signals that the arrangement was essentially a personal service to Woodruff—the real long-term relationship.

Like many other similar situations in the Depression, such favors often came with a legal price tag. For Stetson, this included being sued along with Woodruff and other White directors and officers in both Ohio and New

---

[22] Hritsko, "The White Motor Story," 115–19, 125; White Motor Corporation, *Annual Report* (Cleveland: White Motor Corp., 1933); White Motor Corporation, *Annual Report* (Cleveland: White Motor Corp., 1934); White Motor Corporation, *Annual Report* (Cleveland: White Motor Corp., 1935); White Motor Corporation, *Annual Report* (Cleveland: White Motor Corp., 1936); White Motor Corporation, *Annual Report* (Cleveland: White Motor Corp., 1937); White Motor Corporation, *Annual Report* (Cleveland: White Motor Corp., 1938); White Motor Corporation, *Annual Report* (Cleveland: White Motor Corp., 1939); White Motor Corporation, *Annual Report* (Cleveland: White Motor Corp., 1940); White Motor Corporation, *Annual Report* (Cleveland: White Motor Corp., 1941); White Motor Corporation, *Annual Report* (Cleveland: White Motor Corp., 1943).

York courts by disgruntled White shareholders. Both suits complained about the sale to Studebaker, particularly the distribution of some 15,000 shares of White treasury stock to White's executive employees as part of the deal. They also argued that the sale was unduly favorable to Studebaker. Because Stetson and Teagle were directors on the committee that decided who would get the key employee stock, they were named as defendants.[23]

For Stetson's banking career, the most important aspect of the lawsuits was that they revealed the depth of the relationship between Stetson and Woodruff. Prior to the sale Stetson was consulted on numerous details by Woodruff, Teagle, and Erskine. Stetson made it clear to Woodruff that he would not make any decision on the 15,000 shares of treasury stock without Woodruff's approval. The correspondence between the men during the sale negotiations indicated a trust and friendship that went beyond business transactions. Woodruff, for example, wished Stetson a Merry Christmas with friendly sarcasm: "You've got it coming to you. I'll bend the elbow once or twice to you." Woodruff offered condolences to Stetson when Charles Sabin died in the fall of 1933. Stetson, for his part, did not hesitate to ask Woodruff to schedule Coca-Cola directors' meetings around his trips to Georgia.[24]

The White lawsuits tested this relationship. On 20 October 1933, Woodruff, Stetson, their lawyers, and Teagle's lawyers met in Washington for several hours to discuss the plaintiffs' claims. Stetson was outspoken on a number of legal and strategic issues. By this time a confirmed Morganite, he complained about the Depression-era politics of the case: "I think this is a strike suit and I think the fact that I am connected with [Guaranty] and the fact that Teagle is Teagle and Standard Oil—they are going to make a desperate play to put us in a hole." In response to the plaintiffs' complaints about the sale's fairness, Stetson remarked that some of his colleagues at Guaranty thought that it was Studebaker, not White, that did not get much

[23] A. R. Erskine to The White Motor Company, 13 September 1932, John A. Sibley Papers.

[24] A. R. Erskine to Robert W. Woodruff, 19 November 1932; Eugene W. Stetson to Robert W. Woodruff, 30 November 1930; 13 December 1932; Robert W. Woodruff to Eugene W. Stetson, 8, 20 December 1932; 15 October 1933, John A. Sibley Papers.

from it. This philosophy supported his conclusion that White's shareholders were the primary beneficiaries of the sale and should not be complaining.[25]

The meeting showed how well Stetson and Woodruff worked together. Woodruff said that Studebaker's Erskine had initiated merger discussions. He traveled to New York with Erskine to discuss the possibility with Stetson as soon as the offer was on the table. Stetson had agreed "it would be a fine financial and commercial thing for both companies." Woodruff and a few others, including Stetson, came up with the terms of exchange. Before the sale, all of the directors agreed it was a very good arrangement for White.[26]

Stetson detailed the reasons for Studebaker's receivership. Erskine, contrary to his and others' advice, made the mistake of thinking he would get control of White's cash. Erskine promised his company's creditors that with White's money assets he could pay them in full. Although Studebaker obtained almost all of White's shares, the complete integration of the companies fell through, and thus Studebaker did not absorb White's cash. Stetson stated that Guaranty was ready to extend an $8 million letter of credit to Studebaker if other banks agreed. Without the support of its other bankers, however, Studebaker was forced into the receivership by its creditors, and Erskine's self-inflicted demise followed.[27]

At the 20 October 1933 meeting, in front of the lawyers and White executives, Stetson asked Woodruff if despite this unfortunate turn, White shareholders were better off with the receivership. Woodruff agreed they were. Woodruff put the problem in the context of the Depression: "When we consider that everything anybody has done with good intention in the last four years has turned out wrong, this has not turned out too damned

---

[25] Eugene W. Stetson to Robert W. Woodruff, 10, 16 October 1933; "Freeman v. Bean et al., Memorandum of Conference Held at Washington," 20 October 1933, John A. Sibley Papers.

[26] "Freeman v. Bean et al., Memorandum of Conference Held at Washington," 20 October 1933, John A. Sibley Papers.

[27] Ibid.

wrong. I would say that every one's intention in this deal was just as wide open and above board as it is possible for a man's intention to be."[28]

When the discussion turned to the part of the deal that gave a stock bonus to White's executive employees, the lawyers pressed Woodruff. He needed to come up with an explanation as to why the bonus was not really a bribe to get the support of the officers for the sale. Woodruff had difficulty confronting the question, so Stetson jumped in with a flattering defense. Stetson argued the officers' support was unnecessary. Only the large shareholders, like Woodruff and Teagle and the directors, mattered. More bluntly, according to Stetson, "Woodruff can't answer the question like I can because in asking him the question he can't say that his influence controlled the entire board as against the influence of all the other officers." Stetson's bottom line was that "Mr. Woodruff made the deal and my confidence in him would always make me feel that any deal that he made would be an attractive deal because I have been associated with him for 10 or 12 years in another company and that has always been my experience." In approving the sale, the rest of White's leadership had apparently agreed.[29]

Spurred by Stetson's remarks, Woodruff defended the bonus as representative of his management style. Back "in 1925 the people [his father Ernest, primarily] who ran Coca-Cola paid me very little and we had a good year. [At a Coca-Cola board meeting] Gene [Stetson] got up and said: We want to pay Mr. Woodruff $25,000 in appreciation, etc., and pass[ed] a lot of resolutions and [gave] them to me, and I stood up immediately and said: I will not accept that unless you vote $75,000 more to be distributed among the other officers." By analogy, in White's situation the White sales manager was making $15,000 a year while his equal at Studebaker was making $100,000. Those considerations put it in Woodruff's mind that the White employees "ought to have a break." Stetson added there was no hint of self-dealing because Woodruff took no fee for making the deal.[30]

---

[28] Ibid.
[29] Ibid.
[30] Ibid.

The day-long meeting demonstrated Stetson's relationship banking at work. Woodruff had called his friend Stetson to help provide financial advice for White. Stetson responded with the kind of knowledge and tact that had earned Woodruff's confidence in the first place. In the final analysis Stetson's confidence in Woodruff's ability to run a profitable business defined the banker's role. Both men were adept at the personal, political, legal, and business implications of corporate leadership. This did not prevent them from making mistakes. But it allowed a sharing of expertise in complex and ever changing business conditions.

As for the lawsuits, after a lengthy period of legal wrangling both cases ended without much drama. The parties settled the Ohio proceeding and the Court of Appeals dismissed the New York case on a procedural point. Neither Woodruff nor Stetson had to test their conception of the White sale on the witness stand.[31]

Friendship

As the years passed the Woodruff-Stetson relationship extended to include an ever widening range of issues. During the 1930s, Stetson warned Woodruff that President Franklin Roosevelt's polices would lead to massive inflation. He urged Woodruff to buy sugar at the current low prices and send his cash out of the country, preferably to Canada or Britain. Stetson also kept up with legislation relevant to Coca-Cola, such as the 1934 Jones-Costigan bill, which paid bounties to United States sugar producers and restricted sugar imports. The men discussed the appointment of a state judge in Georgia. Stetson frequently saw Woodruff at Coca-Cola board meetings, although he apparently did not believe his own presence was always necessary. After missing one meeting, he wrote: "I know you will forgive me as I have a pretty good record of being with you whenever you really need me." Woodruff's personal money matters were also a frequent topic of discussion. Woodruff informed Stetson in November 1934 that he

---

[31] James H. Hayes to Walter C. Teagle, 30 October 1934, John A. Sibley Papers; *Freeman v. Bean*, 266 N.Y. 657 (1935).

did not owe Guaranty anything for the first time in years. Still, he thought he might like to become a borrower again.[32]

In the 1930s and 1940s Stetson and Woodruff developed a deep friendship. In 1935 Stetson asked Woodruff for an autographed photograph, something he requested of only four or five others. Stetson expressed an interest in buying Coca-Cola bottling facilities for family members. He invited Woodruff to join the Jekyll Island Club, an elite group who owned the coastal Georgia island and used it as a winter retreat. Woodruff accepted but was never an active member. In 1936, Stetson sent Woodruff a copy of Margaret Mitchell's new novel, *Gone with the Wind*, which he highly recommended. Not known as an avid reader, Woodruff politely thanked Stetson, adding that it was "very interesting so far, but it's a little long—don't you think"? Three years later, when the novel became a movie, Stetson asked Woodruff if he could get tickets to the Atlanta premier. Stetson invited Woodruff to a celebratory dinner for Averell Harriman in June 1943, and Woodruff attended a dinner in honor of Stetson in 1942. The two men played the obligatory executive game, golf, and Stetson was a frequent guest at Woodruff's Georgia plantation, Ichuaway, where hunting was the dominant sport. In 1941, Stetson gave Woodruff advice about establishing a "philanthropic foundation." Perhaps the best symbol of the relationship was that Stetson's birthday was listed in Woodruff's appointment book, which contained only about thirty-five names, including Bobby Jones the golfer, John Sibley and Hughes Spalding, Coca-Cola attorneys, and his father and wife.[33]

Still, the core of the relationship was always business—especially Coca-Cola business. In the 1940s and 1950s Stetson had a habit of sending

---

[32] Eugene W. Stetson to Robert W. Woodruff, 3 January, 20 March, 12, 16 April, 9 May, 7, 27 July, 14 August 1934; Robert W. Woodruff to Eugene W. Stetson, 8 January, 9 February, 23 May, 10 November 1934; "Memorandum," W. H. Strelow Jr. to Eugene W. Stetson, 9 May 1934, Robert W. Woodruff Papers.

[33] "1941 Appointment Book"; "1942 Appointment Book"; "1947 Appointment Book"; "Pamphlet, Jekyll Island Club, 1938–1939"; M. L. DeZutter to Robert W. Woodruff, 5 October 1938; Eugene W. Stetson to Robert W. Woodruff, 9 January 1935; 19 April, 6 December 1937; 9 November 1939; 4 January, 4 February 1941; 14 May 1943; Robert W. Woodruff to Eugene W. Stetson, 14 January, 19 July, 7 November 1935, Robert W. Woodruff Papers.

Woodruff reports from New York that analyzed the prospects of Coca-Cola prepared by Harold Stanley, the former Guaranty employee and then president of Morgan Stanley. On occasion he passed along information about the competition, including Canada Dry, despite his former connection to that company. The intertwining of Woodruff, Coca-Cola, and Stetson's Guaranty was officially confirmed in 1945, when Woodruff agreed to become a member of Guaranty's board. At the time, Stetson was its chairman. For his part, Woodruff was "very pleased to be a little more closely associated with [Bill] Potter, Stetson, et al. at the Guaranty Trust Company."[34]

In addition, Coca-Cola owned a large portion of the Air Reduction Company, for which Stetson was a long-time executive committee member. The interconnections extended further. Woodruff had a substantial personal account at Guaranty and Stetson was a board member of the Coca-Cola Bottling Company of Boston, a company subsidiary. In all these relations a large part of Stetson's appeal to Woodruff must have been his unflagging loyalty. Stetson eagerly took on the role of company advocate at large. He solicited business for Coca-Cola from his many contacts, such as railroad companies. He was on the lookout for trademark violations, at one point warning Woodruff that Jello might introduce a cola-flavored gelatin. When Coca-Cola lost legal disputes involving competitors Nehi and Pepsi, an empathetic Stetson told Woodruff they would have to "take it on the chin." After he bumped into an attorney for Pepsi in a New York subway he bothered to send Woodruff a note about their conversation. All this was the essential stuff of relationship banking.[35]

---

[34] Eugene W. Stetson to Robert W. Woodruff, 18 June, 6 October 1936; 4 June, 22 November 1937; 19 October 1938; 14 August 1939; 9 May, 31 July 1940; 4 January, 22 July, 4 December 1941; 2 February, 21 April 1942; 9 September 1943; "Memorandum to Robert W. Woodruff," 16 July 1945; John Sibley to Robert W. Woodruff, 25 April 1940; William C. Potter to Robert W. Woodruff, 4 June 1944; Robert W. Woodruff to William C. Potter, 19 April 1944; Robert W. Woodruff to Richard Tift, 27 July 1945, Robert W. Woodruff Papers.

[35] Ibid.

More Opportunities

Three matters in which Stetson took a special interest in the 1940s and 1950s further illustrate the broad scope of his relationship with Coca-Cola. They include work for the Coca-Cola board of directors, a trademark dispute against Life Savers, and the company's hiring of Democratic Party leader James Farley.

First, Stetson participated in several special projects as a board member. For example, he was interested in employee compensation, including benefits. Guaranty was frequently an administrator of pension plans for client corporations. At various times Stetson was chairman of Coca-Cola's salary committee for officers and a member of the committee on employee retirement insurance. In the late 1940s, moreover, Stetson joined in discussions about establishing a pension plan at Coca-Cola and whether Guaranty should be its trustee. Stetson told Bob Woodruff that in 1919, thirty years earlier, in a meeting with Albert Wiggin of Chase and Ernest Woodruff, that Bob's father demanded any "perquisites" of the Coca-Cola sale, presumably including pension administration, should go to the Trust Company of Georgia. Stetson had agreed. With that memory, he felt bound thirty years later to support the appointment of the Trust Company as trustee of Coca-Cola's pension fund, although it cost Guaranty substantial business.[36]

The Life Savers matter is a revealing example of Stetson's interest in company affairs beyond finance. By the late 1930s, Coca-Cola was famous for the aggressive protection of its trademark. Just before World War II, the company engaged in a climatic legal battle with Pepsi, in which the courts were asked to decide whether it controlled the word "cola." While

[36] Edmund W. Pugh to Eugene W. Stetson, 11 August 1955; S. K. Bamers to Robert W. Woodruff, 30 January 1958; Eugene W. Stetson to George T. Adams, 7 March 1940; Robert W. Woodruff to Eugene W. Stetson, 10 February 1948; Eugene W. Stetson to Robert W. Woodruff, 31 March 1931; 2 February 1948, Robert W. Woodruff Papers.

that dispute was pending, a disagreement with Life Savers arose when that company began marketing "Cola Life Savers."[37]

Coca-Cola noticed the cola Life Savers advertising campaign and complained to Life Savers executives. Stetson was brought into the dispute because he knew Edward Noble, the chairman of Life Savers. Once again the chain of networks affecting Stetson's banking was broad, deep, and ever productive of new business. In the early 1930s, Stetson had been associated as a director with Drug, Inc., a holding company that included several drugstore related businesses, including Life Savers.[38]

On 29 May 1940, Harrison Jones of Coca-Cola met with Noble in Washington. Jones articulated the company line: Coca-Cola's value was based on its hard-earned trademark, and Life Savers was stealing that value. Noble replied that the issue had already occurred to him, but that there could not be any customer confusion between "cola" and "Coca-Cola." A subsequent meeting with O. T. Kappes, president of Life Savers, turned out even less successfully. Life Savers was aware of Coca-Cola's current legal battle over the ownership of "cola" and it took the position that the courts would eventually decide "cola" could not be trademarked. Jones tried to shift his company's complaint from legal to ethical grounds—"You are taking a free ride on our goodwill and on our name." Life Savers did not agree. Instead, Life Savers executives simply did "not understand why you Southerners always come up here with all this talk about 'ethics.'" We "are in this thing to make money for ourselves and our stockholders. It is not a question of 'ethics' at all; it is a question of making money and doing what you can to get away with it. It is purely business." Coca-Cola should sue if it had a complaint.[39]

Negotiations continued for months, during which Jones, Stetson, and Woodruff again appealed to Life Savers. Stetson and Woodruff, in particular, tried to use their connections with Noble to advantage. To save

---

[37] "Statement of Harrison Jones, In Re Life Savers," Box 10, Robert W. Woodruff Papers; Jerome H. Spingarn, "Of Coca, Cola, and the Courts," *The Nation* 152 (7 June 1941): 666–68.

[38] "Statement of Harrison Jones, In Re Life Savers," Box 10, Robert W. Woodruff Papers.

[39] Ibid.

face, and recoup some of the early costs of the product, Noble began suggesting that his company needed something like $150,000 to settle the matter. This did not make his inferiors at Life Savers happy. They did not want to get along with Woodruff. Noble, however, eventually conceded the obvious. His company was "riding on [Coca-Cola's] name" and was intentionally trying to match the Coca-Cola flavor.[40]

Initially, Woodruff balked at a payoff: "[I]f you quit this thing, which you ought to do—it ain't right and you know it ain't right—then, in my opinion, it ought, within the next few years, to be worth many times $150,000 to you." Woodruff reiterated the ethics theme to Noble, even getting his friend, former Governor Max Gardner of North Carolina, to let Noble know he was disappointed in Noble's business practices. At a lunch with Stetson, Woodruff, and Noble, Stetson suggested the matter could be resolved if Coca-Cola refunded Life Savers' out of pocket expenses in exchange for dropping the cola candy. Stetson later offered the possibility that Coca-Cola give a license to Life Savers to produce a "cola" product. Ever the proponent of consolidation, Stetson also raised the prospect of a Life Savers-Coca-Cola merger, but this "was discarded by all concerned with a few facetious observations." In July 1940, tired of waiting, Coca-Cola obtained legal advice from John Sibley. According to Sibley, a long-time trademark warrior, Life Savers had "joined the business chislers." Not only had it stolen the word "cola" and the company's flavor, its advertising ripped them off by using a red color and showing a glass pouring a very familiar-looking drink into the shape of a Life Savers.[41]

The dispute dragged on for two more years. In 1942, Life Savers agreed to stop making the cola candy if Coca-Cola purchased all materials related to the product. This was approximately $25,000 worth of labels, wrappers, caffeine, "essential oils," phosphoric acid, and extract of coca

---

[40] "Statement of Harrison Jones, In Re Life Savers," "Jones' Third Conference," "Statement of Mr. Woodruff," "Statement of Mr. Eugene Stetson," Box 10; Eugene W. Stetson to Harrison Jones, 27 August 1940; John Sibley to Robert W. Woodruff, 2 July 1940, Robert W. Woodruff Papers.

[41] Ibid.

leaves. Stetson played a crucial role in the final negotiations, once again using his connections to good effect.[42]

After the settlement a question arose as to whether Stetson should be compensated for his time. Stetson wrote Sibley that he "should accept nothing or something substantial and, frankly, I am quite agreeable either way." Predictably, perhaps, Woodruff and Sibley decided there would be no compensation. According to Sibley, originally Stetson "had made it quite plain…that [he] wanted to render any service [he] could to the Company, and that the question of compensation was quite secondary." Sibley further noted that any payments to a director would be subject to scrutiny, and in this case not paying a director anything would avoid all possible criticism. Stetson's reward consisted of "keen appreciation for the services."[43]

Another example of Stetson's services to Coca-Cola involved the recruitment of James A. Farley as head of the Coca-Cola Export Corporation. The export subsidiary managed the company's overseas operations. Farley, a New Yorker, was in 1940 perhaps the most politically connected man in America. He had just finished seven years as Postmaster General under President Franklin Roosevelt. More importantly, he had chaired the Democratic National Committee since 1932 and managed both of FDR's very successful presidential campaigns. In the late 1930s, when it was not yet clear that Roosevelt would seek a third term, Farley seriously considered his own run for the Presidency. A profitable move to the private sector was also possible. In July 1940 Roosevelt accepted the Democratic nomination for president for a third time and a disapproving Farley resigned his office. Farley entered into employment discussions with the

---

[42] "Memorandum to Mr. R. W. Woodruff, Life Savers Corporation Matter," 7 September 1942; Eugene W. Stetson to John A. Sibley, 3 August 1942; John A. Sibley to Eugene W. Stetson, 22 July, 27 October 1942; Eugene W. Stetson to Robert W. Woodruff, 1, 3 April 1942, Robert W. Woodruff Papers.

[43] Ibid.

Willys-Overland Company in Toledo, a manufacturer of Jeeps. He also considered an ownership stake in the New York Yankees baseball club.[44]

Coca-Cola, however, made its own bid for Farley's services. Farley was an attractive hire because he was well-liked, but also because he was a nationally known Democrat. These qualities were appealing to the southerners who ran the company. Even better, he had separated himself from the more liberal wing of the Democratic Party, which was anathema to Woodruff. On 5 August 1940, Farley met with Woodruff and Cliff Roberts, a New York banker who had Coca-Cola interests in South America. Woodruff gave Farley a lot of advice, including not to sell his name for immediate advantage, that Willys was not likely to become particularly successful, and that the Yankees were simply too expensive. Getting quickly to the point, he offered Farley the job as president of the Export Company at $50,000 a year.[45]

According to Woodruff, Farley was needed right away to straighten some problems with South American franchises. The next day the two met again and this time Farley had his attorney present, while Woodruff brought Stetson. Woodruff again made the sales pitch, telling Farley that he could be a big help in international business. Everyone else chimed in and, according to Farley, "were most generous in their praise of me." Within a few hours the deal was done and Farley joined the Coca-Cola family. The selection was a hit. Former Governor Max Gardner of North Carolina told Farley that he heard the announcement by radio with some blue-collar workers, and they thought it was "a grand thing for the country."[46]

---

[44] Thomas B. Doe to James A. Farley, 5 April 1939; Thomas Gagan to James A. Farley, 9 May 1939; James A. Farley to Claude Bowers, 13 June 1939; 8 February, 3 July 1940; Claude Bowers to James A. Farley, 17 May 1939; W. W. Eubank to James A. Farley, 9 July 1940; Robert Butler to James A. Farley, 5 August 1940, James A. Farley Papers, Library of Congress, Manuscripts Division, Washington, DC.

[45] "Private File," 12, 21, 26 June, 1, 5, 6 August 1940; O. Max Gardner to James A. Farley, 14 August 1940, James A. Farley Papers. In 2007 dollars the Farley offer was the equivalent of approximately $740,000 under a consumer price index measurement. See "Six Ways to Compute the Relative Value of a U.S. Dollar Amount," http://measuringworth.com/calculators/uscompare/.

[46] Ibid.

Although Stetson's role was minor, this was yet another demonstration of the considerable confidence Woodruff placed in his ability. Bringing Stetson, a representative of one of the largest banks in the country, to the Farley meeting confirmed the national and even international status achieved by Coca-Cola in just over twenty years. And when Woodruff wanted assurances that Farley would not move quickly to another position if he left Coca-Cola, Farley promised he had no political ambition except perhaps to run for President in 1944. Such a goal for a mere employee of Coca-Cola would have been laughable in 1919, but it seemed entirely reasonable in 1940.[47]

In fact, a few months after taking the Coca-Cola job, Farley visited FDR in the White House. The Second World War was already underway in Europe and Asia. However, knowing of Farley's new position, the President of the United States took the time to suggest that Coca-Cola might be interested in making a Brazilian drink that combined orange juice and bark. Farley knew quite well that the company was not going to sell anything but Coca-Cola, but he listened politely. Almost off-handedly, Roosevelt then told Farley that Adolf Hitler would be defeated, but that it would take at least a year. Coca-Cola and Hitler were an improbable combination for discussion, but the fact that the Georgia soft drink occupied the attention of an American president in a moment of world crisis was something John Pemberton or Asa Candler never could have imagined. Coca-Cola was truly the national drink.[48]

Closing Acts

Stetson's career with Coca-Cola ended only with his death in July 1959. He remained a board member through the 1950s, although he attended fewer meetings as the years passed. Correspondence with Woodruff, however, continued. They seemed to have discussed the emerging Civil Rights Movement, as Stetson sent Woodruff a newspaper clipping describing Abraham Lincoln's reactionary views on racial equality. Neither southerner seemed to think much change was likely. More

---

[47] "Private File," 5, 6 August 1940; 4 January 1941, James A. Farley Papers.
[48] Ibid.

positively, a grateful Woodruff sent cases of his drink to Stetson's office at Guaranty as well as to Stetson's house in Greens Farms, Connecticut.[49]

There was always time for discussions of Coca-Cola ownership, the topic that brought Stetson and the Woodruffs together in the first place. By 1953 Stetson had placed in trust for his children more than 14,000 shares of Coca-Cola stock, mostly International. The trust was created in the early 1920s and was due to be distributed in 1954. As part of a readjustment of the trust, the beneficiaries planned to dispose of 500 shares of International. In 1953 each share of International could be exchanged for eight shares of Coca-Cola common. Only a few years earlier there were less than 800 International shareholders in the world, so the planned disposal was a significant transaction. Stetson wrote Woodruff about the sale as a courtesy, "to see if you have any suggestions as to where [these shares] should be placed." The letter reflected the strength of a relationship that stretched back over decades. It suggested the potential for financial gain to banker and client, the critical balance of ownership and control, and the necessity of trust. It was an appropriate end to a long and successful episode in relationship banking.[50]

Stetson's dealings with Coca-Cola and the Woodruffs provide a useful case study in twentieth century commercial relationship banking. Stetson was not simply one of the New York bankers who helped arrange the purchase from the Candlers, and Guaranty was not just another New York bank in the sale. For forty years after the deal Stetson and his bank became a constant source of information, advice, and advocacy for the company and its leadership. The range of Stetson's service to Coca-Cola is remarkable: director; long-time member of the executive committee; director of Coca-Cola International; provider of advice on the initial purchase and on later securities issues; negotiator in the initial contract dispute with the bottlers; facilitator of a possible merger with Canada Dry; lender to Robert Woodruff; provider of information and connections about political matters;

---

[49] Eugene W. Stetson to Robert W. Woodruff, 3 June 1957; 18 June 1959; Edmund W. Pugh to Eugene W. Stetson, 11 August 1955; 6 December 1956, Robert W. Woodruff Papers.

[50] Eugene W. Stetson to Robert W. Woodruff, 28 December 1953; 18 June 1959, Robert W. Woodruff Papers.

director of the White Motor Company; watchdog and negotiator on trademark matters; recruiter, in the case of James Farley, of executive talent; personal friend of Robert Woodruff; and all-around promoter and salesman for Coca-Cola.

The relationship's long-term impact on the Woodruffs and Stetson's home state was also impressive. The Stetson-Woodruff connection was immeasurably strengthened and shaped by shared Georgia roots. Woodruff made sure that the fabulous wealth generated by Coca-Cola was not siphoned off to New York. In 1937, he established the Trebor Foundation as a philanthropic device. As already noted, Stetson encouraged Woodruff's philanthropy, and advised him to set up a charitable foundation. In 1979, the Woodruff family gave $105 million in Coca-Cola stock to Emory University, at the time the largest unrestricted gift to an American university. Trebor was renamed the Robert W. Woodruff Foundation after Woodruff's death in 1985, and the foundation focused its charitable efforts on education, health care, services for children, economic development, culture, and the environment. In 2007, the Foundation possessed assets in excess of $2.7 billion and issued almost $100 million in grants.[51]

Another example of Woodruff's philanthropy involved land in south Georgia. In 1929 Woodruff and Walter White of the White Motor Company assembled tracts of land along the Flint River in southwest Georgia to create Ichauway Plantation, a 29,060-acre quail-hunting reserve. This was one of the first and biggest land reserves to be scientifically managed. Ichauway Plantation was also used to study and treat malaria.

---

[51] On the Woodruff Foundation, see "About the Foundation," http://woodruff.org/about_rww.aspx. The impact of this wealth goes well beyond the Woodruff Foundation. For example, Robert Woodruff's brother, George W. Woodruff, is the largest single benefactor of Mercer University's law school as well as the School of Mechanical Engineering at the Georgia Institute of Technology, which is named in his honor. See "The George W. Woodruff School of Mechanical Engineering," http://files.asme.org/ASMEORG/Communities/History/Landmarks/1293.pdf and "Top Twenty Law Schools By Size of Endowment," http://leiterlawschool.typepad.com/leiter/2006/09/top_20_law_scho.html. In 2006 Mercer's law school had the sixteenth largest law school endowment in the United States and the fourth largest in terms of per-student value, behind only Harvard, Yale, and Notre Dame.

Later, it became the Emory University Field Station, jointly administered by the Emory School of Medicine, the United States Public Health Service, and the United States Geological Survey. After Woodruff's death, the board and officers of the Woodruff Foundation established the Joseph W. Jones Ecological Research Center at Ichauway.[52]

Stetson drew enormous personal benefits from his connection to Coca-Cola and the Woodruffs. It was of prime importance to his Guaranty career, as Coca-Cola needed precisely the kind of services the bank aimed to provide. Stetson's participation in the 1919 sale occurred near the beginning of his employment at the bank, when he was under forty years old. The sale further enriched his boss, Charles Sabin, and culminated during the early 1920s, a time when the bank was suffering through the massive loss occasioned by the Mercantile Bank of the Americas disaster. As a result, when Thomas Lamont and other Morgan partners assessed Guaranty in the 1920s, Stetson and his activities with Coca-Cola could not have escaped their notice. Further, the experience led to other banking relations, such as directorships with Canada Dry and the Air Reduction Company. Stetson even tried to bring Coca-Cola and Canada Dry together, a feat that would have drastically changed the American soft drink landscape. What mattered most, however, was that he was committed to the success of Coca-Cola. As a result, Stetson's attitude and performance precisely reflected his ideals of relationship banking.

---

[52] On Ichauway, see "Robert Winship Woodruff: Outdoorsman and Conservationist," http://www.sherpaguides.com/georgia/fire_forest/sidebars/robert_woodruff.html.

8

Cuban Sugar

Gene Stetson enjoyed traveling, especially by train, and trips to Cuba were among his favorites. Beginning in the 1910s, Stetson visited the island to oversee Guaranty's loans in sugar plantations. To get there, he made the long journey by rail from New York to Miami. Then, he continued his trip by riding the famous Florida East Coast Railway on to Key West. Finally, he took the short but often bumpy boat ride to Havana. In the 1930s Stetson flew a seaplane across the water between Miami and Cuba. Missing Key West was no great loss—he never liked the rolling waves, which made him seasick. When Stetson got to Cuba he went on steam locomotives into the heart of the rural countryside to inspect sugar fields. Perhaps the best thing about the trips, besides the great hospitality of his Cuban hosts, was that they could be made in winter, giving welcome escape from northeastern cold.[1]

Stetson plunged into the agricultural commodity financing business almost from the day he stepped through Guaranty's doors. The essentials of the work were familiar, because he had loaned money to cotton farmers in his native South. After 1919, Stetson's board position at Coca-Cola gave him further insights into the pricing and distribution of the great Cuban commodity: sugar.

Guaranty was already in the sugar business before Stetson came to New York. After 1914, the company's special interest was the Cuba Cane Sugar Corporation, among the most important producers on the island. Guaranty ultimately invested millions in this company and its successors. The bank's activity was part of the enormous overseas expansion of American capital to Latin America before and after World War I. Stetson

---

[1] On Henry Flagler's Florida East Coast Railway and the Key West Extension, completed in 1912, see Gregg Turner, *A Short History of Florida Railroads* (Charleston SC: Arcadia Publishing, 2003) 67–80.

got involved when he was assigned the Cuba Cane account, and the job occupied a good bit of his energies during the 1920s and 1930s. Not surprisingly, Stetson applied the same kinds of relationship banking practices that he did in other contexts. But in this case both economics and politics provided a special test. Ultimately, Cuban sugar proved to be Stetson's most frustrating task.

The Cuban Scene

During the 1920s Havana radiated excitement, exuding Caribbean glamour and sophistication. The four hundred year old city was much more cosmopolitan than Miami, a frontier town just then digging itself out of a swamp. Havana had a unique electric railway. The hotels and restaurants were on par with any in Europe and New York, and they attracted sun-seeking tourists from all over the world. Near the city developers created fancy resorts, such as Irénée DuPont's Varadero Beach. Celebrities and the very wealthy came, including such well-known names as Hershey of chocolate fame, Lindbergh, Astor, Vanderbilt, Harriman, and Will Rogers. Visitors could enjoy winter warmth, play golf, gamble, and drink rum—the latter being a major attraction for parched Americans during Prohibition.[2]

The island featured a diverse mix of ethnicities with a continuing history of turmoil and war. Cubans maintained Spanish language and Catholic religious traditions, despite the violent end of Spain's colonial rule in the 1890s. Overall, the population was a combination of African and European peoples, the former having been brought to the country as slaves. Americans had overwhelmingly supported Cuban independence from Spain. In 1898 their government used as an excuse for armed intervention the mysterious explosion of the *USS Maine* while it was anchored in Havana harbor. The Spanish-American War helped end Spanish control in Cuba, but as a practical matter the war also delivered power over the remains of the Spanish empire into American hands. Although Cuba did not become

---

[2] Rosalie Schwartz, "Invasion of the Tourists," in *The Cuba Reader: History, Culture, Politics*, eds. Aviva Chomsky, Barry Carr, and Pamela Marie Smorkaloff (Durham: Duke University Press, 2003) 244–52.

an American possession, the United States reserved the right to interfere, including with force, in Cuban affairs.[3]

The history of Spanish colonialism and the proximity of a rising and powerful neighbor naturally made many Cubans suspicious of the United States. Most patriotic Cubans did not want to see their country become a de facto colony or a mere satellite of America. On the other hand, Cuba needed capital and the Americans had it. And capital always came with strings attached. In the first decades of the twentieth century, United States investments in Cuban sugar grew from about $200 million to more than $1 billion. As a result, American interests, led by banks such as Guaranty, assumed a dominating position in the Cuban economy, a fact much resented by many Cubans. During his years as a sugar financier Stetson dealt directly with these tensions. He necessarily confronted the Cuban wariness and pride, the desire of some Americans to exploit the island's dependence, and his own bank's eagerness for a return on its investments.[4]

Sugar is among the few commodities, ranking with salt, gold, and silver, that has captured and held human imagination throughout history. Sugar was first brought to Europe during the Middle Ages from the Near East. Christopher Columbus took sugar to the New World from Spain, and it was planted throughout the West Indies. Sugar quickly became the linchpin in the molasses-rum-slavery triangle trade that founded many fortunes in Europe and North America. Cuba became the chief Caribbean producer after the 1791 Haitian revolution that ended plantation slavery in that French colony. Slavery was not abolished in Cuba until 1884. By the 1920s Cuba surpassed every country in the world in cane sugar production, providing almost twenty percent of the global total.[5]

---

[3] See generally Richard Gott, *Cuba: A New History* (New Haven: Yale University Press, 2004) 11–12.

[4] Gott, *Cuba*, 113–46; Luis E. Aguilar, *Cuba 1933: Prologue to Revolution* (Ithaca: Cornell University Press, 1972) 43–48 (Stating U.S. interests controlled more than 51 percent of Cuban sugar production in 1919); Humphrey McQueen, *The Essence of Capitalism: The Origins of Our Future* (New York: Black Rose Books, 2003) 297.

[5] Sidney W. Mintz, *Sweetness and Power: The Place of Sugar in Modern History* (New York: Viking Penguin, 1985) 19–73; United States Cuban Sugar Council, *Sugar: Facts and Figures* (New York: United States Cuban Sugar Council, 1948) 19.

Stetson was in a better position than most to understand the social, political, and economic dynamics of sugar. After all, he came from the American South, where cotton had played a similar role in the economy and culture as sugar played in Cuba. As a life-long New South advocate Stetson knew cotton had an ambiguous history in his native Georgia. The product produced wealth, but because of its dominance and vulnerability to price swings it also stunted broader growth and prevented diversification. It rendered a substantial segment of the workforce unskilled and poorly paid. On a more technical level, cotton work taught Stetson the intricacies of financing a commodity using warehouse receipts as well as more sophisticated funding devices. And he understood that government policy could have a decisive effect on prosperity or failure, particularly given the potential for protectionist tariffs.

The Cuban Partner

In Cuba, as elsewhere, the best measure of Stetson's experience was at the personal or relationship level. People, not simply large economic or political forces, were the object of his banking practice. Stetson's most important partner and client in Cuban sugar was Manuel Rionda y Pelledo. Rionda was an outstanding figure in the history of Cuban sugar. He became a leader in its production and trading and was influential in U.S.-Cuban economic and political relations for decades. Eventually known as the "Sugar Baron," in the early twentieth century Rionda was president of the prominent global sugar-trading and financing house Czarnikow-Rionda. The company operated sugar plantations in Cuba, arranged for the marketing and shipment of sugar from Cuba, and delved deeply into the politics of the international sugar trade. Rionda's activities extended over the incredibly long period from the 1870s to the 1940s.[6]

Rionda's family groomed him for leadership. Born in Spain in 1854, he was brought to Cuba at the age of sixteen. His extended family was already well-established as sugar growers and merchants and had outposts in Cuba,

---

[6] An excellent account of Rionda and his family-related businesses is Muriel McAvoy, *Sugar Baron: Manuel Rionda and the Fortunes of Pre-Castro Cuba* (Gainesville: University Press of Florida, 2003).

New York, and elsewhere in the United States. In fact, after a brief stop in Havana, as a young man Rionda was sent to an apprenticeship in Maine. There he was the guest of the owner of a major sugar refinery. He learned the nuts and bolts of sugar trade—shipping it from the plantation to warehouses in Cuba and then to the United States, crushing and refining sugar, and distributing it to buyers.[7]

Manuel Rionda also learned about the shifting politics and economics of sugar. After the American Civil War, increased global competition threatened Cuban profits. European sugar beet production ballooned from twenty percent of world sugar production in 1860 to forty-six percent in 1878. In tonnage, by the latter date Europeans bested Cuba by three times. This growth resulted from government subsidies to growers. Further, when Cuban slavery was abolished in the 1880s, a key "advantage" of the Cuban system, forced labor, evaporated. Naturally, the imposition of a new cost of production changed the economic and social dynamics of Cuban sugar.[8]

Rionda's generation of sugar growers had to address these changes. As for labor, he supported the hacienda system, which had some resemblance to share-cropping in the post-war American South. The hacienda, however, placed greater responsibility on plantation owners to provide medical care and old-age protections in a paternalistic fashion. The transition to even this modified form of free labor was not easy. In the late 1870s and 1880s parts of the Rionda business became insolvent. A combination of labor costs, expensive new machines, and falling sugar prices proved difficult to overcome.[9]

Rionda, however, did not give up. He went to New York in the mid–1880s and became a sugar broker. He was soon well-known in the city and provided an effective connection between Cuban growers and American buyers. In 1896, Rionda received the break of his life: an invitation to join the New York branch of the London sugar brokerage firm, Czarnikow, McDougall & Co., the largest sugar brokerage in the world. Founder Julius Caesar Czarnikow knew a good opportunity when he saw one. After the revolution against Spanish rule in Cuba began in 1895, although there was

---

[7] Ibid., 7–9.

[8] Ibid., 11–12.

[9] Ibid., 11–18.

much destruction of property, including the burning of sugar fields, Czarnikow seized the chance to expand. He wagered that conditions in the European markets would become more favorable to Cuban sugar. To respond to this opportunity his firm needed someone who knew sugar and Cuba, and Rionda was that man. In the ensuing years Rionda proved his worth. On Czarnikow's death in 1909, the business was reorganized as the Czarnikow-Rionda Company, with Rionda as its president.[10]

Enter Guaranty

In the early twentieth century, leading New York banks aggressively sought investment opportunities overseas, and sugar offered an appealing prospect. Guaranty entered the Cuban picture in earnest in 1914, when it agreed to lend Czarnikow-Rionda up to $1 million on the security of sugar deposited in Cuban warehouses. In return, the bank received a commission of three-eighths of one percent on the cash drawn. With Guaranty's money Rionda aimed to finance Cuban planters directly, "which in our opinion is far better than if they made direct use of credits on the United States, in which cases transactions would not have the guarantees of a house like ours [Czarnikow-Rionda] residing in this country."[11]

In 1915, relations between Rionda and Guaranty grew closer with the creation of the Cuba Cane Sugar Corporation. Guaranty president Sabin joined the company's executive committee. Cuba Cane's purpose, with Rionda at its head, was the purchase, consolidation, and increased capitalization of Cuban sugar plantations. Hopefully, this would produce higher production and efficiency. Other New York investors joined the project. Chase, National City, J. P. Morgan, and J. & W. Seligman, the last

---

[10] Ibid., 14–56.

[11] Manuel Rionda to Guaranty Trust Co., 3 December 1914, Braga Brothers Collection, George A. Smothers Libraries, University of Florida, Gainesville, Florida. On Guaranty's expansive foreign trade services, see Guaranty Trust Company of New York, *Banking Service for Foreign Trade* (New York: Guaranty Trust Company of New York, 1919). For a discussion of American investment in Cuba and the Caribbean, see Mira Wilkins, *The Emergence of Multinational Enterprise: American Business Abroad from the Colonial Era to 1914* (New York: Cambridge University Press, 1970) 149–58.

represented by brothers Albert and Frederick Strauss, were all interested in Cuba Cane. Initially, the investment was a winner. The European war disrupted sugar beet production and prices soared. In its first two years of operation, while Europe burned, the company made a net profit of more than $19 million. During the prosperity Cuba Cane owned seventeen sugar mills, 500,000 acres of land, 500 miles of railroad track, 400 locomotives, and 2,500 cane cars.[12]

Stetson became a key figure for Guaranty in financing Cuban sugar. In 1919, for example, Guaranty provided loans to Cuba Cane on informal security of sugar held in company warehouses in Cuba. This was a typical financing arrangement, meant to facilitate both efficient production as well as secure the best market price. Apparently, however, Guaranty feared the arrangement did not provide enough security, so the bank demanded additional warehouse receipts plus a substantial fee to be deposited with the Guaranty-controlled Havana branch of the Mercantile Bank of the Americas. Rionda complained about the burdensome effect of these requirements, and Stetson agreed to forget about the warehouse receipts. This revealed Stetson's faith in Rionda, as fraud—selling sugar that supposedly was being held in a warehouse—was a common concern for lenders. Stetson's confidence in Rionda's integrity contributed mightily toward the development of their business relationship.[13]

This small episode took place in the midst of growing tension between Rionda and his financial backers. In 1918, allegedly high expenses in Cuba reduced profits to $3 million, and the investors, including Guaranty, National City, Frederick Strauss, and Alfred Jeretski, an attorney with New

[12] McAvoy, *Sugar Baron*, 81, 83, 96–98, 112; Manuel Rionda to W. P. Conway, 22 October 1917; 23, 25 July 1918; Manuel Rionda to Charles Sabin, 27 May 1919; Charles Sabin to Manuel Rionda, 17 November 1916; Carl J. Schmidlapp to Manuel Rionda, 15 August 1916, Braga Brothers Collection; "The Braga Brothers Collection," http://www.uflib.ufl.edu/spec/manuscript/Braga/Braga.htm. On the Strausses and Seligman, see Charles R. Geisst, *The Last Partnerships: Inside the Great Wall Street Money Dynasties* (New York: McGraw-Hill, 2001) 61–62.

[13] McAvoy, *Sugar Baron*, 126. The incident revealed a typical function of the Mercantile Bank.

York's Sullivan and Cromwell firm, became uneasy and suspicious. As a result, the Cuba Cane board arranged an investigation led by General George Washington Goethals, the famous chief engineer of the recently completed Panama Canal. Goethals criticized several aspects of the company, including accounting practices and operating efficiency. His investigation led to corporate reorganization. An important figure on the new Cuba Cane board was Charles Hayden of the Boston investment banking firm, Hayden, Stone and Company. Cuba Cane rebounded quickly from this setback, partly because the United States eliminated price controls on sugar following World War I. Net profits for 1919 exceeded $7 million, and the bankers watched approvingly as sugar prices rose in early 1920.[14]

Unfortunately, at this point the bankers' optimism went too far. Anticipated high profits produced more large loans to Cuba Cane, including from Guaranty and National City, based on the mistaken assumption that high prices would continue. The peak in sugar prices occurred in May 1920, when it exceeded 22.5 cents a pound. By summer, cane dropped to 17.25 cents. In October it fell to seven cents, with the next harvest only weeks away. Prices continued their freefall and by the end of 1921 the glut reached such proportions that one million tons of sugar sat unwanted in Cuban warehouses. When sugar prices reached about two cents a pound, they had suffered a ninety percent decline in just a few months. Important sources of the problem included increased duty-free competition from beet sugar in the western American states and from cane in the United States possessions of Puerto Rico, Hawaii, and the Philippines. For the banks, the Cubans' inability to sell their sugar meant massive default rates on loans, the failure of Cuba banks and, as already discussed, the collapse of the Mercantile Bank of the Americas, which almost dragged Guaranty down with it.[15]

---

[14] McAvoy, *Sugar Baron*, 122–23, 132–35, 148.

[15] Ibid., 148–49, 152–53, 163, 171. A study which cites the role of U.S. monetary policy, increased global production, and speculation, among other factors, as causes of the sharp rise and fall of Cuban sugar prices is Kevin Grogan, "Cuba's Dance of the Millions: Examining the Causes and Consequences of Violent Price Fluctuations in the Sugar Market between 1919 and 1920" (M.A. thesis, University of Florida, 2004).

During this time Stetson was thoroughly enmeshed in sugar and its problems and regularly corresponded with Rionda and his associates. For example, he met with Rionda prior to a Cuban trip in late 1920. Rionda liked and respected the banker. Rionda thought Stetson had "returned [from a trip to the plantations] very well impressed with Cuba—he gave me a very good account of his visit showing not only his enthusiasm but his great ability and I was very well impressed with him.... [H]e is a young man that promises well."[16]

Stetson made important decisions during the sugar crisis. Near the beginning of 1921, he learned of the problems some planters were having selling sugar. Naturally, they needed loans to carry them through. Stetson indicated he would be interested in extending five to ten million dollars to Rionda, but only on condition that the security, the sugar in warehouses, could be looked after by dependable individuals. Stetson's response indicated the extremely broad extent of his lending authority for Guaranty as well as his persistent faith in sugar, even as prices reached their nadir.[17]

Yet the Cuban situation demanded more than a mere $10 million. Soon Strauss, Rionda, Stetson, Sabin, and Jeretski put their collective resources together for an even larger $20 million loan. In the spring of 1921, Jeretski drew up a contract that required protection for the security in Cuban warehouses and a high twelve percent rate of interest on the loans. Guaranty, including Stetson personally, worked closely with Strauss, his Seligman firm, and the investment banking partnership of Brown Brothers in New York in handling these and other Cuban credit matters. Nonetheless, the additional effort was still not enough. When the market price of sugar fell well below the cost of production, the banks' security could not carry the debt.[18]

---

[16] Manuel Rionda to Eugene W. Stetson, 25 October 1920; Manuel Rionda to Victor Zevallos, 18 November 1920, Braga Brothers Collection.

[17] Albert Strauss to Manuel Rionda, 14, 25 March 1921, Braga Brothers Collection.

[18] "Re: Loans to Cuban Planters by American Bankers," 16 April 1921; Thatcher A. Brown to Manuel Rionda, 31 October 1921, Braga Brothers Collection; McAvoy, *Sugar Baron*, 171.

Despite the sobering lessons of the 1921 crisis, neither Guaranty, its J P. Morgan supporters, nor Stetson gave up on the possibility for profit Apparently, the recent record was too promising and it was assumed that worldwide demand could only increase. They sold off the glut of cheap sugar as early as the middle of 1922 and sugar prices once again rose to a respectable level. A Morgan partner expert in overseas ventures, Edward Stettinius, who was part of the rehabilitation of Guaranty after the Mercantile Bank collapse and a member of the Guaranty board, traveled to Cuba in February 1922 to learn more about sugar plantations and the prospects of the current crop. Stettinius's visit showed the New York bankers' interest in expanding their mortgages on Cuban plantations.[19]

For most of the 1920s Stetson served as an influential Cuba Cane board member. He was first elected director in 1923. The position allowed him to cultivate a more personal relationship with Rionda in much the same way he became friends with Averell Harriman and Bob Woodruff. Both Stetson and Rionda appreciated the depth of the recent difficulties. Rionda wrote Stetson in early 1923 that he hoped "the hard struggles we all had in the last two years are over." Stetson traveled to Cuba to look over company property. But the visits, usually timed to escape dreary New York in February, were more than business. They allowed Stetson to exercise his ability to develop meaningful relations with business associates. After one inspection, Stetson wrote Rionda, "I always enjoy being in your home as your cordial, generous and sincere hospitality is never exceeded by anyone." Rionda asked Stetson to attend a dinner at his home in New Jersey with Cuban President Gerardo Machado y Morales, and to lunch with Colonel José Tarafa, the president's European delegate. Stetson added Rionda to his list of Christmas note recipients, a meaningful gesture.[20]

---

[19] McAvoy, *Sugar Baron*, 177; Edward H. Green to Manuel Rionda, 3 February 1922; Manuel Rionda to Victor Zevallos, 14 February 1922, Braga Brothers Collection.

[20] Manuel Rionda to Eugene W. Stetson, 9 January 1923; 22 December 1927 Eugene W. Stetson to Manuel Rionda, 5 February 1924; 24 February, 21, 22 December 1925; 22 December 1926; 25 February, 13 April 1927; Memo from Hayden, Strauss, Stetson & Party to Manuel Rionda, 14 February 1927; Manuel Rionda to Charles Hayden, 14 February 1927; Frederick Strauss to Manuel Rionda 21 February, 18 April 1927, Braga Brothers Collection.

Of course, friendliness did not change the fact that the relationship was built around the financial concerns of Rionda's plantations. Most of the dialogue concentrated on the hope for profits, and Rionda frequently discussed plantation operations. He argued for a reduction of the American tariff on sugar with Stetson, Strauss, Hayden, and other directors, obviously hoping they would use their political connections to that end. He discussed the Cuban government's sugar policies. Rionda circulated information about production conditions with Stetson and others. In turn, Stetson consulted with Frederick Strauss and Hayden about the company's affairs. Unfortunately, disappointment was a common theme. Sugar languished behind other opportunities of the decade, as prices remained low.[21]

Beginning in 1929 and lasting into the mid–1930s, Stetson's involvement with the Cuban sugar business reached its peak. This was partly related to the retirement, departure, or death of some of the other New Yorkers connected to Cuba Cane, including Sabin, Albert Strauss, and Jaretski. Just prior to the great global depression, Cuba Cane faced several threats: a huge bond payment of $25 million, due in January 1930; falling sugar prices; and constant short-term financing pressures. In the summer of 1929, the company's directors agreed that the situation was so dire that yet another corporate reorganization was necessary. For his part, Stetson signaled that Guaranty would no longer continue to hand over multimillion dollar loans. He agreed a new start was in order, despite expected wrangling over the new ownership terms.[22]

[21] Manuel Rionda to Eugene W. Stetson, 30 June 1924; 9 May 1927; 26 December 1928; 6 June 1929; Frederick Strauss to Eugene W. Stetson, 13 April 1928; Eugene W. Stetson to Manuel Rionda, 17 April 1928; Manuel Rionda to Charles Hayden, 19 April 1928; Manuel Rionda to Robert I. Barr, 3 February 1922; "Synopsis of Conversation with Mr. Stetson by telephone," 8 July 1929, Braga Brothers Collection; McAvoy, *Sugar Baron*, 182–206.

[22] "Synopsis of Meeting of Cuba Cane Executive Committee," 2 May 1929, Braga Brothers Collection; McAvoy, *Sugar Baron*, 208–13.

Sugar and Depression

On 25 July 1929, a six-man Reorganization Committee, chaired by Charles Hayden and including Rionda and Stetson, informed the company's bondholders that poor conditions required drastic steps. The company could not meet its obligations. If nothing was done, a forced receivership by creditors was inevitable and with it a long and wasteful legal battle. To avoid this, the committee proposed to dissolve Cuba Cane and create a new corporation, with new issues of participating debentures and common stock. Current debt and equity holders were to exchange their securities and a voting trust would be created. The bondholders, however, needed to agree to significant reductions in interest and delayed payments. The Reorganization Committee held out hope that the process would position the securities holders to benefit from a hoped-for increase in prices.[23]

This was delicate work, combining finance and negotiation, but Stetson enjoyed both the technical and personal aspects. Over the ensuing months the reorganization consumed much of his time. There were frequent meetings where important details were considered, such as the collection of outstanding securities, government relations, and marketing of securities. Predictably, however, not all securities holders believed Cuba Cane's failures resulted from unavoidable conditions, such as low prices. They blamed management and went to federal court, seeking to derail the plan. On Christmas Eve, 1929, however, a court held the reorganization proposal satisfactorily protected creditors and stock holders.[24]

Under the now court-approved plan New York banks controlled the new company, renamed Cuban Cane Products. Equitable Trust, Central

---

[23] "To the Holders of the Convertible Debentures and the Preferred and Common Stock of Cuba Cane Sugar Corporation," 25 July 1929, Braga Brothers Collection; McAvoy, *Sugar Baron*, 216. The banks most closely involved in the reorganization were Guaranty, Central Hanover, and Equitable Trust Company. Sullivan and Cromwell provided legal counsel. See "Plan of Reorganization, Cuba Cane Sugar Corporation," 25 July 1929; "Reorganization Agreement, Cuba Cane Sugar Corporation," 25 July 1929, Braga Brothers Collection.

[24] "Meeting of Reorganization Committee," 7 August 1929; Carter M. Braxton to W. E. Bird, 11 October 1929; "Memorandum, *J. Z. Horter Co. v. Cuba Cane Sugar Corp.*," 24 December 1929; "Telephone Conversation between Mr. Barr and Mr. Rionda," 29 July 1929, Braga Brothers Collection.

Hanover, Chemical Bank, Chase, and Guaranty agreed to provide financing. The old Cuba Cane, created with such hopefulness in 1915, was auctioned on 7 February 1930, and purchased by the Reorganization Committee. Although Rionda retained a large ownership, Hayden, Stetson, and the other New Yorkers dominated the board. Their concerns naturally extended to the details of the operation, such as when Stetson inquired at one Reorganization Committee meeting as to the company's cash position. The answer determined the extent of planting in the 1930 season. By the spring of 1930 the transition was largely complete. Cuban Cane Products appeared on the New York Stock Exchange and each Reorganization Committee member, including Stetson, received a payment of $10,000 for his services.[25]

Of course, even after refinancing, fending off disgruntled investors, and creating a new company, 1930 was not the best time to sink money into sugar. The Republicans' new high tariff helped reduce sales of Cuban sugar in the United States by more than fifty percent, or over two million tons, during next two years. With the onset of the Depression, Stetson, as Guaranty's representative for both Cuban Cane Products and Rionda's other plantations, was about to get a bigger "belly full" of the risks of international trade. Throughout this ordeal he usually managed to keep Rionda's confidence. They met and corresponded frequently, discussing both Cuban Cane Products and financing for Rionda's independent Manati and Francisco plantations. Unfortunately, however, Cuban Cane Products lost more than $3 million in its first year. The 1930 crop sold for a horrific 1.3 cents a pound, well below the cost of production.[26]

---

[25] McAvoy, *Sugar Baron*, 218–20; "Synopsis of Special Meetings of Board of Directors," 11 January 1930; Reorganization Committee to Hayden, Stone & Co., et al., 6 February 1930; "Resolution of Reorganization Committee," 10 March 1930; "Memorandum for M. E. Rionda," 16 May 1930, Braga Brothers Collection.

[26] Manuel Rionda to Eugene W. Stetson, 16 March, 8, 13, 23 July 1931; Eugene W. Stetson to Manuel Rionda, 16 March 1931, Braga Brothers Collection; McAvoy, *Sugar Baron*, 223, 229; McQueen, *The Essence of Captialism*, 298.

Among the immediate casualties of these developments was Rionda's Manatí plantation. In 1931, Manatí's accumulated debt and lack of profitability pushed it toward receivership. Rionda naturally opposed this and tried to convince Stetson that conditions at Manatí were improving. He offered to put up a personal guarantee if Stetson and his bank approved another $1 million in loans. In the end, Stetson's decision in regards to the likelihood of profit made the choice. From his vantage, the risk was insurmountable, and Manatí went into receivership.[27]

Cuban Cane Products met the same fate in April 1932, only two years after its hopeful creation. The company's bank loans exceeded $9.5 million, secured by warehouse sugar, mortgages on plantations, and Cuban government bonds. The price of sugar collapsed to the amazing level of less than six-tenths of a penny per pound, an all-time low. At this rate a ton of raw product was worth about twelve dollars. The receivership, as a result, was a stop-gap measure to avoid liquidation by the mortgage holders. Despite limited options, Stetson, Hayden, Rionda, and Guaranty tried to patch holes in the rapidly sinking ship of Cuban sugar.[28]

The lack of prospects was so severe that after twenty years on the island Stetson and Guaranty now looked to a dramatically different strategy—exit. Stetson's visit to Cuba in February 1933 was certainly less happy than his earlier trips. Meeting with Rionda's associates in Havana, with uncharacteristic pessimism he admitted New York management "had failed and was beaten." Cuban Cane Products still owed the bankers almost $5 million, and Stetson's boss, Bill Potter, put full responsibility on Stetson to resolve the matter. The debt to Guaranty alone was $1.25 million, and $800,000 had already been written off. Stetson was ready to:

> admit he was licked, and call it 'quits', and that this would not break the Guaranty. But…he hated to abandon a thing in which he had so long been connected with, and that it was always against his nature to do a thing like this, that he always wanted to go through to the end in

---

[27] Manuel Rionda to Eugene W. Stetson, 3 April 1931; "Synopsis of Conversation with Mr. E. W. Stetson," 4 January 1932, Braga Brothers Collection; McAvoy, *Sugar Baron*, 235.

[28] "Reorganization Plan, Cuba Cane Products, Inc.," 20 December 1934, Braga Brothers Collection; McAvoy, *Sugar Baron*, 235–37.

> anything which he undertook. [He said] they could write off now the $450,000 and make a nuisance of himself and create a lot of difficulties and obstructions, but that this was not the policy of the Guaranty.[29]

Under the circumstances Rionda clutched at straws. He hoped the new Roosevelt administration would lower the tariff on Cuban sugar or even issue a moratorium on sugar import duties. If only Roosevelt would do that, Rionda thought, the effect would be "magical." Otherwise, given the Cubans' dependence on sugar, America faced a social and economic catastrophe on its doorstep.[30]

Sugar's Environment

Stetson's activities in Cuba showed the continuing effect of government policy on the sugar business. Clients and banks' strategies were always challenged by taxes, regulations, and the powers given to banks and bankers by law. The process of entering into agreements for banking services, such as loans, depended on concepts of property and contract law and relied on judicial enforcement. The core legal concept of "security" defined the legal rights of lenders. An especially pertinent example of the centrality of government policy was the charter under which Guaranty, a New York state bank, operated. The charter allowed the bank to engage in an enormous range of activities, including international banking. In the case of Cuban sugar, governments' direct power over foreign trade also played a critical role.

According to the model of free trade, international competition will result in efficiencies such as economies of scale that deliver goods and services at the lowest price and optimal quality. The theory implies that when two economies can produce the same thing but one has a competitive advantage, such as climate, the disadvantaged economy should yield the business to the advantaged economy and specialize where it has its own competitive advantage. From the historian's perspective, however, there are

---

[29] "Conference between Stetson, Sample, Fanjul and Jose B. Rionda, Held at Fanjul's Office," 8 February 1933, Braga Brothers Collection.

[30] McAvoy, *Sugar Baron*, 248.

problems with the model, including the fact the two potential traders may be hostile or at war with one another. The issue of trade relative to national defense particularly affects agriculture. Most countries want a certain level of self-sufficiency in food, and partly as a result farmers often have special political clout for protection.[31]

A more fundamental historical problem with the free trade model is that many businesspeople and political leaders understand that free trade harms their interests. As one observer put it, free trade "is believed only by those who will gain an advantage from it." During much of Stetson's business life the Republican Party, which was dominated by manufacturing interests, strongly opposed free trade. After Reconstruction, the "protective" tariff was its signature cause. The GOP had a point: the massive growth of the economy in the late nineteenth and early twentieth centuries seemed to support the policy. Did not America transform itself from debtor to creditor nation and from rural to industrial nation under a trade policy devoted to protection? Millionaire industrialists and politicians from Andrew Carnegie to President William McKinley made careers out of their opposition to free trade. Northern workers usually went along because they thought the protection ensured jobs. Only rural interests, such as those represented by southern Democrats, saw tariffs as subsidies to northern manufacturing, paid for by consumers. But of course they too were motivated by economic self-interest, not economic theory or altruism. Southern slaveholders, as exporters of cotton, had usually been strong free traders. South Carolina created a crisis by threatening to break from the Union in the 1830s because of high Yankee tariffs. When southerners did secede in 1860–1861, ascendant Republicans raised import duties before they freed any slaves.[32]

Sugar was an important piece of this trade history. By Stetson's day import taxes on sugar had long helped shape national economic history. An

---

[31] See generally Douglas A. Irwin, *Against the Tide: An Intellectual History of Free Trade* (Princeton: Princeton University Press, 1996).

[32] See "Republican Party," and "Democratic Party," in Cynthia Clark Northrup and Elaine C. Prange Turney, eds., *Encyclopedia of Tariffs and Trade in United States History*, 3 vols. (Westport CT: Greenwood Press, 2003) 1: 112–13, 323–24; McQueen, *The Essence of Capitalism*, 7.

object of the first United States tariff, in 1789, was sugar. Sugar had been famously taxed in colonial days, in the form of British duties on molasses. The Molasses Act of 1733, imposing a tax of sixpence per gallon, was widely disliked and disobeyed. In 1764 Parliament adopted the Sugar Act, which purported to reduce the old tax but actually stepped up collection efforts. The King needed money to help pay for the just-concluded French and Indian War, but Americans shouted "no taxation without representation" during protests against the new British sugar tax.[33]

The stream of legislation continued. Between 1789 and Stetson's troubles in Cuba Congress passed many laws involving sugar. The general trend was protectionist or regulatory. In the early 1930s, under Roosevelt's sweeping Agricultural Adjustment Act, there was an unprecedented effort to regulate sugar production, much more direct than earlier attempts. Congress concluded that market failures in the commodity (including, paradoxically, Hoover's reliance on tariffs), supported protections against competition and new encouragement for domestic production. During World War II sugar became the object of stringent government-controlled rationing.[34]

Yet arguments that tariffs or regulations were the only reason for problems in Cuban sugar were wrong. As Stetson and other bankers discovered, Cuban sugar was adversely affected by market competition, especially after 1920. There were very low production costs in Asia. Several cane areas within American control, such as the Philippines, Puerto Rico, Louisiana, and Hawaii, as well as the sugar beet territory in the heartland, possessed great potential for efficient sugar production. Further, the fact that in the early 1920s most of the world's sugar production was protected by tariffs meant sugar producers all over the world faced barriers. The Cubans' special problem was that their production was so great, their domestic market was small, and they lacked the international clout to force other markets open. This powerlessness, from an investment standpoint, contributed to insufficient returns. Every time Cuban growers (and their

[33] See "Sugar," in Northrup and Turney, eds., *Encyclopedia of Tariffs and Trade*, 1: 352–53.

[34] United States Cuban Sugar Council, *Sugar: Facts and Figures*, 49–55; John E. Dalton, *Sugar* (New York: The Macmillan Co., 1937) 74–144.

bankers) spent money on clearing land and improving capital equipment, a combination of tariff changes and market forces could make the investment unable to repay itself. During the 1930s Stetson and his colleagues in Cuban sugar faced multiple factors that made sugar a losing venture. As Stetson learned, the tension between markets and regulation contributed to the complex responsibilities of the relationship banker.[35]

The Cuban President

The Cuban Cane Products receivership placed many burdens on Stetson. For the longer term, he still looked for an exit strategy, believing that the intricacies of a large sugar company could not "be managed by a lot of American Bankers, [sitting] around a table in New York." The immediately pressing need, however, was short-term financing, without which there might not be a 1933 crop. Stetson proposed extending a new $900,000 credit, and prior to his trip to Cuba in February 1933 he called a meeting of the company's creditors and bluntly dictated terms. Chase was in for a 5/11 share, Guaranty for 3/11, Central Hanover for 2/11, and the Bank of Manhattan for 1/11. Thomas Lamont, Morgan's managing partner, attended the meeting. All present agreed the banks should accept the proposed shares of the extension. Yet there was a quid pro quo. In order to harvest the 1933 crop, "for the sake of the people in the plantations," Stetson was willing to endorse additional financial support only if compromises could be worked out on railroad freight charges, which were under the control of the Cuban government. As a result, lobbying over railroad costs became the focus of Stetson's upcoming Cuban visit.[36]

Rionda's nephew, Higinio Fanjul Rionda, president of Czarnikow-Rionda's Havana subsidiary, the Cuba Trading Company, expressed respect for Stetson and his plans. In turn, Stetson trusted Fanjul, who he believed had good ideas about how to improve the sugar business. Fanjul regretted the current state of Cuban Cane Products and blamed Charles Hayden for excessive meddling. Some problems, he thought, could also be traced to

---

[35] Dalton, *Sugar*, 11, 20; McAvoy, *Sugar Baron*, 185.

[36] "Conference between Stetson, Sample, Fanjul and Jose B. Rionda," 8 February 1933, Braga Brothers Collection.

high administrative expenses. Politics were important as well, including the need for the Cuban government to reduce railroad freight rates. The railroad matter was complicated further by the fact that Cuba was in the midst of a violent revolution spurred by pervasive economic hardship. A special favor to foreign banks, such as lower railroad rates, would not be politically popular.[37]

After arriving in Cuba in February 1933, Stetson was told that special interests in the notoriously corrupt Cuban bureaucracy had to be assuaged before the railroad situation could be fixed. Stetson thought otherwise. He rejected proposals by Fanjul about how to make connections in the bureaucracy. The only key decision makers, he thought, were Cuba's president, Gerardo Machado, and his "right hand man," Viriato Gutiérrez Valladon. Stetson felt that only by going to Viriato and Machado would the railroad problem be addressed. He was aware of the political risks of altering railroad rates at such a tempestuous time. He also knew that President Machado was a military dictator who regularly used demonstrations of force and corruption—a regular "Tropical Mussolini."[38]

Stetson's trip culminated when he and Fanjul went to see Viratio. Viratio recognized the importance of Cuban Cane Products, so obtaining this "audience" was not difficult for Stetson. According to Fanjul's recollections, at the meeting Stetson was in a talkative mood, and began the discussion by reminiscing about his earlier days in Cuba and criticizing the American president-elect, Franklin Roosevelt, who "without being well posted on anything…promised a lot of things to everybody, which…he would not be able to accomplish." Stetson then expressed concerns about the long-term viability of Cuba sugar, including doubts that the tariff would be much adjusted in the near future and that the Philippines was not likely to become independent soon. The latter point meant that Filipino sugar would continue to hold its advantaged position in the American market.

[37] Ibid.; McAvoy, *Sugar Baron*, 241–42.

[38] "Conference between Stetson, Sample, Fanjul and Jose B. Rionda," 8 February 1933, Braga Brothers Collection; Gott, *Cuba*, 129.

Stetson compared the dire situation to that facing cotton farmers in his native Georgia.[39]

With his listeners warmed up, Stetson launched into a sales pitch for lower railroad rates. The performance was revealing. Of course, he did not simply ask for lower rates. Instead, he first told Viriato he had been sent to Cuba as the representative of all the creditors of Cuban Cane Products: Chase, Guaranty, Central Hanover, and the Bank of Manhattan. He informed Viriato about Cuban Cane Product's debt and the fact that with the approval of Thomas Lamont, a name well-known in Cuba, the banks had raised an additional $900,000. He portrayed this as a transitional device before foreclosure and reorganization, given the poor prospects. Second, "[H]e had been coming to Cuba for the last sixteen years and that he was a friend of Cuba and realized that if the Company did not grind [sugar in 1933] a lot of suffering would result to the people around the plantations, and that although the Guaranty was not a philanthropic institution, he morally considered himself bound to do something for [the Cuban] people."[40]

Stetson concluded his appeal for lower railroad rates by announcing that he "wanted to cooperate in anything that would tend to improve the general condition of Cuba." Thus, reduced railroad rates were in the interests of both New York and Cuba, a win-win scenario. Hoping to overcome any language barrier, Stetson dramatically smacked his fists together and said the current situation was like two rams butting heads. He wanted President Machado to pull one of the rams, the higher railroad rates, away. With his point made, Stetson did not feel the need to plead further, ending smartly with the appearance of conceding power to the other side. Respectfully, he was willing to leave the railroad freight matter to Machado and Viriato. Stetson asked to see the president, but Viriato indicated that Machado was not then willing to talk about anything. He promised to discuss the issue with the president the next morning. Stetson's

---

[39] "Memorandum of Meeting at Viriato's House at 9:30 PM. February 8[, 1933]," Braga Brothers Collection.

[40] Ibid.

speech was rendered into Spanish, but Viriato seemed to understand the English version perfectly well.[41]

The next day Viriato visited the president, as promised, to discuss railroad rates and Cuban Cane Products. Machado told him he was sorry not to have seen Stetson. After Viriato conveyed the substance of Stetson's remarks, Machado declared that it would be necessary to make some concessions on railroad freights. He then complained about the behavior of a Cuban Cane Products manager, Gerard Smith. In particular, Machado was not pleased with Smith's criticisms of the government. When Viriato reported this positive result to Fanjul, he asked Fanjul about the reputation of Guaranty, Stetson's bank. Fanjul replied it was as good as National City. Viriato was not impressed: "I don't think much of them." But when Fanjul reminded Viriato that Morgan backed Guaranty and that Stetson mentioned Lamont was head of Guaranty's executive committee, Viriato abruptly changed his mind. Seeking his own piece of the Morgan empire, he later offered to deposit $150,000 with Guaranty. Stetson, however, did not want the money because it would look too much as if a trade had been made.[42]

Before leaving Cuba, Stetson told Fanjul that he was hoping for a "New Deal" for Cuban Cane Products, just as President-elect Roosevelt was promising a New Deal for the American people. He repeated his hope that the company could soon be sold to the Riondas, with Guaranty backing. Fanjul informed Stetson of the Cuban president's favorable decision on railroad rates and passed along Machado's disapproval of Smith, Cuban Cane Products' manager. Stetson responded that the bankers were also dissatisfied with Smith and would handle the matter. That afternoon he departed by plane for Miami.[43]

Stetson's political success was not enough to save Cuban Cane Products. As he feared, despite lower railroad rates, conditions did not improve with the 1933 harvest, and Cuban Cane Products' mortgage holders began foreclosure proceedings. The first foreclosure sale, in May 1933, attracted

---

[41] Ibid.

[42] "Memorandum of Malpi's Interview with Canel in the morning of February 9, 1933," Braga Brothers Collection.

[43] Ibid.

no bidders at a $16.6 million price. Cuban law required two attempted sales with a minimum price, but no bidder met the $12 million minimum, or any other price, at a second attempt in September 1933. Adding insult to injury, the year's crop again sold for less than a penny per pound.[44]

Stetson's successful lobbying is remarkable partly because it occurred in a volatile political environment. The business challenge was not simply that the price of sugar had fallen below a penny a pound. In Cuban politics the deeper issues were foreign domination and nationalism. Hostility to foreign ownership, such as the sugar plantations operated by Cuban Cane Products, became intense in the early 1930s. To many Cubans, American banks represented forces that unfairly fleeced what labor earned by sweat. The hostility was also directed at Cubans, such as Rionda's family, who worked with foreigners. The new slogan was "Cuba for Cubans," and the aim was to "liquidate the colonial structure that has survived in Cuba since independence."[45]

Machado's government sided with American investors and tried but failed to hold on to power. In 1930 workers' wages were reduced or not paid. Mass protests ensued, with the University of Havana becoming a focal point. A general strike erupted and President Machado suspended the Constitution, charging that labor and student uprisings were "following orders from Moscow." The hard line did not restore stability or confidence. After a period of terrorism and murder, in August 1933, less than six months after Stetson's appeal to lower railroad rates, Machado resigned the presidency. He was replaced, briefly, by Carlos Céspedes. In September 1933 an uprising of Army sergeants under the leadership of Fulgencio Batista took control and installed Ramón Grau San Martín as president. The new leadership adopted sweeping changes but was not considered legitimate by the Roosevelt administration. In early 1934 Batista eliminated the Grau government and began the process of consolidating power, this time aided by formal recognition from the United States. Batista remained the dominant force on the island for many years, ruling as dictator for most

---

[44] "Reorganization Plan, Reorganization of Cuban Cane Products, Inc.," 20 December 1934, Braga Brothers Collection; McAvoy, *Sugar Baron*, 245–58.

[45] Aguilar, *Cuba 1933*, 175–82.

of the period until 1959, when he was forced to flee by Fidel Castro, Che Guevera, and their revolutionary army.[46]

For Stetson, the context meant operating in a powder keg filled with conflicting ideologies, festering hatreds, and selfish ambitions. The banker was simultaneously a financier and a diplomat. Not surprisingly, Stetson had little patience for revolutionaries. His interests were investing in the country and making a profit. As he put it, a banker had moral responsibilities, but Guaranty was not a "philanthropic institution." Although there had once been profits, in the 1930s there was an unending stream of losses. Stetson sympathized with Cuba's larger political and social problems. Nothing would have made him happier than high-priced sugar and satisfied workers; but the state of the global sugar markets and the politics of sugar were something neither he nor the Cuban government could fix by investing in sugar production.

In fact, Stetson had no answer for the country's dilemmas. He never seemed troubled by the problem of foreign ownership for Cuban sovereignty, including his own lobbying. His perspective was that the investors and the public were in this together, so it was simply a false issue. Only by cooperating, and taking appropriate risks, could all interests benefit. It was a typically optimistic, and American, perspective, akin to his experiences with New South ideas. If American capital left, he assumed, Cubans would be harmed. For Stetson, the threat to Cuban sovereignty simply took the analysis back to its starting point: no property rights and profits for American business, then no investment, no production, no sales, and no employment for Cubans. Stetson never claimed the system was without costs or faults. But he also never really questioned whether it contributed to the kind of disaster and dictatorship faced by Cubans.

Trying to Get Out

Under the traumatic circumstances of the 1930s, Stetson's plan to back away from Cuban Cane Products and turn its management over to the Riondas went nowhere. He made a revised offer to sell to Rionda in August 1933. The deal depended on another financial reorganization, but there

---

[46] See generally Aguilar, *Cuba 1933*; Gott, *Cuba*, 129–46.

were no realistic means to change ownership and satisfy creditors, there being no likely purchasers who would meet the existing creditors' demands. Certainly the Riondas did not want to be placed in a situation where their management would be controlled by intrusive American lenders. The only good news was that both the bankers and Rionda were pleased by the American government's refusal to recognize Machado's replacement, the radical Grau government.[47]

Cuban Cane Products' reorganization finally moved forward in 1934, after recognition of the Batista-backed government by the Roosevelt administration. The company's final foreclosure sale, following more delays caused by government changes, took place on 30 January 1934. The mortgage holders, the only bidders, offered just over $4.1 million, approximately the same amount as Cuban Cane Products' debt. The new corporation that emerged from the ashes of Cuban Cane Products was Compañia Azuncarera Atlántica del Golfo ("Atlántica"). This was a Cuban entity, named in Spanish to reflect a greater sensitivity to national pride. The banks arranged for Fanjul and other Rionda associates at the Cuban Trading Company in Havana to have management authority. The foreclosed properties were formally transferred to Atlántica in April 1934.[48]

Stetson's actions during the sale and transfer reflected an increasing desire to cut his bank's losses, get out of sugar management, recover as much debt as possible, and place a new operation under Cubans he trusted, the Riondas. Fanjul Rionda was an important supporter. Stetson expressed his gratitude just after the foreclosure sale, thanking Fanjul for his exemplary service. Stetson hand-picked Fanjul to act as Atlantica's leadership, at least temporarily. John J. Sample, Guaranty's on-site representative in Cuba, was frequently in touch with Fanjul and reported good things about him. Stetson told the elder Manuel Rionda's nephew, Manuel E. Rionda, that he believed strongly in the necessity of Cuban management partly because of the political situation. Simply stated, the

[47] McAvoy, *Sugar Baron*, 249–50, 259.

[48] McAvoy, *Sugar Baron*, 262; "Reorganization Plan, Reorganization of Cuban Cane Products, Inc.," 20 December 1934, Braga Brothers Collection.

Rionda family had "access to public officials who will give them a helping hand in time of need."[49]

Unfortunately, legal ambiguities cast doubts over Atlántica's future. New American securities laws, in particular, changed the rules of the game. The 1933 and 1934 securities acts imposed stringent requirements on public issues of stock, drastically changing the old ways of marketing and distributing shares and reorganizing debtor companies. For example, under the new laws, the transfer of ownership from Cuban Cane Products to Atlántica could not lawfully have any hint of self-dealing. As a result, Stetson decided that "Guaranty Trust Co. will not under any circumstances make any profit thru the foreclosure of [Cuban Cane Products,] not wanting to submit themselves to possible criticism and litigation." Moreover, as a director of both Cuban Cane Products and Guaranty, Stetson wanted to avoid personal liability.[50]

Stetson also worried about Cuba's "El Derecho de Tanteo" law, passed during the Grau presidency. This legislation empowered the Cuban government to bid on sugar property for sale, such as Cuban Cane Products. The law threatened the validity of Cuban Cane's January 1934 foreclosure. Initially, it seemed the government would not challenge the sale, but Cuban officials reconsidered and filed a suit asking that it be overturned. Naturally, this outraged the banks, as it put the entire Atlántica project in limbo. Fanjul, in Havana, lobbied hard for the government to drop its suit.[51]

During these unhappy months Fanjul and Stetson continued to rely on each other's good will. When Fanjul considered resigning his temporary position with Atlántica, he remained because he did not want "to offend my good friend Mr. Stetson." Nonetheless, if "Stetson continues having absolute confidence in me, it is necessary that he put his shoulder to the

[49] Eugene W. Stetson to Higinio Fanjul, 5 February, 29 March, 16 April 1934; Manuel E. Rionda to Higinio Fanjul, 9 February 1934; Higinio Fanjul to Eugene W. Stetson, 10 February, 29 March 1934; Thomas Garrett to Higinio Fanjul, 13 February 1934, Braga Brothers Collection.

[50] McAvoy, *Sugar Baron*, 263–64.

[51] Ibid., 264–71; "Reorganization Plan, Reorganization of Cuban Cane Products, Inc.," 20 December 1934; Higinio Fanjul to Manuel Rionda, 10 May 1934, Braga Brothers Collection.

wheel, giving m[e] absolute control and direction of the Company." Fanjul hoped Stetson would use his power to make him Atlántica's permanent president. Fanjul kept Stetson apprised as to conditions on the sugar plantations. Yet after decades of dealing with troublesome New York investors, Fanjul and the other Riondas maintained a safe distance from the bankers, criticized the ineffective use of lawyers, and fretted over what Charles Hayden would do with his large ownership stake.[52]

In May 1934 Stetson once again tried to resolve Cuban problems through lobbying. He traveled to Washington to meet with Sumner Welles, Assistant Secretary of State and former ambassador to Cuba. Although Stetson believed the State Department was sympathetic to Atlántica's efforts to avoid the Cuban government's challenge, he learned it would not take official action. Welles, however, agreed to contact Cuban officials informally. Stetson's argument was that the Cuban government's claim was having a broadly negative effect. Given its threat to property rights, it meant no further investment in the island. In addition, more than 100,000 workers depended on Atlántica, and the company's inability to provide work would produce destitution, setting off a crisis.[53]

Despite Stetson's activity, during the mid–1930s Cuban sugar was only one of his increasing duties at Guaranty, and the Riondas worried about the depth of his interest in Atlántica. Stetson did not spend all his days and nights focusing on sugar, so he was not always fully aware of Fanjul's worries. On several occasions Stetson asked that Fanjul simply "keep his foot on the base," baseball lingo for waiting patiently for further developments, when patience was difficult. On 19 May 1934, Fanjul met with Guaranty's John Sample. He expressed concern that Stetson was losing interest in the company. As reported by Manuel E. Rionda, Sample replied in a manner that showed Stetson's deep and long-standing support for the Cuban business:

---

[52] Higinio Fanjul to Manuel E. Rionda, 10 May 1934; Manuel E. Rionda to Higinio Fanjul, 15 May 1934, Braga Brothers Collection.

[53] Manuel E. Rionda to Higinio Fanjul, 22, 24 May 1934; Eugene W. Stetson to Higinio Fanjul, 24 May 1934, Braga Brothers Collection.

> [A]fter Mr. [Charles] Sabin's death [in 1933], Mr. [Palen] Conway[,] who had been working side by side with Stetson in all of the Bank's business, had been made President, and...Mr. [Potter] had been named Chairman, thus throwing on Mr. Stetson's shoulders all the work that previously had been taken care of by Stetson and Conway.
>
> Mr. Stetson[,] in the winter months, was the last man to leave the Bank, working sometimes till 9 o'clock at night, and that just recently he had turned over the details of the Cuban Cane affair to Mr. [Potter's] brother, as he (Stetson) had too many things to handle, but that nevertheless he still, kept in touch with things, just the same.—[Sample] stated that Stetson for years was the man of action in all the Board handling Cuban Cane's affairs, notwithstanding the fact that the Guaranty Trust had only about 25% interest in the thing, Chase with their 45% being the largest ones interested with Central Hanover and New York Trust, trailing along.—That no one representing these others had ever had any constructive policy to suggest, and that Stetson had always been the ruling mind.
>
> [Sample] went further to say that [from] all the members of the Board, [Sample] had only received encouragement from Stetson and from the New York Trust, and that he never had even a "scratch of the pen" from any of the others.[54]

Sample correctly surmised Stetson's continuing interest in Atlántica. In fact, not long after Sample's reassurances to Fanjul, Stetson increased his efforts on behalf of the company. For example, he was concerned by the fact that many directors of Atlántica were also its creditors, and these same directors had voted to issue a mortgage which would supersede the rights of debenture holders. This raised the possibility of a lawsuit by a debenture holder against the directors for self-dealing. Stetson told Manuel E. Rionda that this could be avoided if the debenture holders were first given a chance

---

[54] Manuel E. Rionda to Higinio Fanjul, 22, 24 May 1934, Braga Brothers Collection.

to pay off the bank debt and obtain new securities. He planned to present this idea to the Atlántica board.[55]

Stetson's new work comforted Fanjul. He was "a little more encouraged by seeing Stetson again taking an active part.—If he is going to steer the boat, I am with him 100%. –If he confides in me I am sure we will come out all right, but I must have the Pilot's wheel, otherwise, let me get out." On 28 May 1934, Fanjul told Stetson that nothing pleased him more than Stetson's leadership. He reminded Stetson that over the preceding decades more than $100 million had been spent to build up the company's properties, ninety-eight percent of which was American capital. Because of this commitment he believed a forced purchase by the Cuban government would be catastrophic.[56]

In July 1934 Fanjul wrote Stetson that the Cuban government's suit challenging the Cuban Cane Products foreclosure sale had finally been withdrawn. Fanjul exclaimed, "[N]o-body was happier than myself, not only because I had as much interest as you in the success of this enterprise, but also because I have carried on my shoulders the worse part of the fight." He detailed the intense lobbying over the suit by key parties in Cuba, from agricultural workers to associates of the Cuban president. Atlantica was widely disliked because of its foreign ownership. In the future, Fanjul thought, the company needed the excellent connections with the Cuban government he could offer. Fanjul further warned Stetson that financing the next crop had to be forthcoming soon or their efforts would be futile. Naturally, Stetson was grateful. He was "fully conscious" of Fanjul's "splendid cooperation and effectiveness." The New York banks once again came forward with additional financing in July 1934.[57]

---

[55] Ibid.

[56] Higinio Fanjul to Manuel E. Rionda, 26 May 1934; Higinio Fanjul to Eugene W. Stetson, 28 May 1934, Braga Brothers Collection.

[57] Higinio Fanjul to Eugene W. Stetson, 24, 27 July 1934; Eugene W. Stetson to Higinio Fánjul, 26 July 1934; Manuel E. Rionda to Higinio Fanjul, 1 August 1934, Braga Brothers Collection. Guaranty's E. A. Potter indicated the bank would prefer bailing out entirely if not for its moral obligation to the security holders, its previous trustee relationship to the company, the option to security holders to acquire the property, the promises made to the State Department to continue

Surprisingly, over the next several months there were signs of improving business conditions. Under FDR's Democrats, trade policy toward Cuba moved in a direction favorable to sugar producers, with a new treaty providing for dramatically reduced sugar duties on sugar produced within a U.S.-determined quota. The bargain included reduction or elimination of duties on American manufactured goods into Cuba. According to Stetson, Fanjul led a valuable campaign in Cuba in support of the treaty. Stetson also attended a celebratory dinner for the agreement, as did Hayden; representatives of Central Hanover; National City; Chase; the Riondas; and the Cuban Secretary of State, Cosme de la Torriente.[58]

Even the long-standing receivership was finally wrapped up. In December 1934 a formal Reorganization Plan was filed in the federal district court where the Cuban Cane receivership had been pending since 1932. In essence, the plan provided for a new company to acquire the existing Atlántica securities and issue 700,000 shares of common stock. Creditors of both Cuban Cane and Atlántica obtained an opportunity to purchase the stock. In March 1935 Cuban Atlantic Sugar was formed, holding Atlántica as a subsidiary. Ever hopeful, the elder Manuel Rionda believed investment in Cuban Atlantic could be profitable.[59]

This complex process produced meetings between Stetson, Sample, and the Riondas with the purpose of finding new owners. The context was the same as it had been for several years: the banks' "great desire" was to get out of the sugar business. The problem was that they were still owed about $7 million and were not going to relinquish control without getting paid. One solution, suggested by the senior Manuel Rionda, was to sell off the

---

production, and similar promises to the Cuban government. "Compañia Zucharera Atlántica Del Golfo, S.A.," 3 August 1934, Braga Brothers Collection.

[58] "Memorandum for Mr. Miller," 6 August 1934; "Lista de las Personas que Asistieron al Almuerzo Dado en el Down Town Club," 5 September 1934; Eugene W. Stetson to Higinio Fanjul, 6 September 1934; Manuel Rionda to Eugene W. Stetson, 31 August 1934, Braga Brothers Collection. The Reciprocity Treaty was in addition to the Jones-Costigan Act of 1934, which fixed sugar production quotas.

[59] "Reorganization Plan, Reorganization of Cuban Cane Products, Inc.," 20 December 1934; "Notice to all Creditors, Security holders and Stockholders of Cuban Cane Products, Inc.," 28 December 1934; Manuel Rionda to Frank C. Tiarks, 18 December 1934, Braga Brothers Collection; McAvoy, *Sugar Baron*, 274.

various plantations owned by the company, piece by piece, with financing arrangements that would satisfy the debt. Rionda argued that the managers and liquidators "should be all Riondas—no outsiders." Yet at a subsequent meeting attended by Stetson, Sample, Manuel Rionda, Manuel E. Rionda, and Fanjul, Stetson indicated that perhaps the whole could be sold to Coca-Cola or the National Sugar Refining Company, although he preferred the Riondas because of their past services.[60]

The senior Manuel, now more than eighty years old, was too seasoned to take Stetson's proposal uncritically. He did not think Coca-Coca really wanted the properties. The action would be foolish for American Sugar to buy them, because as a refiner it could do better on the international market. Although there had been improvement, sugar profits were still slim. He believed, and Stetson conceded, that the current stock price was too high. Stetson countered by suggesting a new company with $3.5 million capital, but Rionda rejected the idea, knowing it would come burdened with the current debt owed the banks. Other owners were discussed: Hayden, according to Rionda, was "able" but "too overpowering and a bad seller." Neither Irénée DuPont nor sugar tycoon Horace Havemeyer seemed desirable or interested. Ultimately it was the same old conversation. Stetson wanted his bank to get paid and exit. The Riondas wanted control, but only under the right terms. And the market for sugar was not promising.[61]

Late in the spring of 1935 the lack of outside investor interest meant that Guaranty, along with Hayden, Chase, and the New York Trust, not the Riondas, became the primary shareholders of the newly formed Cuban Atlantic. The New Yorkers received securities with a face value of $7 million, with Hayden's ownership portion the largest. Guaranty retained a special role, with its John Sample becoming Cuban Atlantic's new president.

---

[60] "Plan of Campaign Toward Solving the Problems of the Former Cuban Cane and Liquidation of the Atlantic Co.," 27 April 1935; "Synopsis of Conference held Friday, May 3, 1935, at Guaranty," Braga Brothers Collection.

[61] "Synopsis of Conference held Friday, May 3, 1935, at Guaranty," Braga Brothers Collection; *New York Times*, 30 August 1935.

All this had the effect of keeping Stetson involved in Cuban sugar, despite his best efforts to get out.[62]

Continued ownership carried further legal burdens. Complaints raised in the protracted Cuban Cane Products receivership attracted the attention of the new federal Securities and Exchange Commission (SEC). In July 1935, the Commission, led by future Supreme Court justices William O. Douglas and Abe Fortas, launched an investigation that focused on self-dealing by insiders, the New York banks, in the 1930s Cuban sugar company reorganizations. The government sought information from Stetson, Hayden, Manuel Rionda, and Earle Bailie of J. & W. Seligman, and scheduled hearings for August 1935. Although Stetson initially argued that certain privileged communications with attorneys should not be released to the government, he and the others later presented evidence and cooperated with the SEC.[63]

The proceeding fit the pattern of other Depression-era securities investigations. It was largely a contest among owners of corporate interests, with the government flexing its new regulatory muscles and seemingly representing the financial losers. Essentially, the government focused on complaints as to which capitalists managed to get paid first from the inadequate remaining assets of the failing sugar company. In August 1935, Manuel Rionda provided oral testimony to Fortas. Fortas concentrated on the capital structure of the company and asked probing questions about the issue of common and preferred stock. Rionda testified that at the original financing of Cuba Cane, in 1915, he was given 30,000 shares of common stock for services to the company. Naturally, as a regulator Fortas was interested in whether any of the shares were then sold to the public, which of course they were, as Cuba Cane was listed on the New York Stock

[62] Eugene W. Stetson to Higinio Fanjul, 23 March 1935; G. E. Sheehy to Eugene W. Stetson, 26 April 1935; "Interview today with Mr. Muestra, Bernando, Manolo and M. R. Being Present," 5 January 1938; "Capitalization of Cuban Sugar Companies Document," 14 March 1936, Braga Brothers Collection.

[63] "Memorandum," 23 July 1935; "Memorandum," 25 July 1935; "Subpoena, Securities and Exchange Commission," 14 August 1935; Samuel O. Clark Jr. to Manuel Rionda, 14 August 1935; Manuel Rionda to Abraham Fortas, 19 August 1935; "Direct Examination of Manuel Rionda," 20[?] August 1935, Braga Brothers Collection; McAvoy, *Sugar Baron*, 275–76.

Exchange. Most interesting to Fortas was that J. & W. Seligman received 470,000 shares of Cuba Cane common based on their agreement to underwrite the $50 million subscription.[64]

In the end the investigation produced hundreds of pages of testimony and documents but little else. The reorganization of Cuban Cane Products into Atlantica was not overturned and no wrongdoing was prosecuted. The worst part of the process, from Guaranty's perspective, was the publicity. Newspapers fed a Depression-stunned public lurid facts. These included the revelation that the protective committees for the creditors were actually headed by the banks and their lawyers, posing a clear conflict of interest. The reorganization's "administrative" costs surpassed $1 million, which included more than $200,000 in fees to the banks and their lawyers. At the time of the SEC investigation, unemployment still exceeded fifteen percent and the average income of an employed worker was just over $1,500 a year. Moreover, insiders, including a millionaire DuPont, received discounted stock prices. Of course the banks explained all this as reasonable business practice and not at all profitable. Hayden told the Commission he lost $600,000. Stetson did not provide testimony at the New York hearings, but he did travel to Washington to represent Guaranty before the SEC.[65]

Stetson and Sugar

Several years after the SEC investigation, and following more than twenty years of turmoil, Guaranty's business relationship with the Riondas and Cuban sugar came to an end. By 1941 the bank had finally managed to unload its stake in Cuban Atlantic. Ironically, Guaranty's departure coincided with the huge demand for sugar created by World War II. When Guaranty exited, Cuban Atlantic was primarily owned by Chase and the Charles Hayden Foundation; Hayden himself died in 1937. The Riondas'

---

[64] "Direct Examination of Manuel Rionda," 20[?] August 1935, Braga Brothers Collection.

[65] L. A. Crosby to Manuel Rionda, 30 August 1935, Braga Brothers Collection; *New York Times*, 22, 28, 30 August 1935. Efforts were made to review official files of the SEC proceedings, but Commission personnel could not locate the investigation records.

role had been reduced to the kind of warehousing and related documentation and governmental services typically provided by Czarnikow-Rionda and the Cuban Trading Company.[66]

As a gesture of thanks, Stetson had helped the Riondas continue this limited function. In early 1936 Cuban Atlantic considered conducting its own warehouse operations, thereby replacing Fanjul's Cuban Trading Company. Fanjul asked Stetson to intervene and help maintain the historic relationship. The banker called a meeting of the Cuban Atlantic board and conveyed Fanjul's concerns. He reminded the directors of the Riondas' loyal service, and he did not "want to see [them] declared or counted out." The Board, in response, agreed to hear Fanjul's side on the warehousing issue. Stetson recognized Fanjul's "good sportsmanship" and conveyed his "deep sense of appreciation of our friendship." In a letter to Stetson, Fanjul outlined his current service to the company, which included warehousing, shipping sugar, and dealing with the Cuba government and its export rules. Stetson turned the letter over to Cuban Atlantic's president, John Sample, and told Fanjul he hoped a satisfactory conclusion could be reached. If not, he would take it up again with the directors. In quick order Sample concluded that Fanjul's assistance would still be useful, and the long-standing business relationship continued.[67]

Thereafter, Stetson's dealings with the Riondas steadily declined. Their last business included the sale of Guaranty's shares in Cuban Atlantic, introductions to other bankers, and the financial reorganization of one of Manuel Rionda's plantations. With the withdrawal of Guaranty, correspondence between Stetson and Rionda became limited to Stetson's annual Christmas cards. Rionda always replied to these in a manner that expressed his "sincere friendship and that of all my associates." In his final letter to

[66] McAvoy, *Sugar Baron*, 283; J. J. Sample to Higinio Fanjul, 14 February 1936; Higinio Fanjul to J. J. Sample, 21 February 1936, Braga Brothers Collection.

[67] Higinio Fanjul to Eugene W. Stetson, 14 March, 6 April 1936; Eugene W. Stetson to Higinio Fanjul, 26 February, 23 March 1936; J. J. Sample to Higinio Fanjul, 1 April 1936; Higinio Fanjul to J. J. Sample, 6 April 1936, Braga Brothers Collection; McAvoy, *Sugar Baron*, 276, 278–79, 283.

Stetson, in late 1942, he nostalgically recalled the "good old days when we traveled together over the Island."[68]

Stetson's long interaction with Cuban sugar is a rich source of information about Guaranty, the practice of international banking in the 1920s and 1930s, and Stetson's performance as a relationship banker. Stetson originally received the account in the boom times just after World War I. High prices in the 1910s allowed sugar to be highly profitable and Stetson's bank naturally saw it as a sound investment. But after a few years of success the risks became unmanageable. By the late 1920s and through the 1930s Stetson's job became one of limiting losses and developing a coherent exit strategy. This meant reorganizing corporate structures, pacifying creditors, lobbying government officials, and issuing new forms of equity and debt. The bank profited only by collecting reorganization fees and attempting to maintain its position as a preferred creditor.

Stetson performed these diverse tasks with the same attention to client relationships he showed in happier contexts. He brought his usual friendliness and respect for clients to the table. He genuinely liked and admired the Riondas. He was also sensitive to many of the cultural and political conditions of conducting foreign business. Especially noteworthy was his conclusion that under prevailing conditions American capitalists could not effectively run Cuban sugar plantations from New York. In addition, the job required intense lobbying, visits to Havana and Washington, and appreciation for the details of sugar production. The Depression in the United States and persistent revolution in Cuba unleashed a radically changing regulatory structure that had to be considered. In the Cuban sugar business there were never easy answers or permanent solutions.

The experience did not shake Stetson's faith in the benefits of international investment, but he recognized failure when he saw it. As he

---

[68] Manuel Rionda to Eugene W. Stetson, 28 April 1936; 23 January 1937; 27 December 1938; 22 December 1939; 23 December 1940; 30 December 1942; "Interview Today with Mr. Muestra, Bernardo, Manolo and M. R. being Present," 5 January 1938; Eugene W. Stetson to Manuel Rionda, 15 December 1936; 20 December 1937; 20 December 1938; 16 December 1939; 20 December 1940; 20 December 1941; 18 December 1942, Braga Brothers Collection.

concluded in 1933, here was a problem that was simply too large for mere capital to fix. Indeed, as many scholars have argued, investment in sugar by Americans had a host of undesirable economic consequences, especially over-reliance on the sweet crop. Stetson was plainly aware of this kind of effect from the history of cotton in Georgia. Maybe this is why he tried for so long to fix the Cuban problems and achieve some level of success. It might also explain why in the end he was determined to get away from Cuban sugar and move on to more promising tasks.

International banking, with its exotic travel and high-level appeals to the Cuban president, was exhilarating. But the experience was disappointing, and replete with massive losses. It shows Stetson in a long-term losing situation. The constant reorganizing, court proceedings, and need for new investors required a particular kind of banking. Obviously even a perennial optimist such as Stetson was more than casually aware that the American business system produced failure along with success. After all, by the time his relations with Cuban sugar ended Stetson had seen southern poverty, experienced the 1907 panic, survived the demise of the Mercantile Bank in the early 1920s, and witnessed the near total collapse of the American economy in the Depression. But Cuba must have been especially frustrating, because it offered the special case of a luxurious island with a population eager to work, but no clear path that would enrich both Cubans and American investors. There is no record of Stetson's reaction to Fidel Castro's triumphant march into Havana in 1959. In that moment it may have seemed to him that the failure of sugar was not merely unfortunate, but a contributor to the worst possible result for the island and its people.

9

Stetson and the Depression

Gene Stetson had the fortune, or misfortune, of being a banker during the 1930s, one of the most dramatic decades in American banking history. When Stetson started in banking, big time investment was still controlled by a handful of private bankers. The money supply was linked to gold and influenced by issues of banking notes by national banks. By the 1920s the wave of the future seemed to be large banking institutions, such as Guaranty, which provided an expansive mix of commercial and investment services for corporate clients. As a Guaranty vice president, Stetson contributed to the great boom of ever larger banks. This included the unprecedented growth of American banking power overseas during and after World War I. The contributions also included a key role in financing new kinds of national industry. Stetson's actions for Coca-Cola and Cuban sugar reflected the opportunities for corporate relationship banking in the new American century.

Then came the 1929 Crash. Whether Stetson was in his office on lower Broadway on the more frenetic days of trading, or whether he happened to wander to nearby Wall Street to witness the chaos of Black Tuesday, 29 October 1929, when a massive sell off sent prices plummeting, is unknown. His response to the nadir of the market in July 1932, when the Dow industrial average dropped to about eleven percent of its 1929 level, is also not recorded. But it is clear that these events and the public reaction to them had a deep effect. His son Charlie, a boy at the time, remembered that his father's "demeanor" changed sharply in the early 1930s. Depression did not mean poverty for the Stetson family, but the finance world, in fact, had been turned upside down, and Stetson felt the shock waves of the convulsion.[1]

---

[1] Charles P. Stetson, interview by L. Kenneth Hammond, 24 April 1982, Jack Tarver Library, Special Collections, Mercer University, Macon, Georgia. A recent

Banking, including banking at Guaranty, was never the same after the Crash. Historians disagree sharply about the causes of the Depression. They also disagree about what its remedies should have been. Stetson's life is helpful in this regard because it shows that the views of a banker on the Wall Street scene cannot be easily stereotyped. Stetson's reaction to the Depression, partly because he and his colleagues lacked the information that comes with several decades of hind-sight, does not fit neatly into any package. The Depression tested the foundations of his beliefs, including his optimism, and it stretched his banking skills, demanding all of his personal and professional resources.

Some of the Depression-era changes resulted from a substantial amount of new federal regulation on banking practice. The meaning of more government in itself can easily be misinterpreted. Banking has always been the subject of government regulation—and has in fact benefited from much of that law and regulation. Every American political tradition since Hamilton and Jefferson has recognized that banking is not like most businesses. Banking is too important. Inherently it has always had a public function and impact in a way that, say, furniture, textiles, or Coca-Cola do not. As a result, Stetson was necessarily interested in political developments and how they affected finance.[2]

After moving to New York he became a Republican, a choice that would have been unacceptable among his fellow native whites in middle Georgia. The Republican Party was, after all, the party of abolition, Lincoln, the Union Army, and Reconstruction, not subjects likely to be viewed positively by the son of a Confederate officer. The Georgia GOP, between 1902 and 1916, when Stetson would have voted there, was weak even by Southern standards and had essentially disintegrated in 1908 after Democrats rammed through a literacy test and property qualifications for voters with the help of fraud, intimidation, and murder in order to disenfranchise blacks, the source of most Republican votes. The Democratic monopoly was such that Republicans in the Peach State did not elect a

---

detailed account of the market's Crash in the fall of 1929 is Maury Klein, *Rainbow's End: The Crash of 1929* (New York: Oxford University Press, 2001) 190–252.

[2] A summary of some of these changes is Benjamin J. Klebaner, *American Commercial Banking* (Boston: Twayne Publishers, 1990) 138–48.

governor until 2002, almost one hundred years later. When Stetson was a young banker in Macon, the lack of political competition meant that perhaps eighty percent of Georgia's voters, white and black, did not even bother to cast ballots.[3]

Perhaps this miserable legacy, along with his natural aversion to public speaking, helps explain why Stetson had little interest in political office. He had no desire to be a "public figure." His direct political activities were few and minor. Many years after he left Georgia, for example, Stetson agreed to become a member of the Republican Finance Committee in his home district in suburban Connecticut. On the other hand, Republicanism was certainly the perspective of choice among Wall Street bankers. In the late 1930s and 1940s Stetson even visited former President Herbert Hoover on several occasions. Perhaps most revealing, he corresponded with and strongly supported Wendell Willkie in the presidential race of 1940 against Franklin Roosevelt, and was "keenly disappointed" in Willkie's defeat.[4]

All this was important, but not so as to show a strong passion for either laissez-faire economics or partisan politics. For Stetson, being a Republican, like his former status as a Democrat in Georgia, was less a function of support for limited government than belief in a certain kind of government—one that favored Wall Street and industry, especially big and international business. His Republicanism was informed by the views of

---

[3] J. Morgan Kousser, *The Shaping of Southern Politisc: Suffrage Restriction and the Establishment of the One-Party South* (New Haven: Yale University Press, 1974) 217–37.

[4] Eugene W. Stetson to Wendell L. Willkie, 3 August 1943; Wendell L. Willkie to Eugene W. Stetson, 29 July 1943; Wendell L. Willkie Mss., Lilly Library, Indiana University, Bloomington, Indiana; "Herbert Hoover's Daily Calendar," 16 September 1937; 16 March 1941; 2 June 1943; 26 May 1946, Herbert Hoover Papers, Herbert Hoover Presidential Library, West Branch, Iowa. Support for Willkie was the norm among Stetson's Guaranty business associates. See, e.g., W. Palen Conway to Wendell L. Willkie, 19 April 1943; William C. Potter to Wendell L. Willkie, 4 May 1943; Mrs. William C. Potter to Wendell L. Willkie, 3 September 1940; and Thomas W. Lamont to Wendell L. Willkie, 5 July 1940, Wendell L. Willkie Papers. On Willkie generally, see Joseph Barnes, *Willkie: The Events He Was Part Of—The Ideas He Fought For* (New York: Simon and Shuster, 1952); Steve Neal, *Dark Horse: A Biography of Wendell Willkie* (Lawrence: University Press of Kansas, 1989).

Alexander Hamilton and Theodore Roosevelt, both of whom believed in a key role for government. Such attitudes were common among both wealthy Republicans and Democrats in the 1920s, Stetson's first decade in New York. Guaranty's most prominent corporate lawyer, and Stetson's friend, was John W. Davis, the Democrats' candidate for president in 1924. Stetson was an even better friend of Georgia's Democratic United States Senator and fellow Mercer student Walter F. George, who suffered intense criticism from President Franklin Roosevelt for his conservatism. FDR even tried to unseat George in the 1938 Georgia Senate election. During Stetson's life Republicans supported policies that increased federal government power: a protective tariff, the Federal Reserve, and the intervention of American armed forces overseas in the Spanish colonies and in World War I. Hoover set new records for federal action, sponsoring massive loans for American industry through the Reconstruction Finance Corporation and defending the notorious Smoot-Hawley tariff of 1930. This was consistent with portions of the larger Republican tradition. On the other hand, the Democrat elected to do something about the Depression, Theodore's cousin Franklin, famously promised a balanced budget and fiscal prudence during the 1932 campaign.[5]

Ultimately, however, when it came to politics and political behavior, Stetson was a pragmatist, not an ideologue. In business, he could work with Averell Harriman the New Deal Democrat as well as with Harriman's Republican partner, Prescott Bush. He agreed with his bank's decision to issue $20 million in notes to the federal government's Recon-struction Finance Corporation, on the government's recommendation, in order to strengthen its capital structure. He supported some forms of increased public action, such as a legal prohibition on loans to bank officers and

[5] Later, in 1950–1951, Stetson was appointed by President Harry S. Truman to an advisory board for the Commodity Credit Corporation. This reflects both his experience with agricultural markets as well as his willingness to integrate business and public policy regardless of the political party in power. *New York Times*, 1 February 1950; 20 June 1951. On Davis's political career, see William Harbaugh, *Lawyer's Lawyer: The Life of John W. Davis* (New York: Oxford University Press, 1973).

directors and increased taxes to support projects to lower unemployment. He wholeheartedly endorsed American involvement in World War I, a foreign military action unprecedented in scope that required conscription, federal control of economic production and prices, and increased income taxes. He lobbied in Washington for government trade policies that mandated an aggressive federal role in foreign affairs.[6]

Stetson's banking challenge in the 1930s went much deeper than simple party politics or the relative size of government. Was Wall Street to blame? Was capitalism flawed? Was the practice of relationship banking partly responsible? Not surprisingly, Stetson gave an unequivocal "No" to such questions. The American public, however, was not so sure, and Stetson was aware of this uncertainty. As a result, he believed it was up to bankers, like himself, to justify his ideals through words and deeds despite the new conditions.

Guaranty and the Crash

The stock market collapse began the process of dramatically shifting the environment in which Stetson and Guaranty operated. On the Thursday before the Crash Wall Street observers saw that the market was "in distress," as J. P. Morgan partner and Guaranty director Tom Lamont put it in classic understatement. Top New York bankers met at Morgan's office on 23 October to discuss ways of propping up the market. Despite the Federal Reserve, Morgan still considered itself the nation's bank of last resort. Guaranty president Bill Potter attended the meeting; along with Albert Wiggin of Chase; Charles Mitchell of National City; and Lamont, chairman of the "rescue team." The banks pledged about $130 million to buy stocks. Prices actually closed higher the next day, but it was too late. Unlike in 1907, there was not enough private money to stem the tide, and the following Monday and Tuesday the market crashed. The bankers'

[6] "Address Before the Georgia Bankers Association, May 25, 1933," Eugene W. Stetson Papers, Jack Tarver Library, Special Collections, Mercer University, Macon, Georgia; Eugene W. Stetson to Thomas J. Watson, 29 October 1931, Thomas J. Watson Sr. Papers, IBM Corporate Archives, Somers, New York.

failure commenced a new era, one in which government would play a more decisive role in managing the economy.[7]

For years most of the news was bad. The Dow Jones Industrial Average sank from a high of 381 in September 1929 to below 42 in July 1932, a loss of almost 90 percent. Average prices of industrials did not regain their 1929 levels until 1951. In late 1931, the Fed raised the discount rate by two percent in two weeks, a one-time record change. Unemployment grew from 3.2 percent in 1929 to 24.9 percent in 1933. Between 1929 and 1933 real income fell by more than 26 percent; current GDP fell from $103.6 billion to $56.4 billion. The bank failure rate accelerated wildly, especially among rural banks. One of the victims was Stetson's old employer, the Exchange National Bank in Fitzgerald. In 1932, massive withdrawals by customers caused many bank failures. Between the late 1920s and the early 1930s the number of American banks fell from over 25,000 to fewer than 15,000. Over 800 banks failed in September and October 1931 alone. Overall, bank assets declined from $72 billion to $51 billion. By 1933, new corporate stock issues had declined 98 percent from 1929.[8]

Guaranty suffered as well, but mildly compared to other institutions. The bank's resources held at about $2 billion during 1930, then fell sharply to $1.5 billion in December 1931, where they remained through 1933. Assets fluctuated between $1.4 and $2 billion for most of the remainder of the 1930s. Only at the end of 1936, when assets approached $2.1 billion, had the high-flying 1920s been eclipsed. Guaranty's common stock price also fell, from a gold-plated $1,000 in 1929 to $168 in June 1932, a loss of more than eighty percent. The directors reduced dividends on the grounds of diminished earning power, partly because of lower lending rates. The

---

[7] On the bankers' meeting, see Charles R. Geisst, *Wall Street: A History* (New York: Oxford University Press, 1997) 191–92; Klein, *Rainbow's End*, 213–14.

[8] Keith L. Bryant and Henry C. Dethloff, *A History of American Business*, 2nd ed. (Upper Saddle River NJ: Prentice-Hall, 1990) 230–33; John Chamberlain, *The Enterprising Americans: A Business History of the United States* (New York: Harper & Row, 1963) 228–29; Arthur S. Link and William S. Catton, *American Epoch: A History of the United States Since 1900*, 5th ed., 2 vols. (New York: Alfred A. Knopf, 1980) 1: 351–52, 363; Jonathan Hughes and Louis P. Cain, *American Economic History*, 7th ed. (Boston: Pearson Education, Inc., 2007) 479–88.

bank even closed on 4 March 1933, first because of the state Bank Holiday declared in New York, and then two days later because of the national Bank Holiday declared by President Roosevelt upon taking office.[9]

Thanks to its relatively strong financial position, Guaranty was among the first institutions to receive its license to reopen after the federal Bank Holiday. In 1932, amidst the banking catastrophe, a brokerage firm included Guaranty among sixteen elite banks still worthy of an investor's confidence. This firm described the company as the largest of the New York "Morgan banks," which were "noted for their high standing and conservative banking practices." The brokers stressed that the cash and government securities held by the bank were equal to fifty percent of deposits, an extremely safe ratio. They also noted Guaranty had paid dividends every year since 1892, the year after the bank was purchased by the Mutual Life, even in years of national economic recession.[10]

On paper, Guaranty weathered the Depression well. On a deeper level the core purposes and functions of the bank were challenged and then transformed over the course of the 1930s. Perhaps most importantly because of the Depression the public and the government lost faith in the pre–1929 system. In the wake of the anti-banker backlash were new federal regulations, investigations, humiliation, and lawsuits. All these left Stetson

---

[9] "Condensed Statements, Guaranty Trust Company of New York," 31 December 1930; 31 December 1931; 31 December 1932; 31 December 1933; 31 December 1934; 31 December 1935; 31 December 1936; 31 December 1937; 31 December 1938; 31 December 1939, J. P. Morgan & Co., Inc. Papers, JPMorgan Chase Archives, New York, New York; L. A. Norton & Co. to Thomas Lamont, 27 November 1934; Thomas Lamont to [Various Guaranty Trust Shareholders] March 1935, Thomas W. Lamont Collection, Baker Library Historical Collections Harvard Business School, Boston, Massachusetts; "The Corporate History of the Guaranty Trust Company of New York (1952)," 51, J. P. Morgan & Co., Inc Papers; Guaranty Trust Company of New York, *One Hundred Years of Banking Service* (New York: Guaranty Trust Company of New York, 1939) 40.

[10] Thomas Lamont to [Various Guaranty Trust Company Stockholders], March 1935; Rackliff, Whittaker, & Loomis, Inc., "Guaranty Trust Company of New York (1932)," Thomas W. Lamont Collection; Guaranty Trust Company, *One Hundred Years*, 40.

and his colleagues in a brave new world, one that required new ways of thinking and imposed new boundaries.

During the 1920s, Guaranty had greatly expanded its investment banking activities. This was a common strategy among New York commercial banks, including Chase and National City. Most notably, as already discussed, Guaranty created the Guaranty Company, a wholly owned subsidiary headed by Harold Stanley. The Guaranty Company contributed to the growth of retail stock marketing in the United States by opening sales offices across the country. In general, investment banking was an exceptionally profitable line of business that related well to the bank's other corporate services. Stetson's participation in the Coca-Cola sale and his work with Harriman and Rionda suggest the large opportunities presented by investment banking.[11]

At the time, the investment banking world was characterized by a strict hierarchy. Smaller firms that dealt in securities developed their own niches, such as municipal or retailer issues, but the top firms, such as J. P. Morgan, managed and assembled syndicates for a wide range of businesses. An uncooperative firm could be punished by being given a small allocation of a desirable issue, or even drummed out of the opportunity. Competition could have altered the composition of the institutional landscape, but some of the more powerful firms, including Morgan, were so entrenched they could not be unseated. This sort of oligopoly, of which the Morgan-directed Guaranty was a part, irritated many consumers, political leaders, and would-be competitors. Further, since neither the top firms nor government supervised all issues, there was a substantial potential for mismanagement. Fraud occurred, especially as a stock market mania created a supply of questionable securities.[12]

---

[11] In 1927–1931 the Guaranty Company ranked third in the nation in security distributions, with more than $4.75 billion, one billion less than the leader, National City. R. W. Goldschmidt, *The Changing Structure of American Banking* (London: George Routledge & Sons, Ltd., 1933) 70–71, 137.

[12] See Samuel L. Hayes III, A. Michael Spence, and David Van Praag Marks, *Competition in the Investment Banking Industry* (Cambridge: Harvard University Press, 1983) 11–20.

By 1929, commercial and investment banks shared the securities business. Traditionally, commercial banks such as Guaranty made money by taking deposits and making loans, taking a spread between the interest rate they paid depositors and the interest rate they charged borrowers. They might provide other services, such as trust work or services geared to business, including international business. An investment bank, by contrast, raised capital from investors on behalf of corporations and governments that issued securities. The investment bank made money by charging fees to the issuer and sometimes by holding the securities on its own books until their prices rose, then selling and creating an even greater profit. The investment bank might also sell part or all of the issue to other banks and to the public. Deciding how big an issue to float, on what terms, and at what rate of return could be extremely profitable, as the Coca-Cola sale demonstrated.[13]

Of course, the difference between the two types of banks is an oversimplification, because during the booming 1920s different kinds of banks often worked together, had the same ownership, or performed both commercial and investment functions. Again, Stetson's relationships with Guaranty, Coca-Cola, Harriman, and Cuban sugar demonstrate how the arrangements could work. The important point is that before 1929, banks, in particular banks like Stetson's Guaranty, operated in a business and legal environment in which the tools of financing were extremely flexible. Skilled relationship bankers, including Stetson, could make a loan (commercial banking) or underwrite a security (investment banking), or both. The line between commercial and investment tasks was blurred, and after World War I Guaranty was among the leading practitioners of both kinds of banking. In fact, Stetson's early career at Guaranty shows precisely how this kind of pre-Depression banking worked at its fundamental levels. Acting on both commercial and investment matters, Stetson could fulfill the functions of "rainmaker" and relationship banker for Guaranty and its clients, in the

---

[13] Samuel L. Hayes III and Philip Hubbard, *Investment Banking: A Tale of Three Cities* (Boston: Harvard Business School Press, 1990) 97–98; Klebaner, *Commercial Banking*, 118–37; Joel Seligman, *The Transformation of Wall Street: A History of the Securities and Exchange Commission and Modern Corporate Finance* (Boston: Houghton Mifflin, 1982) 23–24.

process shaping what interests received capital and therefore helping to determine the direction of the economy.

Backlash

The mingling of commercial and investment banking functions was widely blamed for the Crash and its disastrous aftermath. Banks were seen to have abused the trust of depositors and public investors. The federal government under Roosevelt wanted Wall Street bankers to embrace meaningful remedies, but most, including Stetson, opposed change. The mood was perhaps best expressed in a spectacular Senate investigation directed by attorney Ferdinand Pecora. Pecora was a perfect foil for the big banks. A tough Italian immigrant from New York whose government salary was a mere $250 a month, in the 1920s he had prosecuted other tough guys while working in the United States Attorney's office in Manhattan. The hearings started in early 1933 and lasted over a year. Roosevelt encouraged Pecora's righteous indignation, having campaigned that as president he would expose and punish "the ruthless manipulation of professional gamblers and the corporate system."[14]

For Wall Street banks, the Pecora hearings were a public relations nightmare. They revealed to an irritated public that New York bankers had immense power but had often refused any public accountability. The Pecora hearings were openly hostile to banks and successfully painted the bankers as self-serving and dishonest. Some bankers were forced to admit that their actions had not been ethical and had even harmed the institutions that employed them.[15]

Stetson knew or had worked with several of the prime targets of the hearings. For example, Pecora disclosed that Chase President Albert Wiggin, with whom Stetson collaborated on the Coca-Cola deal, had anticipated price declines and dumped shares in his own bank in 1929,

---

[14] There are many accounts of the Pecora hearings. See, e.g., Geisst, *Wall Street*, 216–27; Ron Chernow, *The House of Morgan: An American Banking Dynasty and the Rise of Modern Finance* (New York: Atlantic Monthly Press, 1990) 355–74; Robert Sobel, *The Life and Times of Dillon Read* (New York: Truman Talley Books/Dutton, 1991) 172–89; Seligman, *Transformation of Wall Street*, 20–38.

[15] Geisst, *Wall Street*, 222–27; Chernow, *House of Morgan*, 355–74.

driving Chase shares downward. He made a fortune from it, using the same foreign corporations that obtained discounted Coca-Cola stock ten years earlier to hide the short-selling and avoid taxes. Thomas Lamont's son engaged in "wash sales" to avoid paying taxes by selling a stock in one tax year only to buy it back in the next year. Despite great personal wealth, he avoided income taxes in a manner not available to the average wage earner.[16]

After some bankers complained about the circus-like atmosphere of the hearings, Jack Morgan was embarrassed by Ringling Brothers sending over a midget to sit on his lap. In one exchange, Morgan admitted to the chairman of the Senate Committee that the honorable Senator would not be allowed to open an account at J. P. Morgan, even in the amount of $100,000. This was more than twice the amount an average American worker could expect to earn in an entire lifetime. Yet according to Morgan, his bank benefited the public by serving major corporations and their executives, not just anyone, such as a United States Senator, with $100,000 to deposit. Then it emerged that Jack Morgan had not paid federal income taxes from 1930 to 1933 and that not one of the twenty very wealthy Morgan partners paid income taxes in 1932 and 1933.[17]

The real problem for Morgan and his Wall Street allies was not legalistic arguments over tax liability. Instead, the Pecora hearings exposed very real fraud, insider trading, excessive banking fees, special privileges to friends, and monopoly in a vastly important business that had an enormous impact on the public. Wall Street did not claim that its operations were limited to private interests. Instead, Wall Street openly admitted its public function. Thus, Morgan could not claim to be both beneficial to the public through sophisticated investing and yet immune to any public scrutiny when there was compelling evidence of unethical behavior in banking or the securities markets. Blatant insider trading and deceptive stock manipulation were rampant. One "friend" would call another to mention that such-and-such a stock was available privately or should be quickly sold. In the end,

---

[16] Chernow, *House of Morgan*, 356, 366; Klein, *Rainbow's End*, 246–47.

[17] Geisst, *Wall Street*, 223–24; Chernow, *House of Morgan*, 365–69; John D. Forbes, *J. P. Morgan Jr., 1867–1943* (Charlottesville: University Press of Virginia, 1981) 176–79.

many so-called Captains of Wall Street appeared ridiculous and dishonest, the beneficiaries of inside deals and outright lies to the "suckers" on the outside.[18]

Stetson did not testify at the Pecora Hearings (Guaranty's president Bill Potter did), but he and his bank certainly felt its backlash. This not only took the form of hostility from the public, but also revolutionary federal regulation. New laws included the Banking Act of 1933, or Glass-Steagall; the Securities Acts of 1933 and 1934; the Banking Act of 1935; and the Public Utilities Holding Company Act of 1935. Together, they created deposit insurance, separated commercial banks from their investment affiliates, imposed regulation on the issue and marketing of securities, disqualified certain persons from serving as bank directors, centralized control over money through the Board of Governors of the Federal Reserve System, and provided a framework for the regulation of public utility holding companies. Like most of his Wall Street colleagues, Stetson opposed much of the new legislation or at least wanted it written and enforced in a way favorable to bankers. In particular, he criticized newly adopted federal deposit insurance, paid for by banks, as something that would create a disincentive for sound banking. Of course, the insurance was intended to create an incentive for smaller depositors, the sort of persons not customers at Stetson's elite bank, to open banking accounts rather than hoard assets. Critical attitudes by bankers such as Stetson were in turn criticized by the press as selfish. As for the Securities Act of 1933, it established a federally regulated procedure for issuing securities to the public. The idea was to provide investors with truthful and complete information about proposed issues. For the first time, a federal agency, the

---

[18] Ferdinand Pecora, *Wall Street Under Oath: The Story of Our Modern Money Changers* (New York: Simon and Schuster, 1939); Seligman, *Transformation of Wall Street*, 26–28. John Brooks describes Guaranty's large ill-fated loans—more than $8 million—to Allan Ryan, son of Thomas F. Ryan, Guaranty's largest shareholder. *Once in Golconda: A True Drama of Wall Street, 1920–1938* (New York: Harper & Row, 1969) 38–39.

Securities and Exchange Commission, was charged with overseeing the 1933 Act and other crucial aspects of the investment process.[19]

Perhaps most important for Stetson and Guaranty was the Glass-Steagall Act of 1933, which banned the mingling of commercial and investment bank functions by requiring their separation. Not surprisingly, Stetson and his bank vigorously opposed Glass-Steagall, as the legislation aimed directly at limiting their most profitable business. After the law was adopted, Guaranty had one year to choose whether it would operate in the future as an investment or commercial bank. The effect of Glass-Steagall cannot be underestimated. In fact, an entire generation of experienced bankers, men such as Stetson who depended on ongoing relationships and worked at commercial banks, suddenly had a large chunk of their livelihood taken away. Given its number of depositors and its profitable trust and business lending operations, Guaranty chose to become a commercial bank. As a result, the company had to dispose of the securities subsidiary, the Guaranty Company, which went into liquidation in June 1934. President Potter hysterically complained that because the new Securities Acts entailed "such great risks and such unpredictable responsibilities on issuing corporations and their directors and upon dealers in securities, that the amounts of sound investment securities will be so limited, and the risk in dealing with them so great, that it will not be possible profitably to continue the securities business under the present terms of the Securities Act." Thanks to the collapse of public confidence, Stetson and Guaranty entered a more regulated era in banking.[20]

---

[19] Geisst, *Wall Street*, 227–37, 244–51; Editorial from *New York Daily News*, 14 May 1935, Folder 220–26, Thomas W. Lamont Collection. On the opposition of the bank to deposit insurance and increased government control of the Federal Reserve embodied in the 1935 Banking Act, see Helen Burns, *The American Banking Community and New Deal Banking Reforms, 1933–1935* (Westport CT: Greenwood Press, 1974) 157. Guaranty paid about $900,000 a year in the 1930s for deposit insurance under the new federal program.

[20] Geisst, *Wall Street*, 230–32; Klebaner, *Commercial Banking*, 145–47. William C. Potter to The Stockholders of the Guaranty Trust Company of New York, 17 January 1934; William C. Potter to The Stockholders of the Guaranty Trust Company of New York, 16 January 1935, J. P. Morgan & Co., Inc. Papers. In early 1933, a retired and ailing Charles Sabin wrote Stetson that he had a special ability to

Glass-Steagall also imposed limits on interest rates, held commercial banks to certain types of investments, constrained their securities underwriting to municipal notes and bonds, limited the geographic reach of banks, and mandated deposit insurance. Investment banks, in contrast, were allowed to underwrite public offerings of new securities, both equity and debt issues. They could trade securities and finance of mergers and acquisitions. But of course they were subject to the regulations of the Securities and Exchange Commission and the new securities laws.[21]

Finally, the new regulatory environment mandated an exodus of private bankers and the directors of other banks from Guaranty's board. The deadline for this purge was delayed until 1940, but even then approximately one-fifth of the Guaranty's directors fell within the ban. They included some of its more important and long-standing members: Averell Harriman, Robert Goelet, George Whitney, and Thomas Lamont. Lamont's departure, because it symbolized a variety of divorce from Morgan, caused much gnashing of teeth. Early in 1940 Guaranty sought a formal legal opinion from the Davis Polk law firm regarding Lamont's status. It agreed he could not remain. On 21 March 1940, Lamont wrote a letter of resignation to Potter, expressing his "strong attachment" to the company. He bought his first shares of Guaranty and became a director in 1910, even before he was a Morgan partner. He had served as chairman of the executive committee since 1912, the year before J. P. Morgan Sr.'s death. Potter's reply revealed the depth of the Morgan link: "I personally

---

succeed in the new environment: "I haven't the slightest criticism of Bill [Potter] or Len [Conway]—they have done a wonderful job and that is the reason for our strong position today but there are going to be new laws and changes which we must meet and beat the rest of the Banks in operating under them. You are the fellow that has the imagination and the ingenuity to aid tremendously in doing that." Charles H. Sabin to Eugene W. Stetson, 15 March 1933, Eugene W. Stetson Papers. Sabin died a few months later.

[21] Chernow, *House of Morgan*, 374–77; Geisst, *Wall Street*, 230–31. J. P. Morgan & Co. chose to become a commercial bank, separating itself from its securities business, Morgan Stanley. Chernow, *House of Morgan*, 385–87. In the ensuing decades political support for the separation of investment and commercial banking faded, leading eventually to the Gramm-Leach-Bliley Act of 1999, which overturned Glass-Steagall's prohibition of bank's offering both investment and commercial services.

have a distinct sense of loss in parting with you as a director of this company, for in the past twenty years [since the Mercantile Bank debacle] it has been a great comfort to me to feel that I was free to call upon you for advice on countless occasions." By 1941 the board no longer contained the large number of private bankers that had characterized it since the Morgan-led mergers of the early 1910s. Now the heads of large industrial, utility, food, transportation, and emerging technology companies, such as Duke Power, American Cynamid, Union Pacific, AT&T, Campbell Soup, the Pennsylvania Railroad, A&P, Anaconda Copper, IBM, and General Electric, filled the bank's board seats. It was Stetson's task to prosper in this new environment.[22]

Litwin

There is a one particularly strong example of how the Crash and the subsequent reaction against Wall Street banks directly affected Stetson. A Depression-induced Congressional investigation, not completed until 1940, looked into the reorganization and receivership of the Chicago, Milwaukee, and St. Paul Railway. The final report, issued by Senators Burton K. Wheeler and Harry S. Truman, presented a tale of conflict of interest, excessive fees, inadequate representation of security holders, and a final reorganization that virtually guaranteed the railroad's failure.[23]

The investigation spawned a legal dispute, *Litwin v. Allen*,[24] a landmark in the American law of director responsibility. The case arose out of several

---

[22] *New York Sun* Clipping, 1 February 1940; C. H. Willard to Eugene W. Stetson, 21 February 1940; Thomas W. Lamont to William C. Potter, 21 March 1940; William C. Potter to Thomas W. Lamont, 1 April 1940, Thomas W. Lamont Collection; "Condensed Statement of Condition, Guaranty Trust Company of New York," 31 December 1941, J. P. Morgan & Co., Inc. Papers.

[23] The report is United States Senate Committee on Interstate Commerce, *Investigation of Railroads, Holding Companies, and Affiliated Companies, Additional Report of the Committee on Interstate Commerce, The 1925–28 Receivership and Reorganization of the Chicago, Milwaukee, and St. Paul Railway Company, Role of the Guaranty Trust Company of New York* (Washington: Government Printing Office, 1940).

[24] 25 N.Y.S.2d 667 (Sup. Ct. 1940). The case continues to be cited in legal journals and by American courts.

decisions of Morgan and Guaranty from the late 1920s through the mid–1930s. Guaranty directors, including Stetson, had approved loans to companies owned by brothers Oris P. and Mantis J. Van Sweringen of Cleveland. The Van Sweringens, who became notorious to the public as a result of the Pecora investigation, used a holding company to acquire control of several railroads, including the Missouri Pacific. The Van Sweringen properties were heavily indebted to J. P. Morgan & Co. and Guaranty. Because Morgan had substantial representation on Guaranty's board at the time of the loan decisions, the plaintiffs in *Litwin* alleged that Morgan's pressure caused Guaranty to approve bad investments in order to prop up the faltering Van Sweringen interests. The plaintiffs in *Litwin* were Guaranty shareholders who sued when the Van Sweringens defaulted. Both Morgan and Guaranty, their shareholders that is, lost millions as a result of the collapse.[25]

The plaintiffs filed the original complaint in New York state court against more than seventy defendants in May 1937. Because he was a member of the Guaranty board at the time of the transactions, Stetson was one of the defendants. Also sued was Guaranty, as well as Bill Potter and other Guaranty officers and directors. J. P. Morgan partners were among the defendants: Lamont, Jack Morgan, and Russell Leffingwell, for example. Coincidentally, apart from the *Litwin* matter, Stetson had been acquainted with the Van Sweringens through Bob Woodruff and the Cleveland-based White Motor Company. Obviously, it was a small financial world, perhaps too small.[26]

A primary theme of Depression-era Congressional investigations, such as the Pecora Hearings, was banking's monopolistic character, particularly the broad reach of the Morgan firm. The *Litwin* complaint adopted this theme, focusing on Morgan's influence at Guaranty. According to the

---

[25] Ibid. See also these discussions of the Van Sweringens: Frederick Allen, *The Lords of Creation* (New York: Harper & Brothers, 1935) 293–303; Matthew Josephson, *The Money Lords: The Great Finance Capitalists, 1925–1950* (New York: Weybright & Talley, 1972); and Klein, *Rainbow's End*, 155–57.

[26] "Complaint"; "Affidavit of Abraham Geller," 27 January 1938, *Litwin v. Allen*, Division of Old Records, New York State Supreme Court, New York County, New York, New York.

plaintiffs, the Morgan firm engaged in a conspiracy to "waste, dissipate, and improperly use [Guaranty's] funds." The plaintiffs alleged that Guaranty, the Guaranty Company, and Morgan jointly floated securities of the Alleghany Corporation, a holding company headed by the Van Sweringens. The banks then purchased Missouri Pacific bonds from the Van Sweringens for $10.5 million, $3 million of which came from Guaranty. The plaintiffs claimed that Guaranty directors were negligent because, at the time, the Van Sweringens were clearly in serious financial trouble and already unable to repay existing loans. At its core, the complaint was that Guaranty, because of its cozy relationships with Morgan and the Van Sweringens, squandered bank assets.[27]

Guaranty and the other defendants vigorously denied any improper influence. In fact, they understood that to admit wrongdoing for this sort of transaction would be to concede that the fundamental character of Wall Street financing was wrongful, because practically every big deal involved influence and cooperation among banks. Their attorneys, including the prominent Davis Polk firm, tried to portray the lawsuit as an attempt by overly litigious persons, some of whom were not real shareholders, to cash in on the Depression's anti-banker sentiment. In fact, there is some evidence that David Feiner, one of the plaintiffs, may have had experience in making similar claims. At any rate, the defendants sought to dismiss a number of shareholders from the case on the ground that they had not legally owned shares in Guaranty. This wrangling produced a new complaint in June 1938 that seemed to settle the standing of the plaintiffs to bring the suit. In the end, the plaintiffs represented only thirty-six of Guaranty's 900,000 outstanding shares. The June 1938 complaint essentially repeated earlier claims, arguing the Van Sweringen arrangement "was for the accommodation and at the behest of the defendant J. P. Morgan & Co. and was for its benefit and profit."[28]

---

[27] Ibid.

[28] "Motion to Dismiss"; "Supplemental and Amended Complaint," *Litwin v. Allen*, Division of Old Records, New York State Supreme Court; "Settlement," 11 April 1934, *Feiner v. Investors Syndicate*, Division of Old Records, New York State Supreme Court, New York County, New York, New York.

In December 1940, Justice Bernard L. Shientag of the New York Supreme Court in Manhattan issued a 119-page ruling that largely vindicated Guaranty, Morgan, and their officers and directors, including Stetson. Despite the plaintiffs' sweeping claims of malfeasance, by the time the case came to trial only four transactions were still under scrutiny: the purchase of Alleghany Corporation common stock by Morgan partners in January 1929; the October 1930, participation by Guaranty Trust and the Guaranty Company in the purchase of $3 million of Missouri Pacific bonds from the Alleghany Corporation, with an option to the seller to repurchase them in six months; the participation by Guaranty Trust to the extent of $11 million in a $39 million loan to certain Van Sweringen enterprises, which was later defaulted on; and the auction of the collateral on this loan in 1935. The court ruled in favor of the defendants on all issues except those involving the Missouri Pacific bonds.[29]

As for the first issue, the stock purchase, the plaintiffs' claim was that officers and directors of the Guaranty Company and Guaranty, probably including Stetson, were given an opportunity to purchase common stock of the newly formed Alleghany Corporation. Alleghany was intended as a holding company to provide funds for investment in railroad securities. When Alleghany was organized, in early 1929, J. P. Morgan purchased a large amount of its common and preferred stock and bonds. In turn, Morgan entered into an agreement with the Guaranty Company that the latter would undertake to sell the public a large number of the common shares and all of the preferred shares. But Morgan retained many common shares, intending to sell them, according to Morgan partner George Whitney, "to men with whom we had had business relations, who we knew were aware of all the implications of buying the common stock of a holding company."[30]

One of these men was Guaranty's Potter, to whom Whitney offered 40,000 shares. Potter accepted 5,000 shares for himself and sold the rest to Guaranty associates, probably including Stetson. The *Litwin* plaintiffs complained because the common shares increased in value and were then sold for a profit. As a result, they thought the 40,000 shares offered to

---

[29] *Litwin*, 25 N.Y.S.2d 667; *New York Times*, 19 December 1940.

[30] *Litwin*, 25 N.Y.S.2d at 679–91.

Potter represented a proper business opportunity for Guaranty, not a personal opportunity for Potter and other Guaranty personnel. Justice Shientag, however, disagreed, holding that the Guaranty Company had no business interest in obtaining the 40,000 shares. Nonetheless, the offer confirmed the close connection between Guaranty and Morgan. According to George Whitney, there was nothing unusual about a Morgan partner's friendly phone call to Guaranty's president offering him, for personal gain, almost $1 million in pre-public sale stock that Guaranty would later market to the public for a substantial profit.[31]

The court also seemed to have little trouble disposing of the plaintiffs' claims that a $39.5 million loan to the Van Sweringens in October 1930, later defaulted upon, was negligence caused by Morgan's self-dealing. Guaranty participated in this loan to the extent of $11 million. The loan, like the stock issue, showed the close cooperation between Morgan, Guaranty, and other leading New York banks. The loan was part of a plan to shore up a previous $30 million note to the Van Sweringen Corporation, which was issued by the Guaranty Company. In October 1930 the security offered by the Van Sweringens was no longer sufficient to support the note. The Van Sweringens came to New York and met with Lamont, Harold Stanley, Potter, and a few others and asked Guaranty and Morgan "as parties interested in their affairs, to come to their relief by giving them a loan." Not surprisingly, the request disappointed the bankers. Yet Guaranty and Morgan decided to consider a collateralized loan. They feared a Van Sweringen collapse would have a huge ripple effect on the already suffering equity markets. Further, as Lamont testified, in the fall of 1930 there was still hope for a quick recovery: "Nobody knew that Central Europe was going to blow up, nor that Great Britain was going off the gold standard and that there was to be a general collapse."[32]

In the end, the banks made a $39.5 million loan. Morgan contributed $11 million, Guaranty $11 million, Chase National $5.5 million, National City $4.5 million, First National Bank, actually George F. Baker personally, $4.5 million, and Bankers Trust put in $3 million. The work was accomplished hurriedly, within a matter of weeks. But, according to Justice

[31] Ibid.

[32] Ibid., 706–22.

Shientag, the *Litwin* plaintiffs did not establish either self-serving activity or negligence by Guaranty or Morgan in constructing the loan. Morgan, in particular, had no special interest in the original loan. As trustee, that was Guaranty's problem. The court even thought this suggested the partners at "J. P. Morgan & Co. were influenced by the Trust Company, rather than it by J. P. Morgan."[33]

Further, in challenging the value of the security for the second loan, the plaintiffs were in the awkward position of questioning the abilities of men such as Guaranty directors Henry De Forest, former chairman of the Southern Pacific Railroad, Albert Harris, vice president of the New York Central, and Averell Harriman, a member of the executive committee of the Union Pacific, to evaluate railroad property. The court ruled the defendants took reasonable precaution and made no personal profits.[34]

The court took little time in ruling against the plaintiffs on a third claim: when the loan went into default and the collateral was auctioned, Morgan and Guaranty officers conspired with the Van Sweringens to allow a new corporation controlled by the Van Sweringens to obtain the collateral at a ridiculously low price. The court believed the collateral auction was properly advertised and that the banks had no agreement or knowledge that the Van Sweringens would offer any bid. The argument that "J. P. Morgan & Co. should conspire with the Van Sweringens to the end of throwing away a large amount of their own money in order to retain the good will and secure the future business of persons known to be insolvent, is a supposition passing the limits of probability." The court also found there was no evidence that Morgan influenced Guaranty or any other sophisticated creditors about the auction.[35]

A fourth claim, concerning Guaranty's purchase of Missouri Pacific debentures, produced a different result: here the court believed the bankers were at fault. On 16 October 1930, just prior to the $39 million dollar loan, Guaranty's board approved the purchase of Missouri Pacific debentures from Alleghany, with an option allowing Alleghany to repurchase the bonds at the original purchase price within six months. The deal required

---

[33] Ibid., 706–27.

[34] Ibid.

[35] Ibid., 728–37.

Guaranty to purchase $3 million in bonds and Morgan to purchase $4.5 million in bonds; the First National Bank would buy the remaining bonds for $3 million. Although ostensibly an investment, the arrangement was actually a loan. Legally, however, it could not be structured as such because Alleghany had reached the limits of its corporate borrowing authority. Not long after the "investment," the Depression deepened, the Missouri Pacific went under, and the unsecured bonds went into default. The bonds lost more than ten percent of their value in the six months after the purchase, and of course Alleghany did not repurchase them under its option. The *Litwin* plaintiffs complained that the arrangement allowed Alleghany to benefit from any rise in price in the six months option period while Guaranty would suffer any losses. For Guaranty the deal was a "heads you win, tails I lose" transaction.[36]

Justice Shientag concluded that the option arrangement was clearly negligence: "What sound reason is there for a bank, desiring to make an investment, short term or otherwise, to buy securities under an arrangement whereby any appreciation will inure to the benefit of the seller and any loss will be borne by the bank?" But Guaranty had a very telling answer, one that summed up the logic of relationship banking: the deal was justified simply because of the overall relationship with the customer. Guaranty accepted a losing "investment" in order to accommodate a valuable long-term client. The court, however, did not think this was an adequate reason in law and found Guaranty's action "so improvident, so risky, so unusual and unnecessary as to be contrary to fundamental conceptions of prudent banking practice." All of the directors who voted for it, including Harriman, Lamont, Potter, and Stetson were personally liable for negligence. Yet the court did not believe that, in making the mistake, there was any undue influence by Morgan or that there was any bad faith or self-dealing.[37]

Justice Shientag appointed a referee to consider appropriate damages. Initially, Guaranty offered $750,000 to settle the claim. Given that the loss from the bond deal was allegedly more than $2 million, the plaintiffs naturally felt the offer was inadequate. They seemed to want at least $1 million, which would mean each defendant's individual share would be

---

[36] Ibid., 691–98.
[37] Ibid., 691–706.

about $50,000. The defendants rejected this deal. Eventually, however, at a hearing on 28 April 1941, the court approved a final undisclosed settlement and entered judgment. The three-year old dispute was over. The bankers wanted out, as by 1941 it must have seemed a troublesome relic of an unpleasant era. Bill Potter and Lamont approved the settlement, as did Stetson, who by this time was Guaranty's president.[38]

Litwin illustrates a number of significant points about Stetson's experience as a Guaranty banker. The case certainly demonstrates the close connections between Guaranty, the Guaranty Company, and Morgan. Morgan felt comfortable involving Guaranty and Guaranty officers and directors in investment opportunities and even expected them to use bank resources to help provide bailouts in critical situations. It had clout, in the persons of Lamont and George Whitney, on the Guaranty board. Lamont and Potter moved together to "participate" in loans, purchase securities, and make decisions related to the sale of collateral on defaulted loans. This kind of closeness created enormous potential for conflicts of interest. Were the interests of Guaranty officers, Morgan partners, Guaranty shareholders, and clients of Guaranty and Morgan always the same? The mere appearance of self-dealing, much less the sort of private profit taking as occurred here, raised questions about the stewardship of clients' and investors' funds.

Perhaps most importantly, *Litwin* demonstrated key attributes of relationship banking as practiced by Stetson and Guaranty. The Van Sweringens were viewed as valuable clients. So valuable, in fact, that Morgan, Guaranty, and other New York banks structured a $30 million loan for them in short order despite obvious trouble signs. When sued by disgruntled shareholders for the ensuing collapse, Guaranty openly admitted that client relations were among the reasons it approved the Missouri Pacific bond deal, a deceptive and costly end run around legal lending limits. Thus, good relationship banking was such a dominant ethos that it was viewed as a legal defense to short-term unfavorable banking practices and results. On the whole, however, the *Litwin* result gave bankers

---

[38] "Statement of Dora Strauss," 26 April 1941; "To be Published in Law Journal," *Litwin v. Allen*, Division of Old Records, New York State Supreme Court; William C. Potter to Thomas W. Lamont, 18 March 1941; Folders 221-3-5, 221-7-8, Thomas W. Lamont Collection.

wide discretion, confirming the basic preferences inherent in relationship banking even after the Crash and its regulatory aftermath. Only extreme favoritism—guaranteed loss, in fact, was punished. Legally, at least, there was a future for relationship banking.

Perspectives

The Crash, hard times, and the new role for banks fashioned during the 1930s transformed institutions, including Guaranty. Pecora, federal laws, and even *Litwin* established that a newly vigilant government and a less passive public would not tolerate the more blatant forms of cronyism. The new rules sought to impose a particular balance between capital markets and public welfare. The combination of regulatory and market pressures felt by Guaranty in 1940 contrasted sharply with the free-wheeling world of Wall Street in 1916, when Stetson came to New York.

Stetson was dismayed that the sort of conflicts of interest inherent in relationship banking became a target for federal regulation. He believed his personal variety of "honorable" relationship banking should be distinguished from the kind of self-dealing that brought public scorn on bankers. He thought the new sort of government oversight and involvement in private business practices was doomed to constrict finance. Stetson presumed dishonest bankers would get their due from bankers and customers who would refuse to deal with them, or perhaps from the criminal law of fraud or theft. He knew that even when there was no hard evidence of improper actions, the mere suspicion of unethical practices could destroy confidence in an individual or institution. This should be enough to deter the worst offenses.

Stetson's view underestimated the hardships of the Depression and neglected the fact that the purpose of many of the new regulations was to define wrongdoing and prevent it before it happened—especially in an economy increasingly defined by arms-length transactions in which the parties had little opportunity to educate themselves as to the trustworthiness of sellers of goods or services. Few Americans, unlike the Van Sweringens, Bob Woodruff, or Averell Harriman, had access to the information controlled by Guaranty or Morgan. Relying on after-the-fact impressions of proper "ethics" or even criminal prosecution did not prevent the kind of self-dealing that characterized important segments of Wall Street banking in the 1920s. The new banking and securities laws reflected the public's sense that all financial institutions were capable of impropriety without being detected and that only constant oversight from outside the industry, not the market or traditional criminal law, could address the problem in a proactive manner. In the final analysis, banking had too many "public" dimensions. It was too important to tempt another catastrophe.

Stetson was undoubtedly familiar with this argument. But he adhered to the principle that in banking integrity and trust were matters between individuals and private institutions. He understood conflicts of interest existed, but he believed a banker could and usually would refuse to exploit them. He thought that although bankers were in a position to use the information they worked with for personal gain, to have a conflict of interest was not in and of itself evidence of wrongdoing. The obvious limitation to this view is that there will always be disagreement about what is improper and unethical among individuals. In Stetson's day, for example, it was neither illegal nor considered improper to use advance knowledge of the excellence or worthlessness of a security for personal gain. The new securities laws, however, defined this as illegal insider trading that threatened the credibility and functioning of the market.

Did the passing of new laws change the way bankers such as Stetson behaved, even as they disagreed with them? Neither Pecora, Congress, nor Roosevelt thought law could eliminate all deceptive behavior. The goal of banking regulation was much more modest: to create a climate that would deter swindling and restore confidence in the investment markets. Nonetheless, the new environment did in fact affect the behavior of even an ethically-minded banker, such as Stetson. After 1933, if Stetson recommended a security in a public offering, as he did to his sons during World War II, it would be accompanied by the public prospectus. But compliance came at a heavy personal cost. Stetson enjoyed banking because of its relationships, as evidence by his friendships with Lamont, Woodruff, Watson, Rionda, and Harriman. After the early 1930s, the conditions for creating such relationships were fundamentally altered. The modern banking landscaped emerged partly as a result of what happened in the

1930s. Stetson was at the center of this change, and he and his bank felt its consequences deeply.

10

Relationships

Even during the dark days of the Depression, Gene Stetson loved to organize men's business dinners. They were one of his favorite ways of building relationships with corporate executives. The dinners were a time to relax and to tell and hear some great stories. Stetson liked to hold the events at elite places, and his colleagues at Guaranty, Charles Sabin and Bill Potter, arranged for him to join an exclusive venue, the Links Club, an oasis in Manhattan for corporate bosses.[1]

One night in 1939 Stetson hosted a men's dinner at the Links in honor of Sidney Weinberg, the senior partner of the investment firm Goldman Sachs. Protestants did not generally socialize with their Jewish colleagues on Wall Street. But Stetson enjoyed entertaining, and he recognized Weinberg had done a lot for Goldman Sachs and for American business. Weinberg joined Goldman Sachs in 1907 and became partner in 1927, a position he held until his death in 1969. Weinberg was especially interested in linking business and government, and he advised a number of American Presidents. In 1933, he helped found the Business Council (Averell Harriman headed it in the late 1930s), an organization which gave corporate executives an opportunity to discuss and promote certain govern-ment policies. At the time of Stetson's dinner, Weinberg was about to take a leave of absence from his firm to become assistant to the chairman of the War Production Board. He was later named vice-chairman of that board and eventually awarded the United States Medal of Merit for this service.[2]

---

[1] Many invitations to such dinners are in Box 1, Folder 8, Eugene W. Stetson Papers, Jack Tarver Library, Special Collections, Mercer University, Macon, Georgia.

[2] On Weinberg, see "Everybody's Broker: Sidney Weinberg," *Time* 72 (8 December 1958): 96; Lisa Endlich, *Goldman Sachs: The Culture of Success* (New York: Alfred A. Knopf, 1999) 3–62; Charles R. Geisst, *The Last Partnerships: Inside the Great Wall Street Money Dynasties* (New York: McGraw-Hill, 2001) 289–93. For an

Stetson's dinners might seem trivial, but they reflected his determined persistence in developing relationships inside and outside the bank. Between 1916 and the 1950s, this focus on relationships helped Stetson advance from vice president to president and then chairman of Guaranty. The emphasis thus far in this study has been on Stetson's major outside relationships, such as with Coca-Cola, Cuban sugar, Tom Watson of IBM, and Averell Harriman. Alone, however, these were not enough to propel Stetson to the top of Guaranty. By describing the broader sweep of Stetson's banking relationships, his own career as well as the nature of New York banking during his life becomes clearer.

Professional Director

In 1928, Guaranty Trust had twenty-four vice presidents, each of whom competed for the highest positions in the bank. Eventually, Stetson was a winner in this competition. He acted in ways that received the approval of Bill Potter, and equally important, the Morgan men who had great influence in the company. In part, this was demonstrated by Stet-son's election as a director of the Guaranty Company in 1927, as a director of Guaranty Trust in early 1928, and as a director of the restructured and larger Guaranty created by Guaranty's merger with the National Bank of Commerce in 1929.[3]

Equally impressive was Stetson's ability to place himself on the boards of client corporations. Even among the most successful of Wall Street bankers Stetson's performance in this regard was outstanding. Stetson not only held wide-ranging and influential board memberships, but he used them to cement banking relationships, to get leads for new business, to enhance his social life, and to link clients to one another. In many cases, the

---

official firm biography, see "Our Firm," http://www2.goldmansachs. com/our-firm/index.html. For a self-description of the Business Council, see "The Business Council: About Us," http://www.businesscouncil.com/about/.

[3] *International Banking Directory* (New York: Bankers Publishing Co., 1928) 155. Prior to the 1929 merger, the board of directors consisted of 28 members elected for three-year terms. "By-Laws of the Guaranty Trust Company of New York," 1 September 1923, J. P. Morgan & Co., Inc. Papers, JPMorgan Chase Archives, New York, New York.

connections happily served the interests of several parties, such as with Coca-Cola and its supplier Air Reduction. In other instances, however, as when Stetson served on the boards of both Coca-Cola and Canada Dry, there were potential conflicts of interest.

Stetson's career as a kind of professional director started at the very beginning of his association with Guaranty. In 1919 he was already a director of the Asia Banking Corporation, Bibb Manufacturing Company, Italian Discount and Trust Company, the Morris Plan Company of New York, and Pierce Oil Company. By the early 1920s he had added another twelve corporate directorships, including Barnsdall Corporation; The Coca-Cola Company; Cuba Cane Sugar; European Textile Corporation; Fidelitas Realty; Foreign Bond and Share Corporation; Guaranty Company; Independent Warehouses, Inc. (of which he was also president); Mercantile Bank of the Americas; Textile Banking Company; W. A. Harriman & Company; and the Warehouse Finance Corporation. Ten years later, in the early 1930s, Stetson sat on even more boards, including Automatic Registering Machine; Aviation Corporation; New York Petroleum Royalty Corporation; Niagara Shares Corporation; Selected Industries; Small Issues Corporation; Canada Dry; White Motor Company; Vick Financial Corporation; French-American Banking Corporation; United Stores Corporation; Illinois Central Railroad; Tobacco Products Companies of Delaware and New Jersey; United Drug Company; W. A. Harriman Securities; Ward Baking Company; U.S. Industrial Alcohol; Pure Carbonic; Southeastern Compress and Warehouse Company and Guaranty Trust.[4]

---

[4] Adrienne Moore Bond, *Eugene W. Stetson* (Macon GA: Mercer University Press, 1983) 64, 163; *New York Times*, 27 June, 10 August, 11 November 1918; "Rail Directorate Given to Stetson [1932]," The Coca-Cola Company; John W. Leonard, ed. *Who's Who in Finance and Banking (1920–1922)* (New York: Who's Who in Finance, Inc., 1922) 651; *Directory of Directors in the City of New York, 1919–1920* (New York: Directory of Directors Co., 1919); *Directory of Directors in the City of New York, 1921–1922* (New York: Directory of Directors Co., 1921); *Directory of Directors in the City of New York, 1930–1931* (New York: Directory of Directors Co., 1930). According to these sources, the top leadership at Guaranty had similar records: In the mid-1920s Sabin was a director in 78 corporations, Potter in 22. Although it is difficult to determine Stetson's ownership stake in these businesses, he held a substantial interest in the Bibb Manufacturing Company, to the extent of

Not only did Stetson serve on these boards for long periods, but he was an extremely active director, typically serving on executive committees. Given that executive committees often met on a weekly basis, this meant Stetson spent a large amount of his time helping to run companies that were Guaranty clients. These businesses were diverse, specializing in everything from textiles and beverages to transportation and investments. Altogether, for Stetson, his work as a director was the crucial institutional component of relationship banking from the 1920s through the 1940s.[5]

A key aspect of this board work, and one that helps to explain his popularity as a board member, was Stetson's interest in advertising. A hint of this has already been seen with Coca-Cola, especially in his valuation of the drink maker's trademark. Throughout his career Stetson viewed advertising as a valuable source of corporate worth for any company, especially in the new age of national brands and interstate retailers. As lenders, Stetson argued that banks should evaluate the "intangible good-will created through intelligent sales efforts applied to a product of unquestioned merit." In the 1920s, Stetson thought, there were plenty of good examples: Coca-Cola, Proctor and Gamble, Beech-Nut, Aunt Jemima, Old Dutch Cleanser, Victrola, and the cigarette industry generally. Accordingly, companies built value in their trademarks by using advertising to create confidence among consumers, which translated into instant "character." Like "character," which Stetson believed was "the principal collateral behind many loans and an important factor in all loans," effective advertising showed "that a firm's product and its dealings with the buying public have been honest and efficient, and gives other evidence that the future conduct of a business will be on sound and ethical principles." Stetson further believed that even banks, usually stodgy about advertising, should also seek the right kind of publicity. As he put it, progressive banks

---

2,000 shares of $100 par value stock. They paid dividends of $28,000 in 1924 and 1925. See *Iola Wise Stetson v. Commissioner of Internal Revenue*, 1932 WL 157 (B.T.A. 1932).

[5] Ibid.

"that have had that courage and vision are the institutions which are today leading the financial world both in service rendered and in growth."[6]

The Network

A reconstruction of Stetson's actions as director in selected companies helps demonstrate the intensely interconnected nature of his banking practice. One example of the network effect was his association with Air Reduction Company, a supplier of carbonation to soft drink companies, among other products. Obviously Stetson's knowledge and experience with soft drink producers Coca-Cola and Canada Dry were useful to Air Reduction. In fact, there is evidence that Stetson tried to engineer a merger of one of the soft drink companies with Air Reduction, thereby combining syrup, water, and fizz.

Air Reduction was organized in November 1916, the same month Stetson moved to New York. The company's products evolved from new technology for separating oxygen from air. Purified oxygen was especially useful after the development of the oxygen and acetylene welding torch, the company's core business. During the 1920s Air Reduction expanded into carbon dioxide production, a necessary ingredient of the rapidly expanding soft drinks industry. Carbon dioxide also happened to be a by-product of the manufacture of ethyl alcohol, the primary product of U.S. Industrial Alcohol. This fortuity of chemistry led to a joint venture between Air Reduction and U.S. Industrial Alcohol and the formation of Pure Carbonic, Inc., eventually an Air Reduction subsidiary. Stetson was elected to the boards of all three companies: Air Reduction, U.S. Industrial Alcohol, and Pure Carbonic. By 1941 Air Reduction consisted of five separate corporations, each focused on different aspects of gas production. In the

[6] Eugene W. Stetson, "'Advertising Good-Will' as a Bankable Asset," *The Red Barrel* 3 (May 1924): 3–5. Nine years later Stetson wrote a similar article praising sound advertising, but from the standpoint of the banker-as-director. Eugene W. Stetson, "Banker Sees Continuing Need of Advertising," *Printers' Ink* (23 November 1933): 43–45.

1940s and 1950s Air Reduction further expanded, most notably into medical gases and chemicals.[7]

From Stetson's vantage one thing clearly led to another. He was already a director with U.S. Industrial Alcohol and Pure Carbonic before he went on the Air Reduction board in the late 1930s. By this time Stetson knew Charles Munson, the president of Air Reduction, who was also a Guaranty director. When Air Reduction obtained twenty percent of U.S. Industrial Alcohol's stock in the early 1930s, Munson also became president of Industrial Alcohol. Most likely Stetson and his bank influenced these converging corporate structures and benefited from them through selling bank services. There were other official relationships with Guaranty. For example, Guaranty acted as Air Reduction's stock registrar. Stetson served on the Air Reduction board until 1959.[8]

Both Air Reduction and U.S. Industrial were complex technology-based organizations that adjusted to changing conditions through growth and product modification. Between the mid–1930s and the late 1950s Air Reduction's assets grew from about $40 million to more than $225 million. Its predominantly unionized employees peaked at over 8,000 in the mid–1940s, working in more than 178 plants in 33 states. The company's products included not only carbon dioxide and oxygen, but also acetylene, hydrogen, nitrogen, neon, anesthetic gases, and medical and welding equipment. By the late 1950s, the welding portion of the business remained dominant, but a shift in emphasis, and growth, had been achieved by producing chemicals used in paints, plastics, and other materials. There was

---

[7] Air Reduction Co., Inc., *Air Reduction Co., Inc.: Air Reduction Sales Company, National Carbide Corporation, Wilson Welder and Metals Co., Inc., Pure Carbonic, Inc., The Ohio Chemical & Mfg. Co.* (New York: Air Reduction Co., Inc., 1941). Since Stetson's time, Air Reduction's successors have been merged into the German-based Linde Group. On the Linde Group, see "About BOC," http://www.boc-gases.com/about_us/index.asp In the 1960s, Air Reduction became Airco, which in turn was acquired by the UK's global gas giant Brin's Oxygen Co., Ltd., or BOC, in 1978. BOC's 2006 acquirer, The Linde Group, operates in 70 countries, has more than 50,000 employees, and had recent annual revenues of 12.7 billion euros.

[8] Air Reduction Company, Inc., *Annual Report, 1945* (New York: Air Reduction Co., Inc., 1946); Air Reduction Company, Inc., *Annual Report, 1959* (New York: Air Reduction Co., Inc., 1960).

also international expansion to Canada and Cuba. Typical customers included chemical manufacturers, steel makers, railroads, the military, and metal working operations.[9]

Stetson was director with U.S. Industrial Alcohol and its successor, U.S. Industrial Chemicals, from the 1930s to the 1950s. U.S. Industrial Alcohol formed in New York in 1906 after Congress exempted denatured alcohol, alcohol made unfit to drink, from high federal taxes. Congress reasoned that denatured alcohol could be produced from agricultural products, thus benefiting farmers, manufacturers who would use the product, and consumers. Molasses, a sugar derivative, was the company's primary source for industrial-grade alcohol. U.S. Industrial Alcohol was yet another company with which Stetson was identified that enjoyed substantial profits during World War I. The company helped produce gas masks and acetone, the latter for gun powder.[10]

Flexible product and management strategies were a hallmark of U.S. Industrial in the four decades after World War I. During Prohibition its products were marketed as automobile anti-freeze, solvents, and carbon dioxide for soft drinks. At the end of Prohibition, the company partnered with National Distillers Products Corporation and formed Penn-Maryland, Inc., to manufacture gin, rum, whiskey and other alcoholic beverages. Another use for carbon dioxide, dry ice, was exploited through new levels of cooperation with Air Reduction in the early 1940s. The outbreak of World War II meant a shortage of rubber, and the company manufactured alcohol that was essential in the production of synthetic rubber. Medical supplies and solvents for war production became a high priority. In 1943 the growing diversity of operations produced a merger with its subsidiary, U.S. Industrial Chemicals. By 1947 more than sixty percent of the company's sales were in diversified chemicals used to produce insecticides, foods, and perfume. This was approximately double the sales of the late 1930s, when most business derived from anti-freeze and ethyl alcohol. In the 1950s, the company increasingly emphasized research and developed plastics. In

---

[9] Ibid.

[10] Harry C. Barnes, *From Molasses to the Moon: The Story of the U.S. Industrial Chemicals Co.* (New York: U.S. Industrial Chemicals Co., 1975) 31–36.

addition, the company manufactured a wide variety of basic chemicals, eliminating the liquor and anti-freeze operations.[11]

The histories of Air Reduction, Pure Carbonic, and U.S. Industrial fit common themes in Stetson's banking. The companies experienced increasing size and scope through merger, joint ventures, and national and international expansion. The companies were necessarily responsive not only to technology, but to shifting political events, such as Prohibition and world war. They took advantage of Stetson's relationships with other businesses, especially Coca-Cola and Canada Dry. Clearly Stetson was able to cross industrial boundaries and operate comfortably in very different kinds of business settings. A resolution adopted by the Air Reduction board at Stetson's death described him as having "many natural gifts, among them a fine mind, great ability, a never-failing wisdom, and sound judgment."[12]

Another example of Stetson's diverse directorships was Ward Baking Company. Ward, a nationally prominent mass-consumption food company, had several interesting parallels with Coca-Cola. Most importantly, image and advertising were essential to its success. Instead of conceding that bread is an ordinary product, Ward promoted itself as a high technology producer. Founded by an Irish immigrant, Hugh Ward, the business began in Pittsburgh. In 1903 Ward's first large bakery, described by the company as both safe and scientific, opened in the city. A desire to exploit mass production techniques caused the company to build new plants in Chicago, Cleveland, Boston, and Providence. In 1911 the Ward family moved to New York and organized the Ward Baking Company. The company constructed two new bakeries in Manhattan, with a capacity of more than 500,000 loaves per day. Company literature carefully crafted an image that stressed the "modern" and "clean" baking process. Ward bread was even delivered by "clean cut, healthy salesmen who were uniformed and gloved

---

[11] Ibid., 41–132. In 1951, Air Reduction sold its stock in U.S. Industrial to National Distillers Products Corporation, which led to a merger between National Distillers and U.S. Industrial Chemicals. Ibid., 110–11. U.S. Industrial's operations were eventually absorbed into the international chemical company Millenium Chemicals, Inc., which in turn was acquired by Texas-based Lyondell, one of the world's largest chemical companies. See "Lyondell," http://www.lyondell.com/Lyondell/.

[12] Bond, *Stetson*, 160.

in white." In 1921 Ward operated 16 bakeries in the northeast and Midwest, making almost 90 kinds of breads, rolls, and cakes. In 1924, the "goodwill," or trade name, value of the company, including its "Tip Top" brand, was estimated at $11 million, a sum about half that of Coca-Cola just a few years earlier.[13]

Stetson's banking also took him into the emerging world of the chain store, retail operations with outlets in multiple locations. He became a member of the boards of several interrelated consumer product companies, including United Cigar Stores, Tobacco Products Corporation, and United Stores Corporation. These businesses were national operations, engaged in the manufacture and retailing of tobacco, candy, and grocery products. Unfortunately, United Cigar Stores suffered bankruptcy in the 1930s. Stetson was likely placed on the boards of these businesses because United Stores, eventually the controlling force over the others, was a Guaranty client. In fact, each of the companies had a long history with Guaranty executives, including Potter and Harold Stanley, and some of the bank's most elite clients, such as James B. Duke. Guaranty handled the reorganization of United Cigar in the early 1930s and Stetson was a member of the United Stores board from the 1930s to the 1950s.[14]

---

[13] There is no general history of Ward, but see Ward Baking Company, *The Story of Our Research Products* (New York: Ward Baking Company, 1921) 66–71; Ralph Borsodi, *The Distribution Age: A Study in the Economy of Modern Distribution* (New York: D. Appleton, 1927); "Chronology of the Ward Family and the Ward Baking Company," http://www.wardbakingcompany.com/library/docs/AIB_Ward-BakingCo_hist_2003.pdf.

[14] *Hirson v. United Stores Corp.*, 34 N.Y.S.2d 122 (Sup. Ct. App. Div. 1942); United Cigar Stores Company of America, *Reorganization of the United Stores Company of America* (New York: United Cigar Stores of America and Guaranty Trust Company of New York, 1933); Robert F. Durden, *Bold Entrepreneur: A Life of James B. Duke* (Durham: Carolina Academic Press, 2003) 52; *New York Times*, 29 August 1933. The connection between Tobacco Products, United Cigar, and United Stores is complex, but represents another good example of the interlocking business interests involving Guaranty, Stetson, and his clients. Tobacco Products Corporation was formed in Virginia in 1912, partly with financing from Guaranty. George J. Whelan, head of the United Cigar Stores Company, was a stock owner of Tobacco Products. In 1919, Tobacco Products acquired Philip Morris & Co., which had been jointly owned by British and American interests, and reorganized the company. During the early 1920s, James B. Duke, the tobacco tycoon and

Stetson's work with the United Cigar bankruptcy was typical banker labor in the Depression-mired 1930s. He frequently sat on creditors' committees for insolvent or at-risk debtors, such as that for the International Combustion Engine Corporation, which he chaired in 1933. In that instance, he was charged with developing plans that could salvage the company and satisfy its security holders. He criticized one reorganization plan because it failed to provide preferred shares backed by a first mortgage to creditors, failed to identify a credible new management, and failed to provide sufficient working capital for the company to get back on its feet. In the 1932 United Cigar reorganization the task was similar—to develop a refinancing plan that would satisfy creditors and allow the company to resume business.[15]

---

former Guaranty director, was named to assist in a possible merger of Tobacco Products Corporation with United Retail Stores Corporation, the latter of which had stock control of the United Cigar Stores Company and which had been controlled by Duke since 1901. At this time, Guaranty's Harold Stanley was a Tobacco Products director. In 1929, United Stores Corporation was formed to control United Cigar Stores, Union Tobacco Company, and Tobacco Products Corporation. Stetson was put on the boards of both United Stores and Tobacco Products. Many of the brands sold by this new combination are still well-known: Philip Morris, Beech-Nut, Gillette, and Life Savers. At the head of United Stores were brothers George and Frederick Morrow, two food industry leaders. And among Stetson's fellow directors at United Stores was John Foster Dulles, at the time a lawyer at Sullivan & Cromwell and later Secretary of State under President Dwight Eisenhower. See "Tobacco Merger?", *Time* 1 (30 July 1923): 21; "Two Morrows," *Time* 14 (2 September 1929): 57; *New York Times*, 20 August 1929; "Philip Morris International: Our History," http://www.philipmorrisinternational.com/PMINTL/pages/eng/ourbus/Our_history.asp; "The 'Power Elite' Controls Both Sides," http://www.smokershistory.com/power.htm (relying on reports in *New York Times*).

[15] "Press Release, Guaranty Trust Company of New York," 24 April 1933, J. P. Morgan & Co., Inc. Papers; *New York Times*, 10 April 1933; United Cigar Stores of America, *Reorganization of the United Stores Company*. A similar situation may have been involved when Stetson briefly sat on the board of the Ritz-Carlton Hotel Corporation in the late 1930s. *New York Times*, 28 January 1937. The first American Ritz-Carlton opened in Boston to much fanfare in 1927, and others soon followed in New York, Philadelphia, and a few other cities. All, however, except the Boston hotel had closed by 1940.

Stetson's work for United Stores led to his most important position with a retailer. He became a director and member of the executive committee of the McCrory Stores Corporation in the 1940s and 1950s. McCrory was an early leader in mass retailing. In 1882, John G. McCrory borrowed $550 from an uncle and opened his first variety store near Philadelphia. He followed the then new five-and-dime Woolworth model, which meant mass display of goods, high volume sales, and an extensive chain of stores. By 1901, McCrory operated twenty stores, and in 1915, more than 120. With headquarters in New York, McCrory sold more than $14 million of goods in 1922. He retired from the business in 1931, just before the Depression and the company's bankruptcy. At this point George and Frederick Morrow of United Stores acquired McCrory and its competitor, McLellan Stores, which was also in bankruptcy.[16]

The Morrow-United Stores-Guaranty connection eventually led to Stetson's being placed on the boards of both McCrory and McLellan. Unfortunately, McCrory's attempt to regain its former status proved elusive. At the end of 1945, it held roughly $19 million in assets, primarily in cash, inventory, and real estate. Twenty years earlier, by contrast, assets exceeded $25 million and the company operated significantly more outlets. There was only a qualified rebound after World War II. McCrory and McLellan merged, and sales at McCrory picked up in the late 1940s, growing from $71 million in 1945 to more than $98 million in 1950. Although much was invested in constructing and refurbishing stores, management seemed unwilling to make radical changes. It refused, for example, to expand its business beyond "merchandise normally found in a variety store," which meant it did not carry appliances, furniture, or other

---

[16] Isadore Barmash, *For the Good of the Company: Work and Interplay in a Major American Corporation* (New York: Grosset & Dunlap, 1976) 24–25; McCrory Stores Corporation, *[Annual] Report* (New York: McCrory Stores, 1925); McCrory Stores Corporation, *[Annual] Report* (New York: McCrory Stores, 1945); McCrory Stores Corporation, *[Annual] Report* (New York: McCrory Stores, 1950); *In re McCrory Stores*, 14 F. Supp. 739 (S.D.N.Y. 1935); "Riklis Family Corp.," http://www.fundinguniverse.com/company-histories/Riklis-Family-Corp-Company-History.html; *New York Times*, 27 June, 26 September 1941 (Reporting Stetson elected director of McCrory and McLellan).

more expensive but potentially profitable items that were gaining popularity among consumers in the 1950s.[17]

Stetson and Lamont

Of course, Stetson's expansive business network also included the Morgan firm. Because of Morgan's critical role with Guaranty before 1940, Stetson's career depended on impressing its partners. His able cultivation of nationally and internationally important clients, including Harriman and the Woodruffs, was especially worthy to this audience. In the 1920s, Thomas Lamont, managing partner at Morgan and the leader on Guaranty's board, was well aware that there was increasing competition among New York banks for elite business. This competition could only be advanced by leadership at the highest level of the bank, the directors and officers. Stetson was among the Guaranty officers most eager and willing to accept this challenge.[18]

Stetson's relationship with Lamont was always cordial. For example, prior to a trip to Europe in 1929, Stetson asked Lamont a series of questions about economic trends, apparently so that he might express a standard Guaranty-Morgan perspective to European bankers. This was not

---

[17] McCrory Stores Corporation, *[Annual] Report* (1925); McCrory Stores Corporation, *[Annual] Report* (1945); McCrory Stores Corporation, *[Annual] Report* (1950); *In re McCrory Stores*, 14 F. Supp. 739; Barmash, *For the Good of the Company*, 19, 25; *Cumberland Stores Corp. v. McLellan Stores Co.*, 32 F. Supp. 840 (S.D.N.Y. 1940); *New York Times*, 27 June 1941; "Riklis Family Corp.," http://www.funding universe.com/company-histories/Riklis-Family-Corp-Company-History.html. In the early 1960s, just after Stetson's death, the companies were acquired by Meshulam Riklis, who proceeded to take them through a series of ups and downs over the next decades. Ultimately, Riklis led McCrory into bankruptcy in 1992 and 2001. All McCrory stores closed in the latter year. "Riklis Family Corp.," http://www.fundinguniverse.com/company-histories/Riklis-Family-Corp-Company-History.html. According to *Forbes*, creditors lost more than $600 million in these bankruptcies, while Riklis concluded "a lifetime habit of stripping assets from debt-laden companies—and leaving creditors in the lurch." Nathan Vardi, "The Check is Not in the Mail," *Forbes* 170 (30 September 2002): 67.

[18] "Memo for Mr. Steele," 1 November 1926; W. C. Potter to Thomas W. Lamont, 21 February 1936, Thomas W. Lamont Collection, Baker Library Historical Collections, Harvard Business School, Boston, Massachusetts.

the first time Stetson discussed European issues with Lamont or other Morgan partners. Yet the 1929 questions were especially revealing about the connection between him, his bank, and Morgan. Stetson asked for Lamont's ideas on such wide-ranging issues as the "General feeling about the American Bond Market and the possibility of its shortly being able to absorb foreign loans," "Federal Reserve policy and its possible effect on American business and European Finance," the "Continuous absorption by the Stock Market of funds and what ultimate effect of this will be and if it is likely to continue," "American opinion...as to [the] final solving of the [World War I] Reparation Question through the Young Plan," "General outlook of continuance of business prosperity in the States," and the "Future tariff trend and whether it is likely that the present increases in tariff will be put into effect."[19]

Lamont responded at length, anxious to use the opportunity to convey his thoughts. Ironically, given that the stock market crash and the beginning of the Great Depression were only weeks away, he informed Stetson, "Considering the resources of our own country and the gradual return to prosperous and settled business conditions in the rest of the world (except in China and Russia) I see no reason to doubt the continued economic progress of the United States."[20]

By 1940, when Lamont resigned from the Guaranty board because of New Deal banking laws, Stetson had achieved a solid working relationship with the Morgan banker on matters most pertinent to Guaranty. He and Lamont discussed the difficulty of obtaining good directors for the bank, including fellow southerners. Lamont prodded Stetson in one recruitment matter by suggesting, "The more relations that you can preserve with that splendid old gentleman down there along the line of us fine, old Southern

---

[19] Eugene W. Stetson to Thomas W. Lamont, 26 March 1924; R. F. Loree to Thomas W. Lamont, 30 August 1929; Thomas W. Lamont to R. F. Loree, 17 September 1929, Thomas W. Lamont Collection.

[20] Ibid. About the same time, Lamont argued to Guaranty's board—which included Stetson—that American banks had a duty to help in the economic reconstruction of Europe after World War I. "Lamont Speech," 21 May 1930, Folder 148-3, Thomas W. Lamont Collection.

gentry befo' de wah, the better." When Lamont left Guaranty's board, Stetson expressed his "deep appreciation of what I term the great privilege of sitting next to you during the bi-weekly meetings of the Executive Committee for a period of many years when I was Secretary while you were presiding as Chairman of this committee." Stetson added that Lamont's "uniform courtesy and understanding" of Guaranty's problems "have been a real inspiration to me and I have been most grateful for the association and highly appreciative of your friendship."[21]

Financial Opportunities

Another key relationship that Stetson enjoyed was with the firm J. & W. Seligman & Company. Stetson eventually became a director of two of Seligman's corporate subsidiaries, Tri-Continental and Selected Industries, as well as a director in the Globe and Rutgers Fire Insurance Company, of which Seligman acquired an interest in the 1930s. These relationships evolved from his association with Albert and Frederick Strauss, Seligman partners, both of whom were involved in Guaranty's Cuban sugar investments. During the investment boom of the 1920s, Seligman's Francis Randolph successfully convinced his partners that they should form an investment company. Reflecting the prevailing optimism of the day, the new company was called "Tri-Continental," as it was supposed to invest on three continents. Common and preferred shares in the Tri-Continental investment trust sold out quickly when they were first offered in 1929.[22]

Tri-Continental survived the Depression through several strategies. The company obtained almost half its operating expenses by investment returns from subsidiaries and by providing research to other investment

[21] "Note, Returned to Mr. Stetson with Mr. Lamont's thanks," 2 April 1937 Eugene W. Stetson to Thomas W. Lamont, 1 April 1940; Thomas W. Lamont to Eugene W. Stetson, 6 January 1939, 2 April 1940, Thomas W. Lamont Collection.

[22] Ross L. Muir and Carl J. White, *Over the Long Term: The Story of J. & W Seligman & Co.* (New York: J. & W. Seligman, 1964) 124, 134–37, 140. For additional background on Seligman's Tri-Continental, see Geisst, *The Last Partnerships*, 62, 71–72; Maury Klein, *Rainbow's End: The Crash of 1929* (New York Oxford University Press, 2001) 166.

companies. The company engaged in detailed economic research to a degree that was novel in investment management. In fact, an emphasis on research became the company's hallmark. After the passage of Glass-Steagall, Tri-Continental moved entirely to investment banking. Tri-Continental also obtained interests in several companies to which it sold investment advice: Wedgewood Investing Corporation; Selected Industries, Inc.; Capital Administration Company, Ltd.; and The Broad Street Investing Co., Inc. In the late 1930s, Tri-Continental and Selected Industries were developed as underwriting businesses. A further subsidiary, Union Securities, owned by Tri-Continental and Selected Industries, was formed in 1938 to advance underwriting work. The overall strategy was to have subsidiaries with specific functions, all under the Seligman umbrella. In 1940 these entities helped put together a successful bid for the huge Newport News Shipbuilding and Dry Dock, which was fortuitously accepted just one day before the German army launched its attack on France.[23]

Stetson was a Tri-Continental director in the 1940s and 1950s. He was also on the boards of Selected Industries in the 1940s and Globe and Rutgers Fire Insurance in the 1950s. During these years Tri-Continental and other Seligman affiliates restructured and centralized their research organization in order to control operating costs and reduce conflicts of interest. Seligman and its subsidiaries also expanded their mutual fund business. The rebounding economy of the war period drove up the asset

---

[23] Muir and White, *Over the Long Term*, 140–41, 143, 148–49; "Tricontinental History," http://www.tricontinental.com/public/general/history.html; *New York Times*, 13 May 1931. In 1938, *Time* reported that Union Securities was the underwriting arm of Tri-Continental and Selected Industries. The business was partly driven by the departure of commercial banks from investment banking. It provided a backdoor through which Stetson and other bankers could continue to use their underwriting skills. *Time* suggested that in fact companies such as Union Securities were encouraged by the new SEC and its chairman, future Supreme Court Justice William O. Douglas. The head of Union Securities was Earle Bailie, a lawyer and former Seligman partner who had worked in Roosevelt's Treasury Department. Bailie, as Seligman partner, collaborated with Stetson on Cuban sugar matters. "New Tri," *Time* 32 (17 October 1938): 68–69; "The Eastern Cuba Sugar Situation," *Barron's* 11 (7 September 1931): 17.

values of shares of Tri-Continental and Selected Industries. In the late 1940s and early 1950s Selected Industries and smaller subsidiaries were merged into Tri-Continental, and the company's interest in the Globe & Rutgers Fire Insurance Company was sold.[24]

Stetson served on the boards of other investment companies. As already discussed, this included W. A. Harriman Securities, Inc. during the 1930s. W. A. Harriman Securities was a closely held investment trust formed by the partners of W. A. Harriman & Co. Another investment company was Niagara Share Corporation. Apparently, there were at least three Niagara Share Corporations in the 1930s: Niagara Share of Maryland, and Niagara Share Corporations organized in Delaware and New York, the latter presumably subsidiaries of the Maryland corporation. Stetson held a directorship in at least one of these companies. All were products of the 1920s equity boom. The Maryland parent corporation held more than $33 million in assets in 1933, with the largest share of its investments in the Niagara Hudson Power Corporation, the banking company Marine Midland, and the Niagara Oil Corporation.[25]

Stetson's relationship with other kinds of financial institutions, banks, further demonstrates the incredibly expansive range of his financial activity. Textile Banking Company, Inc., was founded in 1919 with Stetson as one of the incorporators. He remained on the board and was chairman at the time of his death in 1959. Stetson was also a board member of the important Discount Corporation of New York. Formed in the late 1920s by New York

---

[24] Muir and White, *Over the Long Term*, 159–68; "Tricontinental History," http://www.tricontinental.com/public/general/history.html. Charles P. Stetson, Eugene Stetson's son, became a Seligman partner in 1949. Eugene Stetson was probably involved in the sale of Globe & Rutgers, an insurance company that traced its history to the nineteenth century. Stetson was on the board of both Globe & Rutgers and its subsidiary, American Home Fire Assurance Company, in the early 1950s. In 1952 a majority interest in the companies was obtained by what later became the global insurance giant, American International Group, Inc. (AIG). Apparently, Stetson left the boards of the insurance companies at that time. On AIG, see "American International Group, Inc.," http://www.answers.com/topic/american-international-group-inc.

[25] Niagara Share Corporation, *Fifth Annual Report to Stockholders* (Buffalo: Niagara Share Corporation, 1933); Niagara Share Corporation, *Tenth Annual Report to Stockholders* (Buffalo: Niagara Share Corporation, 1938).

banks, Discount Corporation bought and sold bankers' acceptances, at the time a new and evolving source of revenue for banks.[26]

Stetson also served as a director in international banking. Perhaps the best example of this kind of directorship not previously discussed was his work with the French-American Banking Corporation. The relationship began in 1929 when Guaranty merged with New York's National Bank of Commerce and Stetson was elected to French-American's board of directors. French-American was originally a joint venture of the Banque Nationale de Paris, the National Bank of Commerce, and the First National Bank of Boston.[27]

In 1930, Stetson became chairman of French-American's executive committee, a position he held until 1957. Stetson worked closely with the French bank both before and after the German occupation during World War II. In recognition of this work, in 1952 Stetson was named "Chevalier" in the National Order of the Legion of Honor by the French government. The award was based on Stetson's "contribution to the development of Franco-American cooperation in the field of banking and business." On receiving the award, Stetson cited a need for "continued development of the relations of the American business public with French financial and business interests."[28]

Altogether, Stetson's activities as director for companies engaged in finance and banking reveal his many connections on Wall Street and beyond. Morgan, Seligman, and Harriman were among the powerful interests with which he maintained long-term relationships. Often this work

---

[26] J. Peter Federer, "Institutional Innovation and the Creation of Liquid Financial Markets: The Case of Bankers' Acceptances, 1914–1934," *Journal of Economic History*, 63 (September 2003): 666–94. In 1933, Textile Banking was described as one of the largest factoring businesses in New York, serving producers of cotton, wool, rayon, and silk. The company passed on credits and collected accounts receivable. During the Depression it came under the supervision of the New York Superintendent of Banks. See *New York Times*, 6 September 1933 (Textile Banking); 13 January 1928 (Discount Corporation).

[27] Bond, *Stetson*, 115–22, 160–62. The Banque Nationale, now BNP Paribus, took full control of French-American in 1971. See "BNP Paribus: History," http://www.bnpparibas.com/en/history/.

[28] Ibid.

required managing an investment trust or other investment company, tasks which demanded considerable expertise in the securities markets, including the evaluation of companies and investments.

Faith, Philanthropy, and Social Life

Important adjuncts to Stetson's business practice included philanthropy, religion, and community service. Philanthropic interests, in fact, were a central part of the relationship banker ethos at Guaranty. For Stetson, Christianity was a key foundation for this work. He drew deeply on the religious belief and training that dated from his days as a boy in Georgia. When Stetson moved to New York, he changed his church affiliation from Methodist to Episcopal, the latter being the denomination of choice among Wall Street bankers. Faithfully attending Sunday services, Stetson was senior warden of St. James' Episcopal Church, one of the most prominent churches in New York, a church that business leaders attended. As senior warden, the highest lay leadership position, he assisted clergy in management details. He held this position for sixteen years. Stetson and his wife made important financial contributions to several churches, in New York and elsewhere, and he became active in the Episcopal Church nationally.[29] Through his friendship with Henry Knox Sherrill, the presiding bishop and head of the national church, Stetson was among the founders and directors of the Episcopal Church Foundation, a lay group created in 1949 by twenty industrialists, financiers, and lawyers. Prescott Bush was a fellow director, as was George E. Whitney, president of J. P. Morgan & Co., Inc., and Edwin S. S. Sunderland of the Davis Polk law firm.[30]

Stetson also raised substantial sums for non-religious charities, usually medical or educational causes, often with other business leaders. He believed that money was an important tool in accomplishing the larger good. For example, in 1925 he participated in the Beekman Street Hospital

---

[29] *New York Times*, 3 April 1937, 21 July 1959; Bond, *Stetson*, 90–91, 146–47. A more recent description of the St. James' building on Madison Avenue at 71st Street in Manhattan is Christopher Gray, "Streetscapes: St. James' Church; A Metamorphosis Still In Progress," *New York Times*, 20 October 1991.

[30] *New York Times*, 15 April, 8 December 1950.

fund drive, along with Charles Sabin of Guaranty, Thomas Watson, H. F. Guggenheim, William V. Griffin of Time Inc., and Frank Altschul of the investment firm Lazard Freres. Stetson belonged to the advisory committee of the New York City Cancer Committee campaign in 1946. His colleagues included Sidney Weinberg, president of Goldman, Sachs & Co.; Stanton Griffis, chairman of the executive committee of Paramount Pictures; Julius Ochs Adler, vice president and general manager of the *New York Times*; and Douglass B. Simonson, vice president of National City Bank. Stetson was also president of the Council for Heart Diseases in 1946.[31]

World War II provided a dramatic opportunity for philanthropic leadership. He served as chairman of the New York Commerce and Industry Committee of the Red Cross Campaigns between 1941 and 1943 and vice-chairman of the 1944 War Fund of Greater New York. This commitment required considerable time and substantial contact with other business and financial leaders. His bank contributed $250,000 to the Red Cross War Fund in 1943 and 1944, and approximately 900 Guaranty employees enrolled as Red Cross blood donors. On 16 January 1942, Stetson announced a voluntary salary deduction plan for employee purchases of United States Defense Bonds. The plan eventually reached 100 percent participation, with more than $1.1 million of bonds bought.[32]

Such actions were consistent with a broader ideal of civic-minded citizens, including wealthy businessmen, donating money and time for causes that furthered their social values. In Stetson's time, these values most often included religious faith, better health care, and improved education,

---

[31] *New York Times*, 16, 20 July 1930 (Fresh Air Fund used to send poor children to camps out of the city during summer); 15 April 1925 (Beekman Hospital Fund); 11, 21 March, 20 June, 20 December 1946; Charles P. Stetson, interview with L. Kenneth Hammond, 24 April 1982, Jack Tarver Library, Special Collections, Mercer University, Macon, Georgia. Stetson's wife Iola was also involved in many charities. See, for example, *New York Times*, 9 January 1944 (Netherland-America fund).

[32] John P. Stevens to John W. Davis, 22 December 1943, John William Davis Papers, Yale University Library, Manuscripts and Archives, New Haven, Connecticut; "Mr. Stetson," 11 July 1949; "Corporate History of the Guaranty Trust Company of New York (1952)," 58–60, 63, J. P. Morgan & Co., Inc. Papers.

especially higher education. As suggested by his New South efforts in Georgia, Stetson had always linked business and the needs of the community. Moreover, he belonged to a generation that was highly influenced by the philanthropy of Andrew Carnegie, who published an article promoting "The Gospel of Wealth" in 1889. Carnegie said the rich should give away their wealth to be administered as a public trust. During this period John D. Rockefeller established important philanthropic enterprises, including founding two universities. Government also encouraged giving to organizations, as personal and corporate income tax exemption for personal charities was adopted in the 1920s and 1930s. The emerging principles of philanthropy stressed the connection between business leadership and giving, and Stetson's efforts and gifts reflected that trend.[33]

Mercer University in Georgia, where Stetson had been a student from 1897 to 1901, was a special object of Stetson's philanthropy. In 1927 he endowed a chair in economics in his father's name and over the years made other contributions to the university, some anonymously. Mercer awarded him an honorary doctor of laws degree in 1933 and an alumni award for meritorious service in 1953. In 1955 Stetson announced a challenge grant for $500,000 to be split between Mercer and his wife Iola's alma mater, Wesleyan College, also located in Macon. After his death, Iola Stetson gave money to Mercer to establish a new university library, named in her husband's honor. The library eventually outgrew the building, and the University built a larger building to house the library next to the Stetson building. Later, with his family's consent, and in recognition of his support and achievements, Mercer's School of Business and Economics was named after him.[34]

---

[33] For a discussion, see Patricia O'Toole, *Money and Morals in America* (New York: Clarkson Potter, 1998) 142–65; Dwight F. Burlingame and Dennis R. Young, *Corporate Philanthropy at the Crossroads* (Bloomington: Indiana University Press, 1996) 147–49.

[34] *New York Times*, 2 May 1927; "Honorary Degree of LL.D. Bestowed on Mr. Stetson by Mercer University," *The Guaranty News* (June 1933) 5–6; Mercer University, Eugene W. Stetson Memorial Library, *Dedication Ceremonies, The Eugene W. Stetson Memorial Library*, (Macon GA: Mercer University, 1965) 44; Bond, *Stetson*, 65–66, 91–93.

Besides church work and philanthropy, Stetson participated in a wide range of social activities, many of which had clear business and networking benefits. For example, he was a governor of the Union Club, the oldest of the major businessmen's social clubs in New York. He joined the Jekyll Island Club in coastal Georgia. Ironically, the groundwork for the Federal Reserve Act of 1913 had been laid at discussions at Jekyll Island in 1910, when Stetson was a young banker in Macon. Senator Nelson Aldrich of Rhode Island and a small cadre of Wall Street financiers, including Paul Warburg of Kuhn, Loeb, and Morgan's Henry P. Davison drafted a plan for the formation of a central bank during a meeting at the island's clubhouse. The state of Georgia purchased Jekyll from the club in 1947.[35]

Perhaps most importantly, through all of these activities Stetson was able to develop and enhance friendships. Simple examples, involving Guaranty board member and attorney John Davis, help show how Stetson was able to turn business colleagues into friends. At celebratory dinners he hosted for colleagues, Stetson had excellent opportunities to show off his abilities as a good fellow. After one meal, Davis wrote Stetson that it "was a fine dinner you pulled off last night and here are my thanks. I congratulate you on the way in which you conducted the post prandial exercises." Davis was a former candidate for President of the United States and perhaps the

[35] "Eugene W. Stetson," 23 October 1942, J. P. Morgan & Co., Inc. Papers; *Macon Telegraph*, 25 June 1934; Box 1, Folder 8, Eugene W. Stetson Papers (containing numerous invitations to Stetson-sponsored dinners). Stetson had little contact with J. P. "Jack" Morgan, despite the Morgan connection to Guaranty and their common interest in Georgia's Jekyll Island Club. This is partly explained by Morgan's disengagement from his firm's business in the late 1930s. He died in 1943. In fact, there is very little in J. P. Morgan Jr.'s papers that relates to Guaranty Trust. See, e.g., J. P. Morgan Jr. to Mrs. W. C. Potter, 3 December 1935 (referencing a charitable venture); J. P. Morgan Jr. to Guaranty Trust Co., 23 January 1939 (a reference letter for John F. Harjes), J. P. Morgan Jr. Papers, The J. Pierpont Morgan Library, New York, New York. Nonetheless, Morgan visited Jekyll Island and supported the club during the 1930s. See, e.g., J. P. Morgan Jr. to J. P. Morgan & Co., 25 May 1938 (paying $4,000 note of club); John W. Davis to J. P. Morgan Jr., 14 February 1936 (Morgan went to Jekyll Island); Box 104, Folder 306 (correspondence relating to club), J. P. Morgan Jr. Papers. For an introduction to the Jekyll Island Club and the origins of the Federal Reserve, see John Hunter, "Jekyll Island," http://www.georgiaencyclopedia.org/nge/Article.jsp?id=h-928.

outstanding appellate orator in the American bar, so he knew about effective communication. His compliment also shows how far Stetson had overcome his teenaged aversion to public speaking. On another occasion, Stetson wrote Davis informing him of a recent decision of the United States Supreme Court. The case involved the death of a New York shareholder of a Utah corporation, and the Court seemed to permit estate taxes by both New York and Utah. Stetson believed "this information will be of value to you and your associates." Stetson's willingness to write a letter about a court decision to Davis, who had argued more cases before the Supreme Court than anyone in American history, suggests his genuine interest in the work of a colleague as well as his ability to link friendship and work.[36]

Stetson also enjoyed more active forms of recreation, including golf, tennis, and hunting, but these often had a business component as well. In the summer of 1940, a golf match involving Stetson; Bill Potter; Palen Conway; John Davis; Morris W. Kellogg, a Guaranty director; and Cornelius Kelly, president of Anaconda Copper and a Guaranty director, displayed the importance of connections outside the office. After it was over, Stetson kidded Davis that "In view of the fact that Potter, Conway, and Kellogg ruled you, Kelley and myself out from participating in any of the bets and, furthermore, that I collected the fifty cents [wager] from you, I am returning it this morning so that I will have a clear conscience." He added, "A clear conscience is only incidental to the great pleasure I had in playing with you and friend Kelley and I am really glad that it rained because I had an opportunity of listening to words of wisdom from both of you on the present economic situation." Davis replied in kind, noting that since Stetson had "more money than [he knew] what to do with, I will keep it; and if it burns a hole in my pocket I will give it up to my pastor." For

[36] John W. Davis to Eugene W. Stetson, 10 August 1942; 16 November 1943; Eugene W. Stetson to John W. Davis, 6 August 1942, John William Davis Papers. Ironically, when Stetson died in 1959 there was a legal dispute over whether a trust he created should be evaluated under New York law or friendlier Connecticut law. *Stetson v. Morgan Guaranty Trust Co.*, 104 A.2d 239 (Conn. Superior Court 1960).

Stetson these kinds of exchanges were not without significance. They represented the full integration of business, life, and finance.[37]

Home and the Business Culture

As the charitable work and social activities suggest, in some ways Stetson never really took a vacation from banking, even in his personal life. At the least, Stetson's time at home also reflected norms of elite banking. Stetson and his wife Iola raised a typically large family, with five children. Naturally the family was affected by Stetson's business and social contacts, sometimes in very personal ways. Iola Stetson ran the Stetson household, which by the 1930s meant managing the children and two homes, an apartment on Manhattan's upper East Side, which was more used during winter months, and a large shorefront house at Greens Farms, Connecticut, the "Gold Coast" of Fairfield County. The Stetsons lived at the Bretton Hall Hotel at 85th Street and Broadway when they first came to New York and later moved to 929 Park Avenue before choosing 117 East 72nd Street for their in-town residence. Iola was a deeply devoted wife who allowed Stetson to pursue his lofty professional ambitions. She was the ideal partner for a Wall Street banker. The children attended exclusive private schools in New York and elsewhere, and their father always expected high academic and personal performance. Stetson, who purchased the Greens Farms property just after World War I, was one of the pioneers in suburban living along the Connecticut coast.[38]

---

[37] Eugene W. Stetson to John W. Davis, 27 June 1940; John W. Davis to Eugene W. Stetson, June 27, 1940, John William Davis Papers; Josephine Hatcher, interview by Adrienne M. Bond, 1981–1982, Jack Tarver Library, Special Collections, Mercer University, Macon, Georgia.

[38] For Iola Wise Stetson, see Bond, *Stetson*, 145–51; Lillian Otlowski, *Over the Walls of Wall Street with Mrs. O* (New Smyrna Beach FL: Luthers' Publishing, 2000) 28; *New York Times*, 25 February 1978; Josephine Hatcher interview; Charles P. Stetson interview. In 1939, writer Odell Shepard commented on the migration to Connecticut: "I must not forget the region along the shore which I call New York's dormitory. I suppose they will soon fill up all Fairfield County, these people who have come out to us from the most fascinating city in the world realizing that it is not so good as rural Connecticut. Although really as foreign to this soil as our recent immigrants from Europe, they too are good for us, often bringing a deeper

Fairfield County, Connecticut, evolved by the 1930s into a trendy spot for "rural" life, from which top executives such as Stetson took trains to and from New York. Stetson's neighbors included Juan Trippe of Pan American Airways, Charles Munson of Air Reduction, and Smith Richardson of Vick's. Executives, however, were not the only denizens of Fairfield County. There were celebrities, such as Richard Rodgers, Henry Fonda, and the conductor Leopold Stowkowski. By the standards of the wealthy, the houses were not ostentatious, nor were the yacht clubs, little theaters, and country clubs. Of course, this assumes a yacht or country club could avoid ostentation. Nonetheless, the absence of showiness by those who could afford it was the Fairfield hallmark.[39]

In August 1949, *Life* took a somewhat tongue-in-cheek approach to the high-class style in Fairfield, illustrating the necessary accoutrements: a post lantern, a cobbler's bench coffee table, antique windowpanes with air bubbles, a wood-sided station wagon, and the ubiquitous beagle. The magazine praised the commuter communities for taking an interest in local affairs and the arts. A series of photographs almost portrayed the Stetson home. In fact the magazine did show Stetson's grandchildren playing on the nearby Richardson beach, where the sand had been imported. With associates, Stetson commuted to New York via a special club car, also featured in the article. This was a private car bought and managed for its members, who each paid $140 a year for the privileges of air conditioning and being able to play poker. At one of these games, Stetson won with a royal flush, an event recorded for posterity by a photograph and later framed and hung on the wall in his Manhattan apartment. Even in daily routine Stetson's private and professional lives were closely intertwined.[40]

---

concern for what is beautiful and characteristic in the State than is currently found in our native people." Odell Shepard, *Connecticut: Past and Present* (New York: Alfred A. Knopf, 1939) 253–54.

[39] "Fairfield County: Smart New Yorkers are Flocking to It," *Life* 27 (8 August 1949): 74–84.

[40] Ibid.

Southern Ties

Throughout his career Stetson specialized in relationships with businesses from the American South. He always had great expectations for southern economic development. A good expression of this optimism after he came to New York was an article he wrote for William Randolph Hearst's *Atlanta Sunday American* in January 1927. The title, "Why Times are Good in Georgia," might have startled many readers, given a lingering agricultural depression that affected most Georgians. The piece was full of the sort of New South boosterism Stetson learned in younger days: the need for agricultural diversity, not just cotton; the desirability of manufacturing; and the need for sound banking institutions to facilitate growth. Indeed, the article appeared just after Stetson's visit to inspect the facilities of a new industry in the region, electric utilities.[41]

According to Stetson, times were good in his home state because agriculture was throwing off the shackles of cotton. Stetson used statistics to drive home the point. Peanuts, tobacco, corn, and other crops now outpaced the white fiber. Textiles were also gaining, as Georgia had recently passed Rhode Island in its number of spindles. Moreover, the state's cities were growing, as shown by both population and construction. Stetson shrugged off the recent closure of some eighty-six banks as not really significant, given the small size of those banks. Overall, he thought, Georgia banking was in good shape. Perhaps most importantly, the downturn in cotton prices would have its inevitable, and positive, economic effect. It would drive farmers, and perhaps the economy more generally, to seek more diverse and more consistently profitable means of making a living. The evidence for this transformation was the real reason why "times are good in Georgia."[42]

Paradoxically, in Stetson's case loyalty to the South was enhanced not simply by visions of material wealth, but by the personal memory of Confederate veterans, such as his father. This memory, as well as his great admiration for General Lee, influenced him to become a leader in the

---

[41] Eugene W. Stetson, "Why Times Are Good in Georgia," *Atlanta Sunday American* (2 January 1927).

[42] Ibid.

Robert E. Lee Memorial Foundation, which sought to preserve Lee's birthplace at Stratford, Virginia. In 1929 he was appointed treasurer of its national foundation, whose members included then-Governor Franklin D. Roosevelt of New York. A successful campaign resulted in the restoration of Stratford and its opening to the public.[43]

In New York Stetson took every opportunity to use his southern connections for business purposes. This included membership in the city's Southern Society. He attended many events organized by this group and in 1934 was elected its president. The Southern Society consisted of over 1,200 businessmen. Further, when young men from the South, particularly Georgia natives, looked to start careers on Wall Street, Stetson often worked to place them in good positions, including at Guaranty.[44]

Among the many important examples of Stetson's efforts for southern business was his work with North Carolinian Smith Richardson, whose family developed the wildly successfully Vick's VapoRub in the 1880s. Vick's VapoRub formed the product core of the Vick Chemical Company, which manufactured a variety of health remedies. By the 1920s Vick Chemical was publicly traded and had expanded sales outside the United States. Richardson became the company's president in 1919. Vick's success naturally led to more complex financial needs, the kind of needs best met by New York banks. In the 1920s a number of banks aggressively sought Vick's business, including Guaranty. The banks bombarded Richardson with appealing offers of financial support. In 1926 Richardson decided that he could "no longer operate the Vick Chemical Company efficiently without the services of [Guaranty]," so he opened an account there. J. J. Sample communicated Guaranty's welcome to Richardson, telling him to "consider the Guaranty Trust Company as headquarters whenever you are here and to use us in a personal way or otherwise whenever you feel disposed to do so."[45]

---

[43] Bond, *Stetson*, 66; *New York Times*, 4 February 1929.

[44] Bond, *Stetson*, 66; "Eugene W. Stetson," 23 October 1942, J. P. Morgan & Co., Inc. Papers; *Macon Telegraph*, 25 June 1934; Box 1, Folder 8, Eugene W. Stetson Papers; *New York Times*, 20 April 1934.

[45] J. J. Sample to H. Smith Richardson, 14 February 1924, 24 June 1926; H. Smith Richardson to J. J. Sample, 17 June 1926, Richardson-Vicks, Inc. Records,

Richardson met Stetson while shopping for banks. For management reasons Richardson moved to New Jersey in 1926, providing a golden opportunity for a personal relationship. As with other important clients, Stetson did not let the chance slip. He invited Richardson to lunch and golf almost immediately after he came to New Jersey: "I am a poor golfer but would like to take a day off with you some time soon and have game." Eventually they played and within a few years were on a first name basis. Richardson asked Stetson about advice on a New York apartment and schools for his children. He planned to move into the city for the winter, and to "sit around and watch how you financiers do it for a few years before I retire the old horse and let him run around the pasture." As always, Stetson's banking was about more than just financial strategy.[46]

The friendship soon led to Stetson's placement on the board of the Vick Financial Corporation, an investment trust created in 1929. The purpose of the company was to create a sophisticated means of dealing with the large cash reserves of the Vick businesses. Bankers and investment experts, including Stetson, served as directors in order to accomplish this end. Stetson assumed a central role from the beginning. He attended weekly finance committee meetings and was chairman of the executive committee.[47]

Southern Historical Collection, Wilson Library, University of North Carolina, Chapel Hill, North Carolina. A Vicks employee wrote Richardson criticizing National City Bank and promoting a new account with Guaranty: Guaranty "has a splendid [investment] advisory service; and is a bank eager for our business." Other New York banks that aggressively solicited Vicks included Hanover National, Irving Trust, Bankers Trust, and the National Bank of Commerce. See G. R. Dawson to H. Smith Richardson, 15 June 1926; Folder 28, Series 1, Richardson-Vicks, Inc. Records.

[46] "Memorandum to H. Smith Richardson," 18 June 1926; J. J. Sample to H. Smith Richardson, 10 February 1926; Eugene W. Stetson to H. Smith Richardson, 14 February 1926; H. Smith Richardson to Eugene W. Stetson, 10 June 1929, Richardson-Vicks, Inc. Records. As with many of Stetson's business relationships, this impacted his family. Stetson's son, Eugene Jr., married Grace Richardson, Smith Richardson's daughter, in 1933. See "Claudia Egelhoff, Interview with Grace Richardson Stetson," 22 June 1998, Henry Smith Richardson Papers, Southern Historical Collection, Wilson Library, University of North Carolina, Chapel Hill, North Carolina.

[47] "To the Stockholders of Vick Chemical Company, June 13, 1929"; "Vick Financial Corporation, Chronology of Investment Responsibility, February 9,

Of course, the timing was not good for winning investments. By early 1930 Vick Financial Corporation's governance was restructured by disbanding the finance committee and creating a new management with Stetson as its salaried chairman. Although this showed Vick's confidence in Stetson, the stock market was falling. By 1932, the company suspended all fees and salaries to directors. In 1933 the executive committee simplified the portfolio into common stocks. In early 1934 Stetson resigned his position because the new federal banking act prohibited a bank director from serving on an investment trust board. Vick Financial was dissolved in 1936 and reorganized with an emphasis on profit from insurance as the Reinsurance Corporation of New York.[48]

Stetson's relationship with Richardson also included the consolidation and separation of several large retail and pharmaceutical companies. In 1928 Sterling Products, Inc. and United Drug Company, famous for its chain of Rexall Drug Stores, merged to form the unhappily-named Drug, Inc. In 1930 Vick was added to the Drug, Inc., empire, as were the Bristol-Myers and Life Savers corporations, although Vick maintained its separate corporate status and management. However, as with the formation of the Vick Financial Corporation, the timing was poor and the complex behemoth did poorly as the Depression deepened. In 1933 Drug, Inc. was broken up, producing an independent Vick and United Drug. Guaranty and Stetson derived considerable business from these restructurings. Stetson even became a director with the new United Drug—a holding company with retail and manufacturing segments.[49]

To Gene Stetson, banking before, during, and after the Depression was about relationships. Sometimes relationships meant social connections, regional heritage, or philanthropy. But first and foremost they meant connections with large banks, the leaders of investment firms, and corporations. The key opportunity for a banker such as Stetson was to serve as corporate director, which allowed full use of his financial knowledge,

---

1950," Richardson-Vicks, Inc. Records; H. Smith Richardson to Our Stockholders, 10 December 1936, Henry Smith Richardson Papers.

[48] Ibid.

[49] "Drug, Inc.," 21 October 1932 (Folder 787); "Organization of Vick Chemical, Inc." (1933) (Folder 802), Richardson-Vicks, Inc. Records.

negotiating skills, salesmanship, and leadership abilities. In fact, practically all of Stetson's business, personal, religious, and philanthropic relationships were somehow linked to his identity as a Guaranty banker and corporate director. Guaranty clients connected Stetson with both the huge resources of the bank as well as with other institutions that could be useful to banking practice. These relationships, in turn, led to national and international banking opportunities. Because of his success in managing these relationships, they also led to the presidency of Guaranty Trust.

11

At the Top

Stetson's ability to work with other companies always depended on Guaranty and its resources. Fortunately, reconstituted leadership after the Mercantile Bank problem set the stage for Guaranty's strong rebound. Especially important to this rebound was that as early as 1926 discussions began about a possible merger between Guaranty and the National Bank of Commerce. Guaranty's Morgan directors encouraged the move. The Bank of Commerce had a long history with the firm, including solid ties with J. P. Morgan Sr. Originally, the Bank of Commerce grew out of President Andrew Jackson's opposition to the Second Bank of the United States. The demise of that institution and the ensuing economic downturn resulted in special New York legislation for chartering banks, under which the Bank of Commerce was created in 1839. From the beginning, the bank had large aspirations and influential supporters. James Kent, one of the outstanding lawyers and judges of the era, drafted its corporate documents. With almost $2 million in assets and a location in Wall Street, the Bank of Commerce immediately took a leading place in the economic life of the city, investing in and lending money to both government and business. The Bank of Commerce became a national bank in 1864 and was a prominent source of funds for the United States government during the Civil War.[1]

By 1900 the institution had fallen so much under Morgan's sway that it was called "J. Pierpont Morgan's bank." Morgan joined Commerce's board of directors in the 1870s and later became a vice president. In 1903, its

[1] Thomas W. Lamont to George Baker, 19 December 1926, Thomas W. Lamont Collection, Baker Library Historical Collections, Harvard Business School, Boston, Massachusetts; Guaranty Trust Company of New York, *One Hundred Years of Banking Service* (New York: Guaranty Trust Company of New York, 1939) 5–7, 18, 44; "Press Release, Guaranty Trust Company of New York," 2 January 1939, J. P. Morgan & Co., Inc. Papers, JPMorgan Chase Archives, New York, New York.

assets exceeded $165 million, more than twice Guaranty's at the time. Given the Morgan interest in foreign finance, the bank expanded its activities in that direction, becoming a noted shipper of gold to Central and South America. The bank established offices in London, Paris, and Berlin. Moreover, as one of the first member banks in the Federal Reserve System, it was prominent in financing the Allied war effort, buying over $1.2 billion of government securities. In the 1920s, it added to an already extensive securities work.[2]

The merger talks between Commerce and Guaranty reflected Morgan's heavy input (even without Pierpont) and a struggle for supremacy. Guaranty's Potter fought any surrender in administrative control. James S. Alexander, head of Commerce, also wanted power. But it was the Morgan partners who determined the outcome, and they favored Guaranty. Thomas Lamont's papers contain numerous references to the deal, including trenchant comparisons of potential executives. Lamont gave many of the Bank of Commerce's vice presidents low marks. In a cutting memorandum, he described specific individuals as "Lazy, honest, good friends—declining 56"; "Honorable, lawyer, can't do his work"; "Way over his head—fell down—retained because couldn't afford to lose anyone"; "Boot licker—mediocre ability"; and "Able but doing all he can. Can't go ahead." Lamont sold the merger to important Commerce shareholders, including George Baker, to whom he wrote, "I should think it would be a fine thing to house your holdings in an institution as sound as both institutions now are and with the increased earning capacity which the Guaranty would furnish." J. P. Morgan Jr., another Commerce shareholder, supported the deal, as did the super rich Thomas F. Ryan, who owned a substantial block of shares in both companies. Myron Taylor, close friend of Baker and leader of the Morgan-financed United States Steel Corporation, and Henry De Forest,

---

[2] Ron Chernow, *The House of Morgan: An American Banking Dynasty and the Rise of Modern Finance* (New York: Atlantic Monthly Press, 1990) 153–80; Guaranty Trust Company, *One Hundred Years*, 27–38; "The Corporate History of the Guaranty Trust Company of New York 1952," 47–50, J. P. Morgan & Co., Inc. Papers; Rackliff, Whittaker, and Loomis, Inc., "Guaranty Trust Company of New York" (1932), Thomas W. Lamont Collection.

chairman of the Southern Pacific Railroad, prepared a report for the banks' boards that endorsed the union.[3]

When the merger took place on 6 May 1929, Guaranty had clearly won the struggle for control. Not only did the new bank carry the Guaranty name, but Bill Potter became its president. Thomas Lamont was chosen as chairman of the executive committee, a position he held at Guaranty, while Commerce's Alexander had to settle for a short term as chairman of the board. Physically, the merger produced few changes. The main offices of both banks were already adjacent. Together they made up nearly the whole block bounded by Broadway, Liberty, Nassau, and Cedar Streets. The revised Guaranty was an instant powerhouse. Assets jumped from $850 million in December 1927 to an astonishing $2 billion just two years later, making it the third largest bank in the United States. Deposits grew from about $700 million to more than $1.2 billion, while the aggregate of capital funds was larger than of any other American bank. Clearly Guaranty resided in the front ranks of American finance.[4]

The merger had a huge impact on Stetson. He had already made a mark as an up-and-coming vice president. His ability to develop business, to serve effectively on outside corporate boards, and to impress Morgan insiders, including Lamont, led to his elevation in 1927 and 1928 to the boards of the Guaranty Company and Guaranty itself. The Commerce merger made his vice-presidency and the Guaranty directorship substantially more valuable, partly because there was a reduction in both vice presidents and the size of Guaranty's board. Another factor in Stetson's favor was Potter's retirement from the presidency in 1934 and his

---

[3] Thomas W. Lamont to George Baker, 19 December 1926; 19 June 1928; "Comments by Thomas W. Lamont," 28 November 1928; "Presentation of Plan of Merger," 4 March 1929; Thomas W. Lamont Collection; David Rogers, *The Future of American Banking: Managing for Change* (New York: McGraw-Hill, Inc., 1993); "Back-to-Back," *Time* 13 (4 March 1929): 54-56.

[4] "The Corporate History of the Guaranty Trust Company of New York [1952]," 47–48, J. P. Morgan & Co., Inc. Papers; Guaranty Trust Company, *One Hundred Years*, 31; "Condensed Statements," Guaranty Trust Company of New York, 31 December 1927; 31 December 1929, J. P. Morgan & Co., Inc. Papers; Myron Taylor to Thomas W. Lamont, 4 March 1929, Thomas W. Lamont Collection.

replacement by W. Palen Conway. Conway had worked for the Guaranty since 1911, beginning in the Bond Department. He became a vice president during the 1916 expansion and a member of the board in 1924. As part of the openings caused by Potter's resignation, Stetson was elected to Guaranty's executive committee, a place where he could convene weekly with the highest forces in the company, including Lamont. By this time, at age 53, Stetson was clearly the heir apparent to the presidency. His salary in 1935 exceeded $85,000, third highest in the company, below those of only Potter and Conway—it was also more than the salary of President of the United States.[5]

As a top-level leader, Stetson had many opportunities to promote his vision of relationship banking at Guaranty. One example is particularly revealing. In 1936 Potter inaugurated a series of meetings with higher-level staff, in which executives and officers gave talks. Stetson spoke on "Business Development and Work of the Districts," a topic that showed his understanding of salesmanship, the regional nature of the bank's operations, and his thoughts about the company's organizational structure. The key portions of Stetson's remarks focused on the advantages of having the bank's commercial operations divided into seven geographical divisions. The purpose of this arrangement was to "make a little team of officers and assistants definitely responsible for all commercial banking matters in a given region and to assure customers in that region that their needs will be looked after by a group always available, frequently traveling the territory,

---

[5] "Corporate History of the Guaranty Trust Company of New York [1952]," 51–52; "List of Officers," 10 May 1929, J. P. Morgan & Co., Inc. Papers. The executive committee consisted of the chairman of the board, the chairman of the executive committee, the president, and "such number of Directors…as the Board may determine." The executive committee could exercise the powers of the entire board between directors' meetings. "By-Laws of the Guaranty Trust Company of New York," 5 September 1951; "By-Laws of the Guaranty Trust Company of New York," 1 September 1923, J. P. Morgan & Co., Inc. Papers. Stetson's 1935 salary was the equivalent, using a consumer price index measure, of almost $1.3 million in 2007 dollars. According to a Congressional report, William R. Hearst earned the highest salary in the United States in 1935—$500,000. In second place was the actress Mae West, with just over $480,000. *New York Times*, 7 January 1937; "Six Ways to Compute the Relative Value of a U.S. Dollar Amount," http://www.measuringworth.com/calculators/uscompare/result.php.

and experienced in the special problems of that section." New business was the responsibility of officers within the divisions, and officers were assigned to a district with which they were most familiar.[6]

Yet, according to Stetson, efficient organization was only the beginning. Given that the goal was to maximize new business through expertise with client needs, personnel quality was most important. Stetson thought new business could only come from satisfied customers, recommendations from satisfied customers, and direct solicitation. He recognized that the best New York banks had similar strategies, so the "greatest variable among them is the tone, skill, character and personality of their representatives." As a result, Guaranty's success depended on the "dignity, wisdom, personality and energy" of individuals, "from the Chairman down." Altogether, Stetson's definition of successful banking practice meant financial knowledge, dynamic personality, individual initiative, and positive image that could be used to develop lasting relationships with clients. In essence, this was the ideal of relationship banking Stetson practiced at Guaranty.[7]

Guaranty's President

Between 1941 and 1947 the histories of Guaranty and Stetson were more closely intertwined than at any previous time. In January 1941, Bill Potter retired as chairman and "Len" Conway moved from president to chairman, leaving the presidency open. In retiring, Potter explained that he "wished to give way to younger men." While Stetson was popular and clearly in line for the top job, apparently the board hesitated to elect him president. Whatever the cause, to force the issue Stetson went to Robert Lehman of Lehman Brothers, who he had known since the 1920s, and obtained an offer to become one of the senior partners there. Faced with the prospect of loosing Stetson, the Guaranty board offered him the president's job.[8]

---

[6] "Group Lecture Meetings Continue With Five Speakers During October," *The Guaranty News* (October-November 1936): 2–4.

[7] Ibid.

[8] *New York Times*, 16 January 1941. Under the by-laws, the president was defined as "the administrative officer of the Company," with power to act in the

In twenty-five years Stetson's career had come full circle, from the presidency of the Citizens National Bank in Macon to the presidency of Guaranty. In 1941, Guaranty was among the largest financial institutions in the world. The main office remained at 140 Broadway, as it had been since 1913, in the heart of the New York's financial district. It employed almost 4,000 people in New York, London, Paris, Brussels, Liverpool, Havre, and Antwerp. The company owned several affiliates, including the Guaranty Executor and Trustee Company, Ltd., a London-based trustee business, and the Guaranty Safe Deposit Company in New York. The bank maintained relationships with more than 8,000 correspondent banks across the globe. Guaranty's stock, with more than 900,000 shares outstanding, was owned by 24,000 individual and institutional shareholders and had a trading value of several hundred million dollars. Its primary borrowers included some of the nation's most important corporations, including the New York Central, Southern Pacific, and Southern railroads; American Tobacco; Anaconda Copper; General Motors Acceptance Corporation; and Cities Service Corporation.[9]

Although Stetson succeeded in the demanding context of Morgan influence, the problems of the early 1920s, and the new regulatory world of the 1930s, in 1941 the bank was beginning a new era. World War II was underway in Europe and Asia, and the United States became a combatant eleven months after Stetson was elected Guaranty's president. An unanswered question was whether Stetson's leadership and values could benefit Guaranty and the government's military efforts under wartime conditions. Under the circumstances the bank was expected to advance both private and public interests. An additional characteristic of the new era was that the board that chose Stetson was composed of clients, not a phalanx of fellow New York bankers. This reflected Depression-era federal laws regulating bank boards as well as the growing power of industrial corporations relative to financial institutions. Stetson was the first president

---

place of the Chairman of the Board in his absence. "By-Laws of the Guaranty Trust Company of New York," 12, 5 September 1951, J. P. Morgan & Co., Inc. Papers.

[9] On Guaranty's lending, see Tian-Kan Go, *American Commercial Banks in Corporate Finance, 1929–1941* (New York: Garland, 1999) 120–21.

of Guaranty since World War I chosen without the vote of a J. P. Morgan & Co. partner.

The Second World War was the most important external force in Stetson's presidency. The growth of government spending during the war revolutionized the economy in ways unimaginable even at the height of the New Deal. On 11 March 1941, only weeks after Stetson became Guaranty's president, Congress approved $7 billion for production and shipment of war materials to help Great Britain and other nations fight the Nazi threat. Congress approved another $6 billion in October 1941. Japan's attack on Pearl Harbor and Germany's declaration of war against the United States in December 1941 thrust the nation into a massive global conflict. Worldwide military action increased the federal budget from less than $10 billion in 1940 to almost $100 billion in 1945. Approximately $80 billion was for war expenditures. In 1944 and 1945 the federal government spent more money than it did in the entire period from 1789 to 1940.[10]

The effect of these events on Guaranty was generally positive, although in unusual ways. Big banks, despite being the objects of hatred during the Depression years, were expected to wholeheartedly support the war and its gigantic financial demands. Under Stetson, Guaranty met this public duty. While Stetson was president, bank assets rose from just under $2.6 billion in December 1941 to roughly $3.8 billion in 1944–1945. A huge portion of the growth was in the form of United States government securities, a reflection of the bank's preeminent role in wartime financing. Despite increased corporate and income taxes (the top rate for high earners such as Stetson increased to about 90 percent in 1944) only about forty-five percent of the money the government needed to run the war came from taxes. The rest had to be raised by borrowing, a task the government partly placed on banks. Stetson's Guaranty was a major player in this job. At the end of 1939, the bank owned less than $740 million in federal securities. By 1946 it owned $2.69 billion. Given that another $62 million in assets was either Federal Reserve Bank stock or state and local government securities,

---

[10] Arthur S. Link and William S. Catton, *American Epoch: A History of the United States Since 1900*, 5th ed., 2 vols. (New York: Alfred A. Knopf, 1980) 1:472–73, 479, 499–501; Jonathan Hughes and Louis P. Cain, *American Economic History*, 7th ed. (Boston: Pearson Education, Inc., 2007) 526–41.

in 1944 almost two-thirds of the bank's resources were tied to public agencies. By contrast, less than five percent of the bank's assets were invested in public agencies at the end of World War I. The war's radical effects also appeared in the jump in deposits, from $2 billion in late 1939 to $3.4 billion in late 1944, almost all of which was related to war-caused savings and investment.[11]

Stetson's presidency also put a premium on helping corporate clients meet the new military conditions. For Stetson personally, this included continued activity on corporate boards, as many of his companies were directly involved in war-related business. For example, in 1941, on the recommendation of former Guaranty director Averell Harriman, Stetson became chairman of the executive committee of the debt-plagued Illinois Central. President Roosevelt appointed Harriman to administer the Lend-Lease program in Great Britain, and Harriman wanted Stetson to replace him at Illinois Central, a vital source of military transportation. Stetson was also a member of the boards of Air Reduction, Bibb Manufacturing, Coca-Cola, General Shareholdings, Tri-Continental, U.S. Industrial Chemicals, and a subsidiary of the Illinois Central, the Yazoo & Mississippi Valley Railroad Company. In most cases he was also on the corporations' executive committees, and he was chairman of the executive committees of the Gulf Atlantic Warehouse Company, McCrory Stores Corporation, and the French-American Banking Corporation. At the time, no other Guaranty officer was remotely as active in outside corporate governance: Potter was a director in six companies; Conway in one. Twenty-eight officers held about seventy outside directorships, and Stetson alone held about twenty percent of these positions. Equally significant was the variety of Stetson's corporate

---

[11] Link and Catton, *American Epoch*, 1:500–501; Benjamin J. Klebaner, *American Commercial Banking* (Boston: Twayne Publishers, 1990) 168–69; Paul Studenski and Herman Krooss, *Financial History of the United States* (New York: McGraw-Hill, 1963) 448, 452; "Guaranty Trust Company of New York, Condensed Statement," 31 December 1919; 31 December 1939; 31 December 1940; 31 December 1941; 31 December 1942; 31 December 1943; 31 December 31, 1944; 31 December 1945, J. P. Morgan & Co., Inc. Papers.

connections. He worked for companies involved in chemicals, textiles, railroads, food, general retail, and finance.[12]

The war deeply affected Guaranty's day-to-day operations. A large number of employees left for military service, and this required substantial hiring, especially of women. The change represented a shock to the bank's overwhelmingly male culture. Under Stetson's presidency the company promised employees who went into military service that they would retain their positions, or ones equivalent in status and pay with seniority, upon return. Departing servicemen received one month's salary while the bank continued to pay for their life insurance. In 1943 the bank paid $25 to each Guaranty employee in the Armed Forces. Guaranty, along with other large banks in New York, created a bonus plan which increased salaries to help lower paid employees address rapidly increasing costs of living. At the end of 1942, eleven officers and 798 employees were in the armed forces—thirty-eight percent of the pre-war male work force. By war's end, thirty-five employees had been killed.[13]

War finance occupied the employees who remained. Under Stetson Guaranty was heavily involved in financing companies that held war production contracts. In addition, it participated in subscription drives for Victory Loans, beginning in 1942. By the end of 1945, Guaranty was responsible for Victory Loan subscriptions of more than $7.24 billion. It marketed these securities through advertisements at its own expense and offered loans to customers who would purchase them. Further, the bank

---

[12] Stetson was a member of the executive committee of Air Reduction, Bibb Manufacturing, French-American Banking, McCrory Stores, McLellan Stores, Selected Industries, Textile Banking, and U.S. Industrial Chemicals. "Eugene W. Stetson," 23 October 1942; Matthew T. Murray Jr. to Samuel Culviner Jr., 17 April 1945; "Annual Report to the Stockholders for the Year 1947," J. P. Morgan & Co., Inc. Papers; *Directory of Directors in the City of New York, 1945* (New York: Directory of Directors Co., 1945). In 1946 Stetson was also the bank's representative on the Discount Corporation board. Adrienne Moore Bond, *Eugene W. Stetson* (Macon GA: Mercer University Press, 1983) 88.

[13] "Corporate History of the Guaranty Trust Company of New York [1952]," 58–60, 63, J. P. Morgan & Co., Inc. Papers; Lillian Otlowski, telephone interview with author, notes in possession of the author, 8 June 2004; *New York Times*, 8 November 1941.

maintained accounts for the Army and Navy in London amounting to more than $34 million. It participated in a $100 million loan to the Dutch government in 1944, immediately after part of The Netherlands was liberated. The bank also served as disbursing agent for shipbuilders acting under government contracts.[14]

War under Stetson even brought military preparation. Management knew about the potential costs of an air strike, as German bombs destroyed the London branch during the Battle of Britain in 1940. Employee volunteers agreed to patrol the streets outside the bank's Manhattan locations in the event of a similar raid. They held practice drills and designated evacuation points. Blackout curtains covered windows and steel wire netting was installed to reduce the danger of debris from falling glass. The bank's roof provided space for an exercise on how to defuse bombs. Key employees received first aid training on the effects of gas and "the psychology of panic." The bank also established a special war-ready "Control Room" and acquired equipment for a possible attack, including fire extinguishers, hoses, gas masks, and sand. The purchase of long handle shovels was made on the assumption that they might be useful in extinguishing incendiaries in or near the bank.[15]

Although Guaranty experienced growth during these years, it was an atypical kind of growth. Earnings increased from about $14 million in 1941 to more than $16.6 million in 1943. Yet this was largely due to interest on government securities or the financing of war industries—the former being most important. Between 1941 and 1942 government securities held by the bank increased phenomenally, from $1 billion to $1.7 billion. Official reports to shareholders stressed that this was unnatural and expressed concern that because of the low interest rates paid by the government that

---

[14] "Corporate History of the Guaranty Trust Company of New York [1952]," 60–65, J. P. Morgan & Co., Inc. Papers; *New York Times*, 16 January 1941; Siegfried Stern, *The United States in International Banking* (New York: Columbia University Press, 1951) 257.

[15] "Corporate History of the Guaranty Trust Company of New York [1952]," 61–62, J. P. Morgan & Co., Inc. Papers.

banks, and not individuals, were being asked to provide too much war financing, despite successful public bond drives and high taxes.[16]

Stetson took on additional war-related responsibilities while acting as president. As already noted, he was active in raising funds for the Red Cross. He also served for one year as chairman of the Clearing House Committee of the New York Clearing House Association. This organization, founded in 1853, determined the process for clearing checks in New York banks. Over $190 billion in checks were processed the year before Stetson became chairman. Stetson was also elected to the advisory board for the New York Ordnance District, which helped coordinate the production of ordnance in the New York-New Jersey area. In 1943 he was elected president of the New York City group of the New York State Banking Association.[17]

Chairman and "Retirement"

On 19 January 1944, Stetson stepped down as president and was elected chairman of the board of directors. Why he served as president for only three years is not clear. Among the presidents since 1915, Palen Conway, his predecessor, had served for seven years, Bill Potter for thirteen, and Charles Sabin had been president for more than six years—until the Mercantile Bank disaster. Most likely, Stetson, at sixty-two, was easing into retirement, as he knew it was traditional for a former president to serve as chairman of the board and retirement was required at sixty-five. Stetson had nothing against this expectation and, in fact, strongly supported the idea of new leadership. Guaranty's board replaced him with J. Luther

---

[16] *New York Times*, 22 January 1942; 21 January, 14 May 1943; 20 January 1944. Despite record bank revenues and a national unemployment rate of just over one percent, at the 1944 shareholders' meeting Chairman Len Conway announced, "The theory that prosperity can be induced by Government spending has been tried and found wanting." He asked for a return to the peacetime economy as soon as possible. *New York Times*, 20 January 1944.

[17] *New York Times*, 7 October 1942; 6 October, 30 November 1943. After the war, Stetson served on a large committee to help the United Nations establish itself in New York. *New York Times*, 24 March 1946.

Cleveland, a long-time vice president. Bill Potter remained as chairman of the executive committee until his retirement in 1946.[18]

A particularly important fact about Guaranty's leadership from the late 1910s through the mid–1940s was its incredible continuity. Stetson, Potter, Conway, and Cleveland each had been at the company for more than twenty years in 1944. Stetson, Conway, and Potter began serving on the executive committee in the mid–1930s. Stability, in fact, characterized the entire officer ranks of the Guaranty after the early 1920s. Stetson and others, however, realized that this could be a double-edged sword, with positive and negative consequences. Experience was good, but so were new ideas and people. As Stetson put it in 1944, he, Potter, and Conway hoped to "mould a new regime into the policies of an old regime." When the need to replace old with new was not followed in the 1950s, it provided the leading impetus for a merger with J. P. Morgan.[19]

Between 1944 and 1947, when Stetson was chairman, Guaranty faced difficult postwar challenges. The transition to peace, as in 1919–1921, was not easy. In 1946 bank resources dropped from $3.81 billion to $2.89 billion, almost all of which was related to decreases in United States government obligations in the form of United States War Loan Deposit Accounts. In December 1947, bank assets stood at $2.84 billion, approximately where they had been in 1940. Deposits hovered around $2.4 billion, a number that would not change much for years. How to raise assets and revenues proved perplexing. Operating costs, particularly those related

---

[18] "Guaranty Trust Company of New York, Condensed Statement," 31 December 1944; 31 December 1945; 31 December 1946; "Corporate History of the Guaranty Trust Company of New York [1952]," J. P. Morgan & Co., Inc. Papers; Eugene W. Stetson to Thomas J. Watson, 31 January 1944, Thomas J. Watson Sr. Papers, IBM Corporate Archives, Somers, New York. Under the by-laws, the Chairman of the Board "shall direct the policy and management of the Company on behalf of the Board and preside at meetings of the Board." The Chairman and Vice-Chairman of the Executive Committee had power to "exercise general supervision of the business affairs and property of the Company." "By-Laws of the Guaranty Trust Company of New York," 10–12, 5 September 1951, J. P. Morgan & Co., Inc. Papers.

[19] "Corporate History of the Guaranty Trust Company of New York [1952]," J. P. Morgan & Co., Inc. Papers; Eugene W. Stetson to Thomas J. Watson, 31 January 1944, Thomas J. Watson Sr. Papers.

to employees, showed a steady rise, partly because the bank supplemented incomes with cost of living allowances as a result of war-driven inflation. Salaries and wages increased fifty-four percent between 1943 and 1947. The good news was that there was little likelihood of a repeat of the Mercantile Bank disaster. Annual reports to stockholders illustrated the bank's solid position. Undivided profits climbed from $31.3 million in late 1943 to $61.6 million in late 1946, declining slightly to $60.6 million in 1947. Demand for corporate financing in the United States improved, and although destruction caused by the war in Europe and Asia unsettled international business, by 1946 there were increased opportunities overseas.[20]

The growing salaries of Guaranty employees reflected a long-standing policy of providing liberal benefits. Stetson always thought that quality personnel were the most important factor in the bank's success. The bank's pension plan was expanded in 1940 to enroll almost ninety-eight percent of eligible employees. In 1947 a new pension plan eliminated previously required employee contributions. The company even reduced the workweek for hourly workers from forty-four in 1938 to forty in 1940 and 37.5 in 1951. During the 1940s and early 1950s, Guaranty provided substantial bonuses. By 1948, virtually all staff members were insured by group life insurance policies, while health insurance, covering physician bills, was available at least as early as 1951. Employees also earned two to three weeks of paid vacation each year and they were reimbursed for courses taken at the American Institute of Banking. Workers rejected an attempt to unionize the bank in the early 1950s.[21]

Yet, as in earlier years, Guaranty imposed notable restrictions on employees, many of which were intended to maintain the bank's elite reputation. Workers could not leave the building without permission, except for lunch, and they could not discuss company business with non-

---

[20] "Guaranty Trust Company of New York, Condensed Statement," 31 December 1943; 31 December 1944; 31 December 1945; 31 December 1946; 31 December 1947; "Annual Report to Stockholders for the Year 1945," "Annual Report to Stockholders for the Year 1946"; "Annual Report to Stockholders for the Year 1947," J. P. Morgan & Co., Inc. Papers; Lillian Otlowski interview.

[21] "Corporate History of the Guaranty Trust Company of New York [1952]," 53, 57, 59, 66–67; "Employee Handbook, Guaranty Trust Company of New York" (c. 1950), 5–9, J. P. Morgan & Co., Inc. Papers.

employees. Employees could not hold a margin account with a broker, borrow or loan money from other staff members, or promise to pay another person's debt. They were discouraged from obtaining personal loans if there was any doubt about repayment. If there was a possibility of defaulting on a personal loan, it needed to be reported to a superior. They could not serve as a director, officer, or partner in another company, engage in any outside business, or be a trustee or executor without the permission of the company. Unless approved or in other limited circumstances, any outside income they earned belonged to Guaranty. There were express limitations on solicitations, telephone use, smoking, "loud talking," use of the company's name or supplies, and personal mail. The bank had a formal policy against employing married women, and expected women who became engaged to resign.[22]

In April 1946 Stetson wrote Conway and Cleveland that he wished to retire as chairman in early 1947, just after his sixty-fifth birthday. Although the executive committee and the board of directors requested that he remain through 1947, he did not want to stay. After almost fifty years in banking, he sought a change of pace, and to "become associated in a closer advisory capacity with several corporations in which my family own stock or in which I am at present a Director." The most important of these connections was Illinois Central, of which he was already executive committee chairman. As a result, Stetson's exit was facilitated by his lifetime of building relationships. He did not leave his position in order to retire fully from business. Instead, he left to become more closely involved with corporations he had worked with while associated with Guaranty. Tellingly, in the official 1947 roster of Guaranty directors, he listed his occupation as "Chairman of the Executive Committee, Illinois Central Railroad." Stetson considered his departure a significant shift in leadership, the end of the "Potter, Conway and Stetson regime," as he described it to the *Wall Street*

---

[22] "Employee Handbook, Guaranty Trust Company of New York" (c. 1950), 9–25, J. P. Morgan & Co., Inc. Papers. In 1958, the company reported that 42 percent of its employees were women. Guaranty Trust Company of New York, *Annual Report to the Stockholders for the Year 1958*, 29, J. P. Morgan & Co., Inc. Papers.

Journal. Still, he continued on the board and the executive committee and maintained an office at the bank.[23]

A wide range of issues engaged Stetson's attention at the end of his term as chairman. Although he was uncertain about greater earnings, perhaps reflecting his experiences after World War I, they continued to climb, reaching more than $18 million in 1946. In 1946 and 1947 Guaranty approved an increase in capital stock in the form of a one-for-nine dividend distribution. Apparently there was pressure to issue more shares because of an assumption that the price of Guaranty was too high. Stetson opposed this, reasoning that Guaranty stock should be expensive and viewed as an investment, not an opportunity for speculation. This reflected the older idea of Guaranty as an upper-crust Morgan bank. He also thought the number of shareholders, 24,000, was satisfactory, especially considering that more than 23,000 held less than 100 shares each.[24]

At the 1947 shareholders' meeting, Stetson's last as chairman, a new executive compensation plan, linked to earnings levels, proved controversial. Stetson supported it, as did the rest of the board. While Stetson presided over the meeting, two disgruntled shareholders led a persistent series of comments and interruptions. One offered to amend the compensation plan by making it contingent on a minimum level of earnings, which Stetson and the board rejected. The shareholder then offered to "disqualify" Stetson from the limitations of the proposal. This prompted Stetson to reply, to "roars of laughter," that "You will never disqualify me from anything." He explained he was retiring after thirty years and would not benefit from the bonus program. Shareholders approved Stetson's version of the bonus plan and also rejected an attempt to further increase the company's capitalization.[25]

---

[23] *Wall Street Journal*, 16 January 1947. Stetson clearly felt no financial need to continue as chairman. He earned a salary of over $120,000 in 1947, more than super celebrities Rita Hayworth or Ginger Rogers (less, however, than Betty Grable or Fred MacMurray). "These are the Men Who Make More than $75,000 a Year," *The Machinist* 2 (4 September 1947): 4–5.

[24] *New York Times*, 17 January 1946; 9 January 1947.

[25] Ibid., 16 January 1947.

In January 1947 a cover story featuring the retiring chairman appeared in *Forbes*. The piece captured his mindset well, including his reasons for leaving full-time banking. According to the article, Stetson wanted to spend his time with Illinois Central. As for banking, he thought it was "pretty well stabilized and I look forward to something that presents more of a challenge." Recalling his early days as a note-issuing national banker, he thought the Federal Reserve System now "cushioned monetary shocks until banking does not feel them as severely as it once did." But industry and transportation were "still subject to the full jounce of recurring cycles." Clearly Stetson perceived that the role of the banker in the late 1940s was circumscribed by regulation. Railroads, not banks, now seemed to be the "pivotal area" in the economy. There was vitality to transportation, including changing technologies, competition, and the challenges of labor that seemed lacking in banking. Stetson thought the time was the right to leave his former occupation and "enter a field that affords plenty of excitement."[26]

How should Stetson's terms as president and chairman be evaluated? Guaranty grew to unprecedented size between 1941 and 1947. Through 1944 bank assets reached record levels and profits rose accordingly. Moreover, Guaranty continued its long-standing tradition of national and international relationship banking, even though thanks to Depression-era laws this no longer included investment banking. During Stetson's tenure the bank made a substantial contribution to the war effort in terms of public finance and in providing banking services to private industry geared to war production. Guaranty also displayed a high degree of concern for its employees, including those in the military. Further, Stetson provided leadership in many charitable organizations that worked to limit the hardships of the war—a continuation of the kind of civic activity that could be traced as far back as his days as a young banker in Georgia.

Yet the end of Stetson's tenure brought unsettling questions. As he recognized, his decision to "retire" to railroading suggested banking had entered a less appealing phase. Beginning in 1946, Stetson's last year as

---

[26] William Hurd Hillyer, "Eugene Stetson—A Close Up," *Forbes* 60 (15 January 1947): 18–19. In 1946, Stetson served briefly as a director with the Seaboard Air Line Railroad after it emerged from receivership. *New York Times*, 1 August 1946.

chairman, assets fell sharply, inflation was a concern, and there were fears another depression might be imminent. More importantly, the bank's future role relative to its corporate clients after the shocks of the 1930s and world war was unclear, partly because Guaranty could not simply resume the functions of the 1920s. Stetson sensed the drift and believed that given his age a key part of his responsibility was to assist in handing over the challenge to younger leadership. Eventually, in the late 1950s, he would fulfill that role more decisively and in so doing once again change Guaranty's future.

Southern Power

An outstanding example of Stetson's transition from full time banking after 1947 was his role in founding the Southern Company, a major producer and distributor of electric power in the Deep South. The Southern Company, which became one of the largest utility companies in the United States, resulted largely from regional pride. Stetson's contribution came about because of an acquaintance with Thomas Martin, a senior officer at Alabama Power, once a part of the huge Commonwealth & Southern electric utility system.

Martin was a dynamic Alabamian, a lawyer by training who joined his father's law firm and became legal counsel to the fledgling Alabama Power Company in the early years of the twentieth century. This work led to Martin's election as president of Alabama Power in 1920. The 1920s became the golden age of electric utility holding companies, as the young industry passed through a consolidation phase. By 1932, more than seventy-six percent of the nation's electricity was controlled by sixteen holding companies. Despite achieving economies of scale, abuses within tiers of holding companies became common. Precarious financial structures, excessive valuation, and deceptive fees among related companies harmed consumers and risked capital. The dangers of the holding company became apparent in the late 1920s and during the Depression. Between 1929 and

1936 fifty-three holding companies, with par values approaching $2 billion, passed into bankruptcy or receivership.[27]

Commonwealth & Southern, formed in 1929, was a holding company that included Alabama Power among its group of southern and Midwestern utilities. Thomas Martin was brought to Commonwealth & Southern after a hostile takeover of Martin's own holding company. Martin accepted Commonwealth & Southern's presidency, but only briefly. He was soon disappointed in the job and in 1932 returned to Alabama Power. During the Depression, Commonwealth & Southern, like the entire electric industry, experienced fundamental shocks. Martin's eventual successor at Commonwealth was soon-to-be Republican presidential candidate Wendell Willkie, another lawyer who came from a smaller utility that was incorporated within Commonwealth & Southern in 1929.[28]

Under the Roosevelt administration, electric utilities—and especially electric holding companies, became classed with Wall Street banks as Enemies of the People. Not only had their poor financial management contributed to the collapse of the stock market, but they often refused to provide service in rural areas and charged what were believed to be excessive prices where they did serve. In quick order, new federal laws, including the Tennessee Valley Authority and rural electrification, took aim at investor-owned utilities. The holding company form itself was attacked through the Public Utility Holding Company Act of 1935, which made the ultimate

---

[27] "Thomas Wesley Martin," http://www.samford.edu/groups/amhf/chronological.html#; "Thomas Wesley Martin," http://cba.ua.edu/investing/hall_of_fame/74TWM.html; William M. Murray Jr., *Thomas W. Martin—A Biography* (Birmingham: Southern Research Institute, 1978); Charles F. Phillips Jr., *The Regulation of Public Utilities* (Arlington: Public Utilities Reports, Inc., 1988) 229, 572–79; Maury Klein, *Rainbow's End: The Crash of 1929* (New York: Oxford University Press, 2001) 153–55. I am very grateful for information and sources provided to me about Martin and the Southern Company by Leah Rawls Atkins, formerly of Auburn University. She has written a history of Alabama Power that includes a detailed account of the formation of the Southern Company. See *Developed for the Service of Alabama—The Centennial History of the Alabama Power Company, 1906–2006* (Birmingham: Alabama Power Company, 2006) 246–55.

[28] Murray, *Thomas W. Martin*, 87–94, 142.

demise of holding companies, including Commonwealth & Southern, inevitable.[29]

In 1935, the Public Utility Holding Company Act placed utility holding companies under the jurisdiction of the newly-formed Securities and Exchange Commission. The Commission exercised its utility authority cautiously, beginning formal reorganization proceedings of holding companies under the Act in 1940. Even then it went slowly, given concern over the outbreak of war: electricity would be needed for war production. Stated simply, the Holding Company Act intended to eliminate complex holding company structures. Henceforth, only holding companies that could prove real efficiencies in electric service were permitted. The law also imposed reporting requirements. Finally, it took aim at another common object of New Deal legislation. Bankers and directors of banks, including Stetson, were prohibited from becoming directors of utility holding companies.[30]

Because Commonwealth & Southern operated in two regions without interconnecting lines, the Holding Company Act required that it be dissolved. As a result, beginning in 1946 Commonwealth & Southern asked permission from the SEC to create a new electric holding company, which would control only its properties in South Carolina, Georgia, Alabama, Florida, and Mississippi. The company informed the SEC that regional restructuring offered an opportunity to raise much needed capital. The proceedings dragged on for several months, as there was important opposition. The state of Georgia, for example, asked that Georgia Power be left out of the arrangement so Georgians could own it. Finally, on 1 August 1947, the SEC approved a newly-created a Southern Company to hold the properties of the Alabama, Georgia, Mississippi, and Gulf Power Companies. Three weeks later, Justin R. Whiting, president of Commonwealth & Southern, announced the official organization of The

---

[29] Phillips, *The Regulation of Public Utilities*, 228–29, 573–83.
[30] Ibid., 581–83.

Southern Company, with Eugene A. Yates as president. Thomas Martin, as president of Alabama Power, was a member of its first board.[31]

Stetson entered the picture when Martin asked him to help shape the new company's direction. The precise issue that brought Stetson to Southern was reminiscent of power struggles over the role of New York investors at Coca-Cola in the early 1920s. Commonwealth & Southern's leadership disagreed as to whether the new holding company, The Southern Company, would be dominated by New York interests or controlled in the region where it sold electricity. Initially, the dispute focused on the location of company offices and sources of financial advice and support. The new holding company's original by-laws kept the main office in New York. Justin Whiting wanted the company to maintain its headquarters there and for it to continue to employ the same New York-based support services company used by Commonwealth & Southern. However, Southern's president Yates and Martin disagreed. They believed success depended on management presence in the South, in the service area, and they wanted more directors from the region, men who had business interests directly served by the company.[32]

Martin required heavyweight financial support if his strategy was to succeed, and he looked to Stetson. Martin bluntly told Stetson that he and Yates "felt we would be a much stronger company if we could have less domination from a New York group, and that we should have a large number of directors from the South." Yates put the reasons for the southern strategy succinctly: "All the investments of The Southern Company are in the South. The efforts of its officers and staff are in the South. The efforts of its officers and staff will be directed solely toward the successful operation and development of these four southern utilities.... The Southern Company will be an important factor in the future development of this region." Martin asked Stetson to come to their aid as advisor, perhaps eventually taking a more formal role. Predictably, given his pro-southern record, Stetson responded favorably. He fully approved the idea that

---

31 *New York Times*, 23 October 1946; 16, 28 January, 22, 23 August 1947; The Southern Company, *The Southern Company and the Territory it Serves* (Atlanta: The Southern Company, 1952).

32 Murray, *Thomas W. Martin*, 142–43.

Southern "should detach [itself] from the dominating influence of the New York office" of Commonwealth & Southern. As a result, Yates, Martin, and Stetson agreed on "a Southern destiny for the company." In fact, Stetson indicated he would not have anything to do with the new operation unless it fully disconnected itself from the financial and operating location of Commonwealth & Southern.[33]

Martin sought out Stetson because he trusted him and because of Stetson's extensive connections in the money world. Most important among these connections were the principal holders of Commonwealth & Southern stock. Stetson's task was to convince owners and other influential persons he knew to support Martin and Yates's strategy. As a result, he became a leader for the southern faction. To assist this, he had some of the utility experts at Guaranty study the financial end of the idea and prepare a report. He discussed the matter with Bob Woodruff, whose opinion would naturally carry great weight, and John Sibley, Woodruff's Atlanta lawyer and a member of the Georgia Power board. In quick order Stetson effectively carried out his behind-the-scenes assignment, convincing leading parties that links to the old Commonwealth & Southern should be severed.[34]

Stetson also played a critical role in advancing both regulatory and ownership issues for the new Southern Company. This was a slow and tedious process, because each stage required the approval of interests at Commonwealth & Southern and the Securities and Exchange Commission. State utility regulators had to be appeased as well. In early 1948 Stetson spoke with Yates about the sale of the South Carolina Power Company by Commonwealth & Southern, which was required by the SEC. He discussed the matter in New York with potentially large investors in The Southern Company. Another important problem was how to structure the utility's ownership. In a February 1948 letter to Sibley, he suggested that perhaps

---

[33] John Temple Graves, "Notebook of Interviews, Notes, and Manuscript Pages of Book," Southern Research Institute, Birmingham, Alabama; Murray, *Thomas W. Martin*, 143–45.

[34] Graves, "Notebook of Interviews"; Eugene W. Stetson to John A. Sibley, 6 November 1947; 9 January 1948, John A. Sibley Papers, Manuscript, Archives, and Rare Book Library, Emory University, Atlanta, Georgia.

southern ownership could be maximized by waiting to buy the company's stock when it hit the open market.[35]

In 1948 and 1949 Stetson spent time traveling in the South, attending dinners, and talking to the right people about the future of The Southern Company. Sibley thanked Stetson for his performance at one gathering, stating that he "handled the situation beautifully and I think everyone present was convinced that it would be to the interest of all if your suggestions [regarding southern control] materialize." Sibley agreed "that your basic conception of the Southern Company is correct and that you are proceeding along sound lines." Martin arranged for Stetson to visit Alabama Power properties and to speak to Birmingham businessmen.[36]

Instead of taking an antagonistic position with government, Stetson and the others agreed it was essential to maintain smooth relations with both federal and state regulators. Yates and Sibley, for example, wrote Stetson encouraging positive dealings with the federal government. This included not only the Securities and Exchange Commission, but also the Tennessee Valley Authority. Both Sibley and Yates believed The Southern Company could arrange favorable distribution agreements with federal producers. Stetson visited Georgia regulators himself, largely to assure them that the company's intent was to create a southern-based company that would benefit the state. The chairman of the Georgia Public Service Commission was impressed, writing Sibley, "I heartily agree with your entire program and hope there will be no difficulty in your being able to successfully follow it."[37]

The crucial moment came in late 1949, when the necessary legal approvals had been obtained and it was time for Commonwealth & Southern to distribute its Southern shares. Here, perhaps, is where Stetson's impact was greatest. He believed roughly 200,000 persons would purchase

---

[35] Eugene W. Stetson to John A. Sibley, 2 February 1948, John A. Sibley Papers.

[36] John A. Sibley to Eugene W. Stetson, 25 October 1948; Thomas W. Martin to Eugene W. Stetson, 9 December 1948, John A. Sibley Papers.

[37] John A. Sibley to Eugene W. Stetson, 3 November 1948; E. A. Yates to Eugene W. Stetson, 17 November 1948; Matt L. McWhorter to John A. Sibley, 22 September 1949; Eugene W. Stetson to John A. Sibley, 26 September 1949, John A. Sibley Papers.

Southern stock. As he wrote Sibley, recognizing the "possibility of having an undesirable group secure proxies to control the policies of The Southern Company when its stock is distributed, some of the northern as well as the southern officials of the various companies [of Commonwealth & Southern] have asked me to sit in the center of the picture so as to help secure a control of the policies of the four operating companies in order to have what might be termed definitely a southern control of policies." As a result, Stetson agreed to be a designated proxy holder and to "vote for a majority group of Southerners to have control of the policies of the operating companies as well as The Southern Company."[38]

Stetson's purpose was both profit and regional development: a southern-controlled company "would have the opportunity of conferring, from time to time, with the regulatory bodies as well as with the consumers, with a definite purpose in mind; namely, to see that the rates were equitable and fair; to see that dividends were not exorbitant, and any surplus earnings should go for expansion and development purposes in the territory in which the companies were operating." More personally, Stetson remarked that the plan was part of his own long-term efforts for the region's commercial, industrial, and agricultural development.[39]

When the stock was issued, Stetson and the southerners prevailed. Their accomplishment had an enormous impact. In 1947 only three of Southern's eleven directors were from the South. By the early 1950s, southerners dominated the board. The company's headquarters moved to Atlanta. Likewise, support services would not be provided from New York. A subsidiary owned by the four operating utilities, Southern Services, Inc., was formed with headquarters in Birmingham. Banking was partly provided by Guaranty, but Sibley's Trust Company of Georgia and Atlanta's Citizens and Southern Bank also received the utility's business. Sibley, among others,

---

[38] Eugene W. Stetson to John A. Sibley, 1 June 1949, John A. Sibley Papers. Stetson could not resist stating his intention to buy Southern stock "if the price is right." In fact, he advised Sibley that Southern Company would be an excellent buy. This was especially valuable public information intended for Sibley, his trust investors at the Trust Company of Georgia, and his client Bob Woodruff. Eugene W. Stetson to John A. Sibley, 7 July 1949, John A. Sibley Papers.

[39] Eugene W. Stetson to John A. Sibley, 1 June, 7 July 1949, John A. Sibley Papers.

recognized Stetson's crucial role in this transfer of valuable property into southern hands. In December 1949 he thanked Stetson for "splendid leadership" and for "establishing sound policies." He had "never seen a company get off to a better start, especially with the regulatory bodies, which is all important now."[40]

The Public Utility Holding Company Act prohibited Stetson, as a banker, from becoming a director of The Southern Company. The law did not, however, prevent his other efforts on its behalf after it swung into operation. He continued to supply financial advice through the 1950s. When Stetson died in 1959, the Southern board passed a resolution stating its "deep appreciation of the great service which he rendered as our financial advisor in the successful inauguration and direction of the Company from the beginning of its active life in 1947." According to the resolution, Stetson advanced the broader financial success of all four operating companies through consultation and negotiation. His actions revealed a special ability to persuade others. Almost certainly the strongly worded praise was written by the man at Southern who knew Stetson from the beginning, Thomas Martin.[41]

---

[40] Murray, *Thomas W. Martin*, 143–45; John A. Sibley to Eugene W. Stetson, 30 September, 12 December 1949, John A. Sibley Papers.

[41] Bond, *Stetson*, 157–60; "Annual Report, 1959, The Southern Company"; "List of Invited Guests, Southern Company Meeting, May 20–23, 1953," John A. Sibley Papers; James F. Crist, *They Electrified the South: The Story of the Southern Electric System* (S.l.: J. F. Crist, 1981) 97 (Stetson's "advice was of great value"). In 1949, the company had annual revenues in excess of $120 million a year and total capitalization of more than $450 million. See *The Southern Company* (S.l.: The First Boston Corporation; Kidder, Peabody & Co.; Merrill Lynch, Pierce, Fenner & Beane, 1949) 3, 5–6. With the rise of the Sunbelt, it did not take long for the company's enormous potential to be realized. By 1953, total capitalization soared to $720 million, while annual sales neared $160 million. James F. Crist, *The Southern Company: A Story of the System's Background and Development* (S.l.: s.n., 1953) 25. Fifty years later, operating in essentially the same service territory, the company served more than 4.3 million customers, had annual revenue in excess of $15.3 billion, and held total assets of more than $45 billion. Through 2007, Southern had paid dividends every year since 1948. "Southern Company Annual Report, 2007," www.southerncompany.com.

The connection with Martin also linked Stetson to the Alabama Research Institute, a research-for-business organization Martin founded in 1941. Martin invited Stetson to become a trustee and member of its advisory committee. Martin's idea was to provide a center for work in chemistry, engineering, and other fields that would prove beneficial to southern industry. The project was slow to get off the ground, but after its reformation as the Southern Research Institute in 1945, real work began. Martin knew it was essential to attract influential supporters and one of the men he turned to was Stetson. Given Stetson's life-long interest in southern business development, the Institute was a cause he could easily support. During the 1940s and 1950s, while he was associated with the institute, it conducted research in textile technology, chemistry, medicine, and aerospace engineering.[42]

Stetson's experience with The Southern Company and the Southern Research Institute between 1947 and 1959 reflect several larger themes. First, his experience fit well with the kind of southern economic development he had supported since his New South days in Macon. By the 1940s, electricity was vital to the growth of the region, and Stetson believed local control of that resource was essential. Second, it reinforced his established business ties, including with Coca-Cola. Among his closest allies in creating The Southern Company were John Sibley and Robert Woodruff. Sibley was Woodruff's friend and lawyer, but he was also president of the Trust Company of Georgia, Ernest Woodruff's old bank, and Stetson's partner in the Coca-Cola deal with the Candlers. Third, the experience showed Stetson's special ability to link a complex financial strategy, southern control over the company, with the personal and political appeals required for success. Once again, "banking" took on a complex, and personal, meaning. The interlocking threads of Stetson's business career came together in his work for The Southern Company. Perhaps this was

---

[42] Southern Research Institute, *25 Years: The First Quarter Century of Southern Research Institute, 1941–1966* (Birmingham: Southern Research Institute, 1966); John Temple Graves, *History of the Southern Research Institute* (Birmingham: Birmingham Publishing Company, 1955). On the current work of the institute, which is now affiliated with the University of Alabama at Birmingham, see "Southern Research," www.southernresearch.org..

best symbolized when Stetson's Guaranty, working with Woodruff's Trust Company, distributed the initial Southern Company dividends with help from computers and punch cards from Tom Watson's IBM. Stetson was the critical link in this business chain.[43]

[43] Arthur C. Vogt to Steve H. Bomar, 7 December 1949, John A. Sibley Papers.

12

Banking for the Railroad

In the 1950s, Tommy Lyons, Gene Stetson's driver, would take Stetson and his grandchildren in the Plymouth "woody," the wooden door station wagon Stetson loved, from Stetson's Greens Farms home to the station at Croton-on-Hudson. There Stetson picked up the *20th Century Limited,* which ran from New York to Chicago. Stetson enjoyed riding the train to Illinois Central board meetings. The company's offices were located near a street in the center of the city, "Stetson Avenue," which the City of Chicago named after him in 1955. While Stetson could have taken an airplane, that would have been a bit treasonous, and at any rate he much preferred the train. He could relax, read Illinois Central papers, have dinner, and then get some undisturbed sleep listening to the sounds of the train wheels running the rails. He could wake up the next morning and have breakfast in the dining car. Then, he would be off to his meeting, returning the next evening by the same route. Stetson appreciated both the glamour and the practical strengths of railroads.[1]

As an economic and political phenomenon, railroads are unrivalled in American history. Almost single-handedly they changed the way the nation lived. Railroads opened up new lands for agriculture and mining, stimulated the development of financial markets, and pioneered the corporate form of business. The last decades of the nineteenth century, when Stetson was a boy, were a great age of railroad construction. In 1860, the United States had a little over 30,000 miles of track. Fifty years later, in 1910, it had more than 240,000. After the Civil War, railroads were the force that bound

---

[1] Stetson Avenue is located one block east of Michigan Avenue, between Wacker and Randolph Streets, just north of the Art Institute. See "Chicago Streets," www.chicagohs.org/documents/research/resources/streetNameChanges.pdf.

together the states and made them literally "united." They served every town of any size.[2]

Railroads required huge amounts of capital, which naturally meant high finance. Cornelius Vanderbilt, the "Commodore," who started his business life with schooners and steamships before there were railroads, decided to get into railroading when in his late 60s. He bought and consolidated various lines into the New York Central. Polite society in the Gilded Age considered Vanderbilt rough and vulgar, but at the time of his death in 1877 he was the richest man in the United States. Vanderbilt's only son, William, inherited $100 million, including control of the New York Central. In 1879, when William wanted to sell some of his Central shares, J. Pierpont Morgan helped dispose of them. More importantly, Morgan retained the new buyers' proxies and thereby secured a place on the company's board of directors, a tactic he had used in other deals. In the late nineteenth century, Morgan specialized in the financing, consolidation, and reorganization of railroads. He frequently placed himself or a Morgan partner on railroad boards. Morgan's ambitious aim was no less than to rationalize the chaotic industry, thereby clearing the way for greater profit.[3]

---

[2] Rudolph L. Daniels, *Trains Across the Continent: North American Railroad History*, 2nd ed. (Bloomington: Indiana University Press, 2000) 228; Jonathan Hughes and Louis P. Cain, *American Economic History*, 7th ed. (Boston: Pearson Education, Inc., 2007) 287; John F. Stover, *The Life and Decline of the American Railroad* (New York: Oxford University Press, 1970) 3–99.

[3] Edward J. Renehan Jr., *Dark Genius of Wall Street: The Misunderstood Life of Jay Gould, King of the Robber Barons* (New York: Basic Books, 2005) 99–103; Maury Klein, *The Life and Legend of Jay Gould* (Baltimore: The Johns Hopkins University Press, 1986) 78; Daniels, *Trains Across the Continent*, 77–78; Charles R. Morris, *The Tycoons: How Andrew Carnegie, John D. Rockefeller, Jay Gould, and J.P. Morgan Invented the American Supereconomy* (New York: Henry Holt and Company, 2005) 143–44; Albro Martin, *Railroads Triumphant: The Growth, Rejection and Rebirth of a Vital American Force* (New York: Oxford University Press, 1992) 295–96; Charles R. Geisst, *Wall Street: A History* (New York: Oxford University Press, 1997) 89–92; Vincent P. Carosso, *The Morgans: Private International Bankers, 1854–1913* (Cambridge: Harvard University Press, 1987) 230–34; Alfred D. Chandler Jr., *The Visible Hand: The Managerial Revolution in American Business* (Cambridge: Harvard University Press, 1977) 145–87.

During the 1880s and 1890s Morgan used the voting trust to this end, a strategy that came to be called "Morganization." By 1900, hundreds of American railroads were consolidated by voting trusts into six systems controlled by either J. P. Morgan or Kuhn, Loeb. These trusts became the object of political attacks from both the Populist Party of the 1890s and later progressives. Their existence was linked to the banks' "Money Trust" that also came under public scrutiny. Technically, a trust is a legal entity that holds property to be managed, protected, and distributed to others. But in the nineteenth century it also became a device to unify corporate power, enhance banker control, and create monopolies.[4]

Railroads, like banks, raised important issues of public policy, and not simply because of the trust device. As "common carriers," railroads were never viewed as entirely private businesses. Legally, they had duties to serve the public in ways that a manufacturing company did not. Further, railroads typically operated under special government charters and had often received massive grants of public land in order to create incentives for construction. For these reasons and because of the public's dependence on railroads, railroad practices were hot political issues during most of Stetson's life. When a railroad shareholders' trust concentrated power in the hands of one party, potentially against the interests of other parties, such as the public and freight shippers, the public perceived that the trust would run the railroads for the benefit of the trust alone. Naturally, this drove political efforts to regulate rates, services, and the railroad's monopolistic characteristics.[5]

No wonder that a rising young banker such as Stetson was attracted to railroads. Anyone his age would have been familiar with the sounds, sights, and smells of the steam engine. Stetson had even enjoyed the luxury of a

---

[4] On "Morganization," see Ron Chernow, *The House of Morgan: An American Banking Dynasty and the Rise of Modern Finance* (New York: Atlantic Monthly Press, 1990) 66–69; and Martin, *Railroads Triumphant*, 333–34.

[5] On the economics of railroad regulation, see Hughes and Cain, *American Economic History*, 294–300. For the argument that Morgan and others failed to achieve monopoly and looked to federal regulation to avoid destructive competition, see Gabriel Kolko, *Railroads and Regulation, 1877–1916* (New York: W.W. Norton, 1970) 231–39. On Morgan's desire to limit competition, see Chernow, *House of Morgan*, 53–58; Carosso, *The Morgans*, 288.

long train trip in the 1890s, before he went to college. As early as 1906, when he was still in his twenties, Stetson was a board member of a small Georgia lumber railroad. When he came to Guaranty a big portion of his credit work was to review the value of corporate securities, which to a large extent meant railroad stocks and bonds. Some of this effort involved travel by rail to inspect railroad property. Having responsibility over railroad financing was not easy. Competition could be rigorous, and a great many railroad companies were structured badly or managed poorly. Failures were frequent. During the downturn of the 1890s, almost 70,000 miles of track had been foreclosed on by creditors, including that owned by the Union Pacific, Baltimore & Ohio, and Northern Pacific.[6]

Moreover, to a banker the significance of railroads far surpassed the financial condition of the lines themselves. In Stetson's time railroads were necessary, at the very heart of American business development. A loan to a manufacturing company, for example, could depend on its access to rail transportation. As a result, bankers like Stetson knew a lot about the demand for rail transportation and its growth or contraction. Bankers became important business partners to railroads. As Stetson traveled for Guaranty he made important contacts among railroads and was able to display this bankers' expertise. These contacts, in turn, soon led to invitations to serve on the boards of lines, including most notably the Missouri, Kansas & Texas Railroad (The Katy). The railroads' attraction to Stetson, as in other fields, was linked to his understanding and sympathy for their business. One Guaranty client, W. Averell Harriman, a member of one of the great railroad families in American history, became the critical link between Stetson and the Illinois Central.[7]

---

[6] Kolko, *Railroads and Regulation*, 64.

[7] "Appendix to Appellant's Brief," 82, 84, *Guttmann v. Illinois Central R.R.*, United States Court of Appeals for the Second Circuit, No. 21801 (1949), National Archives and Records Administration, New York, New York (hereafter "Appendix"); Wayne A. Johnston, *Eugene Stetson: Loyal Son of Mercer* (S.l.: s.n., 1965) 1–10.

Harriman's Proxy

In 1916, when Stetson arrived in New York, Averell Harriman's family owned a good portion of the Union Pacific, the Southern Pacific, and the Illinois Central. Harriman, who was about ten years younger than Stetson, had the exceedingly good fortune to be the son of one of wealthiest men in American history, the railroad baron Edward H. Harriman. The senior Harriman's financing wizardry and management of western routes built the family fortune, which included a $70 million bequest to Averell when he was still a teenager. Immediately after Yale the young Harriman became a vice president of the Union Pacific and director of the Illinois Central. The Union Pacific owned a large block of Illinois Central stock, so there was a close relationship between the two lines. By the 1930s, Harriman's official positions reflected this connection: he was chairman of the board of the Union Pacific and chairman of the executive committee of the Illinois Central. During his lifetime, Harriman's wide-ranging business interests also included the Merchant Shipbuilding Company; Aviation Corporation; Brown Brothers Harriman; and the development of Sun Valley, Idaho, as a resort.[8]

Harriman moved increasingly into politics. In 1932 he supported Democrat Franklin Roosevelt for President. Harriman was opposed to President Hoover's trade barriers and wanted a voice in Roosevelt's plan to tighten regulation of the securities industry. As a partner in the private bank Brown Brothers Harriman, he had a large stake in Wall Street's future. Harriman's political career started in earnest after he was named President Roosevelt's "Expeditor" in evaluating and delivering arms and war materiel to the British under the Lend-Lease Act in 1941. He gradually grew into a leading American politician. He served as Ambassador to the Soviet Union during World War II, United States Secretary of Commerce (1946–1948), United States coordinator of the Marshall Plan (1948–1953), Governor of New York (1955–1959), Presidential candidate (1952 and 1956), and

[8] See Rudy Abramson, *Spanning the Century: The Life of Averell Harriman, 1891–1986* (New York: W. Morrow, 1992).

representative of President Lyndon Johnson to the Paris peace talks with North Vietnam (1968–1969). He died in 1986 at the age of ninety-four.[9]

Harriman needed trusted lieutenants to watch his economic interests while he pursued a political career. One of these lieutenants was Gene Stetson. As early as 1919, Stetson was in regular contact with Harriman. His family and its business interests maintained large accounts with Guaranty. Part of Stetson's job at the bank was to develop and manage the Harriman fortune, and Stetson frequently solicited Harriman for more Guaranty work. In September 1919 he asked Harriman to consider using Guaranty as a depository for his Merchant Shipbuilding Company. In January 1920, he asked Harriman to promote Guaranty as a potential trustee for the United States Railroad Administration, which had taken over the country's railroads during World War I. Several months later, Stetson, learning that Harriman was a director of a Philadelphia bank, requested that he call the president of the bank and propose that Guaranty handle the bank's New York account. By the late 1920s some of Harriman and Stetson's correspondence concerned the Illinois Central. Stetson, ever his bank's booster, informed Harriman that "should there be an opportunity to have the Illinois Central give us a larger and more active account, we will greatly appreciate it."[10]

Over the years the business and personal relationships deepened. As already discussed, Stetson served as director in W. A. Harriman Securities, and his wife, Iola, invested in that company. Stetson sat on other boards connected to Harriman interests, such as Aviation Corporation. Stetson's son, Eugene Jr., attended Yale and in 1933 was elected to Skull and Bones, Harriman's senior society. Eugene Jr.'s election prompted a friendly exchange of letters between Harriman and the senior Stetson. Eugene Jr. eventually worked for Brown Brothers Harriman. In 1935, Stetson invited Harriman to join Georgia's Jekyll Island Club. Stetson also solicited a donation from Harriman to help a charitable group purchase and restore

---

[9] Ibid.

[10] Eugene W. Stetson to W. Averell Harriman, 5 September 1919; 22 January, 13 October 1920; 4 May 1929; 2 June, 23 November 1931; Matthew W. Murray to W. Averell Harriman, March 6, 1919, W. Averell Harriman Papers, Library of Congress, Manuscripts Division, Washington, DC.

Robert E. Lee's birthplace in Virginia. Much like his dealings with Bob Woodruff, Tom Watson, Thomas Lamont, Smith Richardson, and Manuel Rionda, Stetson's actions reflected the core values and tactics of relationship banking.[11]

Yet the most compelling evidence of the relationship was Stetson's appointment to Illinois Central's board on 23 February 1932. At the time Harriman was chairman of Illinois Central's executive committee. The historical ties between Guaranty, the Harriman family, and the railroad were partly demonstrated by the fact that two other Guaranty directors, Henry W. De Forest and Robert W. Goelet, were also Illinois Central directors. Stetson seems to have initiated conversations with Harriman about becoming a director. He told Harriman he would be interested in the appointment and would resign his directorship with the Missouri, Kansas & Texas Railroad. Harriman was receptive. He discussed Stetson's appointment with Lawrence A. Downs, president of the railroad. Downs, who had earlier served as president of the Illinois Central-controlled Central of Georgia Railroad, met with Stetson and was impressed. Once again, the network mattered. As Stetson put it, the Georgia connection meant "his friends and my friends down there were mutual. Also one of the biggest shippers down there was a big manufacturing company, a big cotton mill [Bibb Manufacturing Company], [and Stetson] was a director in that, and so it brought us a community of interest."[12]

---

[11] Eugene W. Stetson to W. Averell Harriman, 4 May 1929; 13 June 1933; 20 June, 13 November 1935; 22 December 1939; 21 September 1943; W. Averell Harriman to Eugene W. Stetson, 9 February 1948, W. Averell Harriman Papers.

[12] "Appendix," 83; Eugene W. Stetson to W. Averell Harriman, 21 June 1932, W. Averell Harriman Papers. Another dimension to Stetson's appointment was that in 1932 representatives of the New York business community dominated the twelve-member IC board. In addition to New Yorkers Harriman and Stetson, other directors were John Auchincloss, member of the investment firm of Auchincloss Brothers of New York, General Cornelius Vanderbilt of New York, great-grandson of the Commodore, Robert W. Goelet of New York, head of the Ritz-Carlton Hotel Corporation, and Vincent Astor. Carlton J. Corliss, *Main Line of Mid-America: The Story of the Illinois Central* (New York: Creative Age Press, 1950) 439.

As a director Stetson tried to make the most of Harriman's status as a FDR Democrat. In early 1934 the federal Public Works Administration ruled Guaranty would not be a suitable trustee for $35 million in bonds on equipment the Illinois Central wanted to use as collateral for a government loan. Part of the reason was that Harriman and Stetson were directors of the Illinois Central. Stetson complained to Harriman that he could not "conceive of any possible conflict that might arise" and he criticized the government's suggestion that "securing trust business from transportation companies through directors would in itself tend to create unfair competition." He asked Harriman to discuss the matter with Secretary of the Interior Harold Ickes. Moreover, Stetson sent Harriman recommendations for commissioners on the newly created Securities and Exchange Commission. When Congress was considering the Securities Act of 1933, Stetson tried to arrange a meeting between Harriman and a United States senator so that Harriman could express his views about securities regulation.[13]

The Main Line of Mid-America

Stetson was aware of the Illinois Central's historic significance. Arguably, no other line was so important to American commerce and economic development. The railroad facilitated both the settling of the West and the joining of North and South. The company was chartered in 1851 as the first land-grant railroad, under an act sponsored by Illinois Senator Stephen A. Douglas, of Lincoln-Douglas debate fame. His political foe, Abraham Lincoln, was an occasional Illinois Central, or "IC," attorney. Another famous American figure, Mark Twain, piloted Illinois Central steamboats on the Mississippi River from 1859 to 1861.[14]

By 1856, the company's road stretched across the Illinois prairies from the frontier town of Chicago to the Ohio River at Cairo, Illinois, making it

---

[13] Eugene W. Stetson to W. Averell Harriman, 8 May 1933; 13 February 1934; 14 October 1937; W. Averell Harriman to Eugene W. Stetson, 22 December 1938, W. Averell Harriman Papers.

[14] For surveys of the railroad's history, see John F. Stover, *History of the Illinois Central Railroad* (New York: Macmillan Publishing Co., 1975); and Corliss, *Main-Line of Mid-America*.

the longest railroad in the world. Illinois Central service contributed greatly to an economic boom in the state. Chicago grew from a mere 28,000 residents in 1850 to more than 80,000 in 1855. During the Civil War, the railroad transported thousands of Union troops to the South. The Army moved over thirty percent of its men and supplies on the Illinois Central. After the war, officers and engineers from both sides worked for the IC. The company began an aggressive expansion policy, hiring Andrew Carnegie to build a bridge across the Mississippi River at Dubuque, Iowa, in 1869, and then a line clear to the Missouri River at Sioux City, Iowa. In the 1870s IC wanted to commence business in the South, linking Chicago with New Orleans. Agreements with southern lines, by the early 1880s, increased the company's service from Cairo across west Kentucky and Tennessee through the heart of Mississippi to Louisiana. Unfortunately, however, the track north of Cairo was "standard" gauge while the track to the south was "wide" gauge. In one of the amazing feats of railroad history, on 29 July 1881, beginning at dawn and finishing at three that afternoon, more than 3,000 men converted the entire 548-mile southern line to New Orleans to standard gauge. In 1889, Illinois Central opened the four-mile-long Cairo Bridge over the Ohio River at a cost of almost $3 million.[15]

The Illinois Central has been so influential that some of its history has entered into national folklore and popular entertainment. In 1900, a train wreck in Mississippi had one fatality, an engineer named John Luther Jones, nicknamed "Casey." The famous story of Casey Jones's fateful run on Illinois Central's *Cannonball* is the subject of the well-known song by Wallace Saunders, written in 1909, and it even produced a short-lived (and much less popular) television series in the late 1950s. Among the more notable IC trains was *The City of New Orleans*, which ran from Chicago to New Orleans. This also became the inspiration for a song, by Steve Goodman, which was recorded by Arlo Guthrie in the early 1970s.[16]

---

[15] Stover, *Illinois Central*, 56–57, 74, 132–39, 187–88, 202–205, 237.

[16] Ibid., 224–25; "Wallace Saunders," http://www.watervalley.net/users/casey-jones/saunders.htm; "City of New Orleans," http://www.folkblues.com/goodman/cono.htm.

High Speed Finance

The great late nineteenth expansion produced high expectations for the company's future. For many years this optimism was fully justified. In 1905 the Illinois Central controlled more than 4,000 miles of track, had a capital stock value of almost $100 million, and gross receipts of almost $50 million a year. The federal government assumed control of all railroads as a war measure from late 1917 until early 1920, but after this brief interlude, Illinois Central commenced a new period of prosperity. During the 1920s gross revenues exceeded $160 million a year. The company paid annual dividends on its common and preferred stock, while the price of its common soared from $85 a share in 1920 to more than $153 in 1929. The good performance stimulated a massive improvements program on which the company spent more than $300 million. It purchased new engines and rolling stock, built new terminals, replaced steam with electric service for suburban trains in Chicago, and acquired new lines in the South. Yet the improvements were not paid for by earnings. Instead, the company issued more than $18 million in preferred stock and increased its bonded debt with the expectation that good times would continue. By 1930, the outstanding funded debt had increased from $257 million to $359 million. Annual interest charges were $15.8 million.[17]

Debt would not have posed a problem if the company's revenues remained stable, but conditions in the early 1930s exploded assumptions about continued prosperity. Signs of impending doom appeared in the late 1920s, with a decline of passenger to freight revenues caused by the rise of the automobile and highway construction and a leveling off in all revenues. The nationwide economic downturn beginning in late 1929 raised the most pressing threats. The company's common stock fluctuated wildly in 1930 between $65 and $136 a share only to collapse to a low of just over $9 in 1931. It bottomed out at just under $5 a share in 1932, a loss of almost ninety-seven percent of its 1929 value. Put another way, IC market value

---

[17] Stover, *Illinois Central*, 285–313; "Appendix," 458 (Court's Findings of Fact); Wayne Johnston, "The Refinancing Story," Illinois Central Management Seminar, 13–14 April 1953, Eugene W. Stetson Papers, Jack Tarver Library, Special Collections, Mercer University, Macon, Georgia (hereafter Johnston, "Refinancing").

plummeted from approximately $700 million to roughly $3 million. There was no likelihood of quick recovery. The territory served by IC swarmed with the unemployed. Agricultural and mineral prices, including for corn, coal, and cotton, crashed. Illinois Central lost half its annual revenue between 1929 and 1932, and with the massive debt looming, began to run a multimillion-dollar annual deficit. In October 1931, the IC board ordered that payments of common and preferred dividends cease, something that had not happened since the 1850s.[18]

Stetson became a director under these extreme conditions. In 1932, the company faced annual deficits, a huge and complex debt of approximately $379 million, and an interest charge on the debt of more than $16.4 million a year with only $89 million in total annual revenues. The prospects for bankruptcy were high, particularly because there seemed no hope of paying the principal on the bonded debt when it became due. Initially, Stetson played an important but not central role in the company's response to the crisis, as Harriman was still the key board member. Nonetheless, Stetson encouraged the radical economizing measures adopted by the company in the early and mid–1930s, which included stopping dividend payments, reducing operating expenses, cuts in employee pay, and laying off of more than half of IC's employees.[19]

For relief, the railroad could not turn to the usual sources of capital, as these funds dried up with the Depression. Who would invest in the doomed company? Even Harriman was unable to persuade friends at the investment bank Kuhn, Loeb to prop up IC. Stetson and other board members also recognized that operating expense reductions could not solve the debt burden. As a result, Harriman and company president Lawrence A. Downs turned to the federal government. They were able to meet the company's debts by obtaining an initial round of federal loans for almost $5 million through the Reconstruction Finance Corporation and the Railroad Finance Corporation, President Herbert Hoover's antidotes to the failure of private

---

[18] Stover, *Illinois Central*, 314–41; "Mid-America's Main Line," *Time* 57 (13 February 1951): 87–88; Johnston, "Refinancing," 3–4.

[19] "Appendix," 91–93 (Testimony of Eugene W. Stetson); Corliss, *Main Line of Mid-America*, 426–28.

lending. Illinois Central was just one among many large corporations that sought and received federal money in order to survive.[20]

As Stetson gained experience on the IC board, the company's recovery from the Depression, like the nation's, was slow and painful. Through the 1930s its property—stations, tracks, and equipment, declined in value. In 1933 the company borrowed an additional $7.1 million from the Railroad Finance Corporation and revenues fell further from 1932. Although income increased slightly in 1934, there was still a deficit of almost $3 million. Revenues increased once again in 1935, but so did expenses, and the company ended the year almost $10 million in the red, a record loss.[21]

Beginning in 1936, IC emerged from the period of deficits, but for several years its profits were small, particularly relative to the continuing debt obligations, which still exceeded $15 million annually. Stetson, in fact, described 1937 as "the second crisis of the Illinois Central." It was necessary to let 4,000 employees go and return to the federal government for another $10 million loan to pay maturing securities. Altogether, IC borrowed about $35 million from the government's corporate finance programs between 1932 and 1937. The company borrowed another $10 million from the New Deal's Public Works Administration. Stetson concluded there would have been a receivership in 1937 if a three-year, six percent note issued to stockholders had not been paid by a government loan. Stetson also believed depression conditions persisted to 1940 despite the fact that the company did not have a deficit between 1936 and 1940.[22]

Conducting a Railroad

During the late 1930s Stetson began to assume a leading role on the IC board. One reason was a dramatic shift in the board's composition. Decades earlier, reflecting the dominance of New York financial interests, the headquarters were moved from Chicago to New York. In 1938, on

---

[20] Stover, *Illinois Central*, 323; "Appendix," 92–93 (Testimony of Eugene W. Stetson), 185 (Testimony of Robert E. Connolly); Johnston, "Refinancing," 4–6.

[21] Stover, *Illinois Central*, 323, 327–28; "Appendix," 93–94, 115 (Testimony of Eugene W. Stetson), 273 (Testimony of William R. King).

[22] Ibid.

Harriman's suggestion, the IC board ordered an increase in the number of directors, removal of the board's headquarters and meeting place back to Chicago, and most importantly, "filling the vacancies so created, as well as other vacancies, with Directors residing on the company's line of railroad." Part of Harriman's motivation was to attract local business leaders who might help in case of receivership. A committee composed of Harriman, President Downs, and Stetson implemented the plan. Stetson later recalled that the move eschewed gradual change. It forced the immediate resignation of elderly New Yorkers who did not wish to travel to Chicago. During 1938 and 1939 the new places on the board went to big shippers on company's line: Robert E. Wood, chairman of Sears, Roebuck & Company; John W. Rath of Iowa's Rath meat packing company; A. D. Geoghegan, president of Wesson Oil & Snowdrift Company in New Orleans; and William R. King, president of the Memphis-based William R. Moore Dry Goods Company.[23]

Another important factor in Stetson's increased standing was that because Harriman was spending more time with politics, Stetson became the heir apparent to protecting the Harriman holdings. Later, Stetson himself recalled that by late 1939 he was "pinch-hitting" for Harriman on financial issues, an apt metaphor for the former manager of the Mercer University baseball team. Although his board position was still part-time (Stetson was only a few months away from being elected president of Guaranty), he was thoroughly engaged with the problems and possibilities of the railroad and welcomed the leadership opportunities that came with increased status.[24]

Stetson already had a clear vision of how the company should try to escape its problems. The overarching challenge facing Illinois Central was its enormous and complex debt. That debt had to be reduced and restructured. Also, the company had to reinvest in its widely scattered physical assets. According to Stetson, debt reduction and facilities improvements were necessary to create the kind of investor confidence the company's business health required. He vigorously promoted these ideas among the officers and directors. At a director's meeting in late 1940, for

---

[23] Stover, *Illinois Central*, 337–38; "Appendix," 84–85 (Testimony of Eugene W. Stetson); Corliss, *Main Line of Mid-America*, 437.

[24] "Appendix," 96–97 (Testimony of Eugene W. Stetson).

example, he bluntly told a new director that receivership had been narrowly avoided in 1937 and that he "hoped that as a new member of the board that he would pull just as hard as he could for new business for us and that we didn't want to have a new member come on and [then] shortly have to go back" because the company went bankrupt. Short-term palliatives to attract investment, such as paying dividends, were out of the question, because the goal was "to save the railroad for the future benefit of the bondholders and both classes of stockholders, as well as for the benefit of the public."[25]

The Japanese attack on Pearl Harbor in December 1941 propelled Stetson to IC's forefront. Once again, Harriman was the catalyst. Harriman became FDR's special representative to Great Britain and then ambassador to the Soviet Union. He resigned as chairman of IC's executive committee and Stetson assumed his place in February 1942. Stetson would hold that position for the next seventeen years. The move elevated Stetson to the pinnacle of his business career. For the next five years he was either president or chairman of Guaranty and chairman of the IC board's executive committee. His official charge with IC required that he exercise "general supervision over the business, affairs, and property of the company."[26]

At this point, the railroad's economic fortunes were rapidly improving. IC profits rose to more than $10 million in 1941, the best return since 1929. Stetson wanted to make the most of the situation, which in his mind meant debt repayment and facilities improvement. In early 1942, Stetson believed

> [T]he Illinois Central should take all steps to map out a program to have an objective to profit as best it could by reason of the circumstances of increased traffic, both freight and passenger, with the idea of using that money to finally save this railroad and bring it back to a first-class railroad.

---

[25] Ibid., 94–96 (Testimony of Eugene W. Stetson), 274 (Testimony of William R. King).

[26] Ibid., 86–87 (Testimony of Eugene W. Stetson).

> Feeling that very strongly, I mapped out in conjunction with the administrative officers, a general program. That program really started in 1939, in a limited way, to purchase [IC] bonds. That program, however, was predicated on a definite idea of, No. 1, to rehabilitate this property. This property had run down considerably...and it needed rehabilitation to handle this increased traffic, as well as for safety purposes.
>
> I wanted to see the working capital built up. We knew that we could not buy during the War many materials that were necessary, so we had to do a lot of makeshift work in keeping this roadbed up. We were unable to buy as much equipment as we would have liked to have had. Also, there were being located on [IC's service territory] new projects, Government projects, as well as private industry, going to the Mississippi Valley for strategic purposes, getting away from the Atlantic Seaboard.
>
> I felt very strongly that if we had mapped out a definite policy, with a definite objective, conserving our cash, which of course means building up working capital, that we could rehabilitate the road, that we could have a bond purchase program which would lead to an ultimate result whereby we could reduce our interest charges to something under $10,000,000 [per year].

The IC board and officers endorsed Stetson's plan.[27]

Implementing the strategy, however, was complicated. Several financing devices were used to reduce and restructure the debt, which was composed of about thirty mortgages and other debt indentures, as well as notes held by the federal government. Stetson's job, because of his wide-ranging connections in the investment community, was to write the letters, make the phone calls, and button-hole the persons who were necessary to achieve the company's goals. In short, he was to make the most of relationships in order to help his client.[28]

---

[27] Ibid., 96–97 (Testimony of Eugene W. Stetson).

[28] Edwin S. S. Sunderland, *Main Line of Mid-America: The Simplification of its Debt Structure, 1938–1952* (S.l.: Privately Printed, 1952) 1, 4; "Appendix," 96–101 (Testimony of Eugene W. Stetson), 463–67 (Court's Findings of Fact). Sunderland

In the early 1940s a most pressing concern was that a huge portion of the debt, over $188 million, would mature between 1950 and 1955, and most of this, about $134 million, was non-callable and due before 1954. If the bonds had been issued in "callable" form, the company could have paid a premium to redeem them, replacing them with a new issue costing less in interest payments. Not only was the short time frame daunting, the company's poor financial record limited refinancing options. Initial attempts, in 1945 and 1946, to lure some bondholders to exchange their bonds for later maturing securities failed because of high prices and lack of interest. As a result, the most consistent tactic through the 1940s was to use the increased revenues of the war years to repurchase IC bonds on the open market. Another concern was the need to repay $35 million owed the government, for which the company required several time extensions. It finally paid this debt in 1943. The government assisted the company's bond buying by allowing some of the debt to be used to purchase outstanding bonds.[29]

In 1946 a crucial corner had been turned. Because of growing investor confidence, the company used the bond exchange device and offers to purchase non-callable bonds with greater success. A key means of increasing investor confidence was constant contact with the nation's most significant sources of financing. This was yet another demonstration of Stetson's use of networks. Stetson sought and obtained the expert advice of Kuhn, Loeb; Guaranty; the United States Secretary of Commerce; the head of the Reconstruction Finance Corporation; the Interstate Commerce Commission; and legal counsel. The strategy's success allowed the company in 1949 to create a consolidated mortgage on all of its property and finance it through an exchange for bonds that would mature in the 1970s. Altogether, Stetson's policy reduced the company's debt by more than $114

---

was an attorney and member of the IC board of directors. As late as 1945 professional investors were skittish about the future of the IC because of its large debt. See, for example, "Heavy Debt Hangs over IC," *BusinessWeek* (13 October 1945): 73–75, which discussed the company's securities maturing in the 1950s and observed that government loans during the Depression had "saved the day" for the railroad.

[29] Ibid.

million, which in turn lowered annual interest payments by more than $5 million per year.[30]

An important aspect of Stetson's plan was that it took place during a time of huge demands on railroads. In contrast to the surplus capacity of the 1930s, the war brought crowded troop trains and massive shipments of war materiel. Between 1943 and 1945 the company carried more than 150 million passengers. Freight shipments rose phenomenally. For example, the company transported about 273,000 tons of crude petroleum in 1938; in 1943 it shipped more than 7.5 million tons. This new business caused revenues and profits to increase sharply. In 1944 the company's operating income neared $260 million, a far cry from the less than $115 million earned in 1940. Net income surpassed $24 million in both 1942 and 1943. But the effects of more traffic were not all favorable. Giant increases in passenger and freight severely burdened IC equipment and war priorities meant replacements were not always available. The war and its aftermath required substantial outlays for railroad maintenance. Perhaps the largest single repair project was the bridge over the Ohio River at Cairo, which cost more than $6 million.[31]

Battling Directors

Stetson's refinancing plan was executed in a context of changing careers and leadership. In 1946 he turned sixty-five and retired from Guaranty as chairman the following January. In fact, by mid–1946 Stetson was essentially a full-time officer of the railroad and his IC salary was raised from $17,000 to $35,000. One telling example of his power in the company at this time was his contribution to the choice of a new president. When President John L. Bevens died, Harriman and the board of directors delegated the job of nominating a new president to Stetson. Stetson interviewed each of the eager candidates and asked the same question: "If you couldn't be the President, who would you support?" All the candidates named Wayne Johnston. Based on that, Stetson picked Johnston, who

---

[30] Sunderland, *Simplification of its Debt Structure*, 4; "Appendix," 466–67 (Court's Findings of Fact).

[31] Stover, *Illinois Central*, 354–56; "Appendix," 466–71 (Court's Findings of Fact).

became IC president in 1945.[32]

Another factor was Harriman himself, who by 1946 was nearing the end of his ambassadorial service. Despite his absence, Harriman remained a force because of his Union Pacific's ownership of IC stock. Anticipating his return, Stetson wrote Harriman in May 1946 that he was welcome to assume the position of chairman of the board or chairman of the executive committee of Illinois Central, or both, when he came back to the United States. When it became clear that Harriman had no intention of taking control, Stetson indicated his desire to become chairman of the board. The request was not simply a matter of shuffling titles. Under the corporate by-laws, the chairman of the board was the railroad's chief executive officer and superior to the president. When President Bevens died it had been suggested that Stetson become chairman of IC's board, but he rejected the idea because he was still chairman of Guaranty. In 1946, however, with his departure from the bank imminent, Stetson wanted the job. He planned to submit his proposal to become chairman at the IC board meeting on 23 July 1946. Prior to the meeting Stetson solicited the support of Harriman, Johnston, and influential board member Robert Wood. He believed he secured the approval of all three.[33]

At the 23 July meeting Stetson informed the directors that his retirement from the bank would be effective on 15 January 1947. As a result, he could give more time to Illinois Central. Stetson stated that his willingness to give more time to the railroad meant his title should be changed to chairman of the board. That would accurately reflect the new and larger role he intended to assume. Stetson also believed that because he was willing to give up his $100,000 a year salary with Guaranty, the IC should henceforth pay him $50,000 a year. He informed the board that he had already discussed the matter with Harriman and Wayne Johnston and

---

[32] Stover, *Illinois Central*, 370; "Appendix," 89 (Testimony of Eugene W. Stetson).

[33] "Appendix," 4 (Plaintiff's Complaint); Robert E. Wood to W. Averell Harriman, 26 July 1946; Eugene W. Stetson to W. Averell Harriman, 23 August 1946; Eugene W. Stetson to Robert E. Wood, September 1946, W. Averell Harriman Papers.

that they approved. He left the boardroom in order to allow the directors to debate the proposal freely.[34]

At this point Stetson's plan encountered a major obstacle—General Robert E. Wood. Wood was a former military quartermaster who abandoned the army for the more profitable world of retail sales. Sixty-seven years old in 1946, Wood graduated from West Point in 1900, served in the Philippine War, and directed the Panama Railroad Company during the construction of the Panama Canal. He was acting Quartermaster General of the Army during World War I. After the war, Wood saw an opportunity to transform the mail-order business by building a chain of retail stores, and because of this insightful policy he rose through the ranks at Sears, Roebuck, serving as president from 1928 to 1939 and chairman of the board from 1939 to 1954. Perhaps ironically, although initially a supporter of Franklin Roosevelt, Wood opposed United States entry into World War II and the Lend-Lease program that fellow IC director Harriman helped administer. By the mid–1940s Wood wanted General Douglas MacArthur to be President, and eventually he was a whole-hearted supporter of Senator Joseph McCarthy's anti-communist witch-hunt.[35]

After Stetson left the directors' meeting, Wood took charge. He asked the three members of the board who were also officers of the company, including Wayne Johnston, to step out of the room. Wood and fellow executive committee member and Chicago meat packing executive Thomas E. Wilson then announced their opposition to Stetson's proposal. They agreed, however, that Stetson should be paid $50,000 and retained as chairman of the executive committee. The remainder of the men present agreed. When Wood and Wilson informed Stetson of the decision, he was surprised and disappointed.[36]

---

[34] Robert E. Wood to W. Averell Harriman, 26 July 1946; Eugene W. Stetson to Robert E. Wood, September 1946, W. Averell Harriman Papers.

[35] On Wood, see James C. Worthy, *Shaping an American Institution: Robert E. Wood and Sears, Roebuck* (Urbana: University of Illinois Press, 1984).

[36] Robert E. Wood to W. Averell Harriman, 26 July 1946; Eugene W. Stetson to Robert E. Wood, September 1946, W. Averell Harriman Papers.

Stetson, however, did not give up after just one try. Demonstrating the IC's true center of power, several days after the meeting Wood wrote Harriman a long letter about the situation. He sent Stetson a copy only a couple of weeks later. Wood admitted that Stetson approached him about the chairmanship and that he had led Stetson to believe he supported the idea. Wood told Harriman that he changed his mind before the 23 July meeting and decided to express his objection to the board. For some reason, however, he did not bother to tell Stetson. Wood assured Harriman that his opposition was not personal. Stetson was a "mutual friend" and all of the board members were "fond of Gene." On the other hand,

> It was the unanimous opinion of the Board that it would be bad policy to appoint as Chairman of the Board a New York City banker, who resided in New York and was associated with New York, that this would probably nullify the effect of bringing the headquarters of the road to Chicago [in 1938].... Then, too, we felt that it might have a bad effect on the organization, that the officers of the road and the working force would not feel the same when the titular head of the road was in New York.

Oddly, Wood did not perceive it was unlikely that Harriman, a New York-based financier, would be impressed by a criticism of New York banks.[37]

There seems to have been more to Wood's opposition. Wood reported that Stetson was told the board did not want him to be chairman but that it would agree to the salary increase and him staying as chairman of the executive committee. Wood claimed Stetson reacted sharply, saying that if he did not become chairman of the board he would terminate his connection with IC. According to Wood, after Wood suggested that a resolution be delayed until October, Stetson demanded an immediate decision. Wood and the board told Stetson that he could continue as chairman of the executive committee with an increase in salary to $50,000, an offer that would remain open until October. Certainly Wood's account attempted to put Stetson in a bad light. Wood took the opportunity to make his broader conclusion perfectly clear:

---

[37] Robert E. Wood to W. Averell Harriman, 26 July 1946, W. Averell Harriman Papers.

> Frankly, I was surprised and upset at Gene's attitude. I think it would be a mistake to make him Chairman of the Board or for that matter any New York man Chairman. I think the road can get along very well without a Chairman for the time being. I think the fiscal affairs of the road can be worked out by the Board even if Gene prefers to step out. We could put Steven Hord [a partner at Brown Brothers Harriman] on the Executive Committee and he could get us any fiscal advice that might be necessary. If Gene chooses to stay as chairman of the Executive Committee, I shall be glad to see him stay, though I personally have differed with him twice on fiscal policies. I felt that he was too slow in buying up the bonds when we had the opportunity of buying them at a considerable discount.... [And] I was opposed to the recent proposal by which the fiscal structure of the road would be refinanced [through exchanging bonds].

In essence, Wood had no difficulty jettisoning Stetson, primarily because he represented New York bankers, whom Wood disliked on principle, but also because in Wood's judgment Stetson made mistakes in handling IC's debt problems.[38]

Several weeks later Stetson responded to Wood in a letter, which, predictably, he sent to Harriman first. The letter showed Stetson had not lasted more than forty years in corporate tussles by shrinking from challenges. First, Stetson blasted Wood for letting him believe, from May until the 23 July meeting, that he would support Stetson's bid to become board chairman. He was peeved that a supposed friend had failed to explain why he changed his mind. Stetson then attacked Wood's representation to Harriman that the board unanimously opposed Stetson's proposal by pointing out that four men on the fourteen-member Board were excluded from the room and four were absent, leaving a minority of six to make the "unanimous" decision. Stetson contended that a majority of the board, if voting, would have supported his offer. More personally, Stetson complained that Wood had "expressed to me and to others many times [his] general antipathy to New York bankers and it is too bad you have let your natural prejudice, coupled with your impulsiveness and I might add that

---

[38] Ibid.

very forceful desire of yours to put your point over, influence the proper affairs of the Illinois Central Railroad." Ironically, considering Stetson first sent the draft of his letter to Harriman, he complained that Wood had sent his letter to Harriman and mailed a copy to Stetson two weeks later.[39]

Stetson tried to address some of the substantive issues related to his bid to become chairman. He maintained the change in title would "make a good bit of difference to my being able to help the railroad in many directions," a reference to obtaining financial and business assistance. Further, he did not intend to assume responsibilities for the physical operation of the railroad and only desired an advisory relationship with the president, who he thought was doing a good job. Stetson defended his past financial policies, adding that the bond purchase program was based on experts' sound advice. In the end, however, he wanted compromise. He told Wood that the railroad faced a host of post-war problems—labor, inflation, government regulators, and competition, and that as a result he was willing to continue his current position: "[T]he question of a title was not fundamental [but]...results for the railroad's stockholders were fundamental." As far as corporate leadership was concerned, the president should be the chief administrative and operating officer of the road. The chairman of the executive committee should act for the committee and the board when the committee was not in session. Stetson thought this means of governing was either already incorporated in the company by-laws or could be developed by a new agreement.[40]

Ultimately, and from the usual source, Stetson obtained the power he wanted. From Paris, Harriman sent his brother Roland a draft response to Wood. He asked Roland to "go over it with Gene" first. Harriman's letter supported Stetson unequivocally. As a director of the IC for more than thirty years, he felt "strongly" that IC was "very fortunate" to have Stetson as chairman: "He is a man of broad financial experience and has sound

[39] Eugene W. Stetson to Robert E. Wood, September 1946, W. Averell Harriman Papers.

[40] Ibid. Stetson and Wood apparently did not develop any lasting animosity from the conflict. See Robert E. Wood to Eugene W. Stetson, 15 June 1958, Eugene W. Stetson Papers.

judgment. In addition, he knows our territory well.... I am satisfied that we must have a man of Stetson's broad experience to concentrate on its problems or else the company may well find itself in a difficult position." Harriman discounted Wood's concern that Stetson, as chairman of the board, would somehow conflict with the president. The ambassador portrayed Wood's New York banker argument as Midwestern paranoia:

> I cannot take seriously the suggestion that the fact that a man has been a New York banker excludes him from the position of Chairman of the Board. The question is whether Stetson has the capacities, which I am satisfied he has. In my opinion, his standing, character and background will add prestige to the company. After all, he was a small town Georgian who from personal experience knows the psychology of much of our territory. The fact that he has "made good" in the banking world is not a handicap. I was the one responsible for moving the Board of Directors from New York to Chicago. I cannot, therefore, be accused of trying to jeopardize the value of this move.

Harriman urged Wood to support Stetson for chairman.[41]

The Wood-Stetson conflict did not result in Stetson becoming chairman of the board. Nonetheless, it did solidify his position at IC's highest level. Stetson emerged from the conflict as the unofficial leader of the board, title or no title. He had the full backing of Harriman and President Johnston. Apparently Wood had been a thorn in the side for some years, but despite this incident Stetson and Wood tended to agree on the company's broad needs. That agreement formed the basis for renewed unity. The episode must have seemed ironic to Stetson, given that he spent the first thirty-five years of his life in the small town world of middle Georgia, a venue far removed from Wood's hated New York. At any rate, the long-term effect of the contest was that Stetson was able to make the transition in 1946–1947 from banker to full-time railroad executive with only a few bumps along the way.

---

[41] W. Averell Harriman to Robert E. Wood, 4 September 1946; W. Averell Harriman to Roland Harriman, 4 September 1946, W. Averell Harriman Papers.

With a good boardroom fight behind him, Stetson looked forward to his new relationship with Illinois Central. In the cover story published in *Forbes* in January 1947, he suggested that for an executive there was real excitement in transportation. He cited, for example, the factor of organized labor, which flexed its muscles in the late 1940s. Stetson hoped "labor leaders and management will come to their senses before over-drastic measures are resorted to by Congress." Congress, did, in fact, impose new restrictions on unions with the Taft-Hartley Act of 1947. Of equal concern was the public, which seemed ignorant about the needs of the railroads. Competition from airlines, trucks, and cars as well as extensive government regulation offered severe challenges. Despite his Republican affiliation, Stetson expected sound economic leadership from President Harry S. Truman as well as Harriman, who was now Secretary of Commerce. Stetson's personal efforts would "be directed towards the establishment of a four-way equilibrium between labor, management, the various instrumentalities of government and the public—comprising at one and the same time both owners and customers."[42]

Illinois Central continued to experience good times in the years immediately after World War II. Gross revenues in 1946 were $211 million and increased to $295 million in 1951. In addition to being able to use these revenues to reduce the company's debt, large amounts, over $148 million, were spent to improve IC's road and equipment. Much of this work was necessary because of the heavy use and impossibility of repair during the war, increased competition for freight and passengers, and the gradual retirement of steam-driven locomotives. In 1945, the railroad's net income stood at $11 million, in 1947 it was $15 million, and in 1950 $12.5 million.

---

[42] William Hurd Hillyer, "Eugene Stetson—A Close Up," *Forbes* 60 (15 January 1947): 18-19.

By this time, the railroad had earned a profit every year since 1936. Even success, however, led to another big challenge for Stetson and Illinois Central.[43]

[43] Stover, *Illinois Central*, 368–79; "Appendix," 6–8 (Plaintiff's Complaint), 22–23, 107 (Testimony of Eugene W. Stetson).

13

Business Judgment

The morning of 25 April 1950, dawned as a typical early spring day in Manhattan—cloudy, cool, and with rain in the forecast. Although a new baseball season was underway, Gene Stetson, a devoted fan with box seats provided by the bank, was not thinking about the New York Yankees, the New York Giants, or the Brooklyn Dodgers. Those teams were in the midst of a golden age in which a New York club would be in the World Series for ten straight years, winning nine championships.[1]

Instead, Stetson descended in the elevator of his apartment at 117 East 72nd Street and strode out to a waiting Cadillac limousine. The car was one Illinois Central perk he particularly enjoyed. The limousine took him down FDR Drive and on to the Federal Court Building on Washington Street in Brooklyn. In the back of the car, Stetson may have read *The New York Herald Tribune*, his favorite newspaper. Or, perhaps he reviewed pertinent court papers. That day he was the key witness in a trial which would evaluate his life-long banking principles. Alexander Guttmann, a Wall Street broker and shareholder in the Illinois Central Railroad, had sued the company, claiming that since 1937 the railroad had unlawfully failed to pay almost $12 million in dividends to preferred shareholders.[2]

Stetson was a passionate defender of the railroad's management during the trying times of the 1930s and 1940s. As the company's lawyers were well aware, that passion would be necessary in a trial. In fact, as chairman of the executive committee, Stetson was the person most responsible for the policy that Guttmann complained about. The lawsuit proved to be an extended judgment on Stetson's, and the railroad's, assumption about the interrelationship between corporate finance and the roles and

[1] *New York Times*, 25 April 1950.

[2] *Guttmann v. Illinois Central R.R.*, 91 F. Supp. 285 (E.D.N.Y. 1950).

responsibilities of corporate directors. More broadly, it provided yet another test of Stetson's vision of relationship banking.

Surprising as it may seem, mounting profits during the 1940s actually had an unsettling effect on IC shareholders. The reason was that no dividends had been paid since 1931. The failure to pay dividends depressed the trading price of IC stock. Following Stetson's policy, the company's position was that repayment and debt restructuring, as well as improvement of the road's physical condition, had to come before dividends. Of course, shareholders were not without means of applying pressure. Beginning in 1942, some retained attorneys and threatened to sue IC. Their claims rested on the supposed terms of the preferred shares as well as the idea that the company's profitability made the directors' failure to pay dividends unlawful. Shareholder criticisms got louder as profits grew. At the annual meeting in 1946 a shareholder moved to require the board to resume dividends if earnings permitted. The board, however, controlled enough proxies to defeat the proposal. Similar issues surfaced at the 1947 meeting, but the board again refused to declare dividends.[3]

The dissatisfaction climaxed with the beginning of the *Guttmann* lawsuit in 1948. As the case unfolded it became a classic contest between managers, directors, and shareholders in which the law was charged with sorting out the relative rights of each. The case also addressed the role of banks and bankers in corporate governance, a recurring problem in relationship banking. The precise legal question was whether Stetson was correct in assuming that directors had the right to deny dividends to preferred shareholders, even in years of profitability. In the lawsuit, Stetson aggressively defended IC policy, which involved some of the most prominent figures in American law.

---

[3] "Appendix to Appellant's Brief," 97-98 (Testimony of Eugene W. Stetson), *Guttman v. Illinois Central R.R.*, United States Court of Appeals for the Second Circuit, No. 21801 (1949), National Archives and Records Administration, New York, New York (hereafter "Appendix"); John F. Stover, *History of the Illinois Central Railroad* (New York: Macmillan Publishing Co., 1975) 379–80; W. Averell Harriman [?] to Robert P. Vanderpoel, 3 June 1947, W. Averell Harriman Papers, Library of Congress, Manuscripts Division, Washington, DC.

The Complaint

The lawsuit officially commenced on 6 July 1948, when Alexander Guttmann filed a complaint on behalf of all Illinois Central preferred shareholders in Brooklyn federal district court. He owned two hundred shares, which he had purchased in 1944 and 1945. The company issued just over 185,000 shares of preferred stock in the early 1920s in order to finance the electrification of its Chicago commuter line. Guttmann offered several arguments in favor of his claim. First, he maintained that the company wrongfully failed to pay dividends between 1937 and 1947 based on the terms of the preferred stock certificates. The language of the certificates, according to Guttmann, gave him an absolute right to semi-annual dividends if there were sufficient net earnings to pay them. As a back-up argument, he contended that even if the payment of dividends was not mandatory, the board of directors unlawfully abused its discretion by not paying preferred dividends in years in which there was a net profit. According to Guttmann, the annual amount that should have been paid preferred shareholders since 1937 was just over $1.1 million per year, making the total claim roughly $12 million, plus interest.[4]

Of course, by 1948 Stetson was no stranger to legal disputes arising out of his work as an officer or director. As already discussed, almost ten years earlier he, along with other Guaranty directors, had been a defendant in the high profile *Litwin v. Allen* shareholder lawsuit. That case had largely, but not entirely, vindicated the actions of Guaranty's board relative to the ill-fated financing of the Van Sweringen brothers.[5]

Guttmann's claim raised some of the same issues as *Litwin*, but it also had clear differences. Like the *Litwin* plaintiffs, Guttmann challenged the actions of directors, partly on the basis that they had been negligent. Instead of condemning a bad loan, however, he criticized the board's refusal to pay preferred shareholder dividends. This was significant, because the law made

---

[4] *Guttmann*, 91 F. Supp. at 289; "Plaintiff's Complaint," "Plaintiff's Pre-Trial Memorandum," *Guttmann v. Illinois Central R.R.*, No. C9195 (1949), United States District Court for the Eastern District of New York, National Archives and Records Administration, New York, New York.

[5] *Litwin* v. *Allen*, 25 N.Y.S.2d 667 (Sup. Ct. 1940); Robert C. Clark, *Corporate Law* (Boston: Little, Brown, 1986) 127–28.

all claims of director wrongdoing difficult to pursue, but it made efforts to extract dividends especially burdensome. To be sure, IC's directors were obligated to act in good faith with the degree of care that a reasonably prudent person would exercise under similar circumstances and in the belief that their actions were in the best interests of the corporation. Further, any fraud, conflict of interest, or other illegality in performing their duties as directors would be a basis for liability or for overturning director action. The law recognized the complexity of corporate decisions, including decisions to declare dividends. In fact, the law sought to avoid excessive second-guessing. As a result, it shielded directors from liability when they acted without self-interest, with sufficient information, and when they reasonably believed the effects of their business judgment were in the best interests of the corporation. Director action, such as the IC board's decision to deny preferred dividends, could not be made the basis for liability if it was the product of ordinary mistakes. This "business judgment rule" presumed the appropriateness of a board's decision.[6]

Guttmann's lawyers, the Nemerov & Shapiro firm, whose offices were just across Broadway from Stetson's Guaranty, were aware of the high legal barriers to challenging directors' decisions. In an effort to deflate the presumption of legality they stressed that by 1948 IC had earned a profit every year for more than ten years. They also argued that the board was merely a Union Pacific tool—meaning a pawn of Averell Harriman. Supposedly Harriman was most interested in increasing the value of his IC common shares. As a consequence, preferred shareholders like Guttmann were wrongly denied dividends. The plaintiffs also tried to avoid the director discretion rule by alleging that the terms of the preferred stock certificates gave them a right to payment in all years in which there was net income: 1936 through 1948. The language in the stock certificates provided that preferred stockholders "shall be entitled to receive out of the surplus or net profits of the Company, in each fiscal year, dividends at such rate or

---

[6] Clark, *Corporate Law*, 123; Harry G. Henn and John R. Alexander, *Laws of Corporations* (St. Paul: West Publishing Co., 1983) 611–13, 904–18.

rates, not exceeding seven per cent, per annum, as shall be determined by the Board of Directors."[7]

In contrast, IC's attorneys saw that their strength lay in the argument that a corporate board normally has wide discretion, especially in the declaration of dividends. The company used its regular New York lawyers, one of the nation's leading corporate firms, Davis Polk Wardwell Sunderland & Kiendl, to make the case. Theodore Kiendl, who had argued important cases before the United States Supreme Court, and S. Hazard Gillespie Jr., were the partners in charge of the defense. Their strategy relied on mounds of evidence showing the details of Stetson's financial policy. They planned to emphasize the railroad's precarious condition in the 1930s and 1940s. Of course, IC's lawyers also denied that the preferred stock certificates gave any special rights to dividends, and they tried mightily to keep the court's focus on the good works of the directors in seeking to bring the company back to physical and financial health.[8]

The Trial

The trial commenced before Judge Clarence G. Galston, without a jury. Galston, an elderly Hoover appointee, was likely to scrutinize a shareholder suit carefully. The strategy marked out by Guttmann in his pre-trial filings, which emphasized contract rights and used the alleged abuse of discretion by the board as a backup argument, was executed rather weakly at trial. His counsel, Mortimer A. Shapiro, called only one witness, an accountant, whose primary purpose was to show that the company had the resources to pay preferred dividends from 1937 to 1947 from net income. The dull testimony did not last long. Kiendl cross-examined the accountant in an extremely aggressive manner, repeatedly forcing statements that the

---

[7] *Guttmann*, 91 F. Supp. at 286; "Plaintiff's Complaint," "Plaintiff's Pre-Trial Memorandum," *Guttman v. Illinois Central R.R.*, No. C9195 (1949), United States District Court for the Eastern District of New York, National Archives and Records Administration.

[8] "Preliminary Trial Memorandum of the Defendant Illinois Central Railroad Company," "Defendant's Amended Answer," *Guttman v. Illinois Central R.R.*, No. C9195 (1949), United States District Court for the Eastern District of New York, National Archives and Records Administration.

accountant was working on a contingency basis, that he began to consider the financial history of the IC only during the past few months, and that he had scant experience with railroad accounting. Kiendl relished the accountant's admission that the one larger railroad for which he had done work was now bankrupt. Altogether, it was clear that Guttmann had no evidence to support his case other than the stock certificate itself and the fact that the company had earned profits since 1936.[9]

In contrast, IC put on a detailed and careful presentation that lasted several days. It emphasized the real problems of the railroad and the directors and officers' determined efforts to manage those problems. Stetson was the first and most important witness. The reasons for putting him up front were clear. He was a senior executive, almost seventy years old, with a distinguished appearance whose vast experience in finance and railroading would be extremely persuasive. Moreover, it was his policy of debt repayment, maintenance, and postponing dividends that was under attack, so from the company's perspective there simply was no one more suited to defend the IC than the chairman of the executive committee. Perhaps he insisted on the role. Finally, there was the intangible benefit of Stetson's direct and effective speaking style and forthright manner, which would almost certainly have a positive effect on the court. This was Stetson's golden opportunity to communicate the reasons for IC's decision-making.

Gillespie began by establishing Stetson's long service with IC and Guaranty. Stetson discussed his Georgia origins and his broader experience with railroad finance. He made the court aware of the connection between Harriman, Guaranty, and Stetson's appointment to the IC board. Stetson's short and to-the-point responses conveyed a strong impression of expertise. For example, he remarked that his many years in banking "gave me an acquaintanceship throughout the United States in practically every

[9] "Appendix," 59-76 (Testimony of Max W. Holtz).

important city in the United States." Stetson stated that the relationship between Harriman, the president of the railroad, and the board members was excellent. They united in seeking the company's health. Gillespie also asked Stetson about his annual compensation for IC, which had risen to $50,000 by 1947. Although this was a large income, Gillespie used the information to show that Stetson had actually traded a $100,000 a year salary with Guaranty for this lower amount out of devotion to IC. In short, the initial stages of Stetson's testimony did an excellent job of portraying Stetson as a business figure worth respect, a man with unusual experience who was not interested in excessive self-aggrandizement or quick fixes to serious business problems.[10]

Getting to the heart of the case, Gillespie asked Stetson about the railroad's debt and the directors' efforts to address the problem. Stetson rattled off the pertinent figures. He described desperate negotiations with government lenders in the 1930s and the large interest payments facing the company. He made it clear that prior to 1941 the overriding issue for the board was the need to save the railroad for bondholders, shareholders, and the public. Under the circumstances, paying dividends to preferred shareholders was a luxury the company could not afford. After 1941, even with significant increases in revenue, Stetson recalled that the railroad needed to build up working capital for construction and maintenance as well as to concentrate on paying IC's large debt.[11]

Besides outlining the debt repayment policy, Stetson's testimony provided concrete evidence of the issues that motivated the board to proceed with caution during and after World War II. These included the government's exceptional demands pursuant to its enormous loans; the bond purchasing program's high costs; investors' hesitance about the future of the IC because of its debt; a large tax payment to the state of Illinois; the construction of a new terminal in New Orleans; and expensive repairs to the Cairo, Illinois, bridge. Stetson and his fellow board members also feared renewed depression after World War II. All of them were old enough to remember the economic problems of 1919–1921. In fact, Stetson indicated that that this fear was only eliminated by the outbreak of "cold war" in

---

[10] Ibid., 81–91 (Testimony of Eugene W. Stetson).

[11] Ibid., 91–96 (Testimony of Eugene W. Stetson).

1948. The anticipated good times emanating from the threat of communism was one of the motivating factors in causing the company to renew preferred dividend payments that year. Only continued success in lowering debt and increasing working capital caused Stetson's eventual support for dividends for common shareholders, which were approved just prior to the trial, in January 1950.[12]

Finally, in response to Guttmann's claims of undue Union Pacific influence, Stetson testified that IC's board always acted with the best possible advice and was free from outside control. As for the good advice, it came from leading bankers in Chicago and New York, investors, lawyers, and the company's most important government contacts. Stetson also relied on railroad finance experts at Guaranty. He emphasized the IC acted on this expert advice and that the company consistently enjoyed approval from the government. The latter point was especially calculated to impress a federal judge. As for the plaintiff's claim that the board was under the thumb of the Union Pacific and Harriman, Stetson replied:

> Mr. Averell Harriman is a great friend of mine. His brother, Mr. Roland Harriman, who is now chairman of the board of the Union Pacific Railroad, is a great friend of mine. I see Mr. Roland Harriman occasionally. I am going to his home this evening on a Red Cross matter to try and help raise some money for him. We are great friends, but there has never been, directly or indirectly, any effort on the part of the Union Pacific Railroad or any of its officials to dominate, to control, to direct or in any way influence any activity on the part of any official or director of the Illinois Central during my connection with it.

Given the practical difficulty of responding to that kind of personal testimony, Guttmann voluntarily removed the issue of Union Pacific control from the case.[13]

Stetson's cross-examination proved to be the trial's climax. From the plaintiff's perspective, it was critical to show that the board abused its discretion by not paying dividends, and Stetson would have to help provide

---

[12] Ibid., 97–107 (Testimony of Eugene W. Stetson).

[13] Ibid., 107–13 (Testimony of Eugene W. Stetson).

evidence for that contention. Given this goal, the cross examination failed. Shapiro certainly demonstrated that IC's financial position improved through the 1930s and 1940s, that it was not absolutely necessary that bonds maturing the 1950s be bought back in the 1940s, and that funds were available to pay the preferred shareholders. All this Stetson and the company conceded. But these facts fell substantially short of the degree of negligence or abuse required. The cross-examination actually gave Stetson more opportunities to explain the directors' reasonableness while reducing the plaintiff's case to quibbles. For example, prior to the trial Shapiro uncovered evidence of the earlier rift between General Wood and Stetson, but his evidence seemed to suggest that the men only differed on details, and Stetson was able to testify as to the board's solidarity: "General Wood is one of the most brilliant individuals in business that I know but General Wood is a merchant, he is a salesman and a brilliant one at that, as shown by the Sears Roebuck statements and one of the finest directors that we have ever had because he is constantly bringing up matters with the board."[14]

The cross-examination also gave Stetson an opportunity to express his real feelings about Guttmann's claim, sometimes in strong language. He said that recent increases in the preferred shares' market prices, particularly because most preferred shareholders had bought their shares in the depressed market of the 1930s and early 1940s, should be enough reward. He believed shareholders had to rely on the directors to make correct decisions and that the debt retirement program would have been harmed if the directors issued dividends prematurely. Even Shapiro admitted that the board had done an excellent job—except in its decision to deny dividends. In the end, Shapiro's most successful point, although entirely irrelevant to the legal issues, was demonstrating that Stetson bought two hundred shares of IC common stock in late 1949, just weeks before the board declared the first dividend on common shares since the Depression. The purchase had been publicly reported and Stetson readily admitted it, but the implication of self-dealing stung. Ironically, Stetson had little personal interest in IC

---

[14] Ibid., 113–72 (Testimony of Eugene W. Stetson).

shares. Before buying the common shares his only ownership in IC was ten shares of preferred stock, which he purchased in 1932.[15]

The defense then trotted out other witnesses, each of whom supported and added to Stetson's basic contentions. The company's chief accountant, an IC employee for more than forty-seven years, testified as to the poor condition of the company in the 1930s and gradual improvement under the board's policies. The company's general counsel, employed by the company almost fifty-two years, repeated the same information from the standpoint of the legal department. Long-time directors were called to demonstrate the company's contention that it was on the brink of bankruptcy in the 1930s and to expound on the principle that "no company can go broke by paying its debts." Gillespie and Kiendl examined a partner from the investment firm of Kuhn, Loeb, who repeated the refrain that the company was in danger of bankruptcy in the 1930s. The IC's chief engineer, an employee for almost forty years, testified about the awful condition of the road and IC's inability to maintain it at an optimal level because of inadequate funds. Finally, the defense offered Wayne Johnston, the current president, who had been with the railroad since 1919. Johnston focused on the great need for equipment, facilities, and maintenance. Altogether, the defense consumed four days, in which the court had ample opportunity to reflect on the enormous experience of its leaders and the massive problems of one of the nation's largest railroads.[16]

On 26 May, four weeks after the trial, Judge Galston issued an opinion dismissing Guttmann's complaint. He agreed with the defense's theory of the case and was impressed by the large volume of testimony documenting the railroad's problems. In fact, half of the opinion repeated the company's perspective, with several direct references to Stetson's testimony. Even before proceeding to its legal analysis, the court concluded that the board's

---

[15] "Appendix," 113–72 (Testimony of Eugene W. Stetson). The price of Illinois Central stock rose dramatically between 1949 and 1951. Through most of 1949 IC common traded in the 20s; it stood at 29 in mid-November, 1949. In 1950 the price increased to about 40 and by 1951 had reached 75. *New York Times*, 25 April 1950; 11 November 1949; 1 June 1951.

[16] "Appendix," 178–422 (Testimony of Robert E. Connolly, Vernon W. Foster, William R. King, Clifford W. Gaylord, Joseph Birk, George W. Bovenizer, Charles A. Mottier, and Wayne A. Johnston).

fiscal policy "seems neither unreasonable nor arbitrary. The directors were all men of affairs, experienced in business, railroading and finance." The high level of expertise utilized in governing the company, which included advice from the federal government, appears to have been especially persuasive to Judge Galston.[17]

The court's legal analysis was also in favor of IC. It found no authority to support the plaintiff's contention that the stock certificate required the payment of dividends in years in which there was net income. Holding that Illinois law governed the dispute, the court found that Illinois law did not provide a clear answer. As a result, the court looked to New York law and to federal law in holding that only in very unusual circumstances, such as when the language of the securities clearly required the payment of dividends, would payment be necessary. Otherwise, directors had the power to issue dividends limited only by bad faith, arbitrariness, or abuse of discretion. The plaintiff's defeat on the mandatory or discretionary issue led the court to consider whether there had been an abuse of discretion in denying the preferred dividends. Here the IC's trial strategy paid off handsomely. Judge Galston suggested it was not even a close question, considering the national economy during the 1930s and early 1940s, the company's status as a common carrier with an obligation to provide public service, the experience of the company's leaders, and the expert advice obtained. Stetson and the rest of the leadership acted in their best judgment.[18]

The Appeal

Perhaps because of the large amount of money at stake and the likely contingent nature of the plaintiff's legal fees, an appeal followed. For this proceeding, held in the United States Court of Appeals for the Second Circuit, Guttmann brought in an additional attorney, Lloyd Garrison, a superstar advocate from the New York firm Paul, Weiss, Rifkind, Wharton & Garrison. Garrison, the great-grandson of abolitionist William Lloyd Garrison, was a prominent Wall Street lawyer. Earlier, he had participated in the formation of the National Labor Relations Board and was dean of the

---

[17] *Guttmann*, 91 F. Supp. at 286–92.

[18] Ibid., at 293–98.

University of Wisconsin Law School. Shortly after the *Guttmann* appeal, Garrison represented playwright Arthur Miller and poet Langston Hughes when they were called to testify in Congress before the communist-hunting Senator Joseph McCarthy. Garrison's presence vastly increased the plaintiff's credibility, especially when he skillfully shifted the legal focus. The appeal concentrated on a new issue: whether the trial court had been correct in assuming that since preferred shares were non-cumulative, that is, dividends did not cumulate when not paid, the dividends were lost forever if not declared in a given year. Garrison argued that non-cumulative dividends were not lost unless there were no profits, which was not true for IC, or if earnings were spent on capital improvements, which Garrison also contended was not true. Simply stated, Guttmann's new argument was that for the years 1942 through 1947 he was entitled to dividends because of the special rights of IC's non-cumulative preferred shareholders.[19]

Although the revised strategy was good lawyering, IC's counsel was up to the challenge. Kiendl and Gillespie brought in their own superstar, John W. Davis, Stetson's long-time friend and fellow Guaranty director, to help prepare a response. In the early 1950s Davis was perhaps the best-known lawyer in the United States. He was soon to become lead counsel for South Carolina in the Supreme Court case *Brown v. Board of Education of Topeka*. Davis's response to Garrison was to hit hard, as in the trial, on the legal principle that directors have wide discretion to declare dividends and that the carefully presented facts at trial showed IC's directors acted prudently. The defense team also took advantage of the plaintiff's shifting legal theories, pointing out that Guttmann's earlier claims of domination by the Union Pacific had magically disappeared, as had any claims to dividends for the years 1937–1941. The plaintiffs' appeal, as a result, was nothing more than a frantic search for a winning argument. Finally, IC argued that the

---

[19] *New York Times*, 16 October 1991; "Appellant's Brief," *Guttmann v. Illinois Central R.R.*, United States Court of Appeals for the Second Circuit, No. 21801 (1949), National Archives and Records Administration.

trial court was correct in deciding that when a dividend is not declared on non-cumulative shares the right to such a dividend can never be revived.[20]

The Second Circuit appeared to have little trouble rejecting Guttmann's argument. It affirmed the judgment of the trial court on 31 May 1951. The panel that heard the appeal included some of the most esteemed judges in the United States: Learned Hand, Jerome N. Frank, and Harrie B. Chase. Hand was nearing the end of a long and distinguished career as perhaps the highest-regarded federal court of appeals judge in the country. Frank, a former corporate lawyer, had been special counsel to the Reconstruction Finance Corporation in the 1930s, chairman of the Securities and Exchange Commission under Roosevelt, and was an internationally known legal theorist. Hand was also Garrison's good friend, but his opinion quickly disposed of Garrison's argument. First, there could be no question that IC directors acted "well within their discretion in withholding declarations of dividends on the non-cumulative stock up to 1948." The only remaining issue was whether preferred shareholders became entitled to dividends for the years 1942 to 1947, or more precisely, whether the directors had the power to issue dividends for previous years to non-cumulative preferred shareholders. After conceding that Illinois law did not provide a clear answer, Hand looked to federal cases and determined that non-cumulative meant non-cumulative. The IC directors lacked the power to declare dividends for past years. Ultimately, Hand viewed the dispute as a simple matter of contract. Accordingly, fairness was not relevant: "[T]he preferred stockholders are not—like sailors or idiots or infants—wards of the judiciary. As courts on occasions have quoted or paraphrased ancient poets, it may not be inappropriate to paraphrase a modern poet, and to say that 'a contract is a contract is a contract'."[21]

---

[20] "Appellee's Brief," *Guttmann v. Illinois Central R.R.*, United States Court of Appeals for the Second Circuit, No. 21801 (1949), National Archives and Records Administration.

[21] *Guttmann v. Illinois Central R.R.*, 189 F.2d 930 (2d Cir. 1951). Although not as influential as *Litwin*, the *Guttmann* opinion is significant on director discretion in issuing dividends to preferred shareholders. Since 1951 it has been cited by many federal courts and has been mentioned frequently by commentators on corporate law. On Judges Frank and Hand see Robert Jerome Glennon, *The Iconoclast as Reformer: Jerome Frank's Impact on American Law* (Ithaca: Cornell University Press,

Guttmann had one option remaining, the United States Supreme Court, and he tried that. At this stage the difficulty facing his lawyers was that the Supreme Court demanded more than simply an argument that the appeals court decision was wrong. Because the Court possessed the power to choose whether it would hear the case, Garrison and Shapiro had to show that the claim raised a significant issue. Obviously a board of directors' discretion to declare dividends did not rise to the level of something the Supreme Court would normally consider. That involved state law and was heavily shaped by facts, two matters other courts could deal with better than the nine men in Washington. Again finding it necessary to try and shift the focus of the case, Garrison made the ingenious argument that the Supreme Court should care about the case because it raised an important issue under the Court's 1938 decision in *Erie R.R. v. Tompkins.* There the Court held that a federal court should apply state law in cases where federal jurisdiction was based on the fact that the parties in the case were citizens of different states. Garrison contended that, in violation of *Erie*, Judge Hand wrongly relied on a federal case, not state law, in ruling on the non-cumulative dividends issue and that at the very least the Supreme Court should clarify whether that was proper. Of course, Garrison also argued that Hand misinterpreted federal law to bar the payment of dividends.[22]

In response, Davis and Kiendl took their cue from Judge Hand's opinion and argued the Supreme Court should refuse to hear the case. The dispute was ultimately about the meaning of a shareholder's contract between the preferred shareholders and the company. They knew the Supreme Court would never be interested in something so mundane as contract language. Finally, IC's lawyers responded to the *Erie* claim by arguing that the appeals court's decision did not contradict the principle that state law should govern: the contract's language determined the outcome, and further, no state law supported Garrison's views about past payment of dividends to non-cumulative preferred shareholders.

1985), Kathryn P. Griffith, *Judge Learned Hand and the Role of the Federal Judiciary* (Norman: University of Oklahoma Press, 1973), and Gerald Gunther, *Learned Hand: The Man and the Judge* (New York: Knopf, 1994).

[22] "Petition for a Writ of Certiorari," *Guttmann v. Illinois Central R.R.*, No. 285 (27 August 1951), United States Supreme Court.

Apparently, the Supreme Court agreed. On 5 November 1951, it denied Guttmann's petition without explanation. The long legal test of Stetson's assumptions about Illinois Central financing was over.[23]

Getting Credit

The successful conclusion of the *Guttmann* suit was not merely a victory in a narrow legal struggle between the company and a shareholder. It officially ended a long era in the railroad's financial history, giving a formal seal of approval to the manner in which Stetson and the company handled the serious challenges of the 1930s and 1940s. Some celebrating began, and much of the credit for better times was bestowed on Stetson. During the company's centennial, in 1951, President Johnston gave a speech on the railroad's history to the Newcomen Society. In Stetson's presence, Johnston described the debt reduction campaign's success and its principal architect:

> It gives me great satisfaction this evening to acknowledge the special indebtedness of the company to the Chairman of our Executive Committee, Eugene W. Stetson. For several years past, he has devoted a large part of his time, thought, and effort to working out, with infinite patience and discerning judgment, step by step, the multitudinous details of [the] refunding, consolidation, and debt reduction program....The much-improved financial position in which the Illinois Central finds itself today is a tribute more eloquent and impressive than any words of mine can possibly express to the sagacious leadership of Eugene W. Stetson.[24]

---

[23] "Brief of Illinois Central Railroad Company in Opposition," *Guttmann v. Illinois Central R.R.*, No. 285 (2 October 1951), United States Supreme Court; *Guttmann v. Illinois Central R.R.*, 342 U.S. 867 (1951).

[24] Stover, *Illinois Central*, 381–82; Wayne A. Johnston, *The Illinois Central Heritage, 1851–1951: A Centenary Address* (New York: Newcomen Society, 1951) 24–25; Wayne A. Johnston to Eugene W. Stetson, 19 December 1957, Eugene W. Stetson Papers, Jack Tarver Library, Special Collections, Mercer University, Macon, Georgia.

Of course, the new era brought its own problems: dieselization; changing agricultural conditions; and intense competition from airlines, trucks, and automobiles. These service-oriented issues seemed to place finance in the background, but Stetson still found ways to contribute. For example, he sent his friend Thomas Watson at IBM a memo about cost savings to the railroad's accounting department that derived from IBM punch card machines, a technology Stetson encouraged for IC. More importantly, the continuing thinness of the company's profit margins caused the board to persist with Stetson's conservative financial perspective through the 1950s. Particularly burdensome were government requirements that the railroad maintain money-losing passenger service, which cost IC millions each year. Because of lagging revenue, net income dropped from $29 million in 1950 to $11 million in 1960, and the railroad reduced dividend payments in 1958.[25]

Stetson presided over the executive committee of the IC until his death in July 1959. At that time, the board recognized his legacy in a resolution which proclaimed that Stetson's "able leadership was especially significant in planning and carrying forward the consolidation and refunding program, with unprecedented reductions in debt and carrying charge, which placed the Illinois Central Railroad on the sound financial position which it enjoys today." Memories of Stetson at IC lasted well beyond his passing. In 1965, Wayne Johnston vividly recalled Stetson's leadership, which put the long-term interests of the railroad, its owners, and the public it served first. Perhaps remembering the *Guttmann* lawsuit, he repeated the former chairman's admonition that business leadership was not about "running a

[25] Stover, *Illinois Central*, 425, 442–44; Eugene W. Stetson to Thomas J. Watson, 17 October 1951; Thomas J. Watson to Eugene W. Stetson, 2 November 1951, Thomas J. Watson Sr. Papers, IBM Corporate Archives, Somers, NewYork. The company's financial needs were not entirely stable, as IC continued to participate in important new securities transactions during the 1950s. See Edwin S. S. Sunderland to Eugene W. Stetson, 10 December 1954, Eugene W. Stetson Papers (discussing issue of $18 million of debentures).

popularity contest.... We have to do what is right, no matter how difficult it will be to do it."[26]

Stetson's twenty-seven year career with Illinois Central sheds further light on his conception of relationship banking. First, Stetson believed that a railroad corporation should keep its debt to a reasonable minimum, plow profits back into physical improvements, and assume that contingencies could become serious liabilities. These beliefs relied on the values that one might expect from a "conservative" banker, a representative of the investing community. In Stetson's view, a railroad, partly because of its public responsibilities, should appeal to long-term investors. With Illinois Central this was clear not only from the focus on debt repayment, but also from Stetson's reliance on the advice of leading financial entities. For Stetson, the crucial players included investment banks in New York and the federal government, the latter of which was perhaps the most important creditor of the railroad in the 1930s and early 1940s as well as its most important customer during World War II. Stetson believed a company could not surmount financial problems without the cooperation of its creditors.[27]

In execution, Stetson's policies were fundamentally pragmatic. As with his other business experiences, political ideology took a back seat. For example, despite his own political conservatism, which included opposition to much of the New Deal's financial legislation, his actions with Illinois Central did not presuppose a sharp dividing line between the government and railroad business. In the 1930s and 1940s he had no qualms about the IC taking New Deal government assistance, which all IC executives, including Stetson, agreed saved the railroad when private investors proved skittish. The amount borrowed from the federal government, more than $45 million, was more than the net profit of the company for the entire decade of the 1930s. It is also clear that Stetson understood the importance

---

[26] Stover, *Illinois Central*, 401; Johnston, *The Illinois Central Heritage*, 11; Adrienne Moore Bond, *Eugene W. Stetson* (Macon GA: Mercer University Press, 1983) 138–43, 155–56.

[27] For more on these views, see Stetson's 1941 speech to the Georgia Bankers' Association, reprinted in Bond, *Stetson*, 73–83. A later perspective on conflicts of interest between bankers and the companies they serve is Myles L. Mace, *Directors: Myth and Reality* (Boston: Harvard Business School, 1986) 128–53.

of business input from government regulators, as evidenced by his dealings with Harriman. Thus, when Stetson was concerned about what he viewed as the high cost of labor, he looked to federal legislation to resolve the problem. Ultimately, in relationship banking there was no sharp dividing line between the public and private sectors.[28]

Stetson's pragmatism and flexibility also reflected his understanding of the role of the banker as corporate director. With IC, he focused on the long-term needs of larger shareholders. This stands in stark contrast with the stereotyped buccaneering financial practices of nineteenth century railroad barons. Stetson's policy meant denying dividends to the lesser owners who eventually sued the IC, even when money was available to pay the dividends. Stetson assumed, and the *Guttmann* judges agreed, that in a large publicly-traded corporation directors could take a strong stand against the short-term interests of shareholders, particularly speculative investors. Stetson thought his job was to establish a "four-way equilibrium between labor, management, the various instrumentalities of government and the public—comprising at one and the same time both owners and customers." This was an expression of the railroad corporation as quasi-public entity, an institution that had obligations beyond its owners, obligations that it was up to the directors to meet. Of course, Stetson's position was affected by his status as a Harriman protégé, who controlled the largest block of IC stock and who had no interest in short term fixes. The position was also shaped by his belief in the broad public responsibilities of all corporations and their leaders.[29]

Stetson was proud of the contribution he could make to IC as a banker, even a New York banker. In part this was because he was aware of the hostility toward Wall Street on the IC board and in the country at large.

---

[28] See, for example, Bond, *Stetson*, 128, 141–42; William Hurd Hillyer, "Eugene Stetson—A Close Up," *Forbes* 60 (15 January 1947): 18–19.

[29] Hillyer, "Eugene Stetson," 19; Bond, *Stetson*, 102–103. More discussions of the theory and practice of corporate governance in the twentieth century are Carl Kaysen, ed. *The American Corporation Today* (New York: Oxford University Press, 1996) 43–54; Edward S. Herman, *Corporate Control, Corporate Power* (Cambridge: Cambridge University Press, 1981) 5–14; John C. Baker, *Directors and Their Functions* (Boston: Harvard Business School, 1945); Richard Eells, *The Government of Corporations* (New York: Free Press, 1962).

The *Guttmann* lawsuit typified the kind of attacks on financial decision-makers that followed the Depression. Yet Stetson deplored the Wall Street stereotype, as his confrontation with fellow director Robert Wood demonstrated, and he tried to prove its inaccuracy. He envisioned the good banker as someone who could do right by helping the worthy business.

But what was business worthiness? In the late 1940s Stetson defined this ideal by describing the "Four Business Freedoms"—his variation of FDR's famous "Four Freedoms": service and sacrifice; thrift; pay as you go; and the right to work. Along with the anti-union sentiment of the last "freedom," the emphasis was on honesty, public service, caution, and performance. Stetson seemed most interested in supporting business and banking policies that benefited both the corporation and its customers, with the assumption that a corporation should operate in a manner that would allow it to continue indefinitely. According to Stetson, a business was not simply a device to enrich shareholders or reward management. Instead, a business was an entity that had deeper productive value, value that should be extracted in a manner to benefit the public at large.[30]

Stetson also held fiercely to the principle that directors, particularly banker directors, should take an active role in a company's success. They should not be rubber stamps for corporate managers, and in fact should be the managers' superiors. Some directors might be mere stand-ins for the company's officers, collecting their per diem pay and keeping their mouths shut. Stetson rejected that kind of behavior. At Illinois Central he even tried to become the chairman of IC's board, a position normally reserved for the company president. Similarly, Stetson was a salesman, and he demanded that other directors demonstrate their loyalty through direct efforts to produce revenue for the corporation.[31]

Stetson's activities with IC also reveal important personal characteristics. First, although he came to the railroad because of the

[30] Bond, *Stetson*, 126, 130.

[31] On the general problem of management domination, see Mace, *Directors*, 83–85. Stetson's continuing salesmanship was revealed in many ways, such as his placement of the article "Distribution and the Main Line of Mid-America," a discussion of the role of the company's contribution to the economy, in Coca-Cola's official publication, *The Red Barrel*, in 1951.

Guaranty-Harriman connection, his forceful and persuasive personality as well as his ideas established real independence. During the late 1930s and 1940s Stetson delivered the goods as a chairman who was able to unify the board and exert compelling leadership when bankruptcy was imminent. He clearly commanded respect on the board and among the company officers. There was no better demonstration of this personal strength than the fact that he was the key witness in the *Guttmann* case.

Second, Stetson's personality required that he be at the center of things. This was the same sort of ambition that had been apparent from the day he left Macon to accept the sink-or-swim vice-presidency at Guaranty. It was still alive thirty years later in his plan to become chairman of IC's board as a kind of "retirement." He simply informed the railroad's president that he wanted to be chairman with a $50,000 salary and then expected that accomplishing that goal would be nearly automatic. Nonetheless, Stetson's outspoken ambition was tempered with realism, a spirit of compromise, and a desire to do what was best for interests other than his own. When he was successfully opposed for the chairman position by Robert Wood, he settled for an enhanced status at IC without the title, which allowed him to continue his financial program.

Gene Stetson was a leader in American railroad finance during difficult times. His pragmatic policies of economy, simplification of debt structure, willingness to seek governmental assistance, and opposition to what he considered the unreasonable demands of shareholders helped Illinois Central emerge from the Depression and World War II with increased value. It was a genuine accomplishment at a time when positive results were rare among railroads. Perhaps most importantly, the connection to IC was also an extended demonstration of relationship banking. It precisely reflected the mix of skills and behaviors that characterized Stetson's work: financial knowledge, personal connections, a willingness to listen to the expertise of others, ambition, an understanding of a corporation's public responsibilities, and beliefs about the broad obligations of the corporate director.

14

The Last Deal

In 1958, Gene Stetson invited Henry Alexander, head of J. P. Morgan, to his home on East 72nd Street. Stetson initiated the private meeting to explore the possibility of a merger between Guaranty and Morgan. According to Stetson, Guaranty had a leadership problem, a problem that had disturbed him for some time. At first, Alexander was not interested in merging his relatively small but highly prestigious bank. In fact, just a few years earlier, he emphatically told New York real estate developer William Zeckendorf: "Morgan will never merge." In the 1950s, however, big bank mergers were changing the industry. In 1954, Chemical Bank merged with Corn Exchange Bank, and the next year Chase National merged with the Bank of Manhattan.[1]

During the first meeting with Alexander, Stetson undoubtedly sat across from the Morgan banker in the high back chair he loved so much. He would have angled his body, as was his habit, so that he faced Alexander from his left. Would Alexander be interested in a Guaranty-Morgan merger if he could became top man at the fourth largest bank in America?

Despite the early hesitance, Alexander eventually changed his mind. Stetson played an essential role in this change and also in selling the merger to Morgan and Guaranty by effectively bringing together the different

---

[1] Charles P. Stetson to Charles H. Andrews, 9 December 1997, letter in possession of author; William Zeckendorf, *The Autobiography of William Zeckendorf* (New York: Holt, Rinehart, and Winston, 1970) 269–70; John Donald Wilson, *The Chase: The Chase Manhattan Bank, 1945–1985* (Boston: Harvard University Business School Press, 1986) 73; Ron Chernow, *The House of Morgan: An American Banking Dynasty and the Rise of Modern Finance* (New York: Atlantic Monthly Press, 1990) 527–35; Stanley L. Engerman and Robert E. Gallman, eds. *The Cambridge Economic History of the United States*, 3 vols. (Cambridge: Cambridge University Press, 1996–2000) 3: 779; "J. P. Morgan Chase & Co.," http://www.fundinguniverse.com/company-histories/JP-Morgan-Chase-amp;-Co-Company-History.html.

parties. By 1958 Stetson had been thinking merger for years. According to his daughter Josephine, in pushing the deal he "seemed to have the ability to talk to the Morgan people, to the Guaranty people, and to work out an equitable coming together.... He did have the finesse, he did have the ability to listen to other people and to try to work out the problems to suit them all." As a culmination of long-standing relationships, the last deal was an appropriate finale. The Morgan-Guaranty plan was officially announced on 17 December 1958, six months before Stetson died. At the time, Henry Alexander stated simply that the principal reason for the merger was to create "a great new bank, strong in resources, operating principally in the field of commerce, business and industry."[2]

Guaranty's Malaise

While Guaranty made money, retained blue-chip clients, and was a leader in utilizing technology, by the late 1950s its once dynamic momentum had stalled. At the end of 1947, Stetson's last year as chairman, assets were about $2.8 billion and deposits $2.4 billion. Four years later, assets had climbed to $3.1 billion and deposits were $2.7 billion. In December 1958, however, assets remained at just over $3 billion and deposits amounted to $2.6 billion. After accounting for inflation, this meant assets and deposits had actually declined during the preceding ten years, the longest period without meaningful growth since 1891. Symbolic of the lackluster conditions, in 1953 the bank dropped plans to build a new main office because of cost, opting instead to refurbish the existing quarters at 140 Broadway.[3]

---

[2] Adrienne Moore Bond, *Eugene W. Stetson* (Macon GA: Mercer University Press, 1983) 94; *New York Times*, 18 December 1958. Wall Street assumed the new company had no interest in retail banking, but simply wanted to enhance its ability to serve business. The *Times* reported Morgan shares were up more than 13% on the news; Guaranty's shares rose by more than 6%.

[3] Chernow, *House of Morgan*, 237; *Annual Report to the Stockholders for the Year 1948*; *Annual Report to Stockholders for the Year 1949*; *Annual Report to the Stockholders for the Year 1954*; *Annual Report to Stockholders for the Year 1958*; "Condensed Statement, Guaranty Trust Company of New York," 31 December 1947; 31 December 1949; 31 December 1951; 31 December 1953; 30 June 1956; 31 December 1958; "Corporate History of Guaranty Trust Company of New York

Banking historian Ron Chernow explains Guaranty's relative decline as the result of reluctant leadership, describing the institution in the late 1950s as "fat, sleepy, [and] dowdy." He singles out J. Luther Cleveland as a cause. Cleveland became chairman of the board on Stetson's retirement in 1947 and still held that position when Stetson began his discussions with Alexander eleven years later. Cleveland had been chairman longer than anyone in the bank's history, and apparently it was too long. Chernow describes Cleveland as curt and humorless; an autocrat who drove away good employees. He was aloof and unusually unpopular among the bank's staff. Unlike Stetson, Cleveland was not invited to sit on many corporate boards. Instead, Cleveland's version of relationship banking meant periodic telephone calls to the bank's ten most important clients. Supposedly, a list of those ten clients was the only piece of paper on his desk.[4]

Cleveland, in his late 60s when Stetson initiated merger talks, was outdated and overly conservative. His failures were apparently of recent origin and consisted primarily of lost opportunities. They seem to have reflected an inability to comprehend new possibilities offered by the post-war environment and rested on the fact that the bank, after all, was still profitable and wealthy. Cleveland's career had many of same attributes as

---

[1952]," 68A, J. P. Morgan & Co., Inc. Papers, JPMorgan Chase Archives, New York, New York; Lillian Otlowski, telephone interview with author, notes in possession of author, 8 June 2004. The problem of stagnant deposits was widespread. In 1957 Morgan's Russell Leffingwell complained to Henry Alexander that because clearing house member bank deposits had remained flat since 1945 and because of inflation since the war, "the ability of the clearing house banks to meet their customers' needs has dwindled." This especially affected Morgan because it had less than $1 billion in assets in the late 1950s. "Memorandum" (1957), Russell Leffingwell to H. C. Alexander, Russell Cornell Leffingwell Papers, Yale University Library, Manuscripts and Archives, New Haven, Connecticut. See also Wilson, *The Chase*, 59, which notes Guaranty had a difficult time attracting deposits after 1945, and Engerman and Gallman, eds., *Cambridge Economic History*, 3: 773, 775–76, which discusses the general decline of banks as asset holders in the 1950s.

[4] Chernow, *House of Morgan*, 532–33; "Corporate History of Guaranty Trust Company of New York [1952]," 56–57, J. P. Morgan & Co., Inc. Papers; Lillian Otlowski interview. Guaranty was the ninth largest commercial bank in the United States in the late 1950s. First Boston Corporation, "Morgan Guaranty Trust Company of New York (1959)," 2, J. P. Morgan & Co., Inc. Papers.

Stetson's—an outsider who made good. A small-town Texan, he entered banking as an assistant cashier with a national bank in Muskogee, Oklahoma, before World War I. Cleveland landed a job with Guaranty in 1923, after military service in France. He worked his way up to vice president in 1928 and then president in 1944, replacing Stetson. Coming from the Southwest, his specialties were oil and public utilities. In New York he became a highly-regarded expert in financing those industries and in developing new practices. At some point, however, the innovation stopped. At one low moment in his leadership the Ford Motor Company was so appalled at losses in its pension plan that it pulled the account. More significantly, in the 1950s Cleveland defended traditional "wholesale" banking and strongly rejected trends to branch banking and broader appeals to retail customers. He also opposed increasing Guaranty's capital. Such attitudes had the predictable effect of precluding growth.[5]

Equally revealing, Cleveland refused to consider change in asset and liability management, which was rapidly becoming a new force in banking. A Guaranty vice president, Ralph Leach, wanted Guaranty to borrow Federal Reserve Funds from smaller regional banks and use the money to expand its asset base. Leach, who had worked at the New York Federal Reserve and continued to advise the Fed after going to the private sector, went on to become treasurer and chairman of the merged Morgan Guaranty and the chief proponent of using borrowed capital to increase lending. Leach was also an advocate of fixed-interest negotiable certificates of deposit as a way of attracting and building corporate accounts. In the early 1960s certificates of deposit, or CDs, became a way for banks holding large amounts of cash to pay interest to corporate depositors. At the time it was illegal for banks to pay interest on checking accounts. The concept of cash management, however, made companies increasingly aware of the free money windfall they traditionally gave banks under the old rules of

---

[5] *New York Times*, 19 January 1956; 16 January 1958; 4 July 1984.

relationship banking. Naturally they looked for ways to earn a return on their cash, and CDs provided one answer.[6]

The result of Guaranty's lethargy was that Stetson and other board members decided Cleveland had to be pushed out, as he was unwilling to step down on his own. The situation must have been uncomfortable, as Stetson had known Cleveland for more than thirty years. He clearly held a very good opinion of him in the 1940s and had supported his elevation to the presidency and to chairman. In 1947, in fact, Stetson described Cleveland as a "double-barreled" person who was both a money maker and a conservator. By 1958 he apparently felt some obligation to remedy the situation he helped create. In general, Stetson had little patience for incompetence, so perhaps he was even angered by the prospect of continued decline at an institution once considered among the pioneers on Wall Street. Others felt the same way. At the 1956 shareholders' meeting, one disgruntled shareholder openly complained about the bank's fall from third in assets among American banks to seventh.[7]

The Solution

Despite his retirement as chairman and increased work with Illinois Central, during the 1950s Stetson did not abandon lower Broadway. He maintained an office at the bank and was a member of both the Guaranty board and its executive committee. When Stetson and a few other board members began looking to merger as a solution to the leadership problem, J. P. Morgan had special appeal as a partner, especially to Stetson. From the days of Thomas Lamont, Charles Sabin, Bill Potter, and Jack Morgan he could remember the deep and profitable ties between the companies. The Morgan possibility would be a homecoming of sorts, almost taking the bank back to the days before Depression-era laws severed many of their connections.[8]

---

[6] Chernow, *House of Morgan*, 538–40; Dan Krier, *Speculative Management: Stock Market Power and Corporate Change* (Albany: State University of New York Press, 2005) 30–39.

[7] *New York Times*, 16 January 1947; 19 January 1956.

[8] *Poor's Register of Directors and Executives, United States and Canada* (New York: Standard and Poor's Corp., 1957).

But Morgan was not the only option. In considering a merger Stetson's southern connections led him to Harold Helm and Baxter Jackson of the retail-oriented Chemical Corn Exchange Bank. Helm and Jackson were part of a southern executive team that dominated Chemical from the 1920s to the 1960s. Jackson was also part of a Dixie-based social, political, and economic network that included Bob Woodruff, Senator Walter F. George of Georgia, and Governor Max Gardner of North Carolina, all of whom were Stetson associates. Chemical served many southern textile and business interests, including West Point, Milliken, and Mount Vernon. Instead of Guaranty, however, in early 1959 Chemical Bank, under Helm's leadership, merged with the "wholesale" Trust Company of New York and became the Chemical Bank New York Trust Company. When the discussions with Chemical led nowhere, Stetson focused on Morgan.[9]

Not all of the impetus for the merger came from Guaranty. Morgan itself was transformed by the upheavals of the 1930s and 1940s, and not positively. In the early forties, it abandoned the partnership form of organization and became an incorporated business, an earth-shattering shift for the tradition-based bank. Further, Morgan's assets were hit hard by the Depression. They fell to a meager $39 million in 1939. Death also took its toll. Jack Morgan died in 1943, and Thomas Lamont, managing partner and long time chairman of Guaranty's executive committee, passed away in 1948.[10]

By 1958 Morgan's once dominant role in the national banking system was over. The expansion of government as a controller of money and the ability of wealthy corporations to by-pass commercial banks changed the

---

[9] "Helm at the Helm," *Time* 73 (15 June 1959): 92; "The History of Chemical Bank," http://www.chasealum.org/article.html?aid=197; "Interviewee: Mr. James Webb," http://www.nasm.si.edu/research/dsh/TRANSCPT/WEBB2.HTM (Interview with James Webb, administrator of NASA during the 1960s).

[10] Chernow, *House of Morgan*, 467, 472, 480, 486; David Rogers, *The Future of American Banking: Managing for Change* (New York: McGraw-Hill, Inc., 1993) 201–202; Benjamin J. Klebaner, *American Commercial Banking* (Boston: Twayne Publishers, 1990) 179–81, 184–86. In the late 1950s, Morgan was the twenty-second largest commercial bank in the United States. First Boston Corporation, "Morgan Guaranty Trust Company of New York (1959)," 2, J. P. Morgan & Co., Inc. Papers.

game. Morgan had even opted for the commercial bank role in the aftermath of Glass-Steagall. The growth of competition in capital markets also reduced Morgan's former power. As a consequence, during the 1950s there was growing pressure for a merger that would reinvigorate the bank with larger lending limits and economies of scale. The larger question was whether Morgan could retain, or more accurately, revive, its standing as a leading national and international bank. Conveniently, Morgan's president, Henry S. Alexander, already had Guaranty ties. Before going to Morgan he was an attorney at Davis Polk, the firm that represented both Guaranty and Morgan and which for many years placed John Davis on Guaranty's board. Alexander's initial hesitance to merge with Guaranty is not difficult to understand. Morgan may have been the most respected name in banking, but it was a small bank, and the wrong sort of merger could weaken the position of Morgan executives and shareholders. It would have been foolish, in fact, not to consider that a merger with the much bigger Guaranty could result in Morgan's subordination.[11]

Stetson certainly had this concern in mind when he initiated negotiations with Alexander. The regional factor also helped smooth over tensions, as Alexander, like Stetson, was a southerner. He grew up and went to college in Tennessee before going to law school at Yale. Like Stetson, he had made the most of the southern elite's social skills. He used his background to disarm Yankee associates, while his abilities as a salesman, lawyer, and negotiator engendered confidence in the Guaranty deal. Ultimately Stetson and Alexander worked out a deal in which the Morgan leadership essentially won control over Guaranty's assets. When the news got out that Morgan was merging with a bank four times its size, the press rightly said it was "Jonah swallowing the whale."[12]

Neither Stetson nor Alexander had a difficult time clearing the merger's draft over the first hurdle—their respective boards of directors. The Morgan and Guaranty boards voted to approve the merger on 17 December 1958. Stetson's task was made easier because few Guaranty board members had a stake in maintaining the status quo and some, like Stetson,

---

[11] Chernow, *House of Morgan*, 467, 472, 480, 486; "Morgan's Men," *Time* 33 (13 February 1939): 64, 66; "The Big Banker," *Time* 74 (2 November 1959): 82–86, 88.

[12] Chernow, *House of Morgan*, 534; "The Big Banker."

were anxious to bring in new leadership. The Guaranty board consisted of twenty-two men, only four of whom had long service —Cleveland, Stetson, George Allen, and George Roosevelt. Even a partial list of the directors reveals how much the board had been altered since the days of banker domination in the 1920s. They included William Bolenius of AT&T, John Dorrance of Campbell Soup, Walter Franklin of the Pennsylvania Railroad, Thomas Perkins of American Cyanamid, Charles Munson of Air Reduction, Carrol Shanks of Prudential Insurance, Kenneth Towe of the Duke Endowment, Clyde Weed of Anaconda Company, and Robert Woodruff of Coca-Cola. Dale Sharp, younger and more attuned to the employees than Cleveland, had been elected Guaranty's president in 1957 and was also a director.[13]

Among these men, no one had greater reason to be dissatisfied with the current state of affairs than Stetson, the only company insider on the board other than Cleveland and Sharp. Stetson's support for the merger would have carried great weight. He was good personal friends with Charles Munson and Robert Woodruff. Stetson's motivations also won approval from AT&T's Bolenius. In 1958 Bolenius wrote Stetson about the need for more junior leadership at Guaranty's vice president level. He believed "it would seem a grave indictment of the current administration of the bank that candidates' names are not already in hand." The problem was with Cleveland, who seemed "pretty uncertain as to which names he wants to promote." Cleveland was unwilling to step down and provide leadership for the future, much to Bolenius's disappointment: "We do not want to leave him in the position where he can say that he must remain for a longer period because the organization is not experienced enough to carry on."[14]

The Plan

In February 1959 the banks' directors agreed to a final merger plan that reflected Stetson and Alexander's agreement. Both boards immediately

---

[13] Guaranty Trust Company of New York, *Annual Report to Stockholders for the Year 1958*, 6, J. P. Morgan & Co., Inc. Papers.

[14] William C. Bolenius to Eugene W. Stetson, 25 March 1958, Box 1, Eugene W. Stetson Papers, Jack Tarver Library, Special Collections, Mercer University, Macon, Georgia; Lillian Otlowski interview.

submitted the plan for shareholder approval. The special advantages to Morgan were clear. Despite Guaranty's supplying the bulk of the cash, Morgan obtained means to control the future executive committee and board. In addition, Morgan would be merged into Guaranty, meaning the new corporation would operate under the more liberal Guaranty state charter granted in 1864. It also got top billing in the all-important new name: "Morgan Guaranty Trust Company of New York."[15]

Not surprisingly, given that from Guaranty's standpoint the need for new executive talent was the merger's driving force, the new leadership was heavily tilted toward Morgan. Shareholders were told that Dale Sharp, Guaranty's president, would become the new president of Morgan Guaranty. This soothed Guaranty's corporate ego, but it had little impact on the real location of power. Instead, Morgan's president, Alexander, became chairman of the board and chief executive officer, and thus the real head of the company. Guaranty's Cleveland was allotted the chairmanship of a weak executive committee. Even there Morgan power was ensured: H. P. Davison and Thomas S. Lamont, executives at Morgan and the sons of well-known Morgan partners, would be the executive committee's vice-chairmen.[16]

Further details of the leadership structure confirmed Morgan control. The chairman (Alexander) and vice-chairmen (Davison and Lamont) could call special shareholder meetings. The chairman of the executive committee (Cleveland) could not. The right to preside at shareholder meetings was

---

[15] "J. P. Morgan & Co. to Stockholders of J. P. Morgan & Co. Incorporated, Notice of Special Meeting," 6 February 1959; "Henry C. Alexander and H. P. Davison to Stockholders of J. P. Morgan & Co. Incorporated," 6 February 1959, Russell Cornell Leffingwell Papers; "Statement Concerning the Matters to be Considered at the Special Meeting of Stockholders to be Held March 4, 1959," J. P. Morgan & Co., Inc. Papers.

[16] Guaranty Trust Company of New York, *Annual Report to Stockholders for the Year 1958*, 6–7, J. P. Morgan & Co., Inc. Papers. The challenge of finding suitable junior executives was not just a problem for Guaranty. See Howard D. Crosse, *Management Policies for Commercial Banks* (Englewood Cliffs NJ: Prentice-Hall, Inc., 1962) 272; and Homer J. Livingston, *Management Policies in American Banks* (New York: Harper & Bros., 1956) 86–102, which show that many bankers considered this the leading difficulty of the 1950s.

arranged in the following order: chairman (Alexander); vice-chairmen (Davison and Lamont); and in the unlikely event the first three were not present, president (Sharp). The executive committee had to include the chairman of the board (Alexander), the vice-chairmen of board (Davison and Lamont), the chairman of the executive committee (Cleveland), and the president (Sharp), thus ensuring a Morgan majority among the committee's leadership. The chairman of the board (Alexander) was designated the chief executive officer, with the right to preside over board meetings. The vice-chairmen (Lamont and Davison) received essentially the same power in Alexander's absence. Thus, Cleveland, although chairman of the executive committee, could only preside at general board meetings when Alexander, Lamont, and Davison were absent. Predictably, Cleveland retired from the executive committee in 1960 and left the board altogether in 1961.[17]

Guaranty's shareholders learned nothing about the internal leadership disputes that motivated the merger. Instead, the official word was that merger would "enhance our capacity to serve the growing financial needs of business by combining the skills and resources of the two institutions." Total resources would exceed $4 billion, making Morgan Guaranty the fourth largest bank in the United States. Moreover, the new bank would "have one of the highest ratios of capital funds to deposit liabilities of any bank in the country and thus will possess outstanding strength from the depositor's point of view and a solid basis for further growth." Precisely why this could not be achieved with the existing structure was never formally explained.[18]

The First Boston Corporation provided a strongly favorable opinion letter for the proposed new bank in December 1958. It promised the deal "will result in the creation of a large, strongly capitalized, and well managed banking organization, better qualified than either of the present banks to

---

[17] "J. P. Morgan & Co. to Stockholders of J. P. Morgan & Co. Incorporated, Notice of Special Meeting," 6 February 1959; "Henry C. Alexander and H. P. Davison to Stockholders of J. P. Morgan & Co. Incorporated," 6 February 1959, Russell Cornell Leffingwell Papers; "Statement Concerning the Matters to be Considered at the Special Meeting of Stockholders to be Held March 4, 1959," J. P. Morgan & Co., Inc. Papers; *New York Times*, 23 June 1960; 4 July 1984.

[18] Guaranty Trust Company of New York, *Annual Report to Stockholders for the Year 1958*, 6–7, J. P. Morgan & Co., Inc. Papers.

provide broad national and international banking and fiduciary services." The merger would involve an exchange of six million outstanding Guaranty shares for six million Morgan Guaranty shares. Morgan's 350,000 outstanding shares would be exchanged for 1.54 million Morgan Guaranty shares. Guaranty stockholders would therefore own approximately eighty percent of the new Morgan Guaranty. Further, the merger was certain to create the third largest bank in New York, albeit a somewhat distant third behind Chase Manhattan and First National City. The leap in size mattered, First Boston noted, because it meant the new bank could lawfully lend more than $50 million to a single corporate borrower. Before the deal, Morgan could not lend more than $8.7 million, while Guaranty could lend just over $42.1 million. First Boston also favorably compared the potential of the proposed bank with its large New York competitors, including Chase Manhattan, First National City, Manufacturers Trust, Chemical Corn Exchange, and Bankers Trust.[19]

The most revealing statement of the banks' merger goals was a confidential memorandum prepared by the companies for the Superintendent of New York Banks. Under New York law Morgan and Guaranty needed to demonstrate that the merger was in the public interest. This meant showing how the merger would benefit both customers and stockholders and would not lessen competition. Although written in the form of a brief supporting the proposal, the memorandum gave the Superintendent of Banks plenty of straightforward information about the merger's justifications.[20]

Demonstrating the fiscal soundness of the new institution would be easy. The ratio of capital funds as a percentage of deposits, for example, would be the highest of comparable New York City banks. In fact, the ratio would be the highest among the thirty largest banks in the United States. It was also rather obvious that new and broader services would be available. Morgan would now have branches in midtown Manhattan and add 400 correspondent banks to Guaranty's 2,400 correspondent banks around the

[19] First Boston Corporation, "Morgan Guaranty Trust Company of New York," 26 December 1958, J. P. Morgan & Co., Inc. Papers.

[20] "Memorandum on Economic Aspects of Proposed Merger of Guaranty Trust Company of New York and J. P. Morgan & Co. Incorporated," 26 January 1959, J. P. Morgan & Co., Inc. Papers.

world, stock transfer activities would be improved, economies of scale produced, and the purchase of labor saving technology more easily accomplished.[21]

The memorandum to the Superintendent of Banks also discussed the problems that led to the merger. From Morgan's standpoint, its relatively low resources, combined with state law limiting an unsecured loan to ten percent of its capital, meant that it simply could not participate in substantial commercial lending. Morgan told the Superintendent that although a good client recently sought a $19 million loan, the lending limit meant Morgan could not satisfy the request. But the desire to increase lending limits affected both Morgan and Guaranty. Continued increases in loan demand, coupled with the fact that sixty-two of the hundred largest industrial companies were Morgan customers and eighty-three were Guaranty customers, constricted the banks' prospects. What hurt most was that "the great corporations which are clients of either or both the merging banks have outstripped in their growth both Guaranty Trust and Morgan." Since 1947, assets of the top one hundred industrial companies grew 151 percent and gross national product grew by almost ninety percent, yet the combined assets of Morgan and Guaranty increased by an embarrassing nine percent. Deposits grew by only a little more than five percent.[22]

The memorandum also addressed Guaranty's pressing personnel issues. It argued Guaranty would benefit greatly from improved management. The memorandum placed this need in a larger context, quoting a paper from the Federal Reserve Bank of Philadelphia that "the biggest problem and most glaring weakness of bank management today is the matter of successor management," largely because of a widespread failure to prepare younger executives after World War II. Guaranty had recently suffered from "death and resignation," and more experienced men were needed to improve the bank's services. Regarding Guaranty, the reference to "death and resignation" applied specifically to former presidents Bill Potter, who retired from the Guaranty board in 1956 and died in 1957, Palen Conway, who retired in 1948, and to Stetson, who retired as chairman in 1947. Each of these men was between 75 and 80 years old in

---

[21] Ibid.

[22] Ibid.

the mid–1950s. Assuming replacements could not be found through lateral hiring, merger was the best option. In contrast, despite its lack of cash, Morgan boasted that it was in a position to provide new management. The elder Morgan officers, now "senior in status,...have trained a younger group of executives who are assuming major responsibilities in the bank." Twenty-one Morgan men would join the existing fifty-one officers in Guaranty's main office, effectively transforming the leadership cadre.[23]

The memorandum also considered whether the merger would have an adverse effect on competition. Naturally, it maintained it would not, arguing partly that banking was already heavily regulated as to opening branches, interest rates on loans and deposits, loan amounts, acceptable types of investments, and credit standards. Instead, only the nature of service was left to the market, and within the resources of a bank, "size alone is not a factor that militates against the ability of a bank to compete." In terms of asset concentration, the new bank would possess 1.6% of the total deposits of American commercial banks. This was actually a sharp decline from 1940, when together they controlled 4.8% of deposits. Among banks with deposits over $1 billion, Morgan Guaranty would have a combined 5.9% of the assets. This was compared with a whopping 19.8% combined share in 1940.[24]

Larger Forces

As this last point suggested, there were significant changes happening in banking nationally that helped motivate the merger. For example, among Federal Reserve banks, New York's share of bank assets declined dramatically from 32.2 percent in 1940 to 19.1 percent in 1958. Deposits, loans, and capital accounts in New York Federal Reserve banks fell after 1945. In contrast, accounts held outside New York Federal Reserve banks grew by about a third between 1945 and 1958. Morgan and Guaranty used New York's declining position to argue to regulators that the merger would not hinder banking competition. Further, between 1946 and 1957, long-

[23] Ibid.; *New York Times*, 16 August 1974; 3 January 1957.

[24] "Memorandum on Economic Aspects of Proposed Merger of Guaranty Trust Company of New York and J. P. Morgan & Co. Incorporated," 26 January 1959, J. P. Morgan & Co., Inc. Papers.

term debt, retained profits, and stock provided much more money for corporations than bank loans. Insurance companies, savings and loan associations, college endowments, and fraternal orders were increasingly important sources of money for business.[25]

This meant becoming bigger was necessary if the banks meant to maintain relationships with America's largest corporations. Of course both banks had long attracted and retained the richest and largest business clients in the world. Developing this kind of wholesale banking was precisely the aim of older relationship bankers, including Stetson and Luther Cleveland. Businesses held more than ninety percent of the deposits in both banks. Over half the deposits of each bank came from customers with more than $1 million. Three-quarters of their customers had deposited at least $250,000. This was at a time when the median income of an American family was less than $7,000 a year. Of the 750 largest companies listed by *Fortune*, Morgan claimed 240 as clients and Guaranty 379. Given the limited pool of customers, the competition for them through claims of better banking "service," meaning relationships, was intense. In effect, as Stetson undoubtedly understood, the opportunity to create and develop banking relationships with wealthy clients in the post-war environment was the real economic force driving the merger. As the banks stated to the regulators:

> It is opportunities for the rendition of this service which all large banks sedulously cultivate in seeking to establish a relationship with important depositors such as the 750 largest corporations just mentioned. Most of the large corporations with a nation-wide base receive between 200 and 400 personal calls a year from banks in all sections of the country, each offering its services in as much variety as possible. Morgan, for example, estimates that it makes about 4,000 calls a year on corporations outside New York City. Guaranty Trust with its larger staff provides even a more extensive coverage. Fifteen or more of the larger New York City banks do the same. The Chicago, Boston, Philadelphia and Pittsburgh banks are just as active, while such banks as those of San Francisco, Seattle, St. Louis,

[25] Ibid.

> Cleveland, Detroit, Atlanta and Dallas cover the country rather thoroughly but less often. An automobile company estimates that it gets from 350 to 400 bank calls a year; and any one of the leading 500 corporations or larger banks will receive up to five or six visits of solicitation per week from various banks.

The result was a degree of competition unknown twenty years earlier. A specific example of the trend was the experience of one large corporation, which simultaneously maintained loan relationships with eighteen banks scattered from New York to Chicago, Los Angeles, Atlanta and places in between. To Stetson and Alexander this meant competition was cutting the relationship-based foundation of their banks from beneath them. A bank that could not provide expected services to the target clients could not hope to survive in the changing environment. Consolidation, they thought, was an answer to this competition.[26]

A more detailed picture of Guaranty's leading clients suggests the connection between relationship banking, competition, client base, and the merger. They were located, literally, on every populated continent of the globe, although most were in North America. The number of clients was not large, numbering less than 2,750. Approximately 1,000 were individuals in the United States. The remainder included domestic corporations (839), domestic banks (183), foreign banks (216), foreign corporations (224), and foreign individuals (244). Corporate deposits greatly predominated over individual deposits. The largest depositors were a "Who's Who" of American enterprise, representing precisely the kind of client the merger was supposed to serve. These customers testified to Guaranty and Stetson's pursuit of the most elite businesses and their success in cultivating relationships with its clients over the preceding decades. In stark contrast, Guaranty's own employees were not permitted to have accounts, and the tradition had been to pay their wages in cash.[27]

---

[26] Ibid.

[27] A very partial list of the corporate clients includes AT&T, Celanese, Johns-Manville, Metropolitan Life Insurance, Phelps Dodge, Standard Oil of New Jersey, U.S. Steel, Harvard College, Pacific Gas & Electric, Aetna Life Insurance, Atchison, Topeka, and Santa Fe R.R. Co., Bethlehem Steel, Boeing, DuPont de Nemours, Remington Arms, Ford Motor, General Electric, General Motors, Gulf

Passing

Guaranty and Morgan's shareholders, as well as the Superintendent of New York banks, easily approved the merger. On 24 April 1959, Morgan was formally merged into Guaranty Trust. At the time, Stetson had just left for Europe, where he met with Guaranty and Morgan representatives to discuss the new bank. On his return, however, he had little time to enjoy the fruits of his labor, which over the long run would be substantial. Within a few years, the bank was doing more corporate lending than its next five competitors combined. Stetson died of a cerebral hemorrhage on 20 July 1959, after serving as a Morgan Guaranty director for less than three months.[28]

The key participants recognized Stetson's critical importance in shaping the new bank. The Morgan Guaranty board resolved that he: "[P]layed a major role in bringing about the merger of J. P. Morgan and Company, Incorporated, and Guaranty Trust Company of New York...[B]y his wise counsel and his own admirable example of cooperation, he did much to insure a successful blending of the two institutions." More precisely, the merger reflected Stetson and Alexander's goals. It replaced Cleveland with Alexander, a result both Alexander and Stetson agreed on. In addition to distributing the most important offices to Morgan, twelve directors from each company came together to form a new board of twenty-four. Although this suggested equality, given the ratio of hard assets it was actually another concession to Morgan's superior leadership. This also was among Stetson's key interests. As for Guaranty's present or former senior

---

Oil, Lockheed Aircraft, Monsanto Chemical, Proctor and Gamble, Phillips Petroleum, the Pennsylvania Railroad, Northwestern Mutual Life Insurance, Travelers Insurance, Trans World Airlines, Weyerhauser Timber, Morgan Stanley, Dean Witter, Brown Brothers Harriman, New York Life Insurance, B. F. Goodrich, and Scott Paper. "Net Deposits," "Present Domestic Depositors Maintaining Cash Balances of $1,000,000 or more Averages for September 1958 at the Close of December 31, 1957 and the 100 Largest Domestic Depositors," Guaranty Trust Company of New York (1958?), J. P. Morgan & Co., Inc. Papers.

[28] Chernow, *House of Morgan*, 534, 536; Bond, *Stetson*, 154–63; Josephine Hatcher, interview by Adrienne M. Bond, 1981-1982, Jack Tarver Library, Special Collections, Mercer University, Macon, Georgia.

officers, only Stetson, the well-liked Dale Sharp, and Cleveland (briefly), became directors of the new company.[29]

Stetson's contribution was so important that he received a $1 million investment banking fee. The payment came at a time when the annual salary for a top New York banker was much less than that amount. In fact, such investment banking fees did not yet exist. Certainly fees were not paid to an individual or to an insider like Stetson. Only later did rainmakers in the mergers and acquisitions departments of investment banking firms earn similarly large compensation for themselves.[30]

The Morgan-Guaranty merger cannot be fully explained without considering Gene Stetson. Most important is that his actions were the logical outgrowth of more than forty years of banking relationships and a particular understanding of the evolving role of the elite commercial bank. Morgan's history intertwined closely with Guaranty's past and in 1958 Stetson was the strongest remaining link in a chain that stretched back to Pierpont Morgan. The Guaranty-Morgan merger was Stetson's last great effort to advance his vision of relationship banking. This is the primary reason why he believed new leadership was imperative. Stetson knew relationship banking needed new direction, and the fact that the merger was part of a trend that helped push banking into a radically different era helped make it especially appealing. After all, Stetson experienced more than his fair share of change in the long period from post-Reconstruction Georgia to the Space Age.[31]

---

[29] Bond, *Stetson*, 154–55.

[30] Charles P. Stetson to Charles H. Andrews, 9 December 1997.

[31] This new era was symbolized by Morgan's massive mergers between 2000 and 2004. In 2000, Morgan merged with Chase Manhattan, creating JPMorgan Chase. Another huge combination followed in 2004, when JPMorgan Chase merged with Midwestern giant Bank One. In early 2008, JPMorgan Chase was the largest bank in the United States and the eleventh largest bank in the world, with assets of approximately $1.31 trillion. "History of JPMorgan Chase, 1799 to Present," http://www.jpmorganchase.com/cm/BlobServer?blobtable=Document&blobcol=url blob&blobkey=name&blobheader=application/pdf&blobwhere=jpmc/about/history /shorthistory.pdf inc; "Top 50 Banks in the World," http://www.bankersalmanac. com/addcon/infobank/wldrank.aspx

The history of Guaranty Trust and Stetson's role in that history reveal several overarching characteristics of American commercial banking between the late nineteenth century and 1959. A few themes stand out in evaluating Guaranty Trust. First is the relentless commitment to growth. Much of this growth was related to three interrelated factors: connections with external financial institutions, particularly the Mutual Life and J. P. Morgan; territorial expansion, especially international operations; and a willingness to merge with other banks, especially before the Depression. Acquisition by the Mutual Life Insurance Company in 1891 transformed Guaranty into a major bank. It infused capital and attracted personnel with broad connections in New York finance. Beginning in the 1890s the company also entered international banking, a field which it helped define.

Equally important, at Morgan's direction it embarked on a series of mergers that, in 1910, 1912, and 1929 expanded Guaranty into one of the largest banks in the United States and the largest trust company in the world. Morgan placed one of its partners, Lamont, as head of the bank's executive committee in 1912 and exercised even greater control over the company after the Mercantile Bank of the Americas debacle of the early 1920s. Morgan benefited from a friendly relationship with Guaranty because risks on its own loans could be shared and because certain kinds of specialized business not handled by Morgan, such as trust accounts, could be performed by Guaranty. The 1959 merger between Morgan and Guaranty was simply the last step in this long trend of cooperation. To be sure, the merger was a response to different conditions, including the decline of commercial banks' ability to provide corporate finance, but it fell within the general pattern of the inexorable need to expand and join with other financial institutions in order to provide business services, including international services.

Another theme in Guaranty's history was its intimate connection to leading private and public institutions. The bank maintained relationships with many of the most important corporations and wealthy individuals in the world. This success was the result of a number of factors, including the enormous range of sophisticated financial services it provided, its ownership by leading persons and institutions in the banking world, and an aggressive culture of relationship banking. The bank had to sell its services to a relatively small class of sophisticated consumers and attempt to provide an expanding range of domestic and international services. Individual and corporate customers, particularly those with global ambitions, expected as much.

Also revealing was the bank's relationship with government. Bank leaders complained about some forms of regulation, whether it was Hughes's New York insurance investigation in 1905, the federal seizure of the railroads in World War I, or the federal regulation of banking in the 1930s. The separation of commercial and investment banking and the forced divorce from Morgan by 1940 were especially dramatic. Nevertheless, the bank always adapted to and in fact usually benefited from government actions. Guaranty's 1864 charter was a valuable asset assiduously protected in the acquisitions and mergers of 1891, 1929, and 1959. American involvement in World War I proved a massive boon to the bank, as did the business stimulated by total war from 1941–1945. During the 1940s a huge portion of the bank's portfolio resided in government securities. Regulators never stood in the way of its mergers, and government almost always encouraged its international work, even when it meant providing services to communists.

A third outstanding theme in Guaranty's history was the bank's ability to deal with economic and institutional change. There were few periods of easy calm between 1864 and 1959. Those that stand out, such as the 1880s and the 1950s, were years of decline that eventually produced revolutionary mergers. The bank did best when it made connections with other powerful financial institutions, provided services that those institutions could or would not provide, and reacted with innovation to special opportunities in the rapidly changing global financial environment. The development of international banking before 1900, stability in the crisis of 1907, the response to the needs of Europeans in 1914–1918, the problems of the Mercantile Bank in the early 1920s, the creation of the Guaranty Company to venture into the retail securities business in the 1920s, the trials of the Depression, the legal restructuring of financial services in the 1930s, and the return of a different kind of prosperity in the 1940s all offered chances for the bank to stand out, and in most cases it did.

The reconstruction of Gene Stetson's career between 1916 and 1959 adds a human element to this broader history. His work provides a case study in elite twentieth century relationship banking, Guaranty's defining characteristic. Stetson was offered an opportunity at Guaranty in 1916 because even as the president of a small national bank in Georgia he was a proven go-getter, a salesman for bank services who could sit on corporate boards, arrange a wide class of financial deals, accurately analyze the business health of a company, link the work of banks to the public good, and be personally and socially impressive while doing so. He performed essentially the same kind of work at Guaranty, only on a larger and more complex stage. Stetson shaped Guaranty's history because he accepted the values and purposes of relationship banking, viewing the role of the banker as largely a matter of building good relationships inside the bank, with the larger financial community, with government, and with the kinds of large corporations and wealthy individuals the bank sought as customers. A great deal of this relationship building was a matter of obtaining the confidence of the men within these constituencies—a skill that combined knowledge, personality, and willingness to be forceful or conciliatory as conditions demanded.

Within the bank, Stetson's rise to Guaranty's board in 1928, his election to its executive committee in 1934, the presidency in 1941, and as chairman of the board in 1944, suggest the extent of his success. One cannot overestimate the importance of his winning the confidence of Charles Sabin, Bill Potter, and Thomas Lamont, the three men most responsible for governance at Guaranty between 1916 and the 1940s. Sabin hired Stetson and provided him with his first opportunities. Lamont, the Morgan partner, was a dominating presence on the board from 1912 until federal law forced him to leave in 1940. Potter, described by the *New York Times* on his death in 1957 as "one of the world's most powerful bankers and industrialists" between the 1920s and 1940s, came to the fore in the Mercantile crisis, was president when Stetson went on the board, and was still an advisor to the company when Stetson resigned as board chairman. Stetson also developed effective relationships with key directors, such as attorney John Davis, and he recruited allies, such as Bob Woodruff, to the board. A breakdown in leadership in the 1950s, while Luther Cleveland was chairman, caused

Stetson, once a Cleveland supporter, to look to Henry Alexander and Morgan to provide a new direction.

Probably a great deal of this internal achievement would not have mattered much if Stetson had not been able to excel at his role as a relationship banker. His record in the 1940s as a director of more corporations than any other Guaranty officer shows how eagerly he accepted this task as well as how effective he was in convincing executives that he was worth having on their boards. Stetson frequently took a leadership role as director, serving as chairman and executive or finance committee member. The process of building profitable enterprises excited him as a young man and kept him active into the 1950s. Stetson believed deeply in the power of institutions to improve lives, and never drew bright lines between public and private responsibilities. In the end, the creation of Morgan Guaranty provided a fitting conclusion to Stetson's career, strongly reflecting his faith in banking's broad capacity to contribute to business and to American life.

Bibliography

PRIMARY SOURCES

Manuscripts

Braga Brothers Collection. George A. Smathers Libraries, University of Florida, Gainesville, Florida.

Brown Brothers Harriman & Company Collection. New-York Historical Society, New York, New York.

Bush, Prescott Sheldon. Reminiscences. Columbia University Oral History Research Office Collection, New York, New York.

Davis, John William Papers. Yale University Library, Manuscripts and Archives, New Haven, Connecticut.

Farley, James A. Papers. Library of Congress, Manuscripts Division, Washington, DC.

Graves, John Temple. "Notebook of Interviews, Notes, and Manuscript Pages of Book." Southern Research Institute, Birmingham, Alabama.

Harriman, W. Averell Papers. Library of Congress, Manuscripts Division, Washington, DC.

Hoover, Herbert Papers. Herbert Hoover Presidential Library, West Branch, Iowa.

J. P. Morgan & Co., Inc. Papers. JPMorgan Chase Archives, New York, New York.

Lamont, Thomas W. Collection. Baker Library Historical Collections, Harvard Business School, Boston, Massachusetts.

Leffingwell, Russell Cornell Papers. Yale University Library, Manuscripts and Archives, New Haven, Connecticut.

Lovett, Robert Abercrombie Papers. Yale University Library, Manuscripts and Archives, New Haven, Connecticut.

Martin, Harold H. Papers. Manuscript, Archives, and Rare Book Library, Emory University, Atlanta, Georgia.

Mercer University Faculty Minutes, 1898–1907. Jack Tarver Library, Special Collections, Mercer University, Macon, Georgia.

Morgan, J. P., Jr. Papers. The Pierpont Morgan Library, New York, New York.

Pendergrast, Mark Papers. Manuscript, Archives, and Rare Book Library, Emory University, Atlanta, Georgia.

Richardson, Henry Smith Papers. Southern Historical Collection, Wilson Library, University of North Carolina, Chapel Hill, North Carolina.

Richardson–Vicks, Inc. Records. Southern Historical Collection, Wilson Library, University of North Carolina, Chapel Hill, North Carolina.

Sibley, John A. Papers. Manuscript, Archives, and Rare Book Library, Emory University, Atlanta, Georgia.

Stetson, Eugene W. Papers. Jack Tarver Library, Special Collections, Mercer University, Macon, Georgia.

The Coca-Cola Company, Atlanta, Georgia.

Watson, Thomas J., Sr. Papers. IBM Corporate Archives, Somers, New York.

Willkie, Wendell L. Mss. Lilly Library, Indiana University, Bloomington, Indiana.

Woodruff, Robert W. Papers. Manuscript, Archives, and Rare Book Library, Emory University, Atlanta, Georgia.

Interviews and Letters

Gordon, Albert. Statement to Chuck Stetson, 1982.

Hatcher, Josephine. Interview by Adrienne M. Bond. Jack Tarver Library, Special Collections, Mercer University, Macon, Georgia. 1981–1982.

Otlowski, Lillian. Telephone interview by author. Notes in possession of author. 8 June 2004.

Sibley, John A. Interview by L. Kenneth Hammond. Jack Tarver Library, Special Collections, Mercer University, Macon, Georgia. 3 March 1982.

Stetson, Charles P. Interview by L. Kenneth Hammond. Jack Tarver Library, Special Collections, Mercer University, Macon, Georgia. 24 April 1982.

Stetson, Charles P. Letter to Charles H. Andrews, 9 December 1997.

Published Materials

Air Reduction Co., Inc. *Air Reduction Co., Inc.: Air Reduction Sales Company, National Carbide Corporation, Wilson Welder and Metals Co., Inc., Pure Carbonic, Inc., The Ohio Chemical & Mfg. Co.* New York: Air Reduction Co., 1941.

———. *Annual Report, 1945*. New York: Air Reduction Co., Inc., 1946.

———. *Annual Report, 1959*. New York: Air Reduction Co., Inc., 1959.

Asia Banking Corporation. *Asia Banking Corporation*. New York: Asia Banking Corporation, 1918.

———. *Asia Banking Corporation*. New York: Asia Banking Corporation, 1919.
———. *Asia Banking Corporation*. New York: Asia Banking Corporation, 1920.
Atlanta Constitution.
Automatic Voting Machine Corporation. *Annual Report*. Jamestown NY: Automatic Voting Machine Corporation, 1929.
———. *Annual Report*. Jamestown NY: Automatic Voting Machine Corporation, 1930.
"Back to Back." *Time* 13 (4 March 1929): 54-56.
Barnsdall Corporation. *Annual Report*. New York: Barnsdall Corporation, 1919.
———. *Annual Report*. New York: Barnsdall Corporation, 1920.
———. *Annual Report*. New York: Barnsdall Corporation, 1921.
———. *Annual Report*. New York: Barnsdall Corporation, 1927.
———. *Annual Report*. New York: Barnsdall Corporation, 1928.
———. *Annual Report*. New York: Barnsdall Corporation, 1929.
———. *Annual Report*. New York: Barnsdall Corporation, 1930.
Canada Dry Ginger Ale Inc. *Annual Report*. New York: Canada Dry Ginger Ale, Inc., 1929.
———. *Annual Report*. New York: Canada Dry Ginger Ale, Inc., 1934.
———. *Annual Report*. New York: Canada Dry Ginger Ale, Inc., 1941.
———. *Annual Report*. New York: Canada Dry Ginger Ale, Inc., 1946.
———. *Annual Report*. New York: Canada Dry Ginger Ale, Inc., 1950.
Catalogue and Annual Announcement of Mercer University, Macon 1897–1898. Macon GA: J. W. Burke, 1898.
Cushing, Henry. "The New Wall Street." *The World's Work* 32 (June 1916): 215-223.
Directory of Directors in the City of New York, 1919–1920. New York: Directory of Directors Co., 1919.
Directory of Directors in the City of New York, 1921–1922. New York: Directory of Directors Co., 1921.
Directory of Directors in the City of New York, 1930–1931. New York: Directory of Directors Co., 1930.
Directory of Directors in the City of New York, 1945. New York: Directory of Directors Co., 1945.
"Everybody's Broker: Sidney Weinberg." *Time* 72 (8 December 1958): 96.
"Fairfield County: Smart New Yorkers are Flocking to It." *Life* 27 (8 August 1949): 74-84.
"Group Lecture Meetings Continue With Five Speakers During October." *The Guaranty News* (October–November 1936): 2-4.

Guaranty Trust Company of New York. *Banking Service for Foreign Trade*. New York: Guaranty Trust Company of New York, 1919.

———. *One Hundred Years of Banking Service*. New York: Guaranty Trust Company of New York, 1939.

———. *The Fabric of Civilization: A Short Survey of the Cotton Industry in the United States*. New York: Guaranty Trust Company of New York, 1919.

"Heavy Debt Hangs Over IC." *BusinessWeek* (13 October 1945): 73-75.

"Helm at the Helm." *Time* 73 (15 June 1959): 92.

Hillyer, William Hurd. "Eugene Stetson—A Close Up." *Forbes* (15 January 1947): 18-19.

"Honorary Degree of LL.D. Bestowed on Mr. Stetson by Mercer University." *The Guaranty News* (June1933): 5-6.

International Banking Directory. New York: Bankers Publishing Co., 1928.

Leonard, John W., ed. *Who's Who in Finance and Banking (1920–22)*. New York: Who's Who in Finance, Inc., 1922.

McCrory Stores Corporation. *[Annual] Report*. New York: McCrory Stores, 1925.

———. *[Annual] Report*. New York: McCrory Stores, 1945.

———. *[Annual] Report*. New York: McCrory Stores, 1950.

Mercer University Kinetoscope 0.1 (N.p.: n.p. [1901?]).

"Mid-America's Main Line." *Time* 57 (19 February 1951): 87–88.

"Morgan's Men." *Time* 33 (13 February 1939): 64-66.

"New Tri." *Time*, 17 October 32 (17 October 1938): 68–69.

New York Times.

Niagara Share Corporation. *Fifth Annual Report to Stockholders*. Buffalo: Niagara Share Corporation, 1933.

———. *Tenth Annual Report to Stockholders*. Buffalo: Niagara Share Corporation, 1938.

"Our New Vice-President." *The Guaranty News* (November 1916): 324.

Poor's Register of Directors and Executives, United States and Canada. New York: Standard and Poor's Corp., 1957.

Spingarn, Jerome H. "Of Coca, Cola, and the Courts." *The Nation* 152 (7 June 1941): 666–68.

Stetson, Eugene W. 1924. "'Advertising Good-Will' as a Bankable Asset." *The Red Barrel* (May 1924): 3–5.

———. "Banker Sees Continuing Need of Advertising." *Printers' Ink* (23 November 1933): 43–45.

———. "Why Times Are Good in Georgia." *Atlanta Sunday American* (2 January 1927).

"The Big Banker." *Time* 74 (2 November 1959): 82–88.
"The Eastern Cuba Sugar Situation." *Barron's* 11 (7 September 1959): 17.
The Southern Company. S.l.: The First Boston Corporation; Kidder, Peabody & Co.; Merrill Lynch, Pierce, Fenner & Beane, 1949.
The Southern Company. *The Southern Company and the Territory it Serves*. Atlanta: The Southern Company, 1952.
"These are the Men Who Make More than $75,000 a Year." *The Machinist* 2 (4 September 1947): 4–5
"Tobacco Merger?" *Time* 1 (30 July 1923): 21.
"Two Morrows." *Time* 14 (2 September 1929): 57.
United Cigar Stores Company of America. *Reorganization of the United Cigar Stores Company of America*. New York: United Cigar Stores of America and Guaranty Trust Company of New York, 1933.
Ward Baking Company. *The Story of Our Research Products*. New York: Ward Baking Company, 1921.
Wall Street Journal.
Wamsley, Wilbur. "Wall Street's New Leaders." *Munsey's Magazine* 68 (December 1919): 412–27.
White Motor Corporation. *Annual Report*. Cleveland: White Motor Corp., 1928.
———. *Annual Report*. Cleveland: White Motor Corp., 1929.
———. *Annual Report*. Cleveland: White Motor Corp., 1930.
———. *Annual Report*. Cleveland: White Motor Corp., 1931.
———. *Annual Report*. Cleveland: White Motor Corp., 1932.
———. *Annual Report*. Cleveland: White Motor Corp., 1933.
———. *Annual Report*. Cleveland: White Motor Corp., 1934.
———. *Annual Report*. Cleveland: White Motor Corp., 1935.
———. *Annual Report*. Cleveland: White Motor Corp., 1936.
———. *Annual Report*. Cleveland: White Motor Corp., 1937.
———. *Annual Report*. Cleveland: White Motor Corp., 1938.
———. *Annual Report*. Cleveland: White Motor Corp., 1939.
———. *Annual Report*. Cleveland: White Motor Corp., 1940.
———. *Annual Report*. Cleveland: White Motor Corp., 1941.
———. *Annual Report*. Cleveland: White Motor Corp., 1943.

Government Records

Appeal of Ernest Woodruff, 1926 WL 523 (B.T.A. 1926).
Appeal of W. C. Bradley, 1 B.T.A. 111 (1924).

Coca-Cola Bottling Co. v. Coca-Cola Co., Nos. 2650, 2651 (1920), United States Court of Appeals for the Third Circuit, National Archives and Records Administration, Philadelphia, Pennsylvania.
Coca-Cola Bottling Company v. Coca-Cola Co., 296 F. 796 (D. Del. 1920).
Coca-Cola Bottling Co. v. Coca-Cola Co., 654 F. Supp. 1388 (D. Del. 1986).
Coca-Cola Bottling Co. of Elizabethtown v. Coca-Cola Co., 988 F.2d 386 (3d Cir. 1993).
Coca-Cola Bottling Co. of Elizabethtown v. Coca-Cola Co., 98 F.R.D. 254 (D. Del. 1983).
Coca-Cola Bottling Co. of Elizabethtown v. Coca-Cola Co., 95 F.R.D. 168 (D. Del. 1982).
Coca-Cola Bottling Co. of Elizabethtown, Inc. v. Coca-Cola Co., No. 81–48 MMS, United States District Court for the District of Delaware, National Archives and Records Administration, Philadelphia, Pennsylvania.
Coca-Cola Bottling Co. of Shreveport v. Coca-Cola Co., 988 F.2d 414 (3d Cir. 1993).
Cumberland Stores Corp. v. McLellan Stores Co., 32 F. Supp. 840 (S.D.N.Y. 1940).
Feiner v. Investors Syndicate, Division of Old Records, New York State Supreme Court, New York County, New York, New York.
Freeman v. Bean, 266 N.Y. 657 (1935).
Gulf Atlantic Warehouse v. Bennett, 36 Ala. App. 33 (1951).
Guttmann v. Illinois Central R.R., 91 F. Supp. 285 (E.D.N.Y. 1950).
Guttman v. Illinois Central R.R., 189 F.2d 930 (2d Cir. 1951).
Guttmann v. Illinois Central R.R., No. 21801 (1949), United States Court of Appeals for the Second Circuit, National Archives and Records Administration, New York, New York.
Guttmann v. Illinois Central R.R., No. C9195 (1949), United States District Court for the Eastern District of New York, National Archives and Records Administration, New York, New York.
Guttmann v. Illinois Central R.R., 342 U.S. 867 (1951).
Guttman v. Illinois Central R.R., No. 285 (1951), United States Supreme Court.
Hirson v. United Stores Corp., 34 N.Y.S.2d 122 (Sup. Ct. App. Div. 1942).
In re McCrory Stores, 14 F. Supp. 739 (S.D.N.Y. 1935).
Iola Wise Stetson v. Commissioner of Internal Revenue, 1932 WL 157 (B.T.A. 1932).
Litwin v. Allen, Division of Old Records, New York State Supreme Court, New York County, New York, New York.
Litwin v. Allen, 25 N.Y.S.2d 667 (Sup. Ct. 1940).
Metropolitan Life Insurance Co. v. Daniel, 64 Ga. App. 620 (1941).

Stetson v. Morgan Guaranty Trust Co., 104 A.2d 239 (Conn. Superior Court 1960).

Trust Company of Georgia v. Rose, No. 794 (1928), United States District Court for the Northern District of Georgia, National Archives and Records Administration, Atlanta, Georgia.

United States Bureau of the Census. *Fourteenth Census of the United States, State Compendium: Georgia.* Washington: Government Printing Office, 1924.

United States Department of Commerce and Labor. *Statistical Abstract of the United States.* Washington: Government Printing Office, 1910.

United States Senate Committee on Interstate Commerce. *Investigation of Railroads, Holding Companies, and Affiliated Companies, Additional Report of the Committee on Interstate Commerce, The 1925–28 Receivership and Reorganization of the Chicago, Milwaukee, and St. Paul Railway Company, Role of the Guaranty Trust Company of New York.* Washington: Government Printing Office, 1940.

United States v. Coca-Cola, No. 738 (1925), United States District Court for the Northern District of Georgia, National Archives and Records Administration, Atlanta, Georgia.

Woodruff v. Commissioner of Internal Revenue, 46 B.T.A. 727 (1942).

York v. Guaranty Trust Co. of New York, 326 U.S. 99 (1945).

SECONDARY SOURCES

Books, Articles, Theses

Abrahams, Paul Phillips. *The Foreign Expansion of American Finance and its Relationship to the Foreign Economic Policies of the United States, 1907–1921.* New York: Arno Press, 1976.

Abramson, Rudy. *Spanning the Century: The Life of Averell Harriman, 1891–1986.* New York: W. Morrow, 1992.

Aguilar, Luis E. *Cuba 1933: Prologue to Revolution.* Ithaca: Cornell University Press, 1972.

Allen, Frederick. *The Lords of Creation.* New York: Harper & Brothers, 1935.

Allen, Frederick III. *Secret Formula: How Brilliant Marketing and Relentless Salesmanship Made Coca-Cola the Best-Known Product in the World.* New York: Harper Business, 1994.

Anderson, W. D. *A Bench Mark: Bibb Manufacturing Company, Macon, Georgia, USA.* New York: Newcomen Society, 1950.

Atkins, Leah Rawls. *Developed for the Service of Alabama—The Centennial History of the Alabama Power Company, 1906–2006*. Birmingham: Alabama Power Company, 2006.

Baker, John C. *Directors and their Functions*. Boston: Harvard Business School, 1945.

Barmash, Isadore. *For the Good of the Company: Work and Interplay in a Major American Corporation*. New York: Grosset & Dunlap, 1976.

Barnes, Harry C. *From Molasses to the Moon: The Story of the U.S. Industrial Chemicals Co.* New York: U.S. Industrial Chemicals Co., 1975.

Barnes, Joseph. *Willkie: The Events He Was Part Of—The Ideas He Fought For*. New York: Simon and Shuster, 1952.

Bartley, Numan V. *The Creation of Modern Georgia*. Athens: University of Georgia Press, 1983.

Baskin, Jonathan B., and Paul J. Miranti Jr. *A History of Corporate Finance*. New York: Cambridge University Press, 1997.

Berger, Allen N., and Gregory F. Udell. "The Future of Relationship Lending." *The Future of Banking*. Edited by Benton E. Gup. Westport CT: Quorum Books, 2003.

Bibb Manufacturing Company. *The Story of Cotton*. Macon GA: Bibb Manufacturing Co., [1939?].

Bodenhorn, Howard. "Short-Term Loans and Long-Term Relationships: Relationship Lending In Early America." *Journal of Money, Credit and Banking* 35 (August 2003): 485–505.

Bond, Adrienne Moore. *Eugene W. Stetson*. Macon GA: Mercer University Press, 1983.

Boot, Arnoud W. A. "Relationship Banking: What Do We Know?" *Journal of Financial Intermediation* 9 (2000): 7–25.

———. and Anjan V. Thakor. "Can Relationship Banking Survive Competition?" *Journal of Finance* 55 (April 2000): 678–713.

Borsodi, Ralph. *The Distribution Age: A Study in the Economy of Modern Distribution*. New York: D. Appleton, 1927.

Brooks, John. *Once in Golcanda: A True Drama of Wall Street, 1920–1938*. New York: Harper & Row, 1969.

Bruchey, Stuart. *Enterprise: The Dynamic Economy of a Free People*. Cambridge: Harvard University Press, 1990.

Bruner, Robert F. and Sean D. Carr. *The Panic of 1907: Lessons Learned from the Market's Perfect Storm*. New York: Wiley, 2007.

Bryan, T. Conn. *Confederate Georgia*. Athens: University of Georgia Press, 1953.

Bryant, Keith L., and Henry C. Dethloff. *A History of American Business*. 2d ed. Upper Saddle River NJ: Prentice-Hall, 1990.
Burlingame, Dwight F., and Dennis R. Young. *Corporate Philanthropy at the Crossroads*. Bloomington: Indiana University Press, 1996.
Burns, Helen. *The American Banking Community and New Deal Banking Reforms, 1933–1935*. Westport, CT: Greenwood Press, 1975.
Candler, Charles H. *Asa Griggs Candler*. Atlanta: Emory University, 1950.
Carosso, Vincent P. *Investment Banking in America: A History*. Cambridge: Harvard University Press, 1970.
———. *The Morgans: Private International Bankers, 1854–1913*. Cambridge: Harvard University Press, 1987.
Chamberlain, John. *The Enterprising Americans: A Business History of the United States*. New York: Harper & Row, 1963.
Chandler, Alfred O. Jr. *The Visible Hand: The Managerial Revolution in American Business.* Cambridge: Harvard University Press, 1977.
Chernow, Ron. *The Death of the Banker*. New York: Vintage Books, 1997.
———. *The House of Morgan: An American Banking Dynasty and the Rise of Modern Finance.* New York: Atlantic Monthly Press, 1990.
Chorafas, Dimitris N. *The Commercial Banking Handbook: Strategic Planning for Growth and Survival in the New Decade*. London: MacMillan Press Ltd., 1999.
Clark, Robert C. *Corporate Law*. Boston: Little, Brown, 1986.
Cleveland, Harold van B., and Thomas S. Huertas. *Citibank, 1812–1970.* Cambridge: Harvard University Press, 1985.
Coleman, Kenneth, ed. *A History of Georgia*. 2d ed. Athens: University of Georgia Press, 1991.
Corliss, Carlton J. *Main Line of Mid-America: The Story of the Illinois Central.* New York: Creative Age Press, 1950.
Crist, James F. *The Southern Company: A Story of the System's Background and Development*. S.l.: s.n., 1953.
———. *They Electrified the South: The Story of the Southern Electric System*. S.l.: J. F. Crist, 1981.
Crosse, Howard D. *Management Policies for Commercial Banks*. Englewood Cliffs: Prentice-Hall, Inc., 1962.
Current, Richard. *Northernizing the South*. Athens: University of Georgia Press, 1983.
Dalton, John E. *Sugar*. New York: The Macmillan Co., 1937.
Daniels, Rudolph L. *Trains Across the Continent: North American Railroad History.* 2d ed. Bloomington: Indiana University Press, 2000.

Davis, Harold E. *Henry Grady's New South: Atlanta, A Brave and Beautiful City*. Tuscaloosa: University of Alabama Press, 1990.

Dinnerstein, Leonard. *The Leo Frank Case*. Athens: University of Georgia Press, 1997.

Dowell, Spright. *A History of Mercer University, 1833–1953*. Macon GA: Mercer University, 1958.

Durden, Robert F. *Bold Entrepreneur: A Life of James B. Duke*. Durham: Carolina Academic Press, 2003.

Eells, Richard. *The Government of Corporations*. New York: Free Press, 1962.

Endlich, Lisa. *Goldman Sachs: The Culture of Success*. New York: Alfred A. Knopf, 1999.

Engerman, Stanley L., and Robert E. Gallman. *The Twentieth Century*. Volume 3 of *The Cambridge Economic History of the United States*. Cambridge: Cambridge University Press, 1996–2000.

Federer, Peter. "Institutional Innovation and the Creation of Liquid Financial Markets: The Case of Bankers' Acceptances, 1914–1934." *Journal of Economic History* 63 (September 2003): 666–94.

Fohlin, Caroline. "Relationship Banking, Liquidity, and Investment in German Industrialization." *Journal of Finance* 53 (October 2000): 1737–1758.

Foner, Eric. *Reconstruction: America's Unfinished Revolution, 1863–1877*. New York: Harper & Row, 1988.

Forbes, B. C. *Finance, Business, and the Business of Life*. [New York]: The Author, 1915.

Forbes, John D. *J. P. Morgan Jr., 1867–1943*. Charlottesville: University Press of Virginia, 1981.

———. *Stettinius, Sr.: Portrait of a Morgan Partner*. Charlottesville: University Press of Virginia, 1974.

Garrett, Franklin M. Volume 2 of *Atlanta and Environs: A Chronicle of Its People and Events*. New York: Lewis Publishing Company, Inc., 1954.

Geisst, Charles R. *Deals of the Century: Wall Street, Mergers, and the Making of Modern America*. Hoboken NJ: John Wiley and Sons, 2004.

———. *The Last Partnerships: Inside the Great Wall Street Money Dynasties*. New York: McGraw-Hill, 2001.

———. *Wall Street: A History*. New York: Oxford University Press, 1997.

Georgia Writers' Project. *Georgia: The WPA Guide to Its Towns and Countryside*. Columbia: University of South Carolina Press, 1990.

Glennon, Robert Jerome. *The Iconoclast as Reformer: Jerome Frank's Impact on American Law*. Ithaca: Cornell University Press, 1985.

Go, Tian-Kang. *American Commercial Banks in Corporate Finance, 1929–41*. New York: Garland, 1999.
Goldin, Claudia and Frank Lewis. "The Economic Cost of the American Civil War." *Journal of Economic History* 35 (June 1975): 299–326.
Goldschmidt, R. W. *The Changing Structure of American Banking*. London: George Routledge & Sons, Ltd., 1933.
Gott, Richard. *Cuba: A New History*. New Haven: Yale University Press, 2004.
Graves, John Temple. *History of the Southern Research Institute*. Birmingham: Birmingham Publishing Company, 1955.
Gray, Christopher. 1991. "Streetscapes: St. James' Church; A Metamorphosis Still In Progress." *New York Times*, 20 October 1991.
Griffith, Kathryn P. *Judge Learned Hand and the Role of the Federal Judiciary*. Norman: University of Oklahoma Press, 1973.
Grogan, Kevin. "Cuba's Dance of the Millions: Examining the Causes and Consequences of Violent Price Fluctuations in the Sugar Market between 1919 and 1920." M.A. thesis, University of Florida, 2004.
Gunther, Gerald. *Learned Hand: The Man and the Judge*. New York: Knopf, 1994.
Harbaugh, William. *Lawyer's Lawyer: The Life of John W. Davis*. New York: Oxford University Press, 1973.
Harr, Luther and W. Carlton Harris. *Banking Theory and Practice*. New York and London: McGraw-Hill Book Co., Inc., 1936.
Hayes, Samuel L. III and Philip Hubbard. *Investment Banking: A Tale of Three Cities*. Boston: Harvard Business School Press, 1990.
Hayes, Samuel L. III, A. Michael Spence, and David Van Praag Marks. *Competition in the Investment Banking Industry*. Cambridge: Harvard University Press, 1983.
Henn, Harry G., and John R. Alexander. *Laws of Corporations*. St. Paul: West Publishing Co., 1983.
Herman, Edward S. *Corporate Control, Corporate Power*. Cambridge: Cambridge University Press, 1981.
Hickman, John, and Dean Oakes. *Standard Catalog of National Bank Notes*. Iola WI: Krause Publications, 1982.
Horn, Martin. "A Private Bank at War: J. P. Morgan & Co. and France, 1914–1918." *Business History Review* 74 (Winter 2000): 85–112.
Hritsko, Rosemary S. "The White Motor Story." Ph.D. dissertation, University of Akron, 1988.
Hubbard, J. T. W. *For Each, the Strength of All: A History of Banking in the State of New York*. New York: New York University Press, 1995.

Hughes, Jonathan, and Louis P. Cain. *American Economic History*. 7th ed. Boston: Pearson Education, Inc., 2007.
Iobst, Richard W. *Civil War Macon*. Macon GA: Mercer University Press, 1999.
Irwin, Douglas A. *Against the Tide: An Intellectual History of Free Trade*. Princeton: Princeton University Press, 1996.
Jacobs, Michael T. *Short-term America: The Causes and Cures of Our Business Myopia*. Boston: Harvard Business School Press, 1991.
Jacobson, Timothy C., and George D. Smith. *Cotton's Renaissance: A Study in Market Innovation*. New York: Cambridge University Press, 2001.
Johnston, Wayne. *Eugene W. Stetson: Loyal Son of Mercer*. S.l.: s.n., 1965.
———. *The Illinois Central Heritage, 1851–1951: A Centenary Address*. New York: Newcomen Society, 1951.
Josephson, Matthew. *The Money Lords: The Great Finance Capitalists, 1925–1950*. New York: Weybright and Talley, 1972.
Kaysen, Carl, ed. *The American Corporation Today*. New York: Oxford University Press, 1996.
Kazin, Michael. *A Godly Hero: The Life of William Jennings Bryan*. New York: Knopf, 2006.
Kinley, David. *Money: A Study of the Theory of the Medium of Exchange*. New York: Macmillan & Co., 1913.
Klebaner, Benjamin J. *American Commercial Banking*. Boston: Twayne Publishers, 1990.
Klein, Maury. *Rainbow's End: The Crash of 1929*. New York: Oxford University Press, 2001.
———. *The Life and Legend of E. H. Harriman*. Chapel Hill: University of North Carolina Press, 2000.
———. *The Life and Legend of Jay Gould*. Baltimore: The Johns Hopkins University Press, 1986.
Knapp, G. Prather. *How Banks Increase Their Business*. Chicago and New York: Rand McNally & Co., 1926.
Kniffin, William H. *American Banking Practice*. New York: McGraw-Hill Book Co., Inc., 1921.
———. *Better Banking: A Treatise on Bank Management in the Light of the Depression*. New York: McGraw-Hill Book Co., Inc., 1934.
———. *The Business Man and His Bank*. New York: McGraw-Hill Book Co., Inc., 1930.
Kolko, Gabriel. *Railroads and Regulation, 1877–1916*. New York: W.W. Norton, 1970.

Kousser, J. Morgan. *The Shaping of Southern Politics: Suffrage Restriction and the Establishment of the One-Party South*. New Haven: Yale University Press, 1974.

Kouwenhoven, John A. *Partners in Banking: An Historical Portrait of a Great Private Bank, Brown Brothers Harriman & Co.* New York: Doubleday & Co., 1968.

Krier, Dan. *Speculative Management: Stock Market Power and Corporate Change.* Albany: State University of New York Press, 2005.

Lamont, Edward M. *The Ambassador from Wall Street: The Story of Thomas W. Lamont: J. P. Morgan's Chief Executive*. Lanham MD: Madison Books, 1994.

Lamont, Thomas M. *Henry P. Davison: The Record of a Useful Life*. New York: Harper & Brothers, 1933.

Lamoreaux, Naomi R. *Insider Lending: Banks, Personal Connections, and Economic Development in Industrial New England*. Cambridge: Cambridge University Press, 1994.

Langston, L. H. and Nathan R. Whitney. *Banking Practice: A Textbook for Colleges and Schools of Business Administration*. New York: Ronald Press Co., 1921.

Larson, Henrietta. *Jay Cooke: Private Banker*. Cambridge: Harvard University Press, 1936.

Link, Arthur S., and William S. Catton. *An Era of Economic Change, Reform, and World Wars, 1900-1945*.Volume 1 of *American Epoch: A History of the United States Since 1900*. 5th ed. New York: Alfred A. Knopf, 1980.

Livingston, Homer J. *Management Policies in American Banks*. New York: Harper & Bros., 1956.

Livingston, James. *Origins of the Federal Reserve System: Money, Class and Corporate Capitalism, 1890–1913*. Ithaca: Cornell University Press, 1986.

McAvoy, Muriel. *Sugar Baron: Manuel Rionda and the Fortunes of Pre-Castro Cuba*. Gainesville: University Press of Florida, 2003.

McQueen, Humphrey. *The Essence of Capitalism: The Origins of Our Future.* Montreal: Black Rose Books, 2003.

Mace, Myles L. *Directors: Myth and Reality*. Boston: Harvard Business School, 1986.

Maney, Kevin. *The Maverick and his Machine: Thomas Watson Sr. and the Making of IBM*. New York: J. Wiley & Sons, 2003.

Martin, Albro. *Railroads Triumphant: The Growth, Rejection and Rebirth of a Vital American Force*. New York: Oxford University Press, 1992.

Mercer, Lloyd. *E. H. Harriman: Master Railroader*. Boston: Twayne Publishers, 1985.

Mercer University, Eugene W. Stetson Memorial Library. *Dedication Ceremonies, The Eugene W. Stetson Memorial Library, Mercer University*. Macon GA: Mercer University, 1965.

Mills, Harry. *The Rainmaker's Toolkit—Power Strategies for Finding, Keeping, and Growing Profitable Clients*. New York: American Management Association, 2004.

Mintz, Sidney W. *Sweetness and Power: The Place of Sugar in Modern History*. New York: Viking Penguin, 1985.

Mizruchi, Mark and Linda Brewster Stearns. "Getting Deals Done: The Use of Social Networks in Bank Decision-Making." *American Sociological Review* 66 (2001): 647–71.

Moore, Roy W. *Down From Canada Came Tales of a Wonderful Beverage*. Princeton: Newcomen Society, 1961.

Morgan, Bruce W. "Demystifying Relationship Banking." *Journal of Retail Banking* 15 (Winter 1993–94): 9–20.

Morris, Charles R. *The Tycoons: How Andrew Carnegie, John D. Rockefeller, Jay Gould, and J. P. Morgan Invented the American Supereconomy*. New York: Henry Holt and Company, 2005.

Muir, Ross and Carl J. White. *Over the Long Term: The Story of J. & W. Seligman & Co*. New York: J. & W. Seligman, 1964.

Murray, William M. Jr. *Thomas W. Martin—A Biography*. Birmingham: Southern Research Institute, 1978.

Neal, Steve. *Dark Horse: A Biography of Wendell Willkie*. Lawrence: University Press of Kansas, 1989.

Northen, William J., ed. *Men of Mark in Georgia*. Atlanta: A. B. Caldwell, 1912.

Northrup, Cynthia Clark, and Elaine C. Prange Turney, editors. *Encyclopedia of Tariffs and Trade in United States History*. Westport CT: Greenwood Press, 2003.

Otlowski, Lillian. *Over the Walls of Wall Street with Mrs. O*. New Smyrna Beach FL: Luthers' Publishing, 2000.

Pecora, Ferdinand. *Wall Street Under Oath: The Story of Our Modern Money Changers*. New York: Simon and Schuster, 1939.

Pendergrast, Mark. *For God, Country, and Coca-Cola: The Definitive History of the Great American Soft Drink and the Company That Makes It*. rev. ed. New York: Basic Books, 2000.

Phillips, Charles F. Jr. *The Regulation of Public Utilities*. Arlington: Public Utilities Reports, Inc., 1988.

Phillips, Kevin. *American Dynasty: Aristocracy, Fortune, and the Politics of Deceit in the House of Bush*. New York: Viking, 2004.

———. *Wealth and Democracy: A Political History of the American Rich*. New York: Broadway Books, 2002.

Pusey, Merlo J. Volume 1 of *Charles Evans Hughes*. New York: MacMillan Co., 1951.

Ransom, Roger L. "The Economic Consequences of the American Civil War." *The Political Economy of War and Peace*, edited by M. Wolfson. Norwell MA: Kluwer Academic Publishers, 1998.

Redlich, Fritz. *1840-1910*. Volume 2 of *The Molding of American Banking: Men and Ideas*. New York: Hafner Publishing Company, 1951.

O'Toole, Patricia. *Money and Morals in America*. New York: Clarkson Potter, 1998.

Renehan, Edward J. Jr. *Dark Genius of Wall Street: The Misunderstood Life of Jay Gould, King of the Robber Barons*. New York: Basic Books, 2005.

Ritter, Dwight S. *Relationship Banking: Cross-Selling the Bank's Products and Services to Meet Your Customer's Every Financial Need*. Chicago and Cambridge: Bankers Publishing Co., Probus Publishing Co., 1993.

Roberts, Priscilla. "Jewish Bankers, Russia, and the Soviet Union, 1900–1940: The Case of Kuhn, Loeb and Company." *American Jewish Archives Journal* 49 (1997): 9–37.

Rodkey, Robert G. *Sound Policies for Bank Management*. New York: Ronald Press Co., 1944.

Rogers, David. *The Future of American Banking: Managing for Change*. New York: McGraw-Hill, Inc., 1993.

Schwartz, Rosalie. "Invasion of the Tourists." *The Cuba Reader: History, Culture, Politics*, edited by Aviva Chomsky, Barry Carr, and Pamela Marie Smorkaloff. Durham: Duke University Press, 2003.

Schweikart, Larry. "U.S. Commercial Banking: A Historiographical Survey." *Business History Review* 65 (Autumn 1991): 606–61.

Seligman, Joel. *The Transformation of Wall Street: A History of the Securities and Exchange Commission and Modern Corporate Finance*. Boston: Houghton Mifflin, 1982.

Shaw, Barton C. *The Wool-Hat Boys: Georgia's Populist Party*. Baton Rouge: Louisiana State University Press, 1984.

Shepard, Odell. *Connecticut: Past and Present*. New York: Alfred A. Knopf, 1939.

Sobel, Robert. *The Life and Times of Dillon Read*. New York: Truman Talley Books/Dutton, 1991.

Southern Research Institute. *25 Years: The First Quarter Century of Southern Research Institute, 1941–1966.* Birmingham: Southern Research Institute, 1966.

Sprague, O. M. W., ed. *Chapters on the Theory and History of Banking.* New York: G. P. Putnam's, 1904.

Stern, Siegfried. *The United States in International Banking.* New York: Columbia University Press, 1951.

Stover, John F. *History of the Illinois Central Railroad.* New York: Macmillan Publishing Co., 1975.

———. *The Life and Decline of the American Railroad.* New York: Oxford University Press, 1970.

Studenski, Paul, and Herman Krooss. *Financial History of the United States.* New York: McGraw-Hill, 1963.

Strouse, Jean. *Morgan: American Financier.* New York: Random House, 1999.

Sunderland, Edwin S. S. *Main Line of Mid-America: The Simplification of its Debt Structure, 1938–52.* S.l.: Privately Printed, 1952.

Tedlow, Richard S. *The Watson Dynasty: The Fiery Reign and Troubled Legacy of IBM's Founding Father and Son.* New York: Harper Business, 2003.

Timberlake, Richard H. *Monetary Policy in the United States.* Chicago: University of Chicago Press, 1993.

Tindall, George B. *The Emergence of the New South, 1914–45.* Baton Rouge: Louisiana State University Press, 1965.

Trelease, Allen. *White Terror: The Ku Klux Klan Conspiracy and Southern Reconstruction.* New York: Harper & Row, 1971.

Trescott, Paul. *Financing American Enterprise: The Story of Commercial Banking.* New York: Harper & Row, 1963.

Trust Company of Georgia. *Story of the Trust Company of Georgia, Atlanta, on its 60th Anniversary.* Atlanta: Trust Company of Georgia, 1951.

Turner, Gregg. *A Short History of Florida Railroads.* Charleston SC: Arcadia Publishing, 2003.

United States Cuban Sugar Council. *Sugar: Facts and Figures.* New York: United States Cuban Sugar Council, 1948.

Vardi, Nathan. "The Check is Not in the Mail." *Forbes* 17 (30 September 2002): 67.

Watson, Thomas J. Jr., and Peter Petre. *Father Son & Co.: My Life at IBM and Beyond.* New York: Bantam, 1990.

West, Robert C. *Banking Reform and the Federal Reserve, 1863–1923.* Ithaca: Cornell University Press, 1977.

Westerfield, Ray B. *Banking Principles and Practice*. New York: Ronald Press Co., 1928.

White, Eugene N. *The Regulation and Reform of the American Banking System, 1900–1929*. Princeton: Princeton University Press, 1983.

Whitlock, Mary P. "Bibb Manufacturing Company and Payne City, Georgia: An Historical Perspective, 1876–1986." Specialist in Education thesis, Georgia College and State University, 1986.

Wicker, Elmus. *The Great Debate on Banking Reform*. Columbus: Ohio State University Press, 2005.

Wilentz, Sean. *The Rise of American Democracy: Jefferson to Lincoln*. New York: W. W. Norton, 2005.

Wilkins, Mira. *The Emergence of Multinational Enterprise: American Business Abroad from the Colonial Era to 1914*. New York: Cambridge University Press, 1970.

———. "The Neglected Intangible Asset: The Influence of the Trade Mark on the Rise of the Modern Corporation." *Business History*, 34 (January 1992): 66–95.

Williams, Ben Ames. *Bank of Boston 200: A History of New England's Leading Bank, 1784–1984*. Boston: Houghton Mifflin, 1984.

Willis, H. Parker, John M. Chapman, and Ralph West. *Contemporary Banking*. New York: Harper & Bros., 1934.

Wilson, Joan Hoff. *Herbert Hoover: Forgotten Progressive*. Boston: Little, Brown, 1975.

Wilson, John Donald. *The Chase: The Chase Manhattan Bank, 1945–85*. Boston: Harvard Business School Press, 1986.

Woodman, Harold D. *New South—New Law: The Legal Foundations of Credit and Labor Relations in the Postbellum Agricultural South*. Baton Rouge: Louisiana State University Press, 1995.

Woodward, C. Vann. *Origins of the New South, 1877–1913*. Baton Rouge: Louisiana State University Press, 1951.

———. *Tom Watson: Agrarian Rebel*. New York: Macmillan, 1938.

Worthy, James C. *Shaping an American Institution: Robert E. Wood and Sears, Roebuck*. Urbana: University of Illinois Press, 1984.

Zeckendorf, William. *The Autobiography of William Zeckendorf*. New York: Holt, Rinehart, and Winston, 1970.

Zhaojin, Ji. *A History of Modern Shanghai Banking: the Rise and Decline of China's Finance Capitalism*. Armonk NY: M.E. Sharpe, 2003.

World Wide Web Pages

"About BOC." http://www.boc-gases.com/about_us/index.asp.
"About the Foundation." http://woodruff.org/about_rww.aspx.
"About Us: Overview."
http://www.cokecce.com/pages/allContent.asp?page_id=81.
"American International Group, Inc."
http://www.answers.com/topic/american-international-group-inc.
"A Message to Our Valued Clients." http://www.mony.com/.
"Bayberry Land: Rest and Refuge in Southampton."
http://www.town.southampton.ny.us/specialgallery/bayberry/bayberrynobleed.pdf.
"BNP Paribus: History." http://www.bnpparibas.com/en/history/.
Bragg, William H. "Reconstruction in Georgia."
http://www.georgiaencyclopedia.org/nge/Article.jsp?path=/HistoryArchaeology/CivilWarandReconstruction/Topics–12&id=h–2533.
"Canada Dry: Tales of a Wonderful Beverage."
http://www.brandspeoplelove.com/csab/Brands/CanadaDry/CanadaDry/tabid/151/Default.aspx.
"Chicago Streets."
http://www.chicagohs.org/documents/research/resources/streetNameChanges.pdf.
"Chronology of the Ward Family and the Ward Baking Company."
http://www.wardbakingcompany.com/library/docs/AIB_WardBakingCo_hist_2003.pdf.
"City of New Orleans." http://www.folkblues.com/goodman/cono.htm.
"GHCL Acquires Dan River for $17.5 m."
http://www.blonnet.com/2005/12/28/stories/2005122802550200.htm.
Hartley, M. K. "Cola Wars: Coca-Cola vs. PepsiCo."
http://media.wiley.com/product_data/excerpt/16/04717432/0471743216–3.pdf.
"History of JPMorgan Chase, 1799 to Present."
http://www.jpmorganchase.com/cm/BlobServer?blobtable=Document&blobcol=urlblob&blobkey=name&blobheader=application/pdf&blobwhere=jpmc/about/history/shorthistory.pdf.
Hunter, John. "Jekyll Island."
http://www.georgiaencyclopedia.org/nge/Article.jsp?id=h–928.
"Interviewee: Mr. James Webb."
http://www.nasm.si.edu/research/dsh/TRANSCPT/WEBB2.HTM.

Jones, Douglas W. "A Brief Illustrated History of Voting." http://www.cs.uiowa.edu/~jones/voting/pictures/.
"J. P. Morgan Chase & Co." http://www.fundinguniverse.com/company-histories/JP-Morgan-Chase-amp;-Co-Company-History.html.
"Lyondell." http://www.lyondell.com/Lyondell/.
"Membership of the Board of Governors of the Federal Reserve System, 1914-Present." http://www.federalreserve.gov/bios/boardmembership.htm.
Moen, Jon. "Still Playing Catch-Up: Mississippi and the South." July 2006. http://www.olemiss.edu/winterinstitute/documents/econo-study1.pdf.
"Our Firm." http://www2.goldmansachs.com/our-firm/index.html.
"Philip Morris International: Our History." http://www.philipmorrisinternational.com/PMINTL/pages/eng/ourbus/Our_history.asp.
"Riklis Family Corp." http://www.fundinguniverse.com/company-histories/Riklis-Family-Corp-Company-History.html.
"Robert Winship Woodruff: Outdoorsman and Conservationist." http://www.sherpaguides.com/georgia/fire_forest/sidebars/robert_woodruff.html.
"Six Ways to Compute the Relative Value of a U.S. Dollar Amount." http://measuringworth.com/calculators/uscompare/#.
"Southern Company Annual Report, 2007." http://www.southerncompany.com.
"Southern Research." http://www.southernresearch.org.
"SunTrust Selling Coca-Cola Shares Held Since 1919." http://en.epochtimes.com/news/7–5–15/55355.html.
Sutton, Anthony C. "Guaranty Trust Goes to Russia." http://reformed-theology.org/html/books/bolshevik_revolution/.
"The Braga Brothers Collection." http://www.uflib.ufl.edu/spec/manuscript/Braga/Braga.htm.
"The Business Council: About Us." http://www.businesscouncil.com/about/.
"The George W. Woodruff School of Mechanical Engineering." http://files.asme.org/ASMEORG/Communities/History/Landmarks/1293.pdf.
"The History of Chemical Bank." http://www.chasealum.org/article.html?aid=197.
"The 'Power Elite' Controls Both Sides." http://www.smokershistory.com/power.htm.
"Thomas Wesley Martin." http://cba.ua.edu/investing/hall_of_fame/74TWM.html.

"Thomas Wesley Martin."
http://www.samford.edu/groups/amhf/chronological.html#.
"Top 50 Banks in the World."
http://www.bankersalmanac.com/addcon/infobank/wldrank.aspx.
"Top Twenty Law Schools by Size of Endowment."
http://leiterlawschool.typepad.com/leiter/2006/09/top_20_law_scho.html.
"Tricontinental History."
http://www.tricontinental.com/public/general/history.html.
"Wallace Saunders."
http://www.watervalley.net/users/caseyjones/saunders.htm.
Workman, Daniel. "Top Global Brands: World's Most Valuable Trademarks in 2006." http://internationaltrade.suite101.com/article.cfm/top_global_brands.

Index